ACCA

S T U D Y   T E X T

PAPER F7

FINANCIAL REPORTING (INTERNATIONAL)

In this new syllabus first edition approved by ACCA

- We **discuss** the **best strategies** for studying for ACCA exams
- We **highlight** the **most important elements** in the syllabus and the **key skills** you will need
- We **signpost** how each chapter links to the syllabus and the study guide
- We **provide** lots of **exam focus points** demonstrating what the examiner will want you to do
- We **emphasise key points** in regular **fast forward summaries**
- We **test your knowledge** of what you've studied in **quick quizzes**
- We **examine your understanding** in our **exam question bank**
- We **reference all the important topics** in our **full index**

BPP's **i-Learn** and **i-Pass** products also support this paper.

FOR EXAMS IN DECEMBER 2008 AND JUNE 2009

BPP LEARNING MEDIA

First edition 2007
Second edition June 2008

ISBN 9780 7517 4729 4

(Previous ISBN 9780 7517 3298 6)

British Library Cataloguing-in-Publication Data
A catalogue record for this book
is available from the British Library

Published by

BPP Learning Media Ltd
BPP House, Aldine Place
London W12 8AA

www.bpp.com/learningmedia

Printed in the United Kingdom

We are grateful to the Association of Chartered Certified
Accountants for permission to reproduce past
examination questions. The suggested solutions in the
exam answer bank have been prepared by BPP Learning
Media Ltd, except where otherwise stated.

Your learning materials, published by BPP Learning
Media Ltd, are printed on paper sourced from
sustainable, managed forests.

Contents

Review form and free prize draw

How the BPP ACCA-approved Study Text can help you pass

Tackling studying

Studying can be a daunting prospect, particularly when you have lots of other commitments. The **different features** of the text, the **purposes** of which are explained fully on the **Chapter features** page, will help you whilst studying and improve your chances of **exam success**.

Developing exam awareness

Our Texts are completely **focused** on helping you pass your exam.

Our advice on **Studying F7** outlines the **content** of the paper, the **necessary skills** the examiner expects you to demonstrate and any **brought forward knowledge** you are expected to have.

Exam focus points are included within the chapters to highlight when and how specific topics were examined.

Using the Syllabus and Study Guide

You can find the syllabus, Study Guide and other useful resources for F7 on the ACCA web site:

www.accaglobal.com/students/study_exams/qualifications/acca_choose/acca/professional/afm/

The Study Text covers **all aspects** of the syllabus to ensure you are as fully prepared for the exam as possible.

Testing what you can do

Testing yourself helps you develop the skills you need to pass the exam and also confirms that you can recall what you have learnt.

We include **Questions** – lots of them – both within chapters and in the **Exam Question Bank**, as well as **Quick Quizzes** at the end of each chapter to test your knowledge of the chapter content.

Chapter features

Each chapter contains a number of helpful features to guide you through each topic.

Topic list	Tells you what you will be studying in this chapter and the relevant section numbers, together the ACCA syllabus references.
Introduction	Puts the chapter content in the context of the syllabus as a whole.
Study Guide	Links the chapter content with ACCA guidance.
Exam Guide	Highlights how examinable the chapter content is likely to be and the ways in which it could be examined.
Knowledge brought forward	What you are assumed to know from previous studies/exams.
Fast forward	Summarises the content of main chapter headings, allowing you to preview and review each section easily.
Examples	Demonstrate how to apply key knowledge and techniques.
Key terms	Definitions of important concepts that can often earn you easy marks in exams.
Exam focus points	Tell you how specific topics may be examined, or any frequent weaknesses in students' exam answers on these topics.
Formula to learn	Formulae that are not given in the exam but which have to be learnt.
Questions	Give you essential practice of techniques covered in the chapter.
Chapter Roundup	A full list of the Fast Forwards included in the chapter, providing an easy source of review.
Quick Quiz	A quick test of your knowledge of the main topics in the chapter.
Exam Question Bank	Found at the back of the Study Text with more comprehensive chapter questions. Cross referenced for easy navigation.

Studying F7

F7 is a demanding paper covering all the fundamentals of financial reporting. It has five main sections:

1. The conceptual framework of accounting

2. The regulatory framework

3. Preparation of financial statements which conform with IFRS

4. Preparation of consolidated financial statements

5. Analysis and interpretation of financial statements

All of these areas will be tested to some degree at each sitting. Sections 3 and 4 are the main areas of application and you must expect to have to produce consolidated and single company financial statements in your exam.

Some of this material you w#

ill have covered at lower level papers. You should already be familiar with accounting for inventories and non-current assets and preparing simple income statements, balance sheets and cash flow statements. You should know the basic ratios.

F7 takes your financial reporting knowledge and skills up to the next level. New topics are consolidated financial statements (which you may have covered if you did the old 1.1), construction contracts, financial instruments and leases. There is also coverage of the substance of transactions and the limitations of financial statements and ratios. The examiner wants you to think about these issues.

If you had exemptions from lower level papers or feel that your knowledge of lower level financial reporting is not good enough, you may want to get a copy of the study text for F3 Financial Accounting and read through it, or at least have it to refer to. You have a lot of new material to learn for F7 and basic financial accounting will be assumed knowledge.

The way to pass F7 is by practising lots of exam-level questions, which you will do when you get onto revision. Only by practising questions do you get a feel for what you will have to do in the exam. Also, topics which you find hard to understand in the text will be much easier to grasp when you have encountered them in a few questions. So don't get bogged down in any area of the text. Just keep going and a lot of things you find difficult will make more sense when you see how they appear in an exam question.

The exam paper

The exam is a three hour paper with five compulsory questions.

Format of the paper

	Marks
Question 1	25
Question 2	25
Question 3	25
Question 4	15
Question 5	10
	100

Question 1 will be on consolidated financial statements.
Question 2 will be on single company financial statements.
Question 3 is likely to be on cash flow statements or interpretation of accounts
Questions 4 and 5 will be on other areas of the syllabus

A certain number of IFRSs/IASs will be tested in questions 1 and 2. Others will appear in questions 4 and 5.

Important note

Make sure you have the new Practice and Revision Kit (available July 2008). This will be fully updated for the revised IFRS 3.

Analysis of past papers – Professional and Fundamentals levels

The table below provides details of when each element of the syllabus has been examined and the question number and section in which each element appeared. Further details can be found in the Exam Focus Points in the relevant chapters.

Covered in Text chapter		Dec 2007	Pilot Paper
9, 11	**Consolidated statement of financial position including associate**	1	1
3, 7	Single company financial statements	2	2
19,20	Analysis and interpretation of financial statements	3	3
16	Discussion and scenario on leasing	4	
5, 7	**Treatment of development costs and change of accounting policy**	5	
1,15	Discussion and scenario on relevance, reliability and comparability		4
12	Calculate financial statement amounts relating to construction contract		5

1

The conceptual framework

Introduction

The IASB's document *Framework for the preparation and presentation of financial statements* represents the **conceptual framework** on which all IASs are based.

A conceptual framework for financial reporting can be defined as an attempt to codify existing **generally accepted accounting practice (GAAP)** in order to reappraise current accounting standards and to produce new standards.

Study guide

		Intellectual level
A	**A CONCEPTUAL FRAMEWORK FOR FINANCIAL REPORTING**	
1	**The need for a conceptual framework**	
(a)	describe what is meant by a conceptual framework of accounting	2
(b)	discuss whether a conceptual framework is necessary and what an alternative system might be	2
2	**Understandability, relevance, reliability and comparability**	
(a)	discuss what is meant by understandability in relation to the provision of financial information	2
(b)	discuss what is meant by relevance and reliability and describe the qualities that enhance these characteristics	2
(c)	discuss the importance of comparability to users of financial statements	2
3	**Recognition and measurement**	
(a)	define what is meant by 'recognition' in financial statements and discuss the recognition criteria	2
(b)	apply the recognition criteria to:	2
(i)	assets and liabilities	
(ii)	income and expenses	
(c)	discuss revenue recognition issues and indicate when income and expense recognition should occur.	2
(d)	demonstrate the role of the principle of substance over form in relation to recognising sales revenue.	2
(e)	explain the following measures and compute amounts using:	2
(i)	historical cost	
(ii)	fair value/current cost	
(iii)	net realisable value	
(iv)	present value of future cash flows.	
6	**The concept of 'faithful representations' ('true and fair view')**	
(a)	describe what is meant by financial statements achieving a faithful representation.	2
(b)	discuss whether faithful representation constitutes more than compliance with accounting standards.	1
(c)	indicate the circumstances and required disclosures where a 'true and fair' override may apply.	1

1 Conceptual framework and GAAP

1.1 The search for a conceptual framework

A **conceptual framework**, in the field we are concerned with, is a statement of generally accepted theoretical principles which form the frame of reference for financial reporting.

These theoretical principles provide the basis for the development of new accounting standards and the evaluation of those already in existence. The financial reporting process is concerned with providing information that is useful in the business and economic decision-making process. Therefore a conceptual framework will form the **theoretical basis** for determining which events should be accounted for, how they should be measured and how they should be communicated to the user. Although it is theoretical in nature, a conceptual framework for financial reporting has highly practical final aims.

The **danger of not having a conceptual framework** is demonstrated in the way some countries' standards have developed over recent years; standards tend to be produced in a haphazard and fire-fighting approach. Where an agreed framework exists, the standard-setting body act as an architect or designer, rather than a fire-fighter, building accounting rules on the foundation of sound, agreed basic principles.

The lack of a conceptual framework also means that fundamental principles are tackled more than once in different standards, thereby producing **contradictions and inconsistencies** in basic concepts, such as those of prudence and matching. This leads to ambiguity and it affects the true and fair concept of financial reporting.

Another problem with the lack of a conceptual framework has become apparent in the USA. The large number of **highly detailed standards** produced by the Financial Accounting Standards Board (FASB) has created a financial reporting environment governed by specific rules rather than general principles. This would be avoided if a cohesive set of principles were in place.

A conceptual framework can also bolster standard setters **against political pressure** from various 'lobby groups' and interested parties. Such pressure would only prevail if it was acceptable under the conceptual framework.

1.2 Advantages and disadvantages of a conceptual framework

Advantages

(a)   The situation is avoided whereby standards are developed on a patchwork basis, where a particular accounting problem is recognised as having emerged, and resources were then channelled into **standardising accounting practice** in that area, without regard to whether that particular issue was necessarily the most important issue remaining at that time without standardisation.

(b)   As stated above, the development of certain standards (particularly national standards) have been subject to considerable **political interference** from interested parties. Where there is a conflict of interest between user groups on which policies to choose, policies deriving from a conceptual framework will be **less open to criticism** that the standard-setter buckled to external pressure.

(c)   Some standards may concentrate on the **income statement** whereas some may concentrate on the **valuation of net assets** (statement of financial position).

Disadvantages

(a)   Financial statements are intended for a **variety of users**, and it is not certain that a single conceptual framework can be devised which will suit all users.

(b)   Given the diversity of user requirements, there may be a need for a variety of accounting standards, each produced for a **different purpose** (and with different concepts as a basis).

(c)   It is not clear that a conceptual framework makes the task of **preparing and then implementing** standards any easier than without a framework.

Before we look at the IASB's attempt to produce a conceptual framework, we need to consider another term of importance to this debate: generally accepted accounting practice; or GAAP.

1.3 Generally Accepted Accounting Practice (GAAP)

GAAP signifies all the rules, from whatever source, which govern accounting.

In individual countries this is seen primarily as a **combination** of:

- National company law
- National accounting standards
- Local stock exchange requirements

Although those sources are the basis for the GAAP of individual countries, the concept also includes the effects of **non-mandatory sources** such as:

- International accounting standards
- Statutory requirements in other countries

In many countries, like the UK, GAAP does not have any statutory or regulatory authority or definition, unlike other countries, such as the USA. The term is mentioned rarely in legislation, and only then in fairly limited terms.

There are different views of GAAP in different countries. The UK position can be explained in the following extracts from *UK GAAP* (Davies, Paterson & Wilson, Ernst & Young, 5th edition).

> 'Our view is that GAAP is a dynamic concept which requires constant review, adaptation and reaction to changing circumstances. We believe that use of the term 'principle' gives GAAP an unjustified and inappropriate degree of permanence. GAAP changes in response to changing business and economic needs and developments. As circumstances alter, accounting practices are modified or developed accordingly….. We believe that GAAP goes far beyond mere rules and principles, and encompasses contemporary permissible accounting **practice**.
>
> It is often argued that the term 'generally accepted' implies that there must exist a high degree of practical application of a particular accounting practice. However, this interpretation raises certain practical difficulties. For example, what about new areas of accounting which have not, as yet, been generally applied? What about different accounting treatments for similar items – are they all generally accepted?
>
> 'It is our view that 'generally accepted' does **not** mean 'generally adopted or used'. We believe that, in the UK context, GAAP refers to accounting practices which are regarded as permissible by the accounting profession. The extent to which a particular practice has been adopted is, in our opinion, not the overriding consideration. Any accounting practice which is legitimate in the circumstances under which it has been applied should be regarded as GAAP. The decision as to whether or not a particular practice is permissible or legitimate would depend on one or more of the following factors:
>
> - Is the practice addressed either in the accounting standards, statute or other official pronouncements?
> - If the practice is not addressed in UK accounting standards, is it dealt with in International Accounting Standards, or the standards of other countries such as the US?
> - Is the practice consistent with the needs of users and the objectives of financial reporting?
> - Does the practice have authoritative support in the accounting literature?
> - Is the practice being applied by other companies in similar situations?
> - Is the practice consistent with the fundamental concept of 'true and fair'?'

This view is not held in all countries, however. In the USA particularly, the equivalent of a 'true and fair view' is 'fair presentation in accordance with GAAP'. Generally accepted accounting principles are defined as those principles which have 'substantial authoritative support'. Therefore accounts prepared in accordance with accounting principles for which there is not substantial authoritative support are presumed to be misleading or inaccurate.

The effect here is that 'new' or 'different' accounting principles are not acceptable unless they have been adopted by the mainstream accounting profession, usually the standard-setting bodies and/or professional accountancy bodies. This is much more rigid than the UK view expressed above.

A **conceptual framework** for financial reporting can be defined as an attempt to codify existing GAAP in order to reappraise current accounting standards and to produce new standards.

2 The IASB's Framework

The *Framework* provides the conceptual framework for the development of IFRSs/IASs.

In July 1989 the IASB (then IASC) produced a document, *Framework for the preparation and presentation of financial statements* (*'Framework'*). The *Framework* is, in effect, the **conceptual** framework upon which all IASs are based and hence which determines how financial statements are prepared and the information they contain.

The *Framework* consists of several sections or chapters, following on after a preface and introduction. These chapters are as follows.

- The objective of financial statements
- Underlying assumptions
- Qualitative characteristics of financial statements
- The elements of financial statements
- Recognition of the elements of financial statements
- Measurement of the elements of financial statements
- Concepts of capital and capital maintenance

We will look briefly at the preface and introduction to the *Framework* as these will place the document in context with the rest of what you have studied for this paper and in particular the context of the *Framework* in the IASB's approach to developing IASs.

As you read through this chapter think about the impact the *Framework* has had on IASs, particularly the definitions.

2.1 Preface

The preface to the *Framework* points out the fundamental reason why financial statements are produced worldwide, ie to **satisfy the requirements of external users**, but that practice varies due to the individual pressures in each country. These pressures may be social, political, economic or legal, but they result in variations in practice from country to country, including the form of statements, the definition of their component parts (assets, liabilities etc), the criteria for recognition of items and both the scope and disclosure of financial statements.

It is these differences which the IASB wishes to narrow by **harmonising** all aspects of financial statements, including the regulations governing their accounting standards and their preparation and presentation.

The preface emphasises the way **financial statements are used to make economic decisions** and thus financial statements should be prepared to this end. The types of economic decisions for which financial statements are likely to be used include the following.

- Decisions to buy, hold or sell equity investments
- Assessment of management stewardship and accountability
- Assessment of the entity's ability to pay employees
- Assessment of the security of amounts lent to the entity
- Determination of taxation policies
- Determination of distributable profits and dividends
- Inclusion in national income statistics
- Regulations of the activities of entities

Any additional requirements imposed by **national governments** for their own purposes should not affect financial statements produced for the benefit of other users.

The *Framework* recognises that financial statements can be prepared using a **variety of models**. Although the most common is based on historical cost and a nominal unit of currency (ie pound sterling, US dollar etc), the *Framework* can be applied to financial statements prepared under a range of models.

2.2 Introduction

The introduction to the *Framework* lays out the purpose, status and scope of the document. It then looks at different users of financial statements and their information needs.

2.2.1 Purpose and status

The introduction gives a list of the purposes of the *Framework*.

(a)   Assist the Board of the IASB in the **development of future IASs** and in its review of existing IASs.

(b)   Assist the Board of the IASB in **promoting harmonisation** of regulations, accounting standards and procedures relating to the presentation of financial statements by providing a basis for reducing the number of alternative accounting treatments permitted by IASs.

(c)   Assist **national standard-setting bodies** in developing national standards.

(d)   Assist **preparers of financial statements** in applying IASs and in dealing with topics that have yet to form the subject of an IAS.

(e)   Assist **auditors** in forming an opinion as to whether financial statements conform with IASs.

(f)   Assist **users of financial statements** in interpreting the information contained in financial statements prepared in conformity with IASs.

(g)   Provide those who are interested in the work of IASB with **information** about its approach to the formulation of IASs (now IFRSs).

The *Framework* is not an IAS and so does not overrule any individual IAS. In the (rare) cases of conflict between an IAS and the *Framework*, the **IAS will prevail**. These cases will diminish over time as the *Framework* will be used as a guide in the production of future IASs. The *Framework* itself will be revised occasionally depending on the experience of the IASB in using it.

2.2.2 Scope

The *Framework* deals with:

(a)   The **objective** of financial statements

(b)   The **qualitative characteristics** that determine the usefulness of information in financial statements

(c)   The **definition, recognition and measurement** of the elements from which financial statements are constructed

(d)   Concepts of **capital and capital maintenance**

The *Framework* is concerned with **'general purpose' financial statements** (ie a normal set of annual statements), but it can be applied to other types of accounts. A complete set of financial statements includes:

(a)   A statement of financial position

(b)   A statement of comprehensive income

(c)   A statement of changes in financial position (eg a statement of cash flows)

(d)   Notes, other statements and explanatory material

Supplementary information may be included, but some items are not included in the financial statements themselves, namely commentaries and reports by the directors, the chairman, management etc.

All types of financial reporting entities are included (commercial, industrial, business; public or private sector).

Key term

2.2.3 Users and their information needs

We have already looked at the users of accounting information in Chapter 1. They consist of investors, employees, lenders, suppliers and other trade creditors, customers, government and their agencies and the public. You should be able to remember enough to do the following exercise.

Question — Users of financial information

Consider the information needs of the users of financial information listed above.

Answer

(a) **Investors** are the providers of risk capital

    (i)   Information is required to help make a decision about buying or selling shares, taking up a rights issue and voting.

    (ii)   Investors must have information about the level of dividend, past, present and future and any changes in share price.

    (iii)   Investors will also need to know whether the management has been running the company efficiently.

    (iv)   As well as the position indicated by the statement of comprehensive income, statement of financial position and earnings per share (EPS), investors will want to know about the liquidity position of the company, the company's future prospects, and how the company's shares compare with those of its competitors.

(b) **Employees** need information about the security of employment and future prospects for jobs in the company, and to help with collective pay bargaining.

(c) **Lenders** need information to help them decide whether to lend to a company. They will also need to check that the value of any security remains adequate, that the interest repayments are secure, that the cash is available for redemption at the appropriate time and that any financial restrictions (such as maximum debt/equity ratios) have not been breached.

(d) **Suppliers** need to know whether the company will be a good customer and pay its debts.

(e) **Customers** need to know whether the company will be able to continue producing and supplying goods.

(f) **Government's** interest in a company may be one of creditor or customer, as well as being specifically concerned with compliance with tax and company law, ability to pay tax and the general contribution of the company to the economy.

(g) The **public** at large would wish to have information for all the reasons mentioned above, but it could be suggested that it would be impossible to provide general purpose accounting information which was specifically designed for the needs of the public.

Financial statements cannot meet all these users' needs, but financial statements which meet the **needs of investors** (providers of risk capital) will meet most of the needs of other users.

The *Framework* emphasises that the preparation and presentation of financial statements is primarily the **responsibility of an entity's management**. Management also has an interest in the information appearing in financial statements.

2.3 IAS 1 Presentation of financial statements

Much of what IAS 1 states in relation to accounting policies and the formats of financial statements repeats the contents of the *Framework* document. IAS 1 is considered in detail in Chapter 3.

3 The objective of financial statements

FAST FORWARD

The *Framework* states that:

> 'The objective of financial statements is to provide information about the financial position, performance and changes in financial position of an entity that is useful to a wide range of users in making economic decisions.'

Such financial statements will meet the needs of most users. The information is, however, **restricted**.

(a)   It is based on **past events** not expected future events.

(b)   It does not necessarily contain **non-financial information**.

The statements also show the results of **management's stewardship**.

3.1 Financial position, performance and changes in financial position

It is important for users to assess the **ability of an entity to produce cash and cash equivalents** to pay employees, lenders etc.

Financial position information is affected by the following and information about each one can aid the user.

(a)   **Economic resources controlled**: to predict the ability to generate cash

(b)   **Financial structure**: to predict borrowing needs, the distribution of future profits/cash and likely success in raising new finance

(c)   **Liquidity and solvency**: to predict whether financial commitments will be met as they fall due (liquidity relates to short-term commitments, solvency is longer-term)

Key term

> **Liquidity**. The availability of sufficient funds to meet deposit withdrawals and other short-term financial commitments as they fall due.
>
> **Solvency**. The availability of cash over the longer term to meet financial commitments as they fall due.
>
> *(Framework)*

In all these areas, the capacity to adapt to changes in the environment in which the entity operates is very important.

Financial performance (statement of comprehensive income) information, particularly profitability, is used to assess potential changes in the economic resources the entity is likely to control in future. Information about performance variability is therefore important.

Changes in financial position (ie statement of cash flows) information is used to assess the entity's investing, financing and operating activities. They show the entity's ability to produce cash and the needs which utilise those cash flows.

All parts of the financial statements are **interrelated**, reflecting different aspects of the same transactions or events. Each statement provides different information; none can provide all the information required by users.

4 Underlying assumptions

FAST FORWARD

Accruals and **going concern** are the two underlying assumptions in preparing financial statements.

4.1 Accruals basis

Key term

Accruals basis. The effects of transactions and other events are recognised when they occur (and not as cash or its equivalent is received or paid) and they are recorded in the accounting records and reported in the financial statements of the periods to which they relate. *(Framework)*

Financial statements prepared under the accruals basis show users past transactions involving cash and also obligations to pay cash in the future and resources which represent cash to be received in the future.

4.2 Going concern

Key term

Going concern. The entity is normally viewed as a going concern, that is, as continuing in operation for the foreseeable future. It is assumed that the entity has neither the intention nor the necessity of liquidation or of curtailing materially the scale of its operations. *(Framework)*

It is assumed that the entity has no intention to liquidate or curtail major operations. If it did, then the financial statements would be prepared on a **different (disclosed) basis.**

5 Qualitative characteristics of financial statements

FAST FORWARD

The *Framework* states that qualitative characteristics are the attributes that make the information provided in financial statements useful to users.

The four principal qualitative characteristics are understandability, relevance, reliability and comparability.

5.1 Understandability

Users must be able to understand financial statements. They are assumed to have some business, economic and accounting knowledge and to be able to apply themselves to study the information properly. **Complex matters should not be left out** of financial statements simply due to its difficulty if it is relevant information.

5.2 Relevance

The **predictive and confirmatory roles** of information are interrelated.

Key term

Relevance Information has the quality of relevance when it influences the economic decisions of users by helping them evaluate past, present or future events or confirming, or correcting, their past evaluations. *(Framework)*

Information on financial position and performance is often used to predict future position and performance and other things of interest to the user, eg likely dividend, wage rises. The **manner of showing information** will enhance the ability to make predictions, eg by highlighting unusual items.

5.2.1 Materiality

The relevance of information is affected by its **nature and materiality**.

Key term

> **Materiality**. Information is material if its omission or misstatement could influence the economic decisions of users taken on the basis of the financial statements. *(Framework)*

Information may be judged relevant simply because of its nature (eg remuneration of management). In other cases, both the nature and materiality of the information are important. Materiality is not a primary qualitative characteristic itself (like reliability or relevance), because it is merely a threshold or cut-off point.

5.3 Reliability

Information must also be reliable to be useful. The user must be able to depend on it being a **faithful representation**.

Key term

> **Reliability**. Information has the quality of reliability when it is free from material error and bias and can be depended upon by users to represent faithfully that which it either purports to represent or could reasonably be expected to represent. *(Framework)*

Even if information is relevant, if it is very unreliable it may be **misleading to recognise it**, eg a disputed claim for damages in a legal action.

Exam focus point

> The pilot paper has a question on qualitative characteristics of financial information.

5.3.1 Faithful representation

Information must represent faithfully the transactions it purports to represent in order to be reliable. There is a risk that this may not be the case, not due to bias, but due to **inherent difficulties in identifying the transactions** or finding an **appropriate method of measurement or presentation**. Where measurement of the financial effects of an item is so uncertain, entities should not recognise such an item, eg internally generated goodwill.

5.3.2 Substance over form

Faithful representation of a transaction is only possible if it is accounted for according to its **substance and economic reality**, not with its legal form.

Key term

> **Substance over form**. The principle that transactions and other events are accounted for and presented in accordance with their substance and economic reality and not merely their legal form. *(Framework)*

For instance, one party may sell an asset to another party and the sales documentation may record that legal ownership has been transferred. However, if agreements exist whereby the party selling the asset continues to enjoy the future economic benefits arising from the asset, then in substance no sale has taken place. This issue is covered in more detail in Chapter 14.

5.3.3 Neutrality

Information must be **free from bias** to be reliable. Neutrality is lost if the financial statements are prepared so as to influence the user to make a judgement or decision in order to achieve a predetermined outcome.

5.3.4 Prudence

Uncertainties exist in the preparation of financial information, eg the collectability of doubtful receivables. These uncertainties are recognised through disclosure and through the application of prudence. Prudence does not, however, allow the creation of hidden reserves or excessive provisions, understatement of assets or income or overstatement of liabilities or expenses.

5.3.5 Completeness

Financial information must be complete, within the **restrictions of materiality and cost**, to be reliable. Omission may cause information to be misleading.

5.4 Comparability

Users must be able to compare an entity's financial statements:

(a) **Through time** to identify trends
(b) **With other entities' statements**, to evaluate their relative financial position, performance and changes in financial position

The consistency of treatment is therefore important across like items over time, within the entity and across all entities.

The **disclosure of accounting policies** is particularly important here. Users must be able to distinguish between different accounting policies in order to be able to make a valid comparison of similar items in the accounts of different entities.

Comparability is **not the same as uniformity**. Entities should change accounting policies if they become inappropriate.

Corresponding information for **preceding periods** should be shown to enable comparison over time.

5.5 Constraints on relevant and reliable information

5.5.1 Timeliness

Information may become irrelevant if there is a delay in reporting it. There is a **balance between timeliness and the provision of reliable information**. Information may be reported on a timely basis when not all aspects of the transaction are known, thus compromising reliability.

If every detail of a transaction is known, it may be too late to publish the information because it has become irrelevant. The overriding consideration is how best to satisfy the economic decision-making needs of the users.

5.5.2 Balance between benefits and cost

This is a pervasive constraint, not a qualitative characteristic. When information is provided, its benefits must exceed the costs of obtaining and presenting it. This is a **subjective area** and there are other difficulties: others than the intended users may gain a benefit; also the cost may be paid by someone other than the users. It is therefore difficult to apply a cost-benefit analysis, but preparers and users should be aware of the constraint.

5.5.3 Balance between qualitative characteristics

A **trade off between qualitative characteristics** is often necessary, the aim being to achieve an appropriate balance to meet the objective of financial statements. It is a matter for professional judgement as to the relative importance of these characteristics in each case.

5.6 True and fair view/fair presentation

The *Framework* does not attempt to define these concepts directly. It does state, however, that the application of the **principal 'qualitative' characteristics** and of **appropriate accounting standards** will usually result in financial statements which show a true and fair view, or present fairly.

6 The elements of financial statements

> Transactions and other events are grouped together in broad **classes** and in this way their financial effects are shown in the financial statements. These broad classes are the **elements** of financial statements.

The *Framework* lays out these elements as follows.

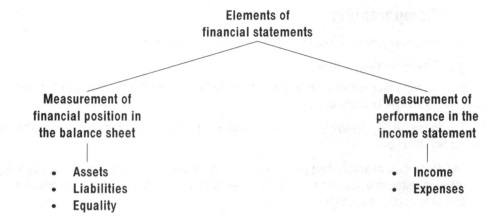

A process of **sub-classification** then takes place for presentation in the financial statements, eg assets are classified by their nature or function in the business to show information in the best way for users to take economic decisions.

6.1 Financial position

We need to define the three terms listed under this heading above.

Key terms

- **Asset**. A resource controlled by an entity as a result of past events and from which future economic benefits are expected to flow to the entity.

- **Liability**. A present obligation of the entity arising from past events, the settlement of which is expected to result in an outflow from the entity of resources embodying economic benefits.

- **Equity**. The residual interest in the assets of the entity after deducting all its liabilities. *(Framework)*

These definitions are important, but they do not cover the **criteria for recognition** of any of these items, which are discussed in the next section of this chapter. This means that the definitions may include items which would not actually be recognised in the statement of financial position because they fail to satisfy recognition criteria particularly, as we will see below, the **probable flow of any economic benefit** to or from the business.

Whether an item satisfies any of the definitions above will depend on the **substance and economic reality** of the transaction, not merely its legal form. For example, consider finance leases (see Chapter 16).

6.2 Assets

We can look in more detail at the components of the definitions given above.

Key term

> **Future economic benefit**. The potential to contribute, directly or indirectly, to the flow of cash and cash equivalents to the entity. The potential may be a productive one that is part of the operating activities of the entity. It may also take the form of convertibility into cash or cash equivalents or a capability to reduce cash outflows, such as when an alternative manufacturing process lowers the cost of production.
>
> *(Framework)*

Assets are usually employed to produce goods or services for customers; customers will then pay for these. **Cash itself** renders a service to the entity due to its command over other resources.

The existence of an asset, particularly in terms of **control**, is not reliant on:

(a)   **physical form** (hence patents and copyrights); *nor*
(b)   **legal rights** (hence leases).

Transactions or events **in the past** give rise to assets; those expected to occur in the future do not in themselves give rise to assets. For example, an intention to purchase a non-current asset does not, in itself, meet the definition of an asset.

6.3 Liabilities

Again we can look more closely at some aspects of the definition. An essential characteristic of a liability is that the entity has a **present obligation**.

Key term

> **Obligation.** A duty or responsibility to act or perform in a certain way. Obligations may be legally enforceable as a consequence of a binding contract or statutory requirement. Obligations also arise, however, from normal business practice, custom and a desire to maintain good business relations or act in an equitable manner.
> *(Framework)*

It is important to distinguish between a present obligation and a **future commitment**. A management decision to purchase assets in the future does not, in itself, give rise to a present obligation.

Settlement of a present obligation will involve the entity giving up resources embodying economic benefits in order to satisfy the claim of the other party. This may be done in various ways, not just by payment of cash.

Liabilities must arise from **past transactions or events**. In the case of, say, recognition of future rebates to customers based on annual purchases, the sale of goods in the past is the transaction that gives rise to the liability.

6.3.1 Provisions

Is a provision a liability?

Key term

> **Provision.** A present obligation which satisfies the rest of the definition of a liability, even if the amount of the obligation has to be estimated.
> *(Framework)*

Question   Definite variables

Consider the following situations. In each case, do we have an asset or liability within the definitions given by the *Framework?* Give reasons for your answer.

(a)   Pat Co has purchased a patent for $20,000. The patent gives the company sole use of a particular manufacturing process which will save $3,000 a year for the next five years.
(b)   Baldwin Co paid Don Brennan $10,000 to set up a car repair shop, on condition that priority treatment is given to cars from the company's fleet.
(c)   Deals on Wheels Co provides a warranty with every car sold.

Answer

(a)   This is an asset, albeit an intangible one. There is a past event, control and future economic benefit (through cost savings).
(b)   This cannot be classified as an asset. Baldwin Co has no control over the car repair shop and it is difficult to argue that there are 'future economic benefits'.

(c)   This is a liability; the business has taken on an obligation. It would be recognised when the warranty is issued rather than when a claim is made.

6.4 Equity

Equity is defined above as a **residual**, but it may be sub-classified in the statement of financial position. This will indicate legal or other restrictions on the ability of the entity to distribute or otherwise apply its equity. Some reserves are required by statute or other law, eg for the future protection of creditors. The amount shown for equity depends on the **measurement of assets and liabilities.** It has nothing to do with the market value of the entity's shares.

6.5 Performance

Profit is used as a **measure of performance**, or as a basis for other measures (eg EPS). It depends directly on the measurement of income and expenses, which in turn depend (in part) on the concepts of capital and capital maintenance adopted.

The elements of income and expense are therefore defined.

Key term

> - **Income**. Increases in economic benefits during the accounting period in the form of inflows or enhancements of assets or decreases of liabilities that result in increases in equity, other than those relating to contributions from equity participants.
> - **Expenses**. Decreases in economic benefits during the accounting period in the form of outflows or depletions of assets or incurrences of liabilities that result in decreases in equity, other than those relating to distributions to equity participants.
>
> *(Framework)*

Income and expenses can be **presented in different ways** in the statement of comprehensive income, to provide information relevant for economic decision-making. For example, distinguish between income and expenses which relate to continuing operations and those which do not.

Items of income and expense can be **distinguished** from each other or **combined** with each other.

6.6 Income

Both **revenue** and **gains** are included in the definition of income. **Revenue** arises in the course of ordinary activities of an entity.

Key term

> **Gains**. Increases in economic benefits. As such they are no different in nature from revenue. *(Framework)*

Gains include those arising on the disposal of non-current assets. The definition of income also includes **unrealised gains**, eg on revaluation of marketable securities.

6.7 Expenses

As with income, the definition of expenses includes losses as well as those expenses that arise in the course of ordinary activities of an entity.

Key term

> **Losses**. Decreases in economic benefits. As such they are no different in nature from other expenses.
> *(Framework)*

Losses will include those arising on the disposal of non-current assets. The definition of expenses will also include **unrealised losses**, eg exchange rate effects on borrowings.

6.8 Capital maintenance adjustments

A **revaluation** gives rise to an increase or decrease in equity.

Key term

Revaluation. Restatement of assets and liabilities. *(Framework)*

These increases and decreases meet the definitions of income and expenses. They are **not included** in the statement of comprehensive income under certain concepts of capital maintenance, however, but rather in equity.

6.9 Section summary

Make sure you learn the important definitions.

- Financial position:
  - Assets
  - Liabilities
  - Equity

- Financial performance:
  - Income
  - Expenses

7 Recognition of the elements of financial statements

FAST FORWARD

Items which meet the definition of assets or liabilities may still not be recognised in financial statements because they must also meet certain **recognition criteria**.

Key term

Recognition. The process of incorporating in the statement of financial position or statement of comprehensive income an item that meets the definition of an element and satisfies the following criteria for recognition:

(a)   it is probable that any future economic benefit associated with the item will flow to or from the entity; and

(b)   the item has a cost or value that can be measured with reliability.

(Framework)

Regard must be given to **materiality** (see Section 5 above).

7.1 Probability of future economic benefits

Probability here means the **degree of uncertainty** that the future economic benefits associated with an item will flow to or from the entity. This must be judged on the basis of the **characteristics of the entity's environment** and the **evidence available** when the financial statements are prepared.

7.2 Reliability of measurement

The cost or value of an item, in many cases, **must be estimated**. The *Framework* states, however, that the use of reasonable estimates is an essential part of the preparation of financial statements and does not undermine their reliability. Where no reasonable estimate can be made, the item should not be recognised, although its existence should be disclosed in the notes, or other explanatory material.

Items may still qualify for recognition **at a later date** due to changes in circumstances or subsequent events.

7.3 Recognition of items

We can summarise the recognition criteria for assets, liabilities, income and expenses, based on the definition of recognition given above.

Item	Recognised in	When
Asset	The statement of financial position	It is probable that the future economic benefits will flow to the entity and the asset has a cost or value that can be measured reliably.
Liability	The statement of financial position	It is probable that an outflow of resources embodying economic benefits will result from the settlement of a present obligation and the amount at which the settlement will take place can be measured reliably.
Income	The statement of comprehensive income	An increase in future economic benefits related to an increase in an asset or a decrease of a liability has arisen that can be measured reliably.
Expenses	The statement of comprehensive income	A decrease in future economic benefits related to a decrease in an asset or an increase of a liability has arisen that can be measured reliably.

8 Measurement of the elements of financial statements

FAST FORWARD

A number of different measurement bases are used in financial statements. They include

- Historical cost
- Current cost
- Realisable (settlement) value
- Present value of future cash flows

Measurement is defined as follows.

Key term

Measurement. The process of determining the monetary amounts at which the elements of the financial statements are to be recognised and carried in the statement of financial position and statement of comprehensive income.   *(Framework)*

This involves the selection of a particular **basis of measurement**. A number of these are used to different degrees and in varying combinations in financial statements. They include the following.

Key terms

Historical cost. Assets are recorded at the amount of cash or cash equivalents paid or the fair value of the consideration given to acquire them at the time of their acquisition. Liabilities are recorded at the amount of proceeds received in exchange for the obligation, or in some circumstances (for example, income taxes), at the amounts of cash or cash equivalents expected to be paid to satisfy the liability in the normal course of business.

Current cost. Assets are carried at the amount of cash or cash equivalents that would have to be paid if the same or an equivalent asset was acquired currently.

Liabilities are carried at the undiscounted amount of cash or cash equivalents that would be required to settle the obligation currently.

Realisable (settlement) value.

- **Realisable value**. The amount of cash or cash equivalents that could currently be obtained by selling an asset in an orderly disposal.

- **Settlement value**. The undiscounted amounts of cash or cash equivalents expected to be paid to satisfy the liabilities in the normal course of business.

Present value. A current estimate of the present discounted value of the future net cash flows in the normal course of business.

(Framework)

Historical cost is the most commonly adopted measurement basis, but this is usually combined with other bases, eg inventory is carried at the lower of cost and net realisable value.

9 Fair presentation and compliance with IFRS

Most importantly, financial statements should **present fairly** the financial position, financial performance and cash flows of an entity. **Compliance with IFRS** is presumed to result in financial statements that achieve a fair presentation.

The following points made by IAS 1 expand on this principle.

(a)   **Compliance with IFRS** should be disclosed

(b)   **All relevant IFRS** must be followed if compliance with IFRS is disclosed

(c)   Use of an **inappropriate accounting treatment** cannot be rectified either by disclosure of accounting policies or notes/explanatory material

There may be (very rare) circumstances when management decides that compliance with a requirement of an IFRS would be misleading. **Departure from the IFRS** is therefore required to achieve a fair presentation. The following should be disclosed in such an event.

(a)   Management confirmation that the financial statements fairly present the entity's financial position, performance and cash flows

(b)   Statement that all IFRS have been complied with *except* departure from one IFRS to achieve a fair presentation

(c)   Details of the nature of the departure, why the IFRS treatment would be misleading, and the treatment adopted

(d)   Financial impact of the departure

This is usually referred to as the **'true and fair override'**.

9.1 Extreme case disclosures

In very rare circumstances, management may conclude that compliance with a requirement in a Standard or interpretation may be so **misleading** that it would **conflict with the objective** of Financial Statements set out in the *Framework*, but the relevant regulatory framework prohibits departure from the requirements. In such cases the entity needs to reduce the perceived misleading aspects of compliance by **disclosing**:

(a)   The title of the Standard, the nature of the requirement and the reason why management has reached its conclusion.

(b)   For each period, the adjustment to each item in the Financial Statements that would be necessary to achieve fair presentation.

IAS 1 states what is required for a fair presentation.

(a)   Selection and application of **accounting policies**

(b)   **Presentation of information** in a manner which provides relevant, reliable, comparable and understandable information

(c)   **Additional disclosures** where required

Chapter roundup

- There are advantages and disadvantages to having a conceptual framework.

- The *Framework* provides the conceptual framework for the development of IFRSs/IASs.

- The objective of financial statements is to provide information about the financial position, performance and changes in financial position of an entity.

- **Accruals** and **going concern** are the two underlying assumptions in preparing financial statements.

- The *Framework* states that qualitative characteristics are the attributes that make the information provided in financial statements useful to users.

- Transactions and other events are grouped together in broad **classes** and in this way their financial effects are shown in the financial statements. These broad classes are the **elements** of financial statements.

- Items which meet the definition of assets or liabilities may still not be recognised in financial statements because they must also meet certain **recognition criteria**.

- A number of different measurement bases are used in financial statements. They include:

    - Historical cost
    - Current cost
    - Realisable (settlement) value
    - Present value of future cash flows

Quick quiz

1   Define a 'conceptual framework'.
2   What are the advantages and disadvantages of developing a conceptual framework?
3   The needs of which category of user are paramount when preparing financial statements?
4   Define 'relevance'.
5   In which two ways should users be able to compare an entity's financial statements?
6   A provision can be a liability. True or false?
7   Define 'recognition'.
8   The cost or value of items in the financial statements is never estimated. True or false?
9   What is the most common basis of measurement used in financial statements?

Answers to quick quiz

1   This is a statement of generally accepted theoretical principles, which form the frame of reference for financial reporting.

2   *Advantages*
    - Standardised accounting practice
    - Less open to criticism
    - Concentrate on statement of comprehensive income or statement of financial position, as appropriate

    Disadvantages
    - Variety of users, so not all will be satisfied
    - Variety of standards for different purposes
    - Preparing and implementing standards not necessarily any easier

3   Needs of investors

4   Information has relevance when it influences the economic decisions of users by helping them evaluate past, present or future events or confirming (or correcting) their past evaluations.

5   - Through time to identify trends
    - With other entities' statements

6   True. It satisfies the definition of a liability but the amount may need to be estimated.

7   See Key Term Section 7.

8   False. Monetary values are often estimated.

9   Historical cost.

Now try the questions below from the Exam Question Bank

Number	Level	Marks	Time
1	Examination	10	18 mins

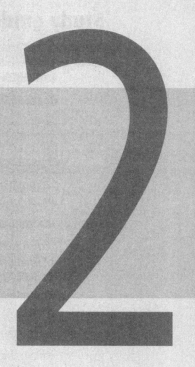

The regulatory framework

Topic list	Syllabus reference
1 The need for a regulatory framework	B1
2 The International Accounting Standards Board (IASB)	B2
3 Setting of International Financial Reporting Standards	B2

Introduction

We have already discussed the IASB and IFRSs to some extent. Here we are concerned with the IASB's relationship with other bodies, and with the way the IASB operates and how IFRSs are produced.

Later in this text we look at some of the theory behind what appears in the accounts. The most important document in this area is the IASB's *Framework for the preparation and presentation of financial statements*. Since it was published, all IFRSs have been based on the principles it contains.

Study guide

		Intellectual level
B	**A REGULATORY FRAMEWORK FOR FINANCIAL REPORTING**	
1	**Reasons for the existence of a regulatory framework**	
(a)	explain why a regulatory framework is needed.	2
(b)	explain why accounting standards on their own are not a complete regulatory framework.	2
(c)	distinguish between a principles based and a rules based framework and discuss whether they can be complementary.	1
2	**The standard setting process**	
(a)	describe the structure and objectives of the IASC Foundation, the International Accounting Standards Board (IASB), the Standards Advisory Council (SAC) and the International Financial Reporting Interpretations Committee (IFRIC).	2
(b)	describe the IASB's Standard setting process including revisions to and interpretations of Standards.	2
(c)	explain the relationship of national standard setters to the IASB in respect of the standard setting process.	2

Exam guide

You may be asked about these topics as part of a longer question.

1 The need for a regulatory framework

1.1 Introduction

The regulatory framework is the most important element in ensuring relevant and reliable financial reporting and thus meeting the needs of shareholders and other users.

Without a single body overall responsible for producing financial reporting standards (the IASB) and a framework of general principles within which they can be produced (the *Framework*), there would be no means of enforcing compliance with GAAP. Also, GAAP would be unable to evolve in any structured way in response to changes in economic conditions.

1.2 Principles-based versus rules-based systems

FAST FORWARD

A principles-based system works within a set of laid down principles. A rules-based system regulates for issues as they arise. Both of these have advantages and disadvantages.

The *Framework* provides the background of principles within which standards can be developed. This system is intended to ensure that standards are not produced which are in conflict with each other and also that any departure from a standard can be judged on the basis of whether or not it is in keeping with the principles set out in the *Framework*. This is a **principles-based** system.

In the absence of a reporting framework, a more **rules-based** approach has to be adopted. This leads to a large mass of regulation designed to cover every eventuality, as in the US. As we have seen over the past few years, a large volume of regulatory measures does not always detect or prevent financial irregularity.

1.3 Problems of a principles-based system

The principles-based system also has its drawbacks. The *Framework* was produced in 1989 by the IASC and adopted by the IASB in 2001. It is now 18 years old and in danger of becoming out of date as constant changes take place in financial reporting. IFRSs are reflecting these changes but the *Framework* which underpins them is not.

For instance, the 'fair value' concept is now an important part of many IFRSs, but is not referred to in the *Framework*. So the IFRSs are running ahead of the *Framework*, rather than vice versa. In this regard, a rules-based system, while more unwieldy, at least has the merit of keeping pace with what is happening.

If it is accepted that the *Framework* should be subject to a continuous process of review and updating, then some machinery will have to be set up to do this, and a rules-based approach could be used to deal with issues which arise between reviews.

The IASB and the FASB are now working to produce a joint conceptual framework which should combine the best of both approaches.

2 The International Accounting Standards Board (IASB)

FAST FORWARD

The organisational structure consists of:

- The IASC Foundation
- The IASB
- The Standards Advisory Council (SAC)
- The International Financial Reporting Interpretations Committee

2.1 Introduction

The International Accounting Standards Board is an independent, privately-funded accounting standard setter based in London.

In March 2001 the IASC Foundation was formed as a not-for-profit corporation incorporated in the USA. The IASC Foundation is the parent entity of the IASB.

From April 2001 the IASB assumed accounting standard setting responsibilities from its predecessor body, the International Accounting Standards Committee (IASC). This restructuring was based upon the recommendations made in the *Recommendations on Shaping IASC for the Future*.

2.2 How the IASB is made up

The 14 members of the IASB come from nine countries and have a variety of backgrounds with a mix of auditors, preparers of financial statements, users of financial statements and an academic. The Board consists of 12 full-time members and two part-time members.

2.3 Objectives of the IASB

The formal objectives of the IASB, formulated in its mission statement are:

(a) To develop, in the public interest, a single set of high quality, understandable and enforceable global accounting standards that require high quality, transparent and comparable information in general purpose financial statements

(b) To provide the use and vigorous application of those standards

(c) To work actively with national accounting standard setters to bring about convergence of national accounting standards and IFRS to high quality solutions.

2.4 Structure of the IASB

The structure of the IASB has the following main features.

(a)   The IASC Foundation is an independent corporation having two main bodies – the Trustees and the IASB. The IASC Foundation holds the copyright of IFRSs and all other IASB publications.

(b)   The IASC Foundation trustees appoint the IASB members, exercise oversight and raise the funds needed.

(c)   The IASB has sole responsibility for setting accounting standards.

(d)   There are also two further bodies, the Standards Advisory Council and the International Financial Reporting Interpretations Committee (see below).

The structure can be illustrated as follows.

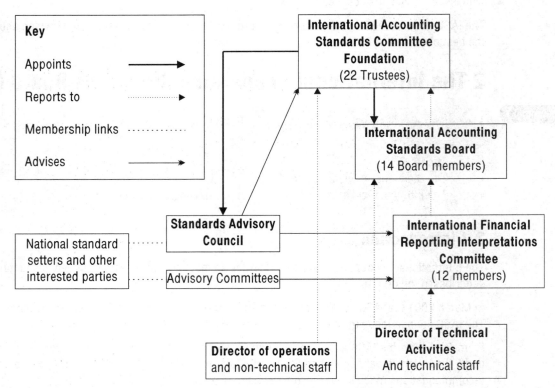

Trustees. The Trustees comprise a group of twenty two individuals, with diverse geographic and functional backgrounds. The Trustees appoint the Members of the Board, the International Financial Reporting Interpretations Committee and the Standards Advisory Council. In addition to monitoring IASC's effectiveness and raising its funds, the Trustees will approve IASC's budget and have responsibility for constitutional changes. Trustees were appointed so that initially there were six from North America, six from Europe, four from Asia Pacific, and three others from any area, as long as geographic balance is maintained.

(a)   The International Federation of Accountants (IFAC) suggested candidates to fill five of the nineteen Trustee seats and international organisations of preparers, users and academics each suggested one candidate.

(b)   The remaining eleven Trustees are 'at-large' in that they were not selected through the constituency nomination process.

Standards Advisory Council. The Standards Advisory Council provides a formal vehicle for further groups and individuals with diverse geographic and functional backgrounds to give advice to the Board and, at times, to advise the Trustees. It comprises about fifty members and meets at least three times a year. It is consulted by the IASB on all major projects and its meetings are open to the public. It advises the IASB on prioritisation of its work and on the implications of proposed standards for users and preparers of financial statements.

International Financial Reporting Interpretations Committee. The IFRIC provides timely guidance on the application and interpretation of International Financial Reporting Standards. It deals with newly identified financial reporting issues not specifically addressed in IFRSs, or issues where unsatisfactory or conflicting interpretations have developed, or seem likely to develop.

2.5 Other international influences

There are a few **other international bodies** worth mentioning. You are not required to follow their workings in detail, but knowledge of them will aid your studies and should help your general reading around the subject area

2.5.1 IASB and the EC/intergovernmental bodies

The European Commission has acknowledged the role of the IASB in harmonising world-wide accounting rules and EC representatives attend IASB Board meetings and have joined Steering Committees involved in setting IFRSs. This should bring to an end the idea of a separate layer of European reporting rules.

The EC has also set up a committee to investigate where there are conflicts between EU norms and international standards so that compatibility can be achieved. In turn, the IASB has used EC directives in its work.

All listed entities in member states must use IFRSs in their consolidated financial statements from 2005.

The IASB also works closely with the United Nations Working Groups of Experts on International Standards of Accounting and Reporting (UN IASR group), and with the Working Group in Accounting Standards of the Organisation for Economic Co-operation and Development (OECD Working group). These bodies support harmonisation and improvement of financial reporting, but they are not standard-setting bodies and much of their output draws on the work of the IASB (eg using the IASB's *Framework* document).

2.5.2 United Nations (UN)

The UN has a Commission and Centre on Transnational Reporting Corporations through which it gathers information concerning the activities and reporting of multinational companies. The UN processes are highly **political** and probably reflect the attitudes of the governments of developing countries to multinationals. For example, there is an inter-governmental working group of 'experts' on international standards of accounting and reporting which is dominated by the non-developed countries.

2.5.3 International Federation of Accountants (IFAC)

The IFAC is a private sector body established in 1977 and which now consists of over 100 professional accounting bodies from around 80 different countries. The IFAC's main objective is to co-ordinate the accounting profession on a global scale by issuing and establishing international standards on auditing, management accounting, ethics, education and training. You are already familiar with the **International Standards on Auditing** produced by the IAASB, an IFAC body. The IFAC has separate committees working on these topics and also organises the World Congress of Accountants, which is held every five years. The IASB is affiliated with IFAC.

2.5.4 Organisation for Economic Co-operation and Development (OECD)

The OECD was established in 1960 by the governments of 21 countries to 'achieve the highest sustainable economic growth and employment and a rising standard of living in member countries while maintaining financial stability and, thus, to contribute to the world economy'. The OECD supports the work of the IASB but also undertakes its **own research** into accounting standards via *ad hoc* working groups. For example, in 1976 the OECD issued guidelines for multinational companies on financial reporting and non-financial disclosures. The OECD appears to work on behalf of developed countries to protect them from the extreme proposals of the UN.

2.6 Generally Accepted Accounting Practice (GAAP)

We also need to consider some important terms which you will meet in your financial accounting studies. GAAP, as a term, has sprung up in recent years and signifies **all the rules, from whatever source, which govern accounting**. The rules may derive from:

(a) Local (national) company legislation
(b) National and international accounting standards
(c) Statutory requirements in other countries (particularly the US)
(d) Stock exchange requirements

2.7 True and fair view (or presented fairly)

It is a requirement of national legislation (in some countries) that the financial statements should give a true and fair view of (or 'present fairly, in all material respects') the financial position of the entity as at the end of the financial year.

The terms 'true and fair view' and 'present fairly, in all material respects' are not defined in accounting or auditing standards. Despite this, a company's managers may depart from any of the provisions of accounting standards if these are inconsistent with the requirement to give a true and fair view. This is commonly referred to as the 'true and fair override'. It has been treated as an important **loophole** in the law in different countries and has been the cause of much argument and dissatisfaction within the accounting profession.

| Question | Harmonisation |

In accounting terms what do you think are:

(a) The advantages to international harmonisation?
(b) The barriers to international harmonisation?

| Answer |

(a) Advantages of global harmonisation

The advantages of harmonisation will be based on the benefits to users and preparers of accounts, as follows.

(i) Investors, both individual and corporate, would like to be able to compare the financial results of different companies internationally as well as nationally in making investment decisions.

(ii) Multinational companies would benefit from harmonisation for many reasons including the following.

  (1) Better access would be gained to foreign investor funds.
  (2) Management control would be improved, because harmonisation would aid internal communication of financial information.
  (3) Appraisal of foreign entities for take-overs and mergers would be more straightforward.
  (4) It would be easier to comply with the reporting requirements of overseas stock exchanges.
  (5) Preparation of group accounts would be easier.
  (6) A reduction in audit costs might be achieved.
  (7) Transfer of accounting staff across national borders would be easier.

(iii) Governments of developing countries would save time and money if they could adopt international standards and, if these were used internally, governments of developing countries could attempt to control the activities of foreign multinational companies in their own country. These companies could not 'hide' behind foreign accounting practices which are difficult to understand.

(iv)　Tax authorities. It will be easier to calculate the tax liability of investors, including multinationals who receive income from overseas sources.

(v)　Regional economic groups usually promote trade within a specific geographical region. This would be aided by common accounting practices within the region.

(vi)　Large international accounting firms would benefit as accounting and auditing would be much easier if similar accounting practices existed throughout the world.

(b)　Barriers to harmonisation

(i)　Different purposes of financial reporting. In some countries the purpose is solely for tax assessment, while in others it is for investor decision-making.

(ii)　Different legal systems. These prevent the development of certain accounting practices and restrict the options available.

(iii)　Different user groups. Countries have different ideas about who the relevant user groups are and their respective importance. In the USA investor and creditor groups are given prominence, while in Europe employees enjoy a higher profile.

(iv)　Needs of developing countries. Developing countries are obviously behind in the standard setting process and they need to develop the basic standards and principles already in place in most developed countries.

(v)　Nationalism is demonstrated in an unwillingness to accept another country's standard.

(vi)　Cultural differences result in objectives for accounting systems differing from country to country.

(vii)　Unique circumstances. Some countries may be experiencing unusual circumstances which affect all aspects of everyday life and impinge on the ability of companies to produce proper reports, for example hyperinflation, civil war, currency restriction and so on.

(viii)　The lack of strong accountancy bodies. Many countries do not have strong independent accountancy or business bodies which would press for better standards and greater harmonisation.

2.8 The IASB and current accounting standards

The IASB's predecessor body, the IASC, had issued 41 International Accounting Standards (IASs) and on 1 April 2001 the IASB adopted all of these standards and now issues its own International Financial Reporting Standards (IFRSs). So far eight new IFRSs have been issued.

2.9 The IASB and FASB

The IASB is currently involved in a joint project with the FASB (Financial Accounting Standards Board) to develop a common conceptual framework This would provide a sound foundation for developing future accounting standards. The aim is that future standards should be principles-based and internationally-converged. This represents a movement away from the rules-based approach which has characterised US accounting standards.

The new framework will build upon the existing IASB and FASB frameworks and take into account subsequent developments.

2.10 European Commission and IFRSs

All listed entities in member states have been required to use IFRSs in their consolidated financial statements from 2005.

To this end the IASB undertook an **improvements project**, dealing with **revisions to IFRS**, for example in the area of materiality, presentation, leases, related parties and earnings per share. This has been matched in, for example, the UK, by a **convergence project**, bringing UK GAAP into line with IFRSs where these are better.

3 Setting of International Financial Reporting Standards

IFRSs are developed through a formal system of due process and broad international consultation involving accountants, financial analysts and other users and regulatory bodies from around the world.

3.1 Due process

The overall agenda of the IASB will initially be set by discussion with the Standards Advisory Council. The process for developing an individual standard would involve the following steps.

Step 1 During the early stages of a project, IASB may establish an **Advisory Committee** to give advice on issues arising in the project. Consultation with the Advisory Committee and the Standards Advisory Council occurs throughout the project.

Step 2 IASB may develop and publish **Discussion Documents** for public comment.

Step 3 Following the receipt and review of comments, IASB would develop and publish an **Exposure Draft** for public comment.

Step 4 Following the receipt and review of comments, the IASB would issue a final **International Financial Reporting Standard**.

The period of exposure for public comment is normally 90 days. However, in exceptional circumstances, proposals may be issued with a comment period of 60 days. Draft IFRIC Interpretations are exposed for a 60 day comment period.

3.2 Co-ordination with national standard setters

Close co-ordination between IASB due process and due process of national standard setters is important to the success of the IASB's mandate.

The IASB is exploring ways in which to integrate its due process more closely with national due process. Such integration may grow as the relationship between IASB and national standard setters evolves. In particular, the IASB is exploring the following procedure for projects that have international implications.

(a) IASB and national standard setters would co-ordinate their work plans so that when the IASB starts a project, national standard setters would also add it to their own work plans so that they can play a full part in developing international consensus. Similarly, where national standard setters start projects, the IASB would consider whether it needs to develop a new Standard or review its existing Standards. Over a reasonable period, the IASB and national standard setters should aim to review all standards where significant differences currently exist, giving priority to the areas where the differences are greatest.

(b) National standards setters would not be required to vote for IASB's preferred solution in their national standards, since each country remains free to adopt IASB standards with amendments or to adopt other standards. However, the existence of an international consensus is clearly one factor that members of national standard setters would consider when they decide how to vote on national standards.

(c) The IASB would continue to publish its own Exposure Drafts and other documents for public comment.

(d) National standard setters would publish their own exposure document at approximately the same time as IASB Exposure Drafts and would seek specific comments on any significant divergences between the two exposure documents. In some instances, national standard setters may include in their exposure documents specific comments on issues of particular relevance to their country or include more detailed guidance than is included in the corresponding IASB document.

(e)   National standard setters would follow their own full due process, which they would ideally choose to integrate with the IASB's due process. This integration would avoid unnecessary delays in completing standards and would also minimise the likelihood of unnecessary differences between the standards that result.

3.3 IASB liaison members

Seven of the full-time members of the IASB have formal liaison responsibilities with national standard setters in order to promote the convergence of national accounting standards and International Accounting Standards. The IASB envisages a partnership between the IASB and these national standard setters as they work together to achieve convergence of accounting standards world-wide.

The countries with these liaison members are Australia and New Zealand, Canada, France, Germany, Japan, UK and USA.

In addition all IASB members have contact responsibility with national standards setters not having liaison members and many countries are also represented on the Standards Advisory Council.

Exam focus point

This topic is likely to be examined as a short discussion question.

3.4 Current IASs/IFRSs

The current list is as follows.

International Accounting Standards		Date of issue
IAS 1 (revised)	Presentation of financial statements	Sep 2007
IAS 2	Inventories	Dec 2003
IAS 7	Statements of cash flows	Dec 1992
IAS 8	Accounting policies, changes in accounting estimates and errors	Dec 2003
IAS 10	Events after the reporting period	Dec 2003
IAS 11	Construction contracts	Dec 1993
IAS 12	Income taxes	Nov 2000
IAS 16	Property, plant and equipment	Dec 2003
IAS 17	Leases	Dec 2003
IAS 18	Revenue	Dec 1993
IAS 19 *	Employee benefits	Dec 2004
IAS 20	Accounting for government grants and disclosure of government assistance	Jan 1995
IAS 21	The effects of changes in foreign exchange rates	Dec 2003
IAS 23 (revised)	Borrowing costs	Jan 2008
IAS 24	Related party disclosures	Dec 2003
IAS 26 *	Accounting and reporting by retirement benefit plans	Jan 1995
IAS 27 (revised)	Consolidated and separate financial statements	Jan 2008
IAS 28	Investments in associates	Dec 2003
IAS 29 *	Financial reporting in hyperinflationary economies	Jan 1995
IAS 30 *	Disclosure in the financial statements of banks and similar financial institutions (not examinable)	Jan 1995
IAS 31 *	Interests in joint ventures	Dec 2003
IAS 32	Financial instruments: presentation	Dec 2003

International Accounting Standards		Date of issue
IAS 33	Earnings per share	Dec 2003
IAS 34	Interim financial reporting	Feb 1998
IAS 36	Impairment of assets	Mar 2004
IAS 37	Provisions, contingent liabilities and contingent assets	Sept 1998
IAS 38	Intangible assets	Mar 2004
IAS 39	Financial instruments: recognition and measurement	Dec 2004
IAS 40	Investment property	Dec 2003
IAS 41 *	Agriculture	Feb 2001
IFRS 1	First time adoption of International Financial Reporting Standards	June 2003
IFRS 2 *	Share-based payment	Feb 2004
IFRS 3 (revised)	Business combinations	Jan 2008
IFRS 4 *	Insurance contracts	Mar 2004
IFRS 5	Non-current assets held for sale and discontinued operations	Mar 2004
IFRS 6 *	Exploration for and evaluation of mineral resources	Dec 2004
IFRS 7	Financial instruments: disclosures	Aug 2005
IFRS 8 *	Operating segments	Nov 2006

* These standards are not examinable at F7.

Various exposure drafts and discussion papers are currently at different stages within the IFRS process, but these are not of concern to you at this stage. By the end of your financial accounting studies, however, you will know *all* the standards, exposure drafts and discussion papers!

3.5 Alternative treatments

Many of the old IASs permitted two accounting treatments for like transactions or events. One treatment was designated as the **benchmark treatment** (effectively the **preferred treatment**) and the other was known as the **alternative treatment**. This is no longer the case. The last standard to have a benchmark alternative was IAS 23 which has now been revised to remove the benchmark treatment. Under the revised standard allowable borrowing costs **must** be capitalised.

3.6 Interpretation of IFRSs

The IASB has developed a procedure for issuing interpretations of its standards. In September 1996, the IASC Board approved the formation of a **Standing Interpretations Committee (SIC)** for this task. This was renamed under the IASB as the **International Financial Reporting Interpretations Committee** (IFRIC).

The duties of the IFRIC are:

(a) To interpret the application of International Financial Reporting Standards and provide timely guidance on financial reporting issues not specifically addressed in IFRSs or IASs in the context of the IASB's Framework, and undertake other tasks at the request of the Board.

(b) To have regard to the Board's objective of working actively with national standard setters to bring about convergence of national accounting standards and IFRSs to high quality solutions.

(c) To publish, after clearance by the Board, Draft Interpretations for public comment and consider comments made within a reasonable period before finalising an Interpretation.

(d) To report to the Board and obtain Board approval for final Interpretations.

In developing interpretations, the 12-person IFRIC will work closely with **similar national committees**. If no more than three of its members vote against an interpretation, the SIC will ask the Board to approve the interpretation for issue; as is the case for IFRSs, three-quarters of the Board must vote in favour of an interpretation. Interpretations will be formally published after approval by the Board.

3.7 Scope and application of IFRSs

3.7.1 Scope

Any limitation of the applicability of a specific IFRS is made clear within that standard. IFRSs are **not intended to be applied to immaterial items, nor are they retrospective**. Each individual IFRS lays out its scope at the beginning of the standard.

3.7.2 Application

Within each individual country **local regulations** govern, to a greater or lesser degree, the issue of financial statements. These local regulations include accounting standards issued by the national regulatory bodies and/or professional accountancy bodies in the country concerned.

The IASC **concentrated on essentials** when producing IFRSs. This means that the IASC tried not to make IFRSs too complex, because otherwise they would be impossible to apply on a worldwide basis.

3.8 World-wide effect of IFRSs and the IASB

The IASB, and before it the IASC, has now been in existence for around 25 years, and it is worth looking at the effect it has had in that time.

As far as **Europe** is concerned, the consolidated financial statements of many of Europe's top multinationals are now prepared in conformity with national requirements, EC directives and IFRSs. Furthermore, IFRSs are having a growing influence on national accounting requirements and practices. Many of these developments have been given added impetus by the internationalisation of capital markets.

In **Japan**, the influence of the IASC had, until recently, been negligible. This was mainly because of links in Japan between tax rules and financial reporting. The Japanese Ministry of Finance set up a working committee to consider whether to bring national requirements into line with IFRSs. The Tokyo Stock Exchange has announced that it will accept financial statements from foreign issuers that conform with home country standards.

This was widely seen as an attempt to attract foreign issuers, in particular companies from Hong Kong and Singapore. As these countries base their accounting on international standards, this action is therefore implicit acknowledgement by the Japanese Ministry of Finance of IFRS requirements.

America and Japan have been two of the developed countries which have been most reluctant to accept accounts prepared under IFRSs, but recent developments suggest that such financial statements may soon be acceptable on these important stock exchanges.

In **America**, the Securities and Exchange Commission (SEC) agreed in 1993 to allow foreign issuers (of shares, etc) to follow IFRS treatments on certain issues, including cash flow statements under IAS 7. The overall effect is that, where an IFRS treatment differs from US GAAP, these treatments will now be acceptable. The SEC is now supporting the IASB because it wants to attract foreign listings.

3.9 Criticisms of the IASB

You need to be able to understand the problems that can arise.

We will begin by looking at some of the general problems created by **accounting standards**.

3.9.1 Accounting standards and choice

It is sometimes argued that companies should be given a choice in matters of financial reporting on the grounds that accounting standards are detrimental to the quality of such reporting. There are arguments on both sides.

In favour of accounting standards (both national and international), the following points can be made.

- They reduce or eliminate confusing variations in the methods used to prepare accounts.
- They provide a focal point for debate and discussions about accounting practice.
- They oblige companies to disclose the accounting policies used in the preparation of accounts.
- They are a less rigid alternative to enforcing conformity by means of legislation.
- They have obliged companies to **disclose more accounting information** than they would otherwise have done if accounting standards did not exist, for example IAS 33 *Earnings per share*.

Many companies are reluctant to disclose information which is not required by national legislation. However, the following arguments may be put forward **against standardisation** and **in favour of choice**.

- A set of rules which give backing to one method of preparing accounts might be **inappropriate in some circumstances**. For example, IAS 16 on depreciation is inappropriate for investment properties (properties not occupied by the entity but held solely for investment), which are covered by IAS 40 on investment property.
- Standards may be subject to **lobbying or government pressure** (in the case of national standards). For example, in the USA, the accounting standard FAS 19 on the accounts of oil and gas companies led to a powerful lobby of oil companies, which persuaded the SEC (Securities and Exchange Commission) to step in. FAS 19 was then suspended.
- Many national standards are not based on a **conceptual framework of accounting**, although IFRSs are.
- There may be a **trend towards rigidity**, and away from flexibility in applying the rules.

3.9.2 Political problems

Any international body, whatever its purpose or activity, faces enormous political difficulties in attempting to gain **international consensus** and the IASB is no exception to this. How can the IASB reconcile the financial reporting situation between economies as diverse as third-world developing countries and sophisticated first-world industrial powers?

Developing countries are suspicious of the IASB, believing it to be dominated by the **USA.** This arises because acceptance by the USA listing authority, the Securities and Exchange Commission (SEC), of IASs is seen as a major hurdle to be overcome. For all practical purposes it is the American market which must be persuaded to accept IFRSs.

Developing countries are being catered for to some extent by the issue of a standard on **agriculture**, which is generally of much more relevance to such countries.

There are also tensions between the **UK/US model** of financial reporting and the **European model**. The UK/US model is based around investor reporting, whereas the European model is mainly concerned with tax rules, so shareholder reporting has a much lower priority.

The break-up of the former USSR and the move in many **Eastern European countries** to free-market economies has also created difficulties. It is likely that these countries will have to 'catch up' to international standards as their economies stabilise.

You must keep up to date with the IASB's progress and the problems it encounters in the financial press. You should also be able to discuss:

- **Due process** of the IASB
- **Use and application** of IFRSs
- **Future work** of the IASB
- **Criticisms** of the IASB

Chapter Roundup

- A principles-based system works within a set of laid down principles. A rules-based system regulates for issues as they arise. Both of these have advantages and disadvantages.

- The organisational structure consists of:

  - the IASC Foundation
  - the IASB
  - the Standards Advisory Council (SAC)
  - the International Financial Reporting Interpretations Committee (IFRC)

- IFRSs are developed through a formal system of due process and broad international consultation involving accountants, financial analysis and other users and regulatory bodies from around the world.

Quick Quiz

1   What recent decisions will have a beneficial effect on global harmonisation of accounting?

2   One objective of the IASB is to promote the preparation of financial statements using the euro.

    True   ☐

    False   ☐

3   How many IASs and IFRSs have been published?

4   A conceptual framework is:

    A   A theoretical expression of accounting standards

    B   A list of key terms used by the IASB

    C   A statement of theoretical principles which form the frame of reference for financial reporting

    D   The proforma financial statements

5   Which of the following are chapters in the IASB *Framework?*

    A   Subsidiaries, associates and joint ventures

    B   Profit measurement in financial statements

    C   The objective of financial statements

    D   Accounting for interests in other entities

    E   Recognition of the elements of financial statements

    F   Presentation of financial information

    G   Substance of transactions in financial statements

    H   Qualitative characteristics of financial statements

    I   Quantitative characteristics of financial statements

    J   Measurement of the elements of financial statements

6   What development at the IASB aided users' interpretation of IFRSs?

7   Which of the following arguments is not in favour of accounting standards, but is in favour of accounting choice?

    A   They reduce variations in methods used to produce accounts

    B   They oblige companies to disclose their accounting policies

    C   They are a less rigid alternative to legislation

    D   They may tend towards rigidity in applying the rules

1   The IOSCO endorsement, and the EC requirement that listed companies should use IFRS from 2005.

2   False

3   41 IASs and 8 IFRSs

4   C

5   C, E, H, J.

6   The formation of the International Financial Reporting Interpretations Committee (IFRIC).

7   D   The other arguments are all in favour of accounting standards.

Now try the question below from the Exam Question Bank

Number	Level	Marks	Time
2	Examination	10	18 mins
3(a)	–	5	9 mins

Presentation of published financial statements

Topic list	Syllabus reference
1 IAS 1 (revised) Presentation of financial statements	C10
2 Statement of financial position	C10
3 The current/non-current distinction	C10
4 Statement of comprehensive income	C10
5 Income statement	C10
6 Revision of basic accounts	C10
7 Changes in equity	C10
8 Notes to the financial statements	C10

Introduction

The bulk of this Study Text looks at the accounts of limited liability companies, either single companies or groups of companies.

We begin in this chapter by looking at the overall **content and format** of company financial statements. These are governed by IAS 1 (revised) *Presentation of financial statements*.

Study guide

		Intellectual level
10	**Regulatory requirements relating to the preparation of financial statements**	
(a)	describe the structure (format) and content of financial statements presented under IFRS.	2
(b)	prepare an entity's financial statements in accordance with the prescribed structure and content.	2
11	**Reporting financial performance**	
(a)	prepare and explain the contents and purpose of the statement of changes in equity.	2
(b)	describe and prepare a statement of changes in equity.	2

Exam guide

Knowledge of IAS 1 will be assumed to be 'second nature' at this level.

1 IAS 1 (revised) Presentation of financial statements

FAST FORWARD

> IAS 1 covers the form and content of financial statements. The main components are:
>
> – Statement of financial position
> – Statement of comprehensive income
> – Statement of changes in equity
> – Statement of cash flows
> – Notes to the financial statements

IAS 1 *Presentation of financial statements* give substantial guidance on the form and content of published financial statements. It was revised in September 2007. The standard looks at the statement of financial position and statement of comprehensive income (the statement of cash flows is covered by IAS 7). First of all, some general points are made about financial statements.

1.1 Profit or loss for the period

The statement of comprehensive income is the most significant indicator of a company's financial performance. So it is important to ensure that it is not misleading.

IAS 1 stipulates that all items of income and expense recognised in a period shall be included in profit or loss unless a **Standard** or an **Interpretation** requires otherwise.

Circumstances where items may be excluded from profit or loss for the current year include the correction of errors and the effect of changes in accounting policies. These are covered in IAS 8.

1.2 How items are disclosed

IAS 1 specifies disclosures of certain items in certain ways.

- Some items must appear on the face of the statement of financial position or statement of comprehensive income
- Other items can appear in a **note to the financial statements** instead
- **Recommended formats** are given which entities may or may not follow, depending on their circumstances

Obviously, disclosures specified by **other standards** must also be made, and we will mention the necessary disclosures when we cover each statement in turn. Disclosures in both IAS 1 and other standards must be made either on the face of the statement or in the notes unless otherwise stated, ie disclosures cannot be made in an accompanying commentary or report.

1.3 Identification of financial statements

As a result of the above point, it is most important that entities **distinguish the financial statements** very clearly from any other information published with them. This is because all IASs/IFRSs apply *only* to the financial statements (ie the main statements and related notes), so readers of the annual report must be able to differentiate between the parts of the report which are prepared under IFRSs, and other parts which are not.

The entity should **identify each** financial statement and the notes very clearly. IAS 1 also requires disclosure of the following information in a prominent position. If necessary it should be repeated wherever it is felt to be of use to the reader in his understanding of the information presented.

- **Name** of the reporting entity (or other means of identification)
- Whether the accounts cover the **single entity** only or a group of entities
- The **date of the end of the reporting period** or the period covered by the financial statements (as appropriate)
- The **presentation currency**
- The **level of rounding** used in presenting amounts in the financial statements

Judgement must be used to determine the best method of presenting this information. In particular, the standard suggests that the approach to this will be very different when the financial statements are communicated electronically.

The **level of rounding** is important, as presenting figures in thousands or millions of units makes the figures more understandable. The level of rounding must be disclosed, however, and it should not obscure necessary details or make the information less relevant.

1.4 Reporting period

It is normal for entities to present financial statements **annually** and IAS 1 states that they should be prepared at least as often as this. If (unusually) the end of an entity's reporting period is changed, for whatever reason, the period for which the statements are presented will be less or more than one year. In such cases the entity should also disclose:

(a)   the **reason(s) why** a period other than one year is used; and
(b)   the fact that the comparative figures given **are not in fact comparable**.

For practical purposes, some entities prefer to use a period which **approximates to a year**, eg 52 weeks, and the IAS allows this approach as it will produce statements not materially different from those produced on an annual basis.

1.5 Timeliness

If the publication of financial statements is delayed too long after the reporting period, their usefulness will be severely diminished. The standard states that entities should be able to produce their financial statements **within six months of the end of the reporting period.** An entity with consistently complex operations cannot use this as a reason for its failure to report on a timely basis. Local legislation and market regulation imposes specific deadlines on certain entities.

IAS 1 looks at the statement of financial position and statement of comprehensive income. We will not give all the detailed disclosures as some are outside the scope of your syllabus. Instead we will look at a **'proforma' set of accounts** based on the Standard.

2 Statement of financial position

FAST FORWARD ❯❯

> IAS 1 suggests a format for the statement of financial position. Certain items are specified for **disclosure on the face of the financial statements**.

IAS 1 discusses the distinction between current and non-current items in some detail, as we shall see in the next section. First of all we can look at the **suggested format** of the statement of financial position (given in an appendix to the standard) and then look at further disclosures required.

2.1 Statement of financial position example

The example given by IAS 1 revised is as follows.

XYZ GROUP – STATEMENT OF FINANCIAL POSITION AT 31 DECEMBER

	20X7 $'000	20X6 $'000
Assets		
Non-current assets		
Property, plant and equipment	350,700	360,020
Goodwill	80,800	91,200
Other intangible assets	227,470	227,470
Investments in associates	100,150	110,770
Available-for-sale financial assets	142,500	156,000
	901,620	945,460
Current assets		
Inventories	135,230	132,500
Trade receivables	91,600	110,800
Other current assets	25,650	12,540
Cash and cash equivalents	312,400	322,900
	564,880	578,740
Total assets	1,466,500	1,524,200
Equity and liabilities		
Equity attributable to owners of the parent		
Share capital	650,000	600,000
Retained earnings	243,500	161,700
Other components of equity	10,200	21,200
	903,700	782,900
Non-controlling interest	70,050	48,600
Total equity	973,750	831,500
Non-current liabilities		
Long-term borrowings	120,000	160,000
Deferred tax	28,800	26,040
Long-term provisions	28,850	52,240
Total non-current liabilities	117,650	238,280
Current liabilities		
Trade and other payables	115,100	187,620
Short-term borrowings	150,000	200,000
Current portion of long-term borrowings	10,000	20,000
Current tax payable	35,000	42,000
Short-term provisions	5,000	4,800
Total current liabilities	315,100	454,420
Total liabilities	492,750	692,700
Total equity and liabilities	1,466,500	1,524,200

IAS 1 (revised) specifies various items which must appear on the **face of the statement of financial position** as a minimum disclosure.

(a)   Property, plant and equipment (Chapter 4)
(b)   Investment property (Chapter 4)
(c)   Intangible assets (Chapter 5)
(d)   Financial assets (excluding amounts shown under (e), (h) and (i)) (Chapter 14)
(e)   Investments accounted for using the equity method (Chapter 11)
(f)   Biological assets (outside the scope of the syllabus)
(g)   Inventories (Chapter 12)
(h)   Trade and other receivables
(i)   Cash and cash equivalents (Chapter 21)
(j)   Assets classified as held for sale under IFRS 5
(k)   Trade and other payables
(l)   Provisions (Chapter 13)
(m)   Financial liabilities (other than (j) and (k))
(n)   Current tax liabilities and assets as in IAS 12 (Chapter 17)
(o)   Deferred tax liabilities and assets
(p)   Liabilities included in disposal groups under IFRS 5
(q)   Non-controlling interests (Chapter 9)
(r)   Issued capital and reserves

We will look at these items in the chapters marked.

Any **other line items**, headings or sub-totals should be shown on the face of the statement of financial position when it is necessary for an understanding of the entity's financial position.

The example shown above is for illustration only (although we will follow the format in this Study Text). The IAS, however, does not prescribe the order or format in which the items listed should be presented. It simply states that they **must be presented separately** because they are so different in nature or function from each other.

Whether additional items are presented separately depends on judgements based on the assessment of the following factors.

(a)   **Nature and liquidity of assets and their materiality**. Thus goodwill and assets arising from development expenditure will be presented separately, as will monetary/non-monetary assets and current/non-current assets.

(b)   **Function within the entity.** Operating and financial assets, inventories, receivables and cash and cash equivalents are therefore shown separately.

(c)   **Amounts, nature and timing of liabilities**. Interest-bearing and non-interest-bearing liabilities and provisions will be shown separately, classified as current or non-current as appropriate.

The standard also requires separate presentation where **different measurement bases** are used for assets and liabilities which differ in nature or function. According to IAS 16, for example, it is permitted to carry certain items of property, plant and equipment at cost or at a revalued amount.

2.2 Information presented either on the face of the statement of financial position or by note

Further **sub-classification** of the line items listed above should be disclosed either on the face of the statement of financial position or in the notes. The classification will depend upon the nature of the entity's operations. As well as each item being sub-classified by its nature, any amounts payable to or receivable from any **group company or other related party** should also be disclosed separately.

The sub-classification details will in part depend on the requirements of IFRSs. The size, nature and function of the amounts involved will also be important and the factors listed above should be considered. **Disclosures** will vary from item to item and IAS 1 gives the following examples.

(a)   **Property, plant and equipment** are classified by class as described in IAS 16, *Property, plant and equipment*

(b)   **Receivables** are analysed between amounts receivable from trade customers, other members of the group, receivables from related parties, prepayments and other amounts

(c)   **Inventories** are sub-classified, in accordance with IAS 2 *Inventories,* into classifications such as merchandise, production supplies, materials, work in progress and finished goods

(d)   **Provisions** are analysed showing separately provisions for employee benefit costs and any other items classified in a manner appropriate to the entity's operations

(e)   **Equity capital and reserves** are analysed showing separately the various classes of paid in capital, share premium and reserves

The standard then lists some **specific disclosures** which must be made, either on the face of the statement of financial position or in the related notes.

(a)   **Share capital disclosures** (for each class of share capital)

    (i)   Number of shares authorised

    (ii)   Number of shares issued and fully paid, and issued but not fully paid

    (iii)   Par value per share, or that the shares have no par value

    (iv)   Reconciliation of the number of shares outstanding at the beginning and at the end of the year

    (v)   Rights, preferences and restrictions attaching to that class including restrictions on the distribution of dividends and the repayment of capital

    (vi)   Shares in the entity held by the entity itself or by related group companies

    (vii)   Shares reserved for issuance under options and sales contracts, including the terms and amounts

(b)   Description of the nature and purpose of **each reserve** within owners' equity

Some types of entity have no share capital, eg partnerships. Such entities should disclose information which is **equivalent** to that listed above. This means disclosing the movement during the period in each category of equity interest and any rights, preferences or restrictions attached to each category of equity interest.

3 The current/non-current distinction

FAST FORWARD

> You should appreciate the distinction between current and non-current assets and liabilities and their different treatments.

3.1 The current/non-current distinction

An entity must present **current** and **non-current** assets as separate classifications on the face of the statement of financial position. A presentation based on liquidity should only be used where it provides more relevant and reliable information, in which case all assets and liabilities must be presented broadly **in order of liquidity**.

In either case, the entity should disclose any portion of an asset or liability which is expected to be recovered or settled **after more than twelve months**. For example, for an amount receivable which is due in instalments over 18 months, the portion due after more than twelve months must be disclosed.

The IAS emphasises how helpful information on the **operating cycle** is to users of financial statements. Where there is a clearly defined operating cycle within which the entity supplies goods or services, then information disclosing those net assets that are continuously circulating as **working capital** is useful.

This distinguishes them from those net assets used in the long-term operations of the entity. Assets that are expected to be realised and liabilities that are due for settlement within the operating cycle are therefore highlighted.

The liquidity and solvency of an entity is also indicated by information about the **maturity dates** of assets and liabilities. As we will see later, IFRS 7 *Financial instruments: disclosures* requires disclosure of maturity dates of both financial assets and financial liabilities. (Financial assets include trade and other receivables; financial liabilities include trade and other payables.) In the case of non-monetary assets, eg inventories, such information is also useful.

3.2 Current assets

Key term

An asset should be classified as a **current asset** when it:

- is expected to be realised in, or is held for sale or consumption in, the normal course of the entity's operating cycle; or

- is held primarily for trading purposes or for the short-term and expected to be realised within twelve months of the end of the reporting period; or

- is cash or a cash equivalent asset which is not restricted in its use.

All other assets should be classified as non-current assets. *(IAS 1)*

Non-current assets includes tangible, intangible, operating and financial assets of a long-term nature. Other terms with the same meaning can be used (eg 'fixed', 'long-term').

The term 'operating cycle' has been used several times above and the standard defines it as follows.

Key term

The **operating cycle** of an entity is the time between the acquisition of assets for processing and their realisation in cash or cash equivalents. *(IAS 1)*

Current assets therefore include inventories and trade receivables that are sold, consumed and realised as part of the normal operating cycle. **This is the case even where they are not expected to be realised within twelve months**.

Current assets will also include **marketable securities** if they are expected to be realised within twelve months after the reporting period. If expected to be realised later, they should be included in non-current assets.

3.3 Current liabilities

Key term

A liability should be classified as a **current liability** when it:

- Is expected to be settled in the normal course of the entity's operating cycle; or

- Is held primarily for the purpose of trading; or

- Is due to be settled within twelve months after the reporting period; or

- The entity does not have an unconditional right to defer settlement of the liability for at least twelve months after the reporting period.

All other liabilities should be classified as non-current liabilities. *(IAS 1)*

The categorisation of current liabilities is very similar to that of current assets. Thus, some current liabilities are part of the **working capital** used in the normal operating cycle of the business (ie trade payables and accruals for employee and other operating costs). Such items will be classed as current liabilities **even where they are due to be settled more than twelve months after the end of the reporting period.**

There are also current liabilities which are not settled as part of the normal operating cycle, but which are due to be settled within twelve months of the end of the reporting period. These include bank overdrafts, income taxes, other non-trade payables and the current portion of interest-bearing liabilities. Any interest-bearing liabilities that are used to finance working capital on a long-term basis, and that are not due for settlement within twelve months, should be classed as **non-current liabilities**.

A **non-current financial liability** due to be **settled within twelve months** of the end of the reporting period should be classified as a **current liability**, even if an agreement to refinance, or to reschedule payments, on a long-term basis is completed after the end of the reporting period and before the financial statements are authorised for issue.

End of the reporting period	Agreement to refinance on long-term basis	Date financial statements authorised for issue	Settlement date <12 months after end of the reporting period therefore current liability

A **non-current financial liability** that is payable on **demand** because the entity **breached** a **condition** of its loan agreement should be classified as **current** at the end of the reporting period even if the **lender** has agreed **after the end of the reporting period**, and **before** the financial statements are **authorised for issue**, **not** to **demand payment** as a consequence of the breach.

Condition of loan agreement breached. Non-current liability becomes payable on demand	End of the reporting period	Lender agrees not to enforce payment resulting from breach	Date financial statements are authorised for issue. Loan shown as **current** liability

However, if the **lender** has **agreed** by the **end of the reporting period** to provide a **period of grace** ending **at least twelve months after the end of the reporting period** within which the entity can rectify the breach and during that time the lender cannot demand immediate repayment, the liability is classified as **non-current**.

4 Statement of comprehensive income

IAS 1 (revised) requires all items of income and expense in a period to be shown in a **statement of comprehensive income**.

The revision of IAS 1 in 2007 introduced a new statement, the **statement of comprehensive income**. This shows both income statement items and items which would previously have gone to the statement of recognised income and expense.

4.1 Statement of comprehensive income – format

IAS 1 (revised) allows income and expense items to be presented either:

(a)   in a single statement of comprehensive income; or
(b)   in two statements: a separate income statement and statement of other comprehensive income.

The format for a single statement of comprehensive income is shown as follows in the standard. The section down to 'profit for the year' can be shown as a separate 'income statement' with an additional 'statement of other comprehensive income'. Note that not all of the items which would appear under 'other comprehensive income' are included in your syllabus.

Exam focus point

In the examinations, if a 'Statement of Comprehensive Income' is referred to, this will always relate to the single statement format. If 'Income Statements' are referred to, this relates to the statement from 'Revenue' to 'Profit for the year'. Exams may refer to 'Other Comprehensive Income' which relates to the 'other comprehensive income' section of the statement. In practice, the item of 'other comprehensive income' you are most likely to meet is a revaluation gain. Where we have used 'income statement' in this text, this can be taken to refer to the income statement section of the statement of comprehensive income or separate income statement.

XYZ GROUP – STATEMENT OF COMPREHENSIVE INCOME FOR THE YEAR ENDED 31 DECEMBER 20X7

	20X7	20X8
	$'000	$'000
Revenue	39,000	355,000
Cost of sales	(245,000)	(230,000)
Gross profit	145,000	125,000
Other income	20,667	11,300
Distribution costs	(9,000)	(8,700)
Administrative expenses	(20,000)	(21,000)
Other expenses	(2,100)	(1,200)
Finance costs	(8,000)	(7,500)
Share of profit of associates	35,100	30,100
Profit before tax	161,667	128,000
Income tax expense	(40,417)	(32,000)
Profit for the year from continuing operations	121,250	96,000
Loss for the year from discontinued operations	–	(30,500)
Profit for the year	121,250	65,500
Other comprehensive income:		
* Exchange differences on translating foreign operations	5,334	10,667
Available-for-sale financial assets	(24,000)	26,667
*Cash flow hedges	(667)	(4,000)
Gains on property revaluation	993	3,367
*Actuarial gains (losses) on defined benefit pension plans	(667)	1,333
Share of other comprehensive income of associates	400	(700)
Income tax relating to components of other comprehensive income	4,667	(9,334)
Other comprehensive income for the year, net of tax	(14,000)	28,000
Total comprehensive income for the year	107,250	93,500
Profit attributable to:		
Owners of the parent	97,000	52,400
Non-controlling interest	24,250	13,100
	121,250	65,500
Total comprehensive income attributable to		
Owners of the parent	85,800	74,800
Non-controlling interest	21,450	18,700
	107,250	93,500
Earnings per share (in currency units)	0.46	0.30

*Not in the F7 syllabus

Companies are given the option of presenting this information in two statements as follows:

XYZ GROUP – STATEMENT FOR THE YEAR ENDED 31 DECEMBER 20X7

	20X7	20X8
	$'000	$'000
Revenue	39,000	355,000
Cost of sales	(245,000)	(230,000)
Gross profit	145,000	125,000
Other income	20,667	11,300
Distribution costs	(9,000)	(8,700)
Administrative expenses	(20,000)	(21,000)
Other expenses	(2,100)	(1,200)
Finance costs	(8,000)	(7,500)
Share of profit of associates	35,100	30,100
Profit before tax	161,667	128,000
Income tax expense	(40,417)	(32,000)
Profit for the year from continuing operations	121,250	96,000
Loss for the year from discontinued operations	–	(30,500)
Profit for the year	121,250	65,500
Profit attributable to:		
Owners of the parent	97,000	52,400
Non-controlling interest	24,250	13,100
	121,250	65,500

XYZ GROUP STATEMENT OF COMPREHENSIVE INCOME FOR THE YEAR ENDED 31 DECEMBER 20X7

	20X7	20X8
	$'000	$'000
Profit for the year	121,250	65,500
Other comprehensive income:		
*Exchange differences on translating foreign operations	5,334	10,667
Available-for-sale financial assets	(24,000)	26,667
*Cash flow hedges	(667)	(4,000)
Gains on property revaluation	933	3,367
*Actuarial gains (losses) on defined benefit pension plans	(667)	1,333
Share of other comprehensive income of associates	400	(700)
Income tax relating to components of other comprehensive income	4,667	(9,334)
Other comprehensive income for the year, net of tax	(14,000)	28,000
Total comprehensive income for the year	107,250	93,500
Total comprehensive income attributable to		
Owners of the parent	85,800	74,800
Non-controlling interest	21,450	18,700
	107,250	93,500

*Not in the F7 syllabus

5 Income statement

IAS 1 offers two possible formats for the income statement section or separate income statement - by function or by nature. Classification by function is more common.

5.1 Examples of separate income statements

XYZ GROUP
INCOME STATEMENT FOR THE YEAR ENDED 31 DECEMBER 20X8

Illustrating the classification of expenses by function

	20X8	20X7
	$'000	$'000
Revenue	X	X
Cost of sales	(X)	(X)
Gross profit	X	X
Other income	X	X
Distribution costs	(X)	(X)
Administrative expenses	(X)	(X)
Other expenses	(X)	(X)
Finance costs	(X)	(X)
Share of profit of associates	X	X
Profit before tax	X	X
Income tax expense	(X)	(X)
Profit for the year	X	X
Attributable to:		
Owners of the parent	X	X
Non-controlling interest	X	X
	X	X

Illustrating the classification of expenses by nature

	20X8	20X7
	$'000	$'000
Revenue	X	X
Other operating income	X	X
Changes in inventories of finished goods and work in progress	(X)	X
Work performed by the entity and capitalised	X	X
Raw material and consumables used	(X)	(X)
Employee benefits expense	(X)	(X)
Depreciation and amortisation expense	(X)	(X)
Impairment of property, plant and equipment	(X)	(X)
Other expenses	(X)	(X)
Finance costs	(X)	(X)
Share of profit of associates	X	X
Profit before tax	X	X
Income tax expense	(X)	(X)
Profit for the year	X	X
Attributable to:		
Owners of the parent	X	X
Non-controlling interest	X	X
	X	X

Note: The usual method of presentation is expenses by function and this is the format likely to appear in your exam.

5.2 Information presented in the statement of comprehensive income or separate income statement

The standard lists the following as the **minimum** to be disclosed on the face of the income statement.

(a)   Revenue

(b)   Finance costs

(c)   Share of profits and losses of associates and joint ventures accounted for using the equity method

(d)   Pre-tax gain or loss recognised on the disposal of assets or settlement of liabilities attributable to discontinued operations

(e)   Tax expense

(f)   Profit or loss

The following items must be disclosed in the income statement as allocations of profit or loss for the period.

(a)   Profit or loss attributable to non-controlling interest

(b)   Profit or loss attributable to owners of the parent

The allocated amounts must not be presented as items of income or expense. (These relate to group accounts, covered later in this text.)

Income and expense items can only be **offset** when, and only when:

(a)   It is permitted or required by an IFRS, or

(b)   Gains, losses and related expenses arising from the same or similar transactions and events are immaterial, in which case they can be aggregated.

5.3 Information presented either in the statement or in the notes

An analysis of expenses must be shown either in the income statement section (as above, which is encouraged by the standard) or by note, using a classification based on *either* the nature of the expenses or their function. This **sub-classification of expenses** indicates a range of components of financial performance; these may differ in terms of stability, potential for gain or loss and predictability.

5.3.1 Nature of expense method

Expenses are not reallocated amongst various functions within the entity, but are aggregated in the income statement **according to their nature** (eg purchase of materials, depreciation, wages and salaries, transport costs). This is by far the easiest method, especially for smaller entities.

5.3.2 Function of expense/cost of sales method

You are likely to be more familiar with this method. Expenses are classified according to their function as part of cost of sales, distribution or administrative activities. This method often gives **more relevant information** for users, but the allocation of expenses by function requires the use of judgement and can be arbitrary. Consequently, perhaps, when this method is used, entities should disclose **additional information** on the nature of expenses, including staff costs, and depreciation and amortisation expense.

Which of the above methods is chosen by an entity will depend on **historical and industry factors**, and also the **nature of the organisation**. Under each method, there should be given an indication of costs which are likely to vary (directly or indirectly) with the level of sales or production. The choice of method should fairly reflect the main elements of the entity's performance. **This is the method you should expect to see in your exam**.

5.4 Dividends

IAS 1 also requires disclosure of the amount of **dividends per share** for the period covered by the financial statements. This may be shown either in the income statement or in the statement of changes in equity.

Further points

(a) All requirements previously set out in other Standards for the presentation of particular line items in the statement of financial position and income statement are now dealt with in IAS 1. These line items are: biological assets; liabilities and assets for current tax and deferred tax; and pre-tax gain or loss recognised on the disposal of assets or settlement of liabilities attributable to discontinued operations.

(b) The section that set out the **presentation requirements** for the **net profit or loss** for the period in **IAS 8** has now been **transferred** to **IAS 1** instead.

(c) The following disclosures are no longer required:

　　(i) The results of operating activities, as a line item in the income statement. **'Operating activities'** are **not defined in IAS 1**

　　(ii) **Extraordinary items**, as a line item in the income statement (note that the disclosure of 'extraordinary items' is now **prohibited**)

　　(iii) The **number** of an **entity's employees**

(d) An entity must disclose, in the summary of significant accounting policies and/or other notes, the **judgements** made by management in **applying** the **accounting policies** that have the **most significant effect** on the amounts of items recognised in the financial statements.

(e) An entity must disclose in the notes information regarding **key assumptions** about the **future**, and other sources of **measurement uncertainty**, that have a significant **risk of** causing a **material adjustment** to the carrying amounts of assets and liabilities within the **next financial year**.

6 Revision of basic accounts

FAST FORWARD

The Study Guide requires you to be able to prepare a basic set of company accounts from a trial balance.

In the next part of this text we move on to the mechanics of preparing financial statements. It would be useful at this point to refresh your memory of the basic accounting you have already studied and these questions will help you. Make sure that you understand everything before you go on.

Question   Basics

A friend has bought some shares in a company quoted on a local stock exchange and has received the latest accounts. There is one page he is having difficulty in understanding.

Briefly, but clearly, answer his questions.

(a) What is a statement of financial position?
(b) What is an asset?
(c) What is a liability?
(d) What is share capital?
(e) What are reserves?
(f) Why does the statement of financial position balance?
(g) To what extent does the statement of financial position value my investment?

(a) A **statement of financial position** is a statement of the assets, liabilities and capital of a business as at a stated date. It is laid out to show either total assets as equivalent to total liabilities and capital or net assets as equivalent to capital. Other formats are also possible but the top half (or left hand) total will always equal the bottom half (or right hand) total.

(b) An **asset** is a resource controlled by a business and is expected to be of some future benefit. Its value is determined as the historical cost of producing or obtaining it (unless an attempt is being made to reflect rising prices in the accounts, in which case a replacement cost might be used). Examples of assets are:

  (i) Plant, machinery, land and other **non-current assets**

  (ii) **Current** assets such as inventories, cash and debts owed to the business with reasonable assurance of recovery: these are assets which are not intended to be held on a continuing basis in the business

(c) A **liability** is an amount owed by a business, other than the amount owed to its proprietors (capital). Examples of liabilities are:

  (i) Amounts owed to the government (sales or other taxes)
  (ii) Amounts owed to suppliers
  (iii) Bank overdraft
  (iv) Long-term loans from banks or investors

  It is usual to differentiate between 'current' and 'long-term' liabilities. The former fall due within a year of the end of the reporting period.

(d) **Share capital** is the permanent investment in a business by its owners. In the case of a limited company, this takes the form of *shares* for which investors subscribe on formation of the company. Each share has a **nominal** or **par** (ie face) **value** (say $1). In the statement of financial position, total issued share capital is shown at its par value.

(e) If a company issues shares for more than their par value (at a **premium**) then (usually) by law this premium must be recorded separately from the par value in a 'share premium account'. This is an example of a reserve. It belongs to the shareholders but cannot be distributed to them, because it is a **capital reserve**. Other capital reserves include the revaluation surplus, which shows the surpluses arising on revaluation of assets which are still owned by the company.

  Share capital and capital reserves are not distributable except on the winding up of the company, as a guarantee to the company's creditors that the company has enough assets to meet its debts. This is necessary because shareholders in limited liability companies have 'limited liability'; once they have paid the company for their shares they have no further liability to it if it becomes insolvent. The proprietors of other businesses are, by contrast, personally liable for business debts.

  Retained earnings constitute accumulated profits (less losses) made by the company and can be distributed to shareholders as **dividends**. They too belong to the shareholders, and so are a claim on the resources of the company.

(f) Statements of financial position do not always balance on the first attempt, as all accountants know! However, once errors are corrected, all statement of financial position balance. This is because in **double entry bookkeeping** every transaction recorded has a dual effect. Assets are always equal to liabilities plus capital and so capital is always equal to assets less liabilities. This makes sense as the owners of the business are entitled to the net assets of the business as representing their capital plus accumulated surpluses (or less accumulated deficit).

(g) The statement of financial position is not intended as a statement of a business's worth at a given point in time. This is because, except where some attempt is made to adjust for the effects of rising prices, assets and liabilities are recorded at **historical cost** and on a prudent basis. For example, if there is any doubt about the recoverability of a debt, then the value in the accounts must be reduced to the likely recoverable amount. In addition, where non-current assets have a finite useful life, their cost is gradually written off to reflect the use being made of them.

Sometimes non-current assets are **revalued** to their market value but this revaluation then goes out of date as few assets are revalued every year.

The figure in the statement of financial position for capital and reserves therefore bears **no relationship** to the market value of shares. Market values are the product of a large number of factors, including general economic conditions, alternative investment returns (eg interest rates), likely future profits and dividends and, not least, market sentiment.

| Question | Company financial statements |

The accountant of Fiddles Co, a limited liability company, has begun preparing final accounts but the work is not yet complete. At this stage the items included in the list of account balances are as follows.

	$'000
Land	100
Buildings	120
Plant and machinery	170
Depreciation provision	120
Ordinary shares of $1	100
Retained earnings brought forward	200
Trade accounts receivable	200
Trade accounts payable	110
Inventory	190
Operating profit	80
Loan stock (16%)	180
Allowance for receivables	3
Bank balance (asset)	12
Suspense	1

Notes (i) to (vii) below are to be taken into account.

(i)   The accounts receivable control account figure, which is used in the list of account balances, does not agree with the total of the sales ledger. A contra of $5,000 has been entered correctly in the individual ledger accounts but has been entered on the wrong side of both control accounts.

A batch total of sales of $12,345 had been entered in the double entry system as $13,345, although the individual ledger accounts entries for these sales were correct. The balance of $4,000 on the sales returns account has inadvertently been omitted from the trial balance though correctly entered in the ledger records.

(ii) A standing order of receipt from a regular customer for $2,000, and bank charges of $1,000, have been completely omitted from the records.

(iii) A receivable for $1,000 is to be written off. The allowance for receivables balance is to be adjusted to 1% of receivables.

(iv) The opening inventory figure had been overstated by $1,000 and the closing inventory figure had been understated by $2,000.

(v)   Any remaining balance on the suspense account should be treated as purchases if a debit balance and as sales if a credit balance.

(vi) The loan stock was issued three months before the year end. No entries have been made as regards interest.

Required

(a)   Prepare journal entries to cover items in notes (i) to (v) above. You are not to open any new accounts and may use only those accounts included in the list of account balances as given.

(b) Prepare final accounts for internal use within the limits of the available information. For presentation purposes all the items arising from notes (i) to (vii) above should be regarded as material.

Answer

(a) JOURNAL ENTRIES FOR ADJUSTMENTS

		Debit $	Credit $
(i)	Trade accounts payable	10,000	
	Trade accounts receivable		10,000
	Operating profit	1,000	
	Trade accounts receivable		1,000
	Operating profit	4,000	
	Suspense		4,000
(ii)	Bank	2,000	
	Trade accounts receivable		2,000
	Operating profit	1,000	
	Bank		1,000
(iii)	Operating profit	1,000	
	Trade accounts receivable		1,000
	Allowance for receivables (W1)	1,140	
	Operating profit		1,140
(iv)	Inventories	2,000	
	Operating profit		2,000
	Retained earnings brought forward	1,000	
	Operating profit		1,000
(v)	Suspense	3,000	
	Operating profit		3,000

(b) FIDDLES CO
STATEMENT OF FINANCIAL POSITION

	$	$	$
Assets			
Non-current assets			
Land and buildings		220,000	
Plant and machinery		170,000	
Depreciation		(120,000)	
			270,000
Current assets			
Inventories (190 + 2)		192,000	
Accounts receivable (W1)	186,000		
Less allowance	(1,860)		
		184,140	
Bank (12 + 2 – 1)		13,000	
			389,140
Total assets			659,140
Equity and liabilities			
Equity			
Share capital		100,000	
Retained earnings		271,940	
			371,940
Non-current liabilities			
Loan stock			180,000
Current liabilities			
Accounts payable (110 – 10)		100,000	
Loan stock interest payable		7,200	
			107,200
Total equity and liabilities			659,140

FIDDLES CO

INCOME STATEMENT (note that this is not as per IAS 1, it is purely for internal purposes)

	$
Operating profit (W2)	80,140
Debenture interest ($180,000 × 16% × 3/12)	(7,200)
	72,940
Retained earnings brought forward ($200,000 − 1,000)	199,000
Retained earnings carried forward	271,940

Workings

1	*Accounts receivable*	$
	Per opening trial balance	200,000
	Contra	(10,000)
	Miscasting	(1,000)
	Standing order	(2,000)
	Written off	(1,000)
		186,000
	Allowance b/f	3,000
	Allowance required	1,860
	Journal	1,140

2	*Operating profit*	
		$
	Per question	80,000
	Wrong batch total	(1,000)
	Returns	(4,000)
	Bank charges	(1,000)
	Irrecoverable debt	(1,000)
	Allowance for receivables	1,140
	Inventory (2,000 + 1,000)	3,000
	Suspense (sales)	3,000
		80,140

Note: This question dealt with accounts for **internal** purposes. In accounts produced for publication the income statement would comply with the IAS 1 format. In the following chapter we will be dealing with all the issues involved in producing financial statements for publication.

7 Changes in equity

IAS 1 requires a statement of changes in equity. This shows the movement in the equity section of the statement of financial position. A full set of financial statements includes a statement of changes in equity.

7.1 Format

This is the format of the statement of changes in equity as per IAS 1 (revised).

XYZ GROUP – STATEMENT OF CHANGES IN EQUITY FOR THE YEAR ENDED 31 DECEMBER 20X7

	Share capital	Retained earnings	Available for-sale financial assets	Revaluation surplus	Total	Non-controlling interest	Total equity
	$'000	$'000	$'000	$'000	$'000	$'000	$'000
Balance at 1 January 20X6	600,000	118,100	1,600	–	719,700	29,800	749,500
Changes in accounting policy	–	400	–	–	400	100	500
Restated balance	600,000	118,500	1,600	–	720,100	29,900	750,000
Changes in equity							
Dividends	–	(10,000)	–	–	(10,000)	–	(10,000)
Total comprehensive income for the year	–	53,200	16,000	1,600	70,800	18,700	89,500
Balance at 31 December 20X6	600,000	161,700	17,600	1,600	780,900	48,600	829,500
Changes in equity for 20X7							
Issue of share capital	50,000	–	–	–	50,000	–	50,000
Dividends	–	(15,000)	–	–	(15,000)	–	(15,000)
Total comprehensive income for the year	–	96,600	(14,400)	800	83,000	21,450	104,450
Transfer to retained earnings	–	200	–	(200)	–	–	–
Balance at 31 December 20X7	650,000	243,500	3,200	2,200	898,900	70,050	968,950

Note that where there has been a change of accounting policy necessitating a retrospective restatement, the adjustment is disclosed for each period. So, rather than just showing an adjustment to the balance b/f on 1.1.X7, the balances for 20X6 are restated.

8 Notes to the financial statements

FAST FORWARD

Some items need to be disclosed by way of note.

8.1 Contents of notes

The notes to the financial statements will **amplify** the information given in the statement of financial position, statement of comprehensive income and statement of changes in equity. We have already noted above the information which the IAS allows to be shown by note rather than in the statements. To some extent, then, the contents of the notes will be determined by the level of detail shown on the **face of the statements**.

8.2 Structure

The notes to the financial statements should perform the following functions.

(a)   Provide information about the **basis on which the financial statements were prepared** and which **specific accounting policies** were chosen and applied to significant transactions/events

(b)   Disclose any information, not shown elsewhere in the financial statements, which is **required by IFRSs**

(c)   Show any additional information that is relevant to understanding which is not shown elsewhere in the financial statements

The way the notes are presented is important. They should be given in a **systematic manner** and **cross referenced** back to the related figure(s) in the statement of financial position, statement of comprehensive income or statement of cash flows.

Notes to the financial statements will amplify the information shown therein by giving the following.

(a)   More **detailed analysis** or breakdowns of figures in the statements
(b)   **Narrative information** explaining figures in the statements
(c)   **Additional information**, eg contingent liabilities and commitments

IAS 1 suggests a **certain order** for notes to the financial statements. This will assist users when comparing the statements of different entities.

(a)   Statement of **compliance** with IFRSs

(b)   Statement of the **measurement basis** (bases) and accounting policies applied

(c)   **Supporting information** for items presented in each financial statement in the same order as each line item and each financial statement is presented

(d)   Other disclosures, eg:

      (i)   Contingent liabilities, commitments and other financial disclosures
      (ii)   Non-financial disclosures

The order of specific items may have to be varied occasionally, but a systematic structure is still required.

8.3 Presentation of accounting policies

The accounting policies section should describe the following.

(a)   The **measurement basis** (or bases) used in preparing the financial statements
(b)   The **other accounting policies** used, as required for a proper understanding of the financial statements

This information may be shown in the notes or sometimes as a **separate component** of the financial statements.

The information on measurement bases used is obviously fundamental to an understanding of the financial statements. Where **more than one basis is used**, it should be stated to which assets or liabilities each basis has been applied.

Note: accounting policies are covered in Chapter 4.

8.4 Other disclosures

An entity must disclose in the notes:

(a)   The amount of dividends proposed or declared before the financial statements were authorised for issue but not recognised as a distribution to owners during the period, and the amount per share
(b)   The amount of any cumulative preference dividends not recognised

IAS 1 ends by listing some **specific disclosures** which will always be required if they are not shown elsewhere in the financial statements.

(a)   The domicile and legal form of the entity, its country of incorporation and the address of the registered office (or, if different, principal place of business)
(b)   A description of the nature of the entity's operations and its principal activities
(c)   The name of the parent entity and the ultimate parent entity of the group

Exam focus point

You will have to produce financial statements suitable for publication in your exam, so this chapter is important and you should refer back to it.

The accountant of Wislon Co has prepared the following list of account balances as at 31 December 20X7.

	$'000
50c ordinary shares (fully paid)	450
10% debentures (secured)	200
Retained earnings 1.1.X7	242
General reserve 1.1.X7	171
Land and buildings 1.1.X7 (cost)	430
Plant and machinery 1.1.X7 (cost)	830
Accumulated depreciation	
Buildings 1.1.X7	20
Plant and machinery 1.1.X7	222
Inventory 1.1.X7	190
Sales	2,695
Purchases	2,152
Ordinary dividend	15
Debenture interest	10
Wages and salaries	254
Light and heat	31
Sundry expenses	113
Suspense account	135
Trade accounts receivable	179
Trade accounts payable	195
Cash	126

Notes

(a)   Sundry expenses include $9,000 paid in respect of insurance for the year ending 1 September 20X8. Light and heat does not include an invoice of $3,000 for electricity for the three months ending 2 January 20X8, which was paid in February 20X8. Light and heat also includes $20,000 relating to salesmen's commission.

(b)   The suspense account is in respect of the following items.

	$'000
Proceeds from the issue of 100,000 ordinary shares	120
Proceeds from the sale of plant	300
	420
Less consideration for the acquisition of Mary & Co	285
	135

(c)   The net assets of Mary & Co were purchased on 3 March 20X7. Assets were valued as follows

	$'000
Available-for-sale financial assets	231
Inventory	34
	265

All the inventory acquired was sold during 20X7. The available-for-sale financial assets were still held by Wislon at 31.12.X7. Goodwill has not been impaired in value.

(d)   The property was acquired some years ago. The buildings element of the cost was estimated at $100,000 and the estimated useful life of the assets was fifty years at the time of purchase. As at 31 December 20X7 the property is to be revalued at $800,000.

(e)   The plant which was sold had cost $350,000 and had a net book value of $274,000 as on 1.1.X7. $36,000 depreciation is to be charged on plant and machinery for 20X7.

(f)   The management wish to provide for:

 (i)   Debenture interest due
 (ii)   A transfer to general reserve of $16,000
 (iii) Audit fees of $4,000

(g)   Inventory as at 31 December 20X7 was valued at $220,000 (cost).

(h)   Taxation is to be ignored.

Required

Prepare the financial statements of Wislon Co as at 31 December 20X7. You do not need to produce notes to the statements.

Answer

(a)   Normal adjustments are needed for accruals and prepayments (insurance, light and heat, debenture interest and audit fees). The debenture interest accrued is calculated as follows.

	$'000
Charge needed in income statement (10% × $200,000)	20
Amount paid so far, as shown in list of account balances	10
Accrual: presumably six months' interest now payable	10

The accrued expenses shown in the statement of financial position comprise:

	$'000
Debenture interest	10
Light and heat	3
Audit fee	4
	17

(b)   The misposting of $20,000 to light and heat is also adjusted, by reducing the light and heat expense, but charging $20,000 to salesmen's commission.

(c)   Depreciation on the building is calculated as $\dfrac{\$100,000}{50} = \$2,000$.

The NBV of the property is then $430,000 – $20,000 – $2,000 = $408,000 at the end of the year. When the property is revalued a reserve of $800,000 – $408,000 = $392,000 is then created.

(d)   The profit on disposal of plant is calculated as proceeds $300,000 (per suspense account) less NBV $274,000, ie $26,000. The cost of the remaining plant is calculated at $830,000 – $350,000 = $480,000. The depreciation provision at the year end is:

	$'000
Balance 1.1.X7	222
Charge for 20X7	36
Less depreciation on disposals (350 – 274)	(76)
	182

(e)   Goodwill arising on the purchase of Mary & Co is:

	$'000
Consideration (per suspense account)	285
Assets at valuation	265
Goodwill	20

This is shown as an asset in the statement of financial position. The financial assets, being owned by Wislon at the year end, are also shown on the statement of financial position, whereas Mary's inventory, acquired and then sold, is added to the purchases figure for the year.

(f)   The other item in the suspense account is dealt with as follows.

	$'000
Proceeds of issue of 100,000 ordinary shares	120
Less nominal value 100,000 × 50c	50
Excess of consideration over par value (= share premium)	70

(g)   The transfer to general reserve increases it to $171,000 + $16,000 = $187,000.

We can now prepare the financial statements.

WISLON CO
STATEMENT OF COMPREHENSIVE INCOME FOR THE YEAR ENDED 31 DECEMBER 20X7

	$'000
Revenue	2,695
Cost of sales (W1)	(2,156)
Gross profit	539
Other income (profit on disposal of plant)	26
Administrative expenses (W2)	(437)
Finance costs	(20)
Profit for the year	108
Gain on property revaluation	392
Total comprehensive income for the year	500

Note

The only item of 'other comprehensive income' for the year was the revaluation gain. If there had been no revaluation gain, only an income statement would have been required.

Workings

1   *Cost of sales*

	$'000
Opening inventory	190
Purchases (2,152 + 34)	2,186
Closing inventory	(220)
	2,156

2   *Administrative expenses*

	$'000
Wages, salaries and commission (254 + 20)	274
Sundry expenses (113 − 6)	107
Light and heat (31 − 20 + 3)	14
Depreciation: buildings	2
plant	36
Audit fees	4
	437

WISLON CO
STATEMENT OF FINANCIAL POSITION AS AT 31 DECEMBER 20X7

	$'000	$'000
Assets		
Non-current assets		
Property, plant and equipment		
Property at valuation		800
Plant: cost	480	
Accumulated depreciation	(182)	
		298
Goodwill		20
Available-for-sale financial assets		231
Current assets		
Inventory	220	
Trade accounts receivable	179	
Prepayments	6	
Cash	126	
		531
Total assets		1,880

	$'000	$'000
Equity and liabilities		
Equity		
50c ordinary shares	500	
Share premium	70	
Revaluation surplus	392	
General reserve	187	
Retained earnings	319	
		1,468
Non-current liabilities		
10% loan stock (secured)		200
Current liabilities		
Trade accounts payable	195	
Accrued expenses	17	
		212
Total equity and liabilities		1,880

WISLON CO
STATEMENT OF CHANGES IN EQUITY
FOR THE YEAR ENDED 31 DECEMBER 20X7

	Share capital $'000	Share premium $'000	Retained earnings $'000	General reserve $'000	Revaluation Surplus $'000	Total $'000
Balance at 1.1.X7	450	–	242	171	-	863
Issue of share capital	50	70				120
Dividends			(15)			(15)
Total comprehensive income for the year			108		392	500
Transfer to reserve			(16)	16		
Balance at 31.12.X7	500	70	319	187	392	1,468

Note that the total comprehensive income is analysed into its components.

Chapter Roundup

- IAS 1 covers the **form and content of** financial statements. The main components are:
  - Statement of financial position
  - Statement of comprehensive income
  - Statement of changes in equity
  - Statement of cash flows (see Chapter 20)
  - Notes to the financial statements

- Each component must be **identified clearly**.

- IAS 1 suggests **formats** for the statement of financial position and statement of comprehensive income, but these are not rigid. Certain items are specified, however, for **disclosure on the face of the financial statements.**

- You should appreciate the distinction between **current and non-current** assets and liabilities and their different treatments.

- IAS 1 (revised) requires all items of income and expense in a period to be shown in a **statement of comprehensive income**.

- IAS 1 offers **two** possible formats for the income statement – by function or by nature. Classification by function is more common.

- IAS 1 requires a statement of changes in equity. This shows the movement in the equity section of the statement of financial position. A full set of financial statements includes a statement of changes in equity.

1   Which of the following are examples of current assets?

(a)   Property, plant and equipment
(b)   Prepayments
(c)   Cash equivalents
(d)   Manufacturing licences
(e)   Retained earnings

2   Provisions must be disclosed in the statement of financial position.

True ☐

False ☐

3   Which of the following must be disclosed on the face of the income statement?

(a)   Tax expense
(b)   Analysis of expenses
(c)   Net profit or loss for the period.

4   Where are revaluation gains shown in the financial statements?

Answers to Quick Quiz

1   (b) and (c) only
2   True
3   (a) and (c) only. (b) may be shown in the notes.
4   In the statement of comprehensive income and the statement of changes in equity.

Now try the questions below from the Exam Question Bank			
Number	Level	Marks	Time
4	Examination	25	45 mins

Non-current assets

4

Topic list	Syllabus reference
1 IAS 16 Property, plant and equipment	C2
2 Depreciation accounting	C2
3 IAS 20 Government grants	C2
4 IAS 40 Investment property	C2
5 IAS 23 Borrowing costs	C2

Introduction

IAS 16 should be familiar to you from your earlier studies, as should the mechanics of accounting for depreciation, revaluations of non-current assets and disposals of non-current assets. Some questions are given here for revision purposes.

IAS 20 on government grants is a straightforward standard and you should have few problems with it.

IAS 40 deals with investment properties, which can be treated differently from other property under IAS 16.

Study guide

		Intellectual level
C2	**Tangible non-current assets**	
(a)	define and compute the initial measurement of a non-current (including a self-constructed) asset.	2
(b)	identify subsequent expenditure that may be capitalised (including borrowing costs), distinguishing between capital and revenue items.	2
(c)	discuss the requirements of relevant accounting standards in relation to the revaluation of non-current assets.	2
(d)	account for revaluation and disposal gains and losses for non-current assets.	2
(e)	compute depreciation based on the cost and revaluation models and on assets that have two or more significant parts (complex assets).	2
(f)	apply the provision of relevant accounting standards in relation to accounting for government grants.	2
(g)	discuss why the treatment of investment properties should differ from other properties.	2
(h)	apply the requirements of relevant accounting standards for investment property.	2

1 IAS 16 Property, plant and equipment

FAST FORWARD

IAS 16 covers all aspects of accounting for property, plant and equipment. This represents the bulk of items which are **'tangible' non-current assets.**.

1.1 Scope

IAS 16 should be followed when accounting for property, plant and equipment *unless* another international accounting standard requires a **different treatment**.

IAS 16 **does not apply** to the following.

(a) Biological assets related to agricultural activity
(b) Mineral rights and mineral reserves, such as oil, gas and other non-regenerative resources

However, the standard applies to property, plant and equipment used to develop these assets.

1.2 Definitions

The standard gives a large number of definitions.

Key terms

> - **Property, plant and equipment** are tangible assets that:
>   - are held for use in the production or supply of goods or services, for rental to others, or for administrative purposes; and
>   - are expected to be used during more than one period.
>
> - **Cost** is the amount of cash or cash equivalents paid or the fair value of the other consideration given to acquire an asset at the time of its acquisition or construction.
>
> - **Residual value** is the net amount which the entity expects to obtain for an asset at the end of its useful life after deducting the expected costs of disposal.

- **Entity specific value** is the present value of the cash flows an entity expects to arise from the continuing use of an asset and from its disposal at the end of its useful life, or expects to incur when settling a liability.

- **Fair value** is the amount for which an asset could be exchanged between knowledgeable, willing parties in an arm's length transaction.

- **Carrying amount** is the amount at which an asset is recognised in the statement of financial position after deducting any accumulated depreciation and accumulated impairment losses.

- An **impairment loss** is the amount by which the carrying amount of an asset exceeds its recoverable amount.

(IAS 16)

1.3 Recognition

In this context, recognition simply means incorporation of the item in the business's accounts, in this case as a non-current asset. The recognition of property, plant and equipment depends on two criteria.

(a)   It is probable that **future economic benefits** associated with the asset will flow to the entity
(b)   The cost of the asset to the entity can be **measured reliably**

These recognition criteria apply to **subsequent expenditure** as well as costs incurred initially. There are no longer any separate criteria for recognising subsequent expenditure.

Property, plant and equipment can amount to **substantial amounts** in financial statements, affecting the presentation of the company's financial position and the profitability of the entity, through depreciation and also if an asset is wrongly classified as an expense and taken to profit or loss.

1.3.1 First criterion: future economic benefits

The **degree of certainty** attached to the flow of future economic benefits must be assessed. This should be based on the evidence available at the date of initial recognition (usually the date of purchase). The entity should thus be assured that it will receive the rewards attached to the asset and it will incur the associated risks, which will only generally be the case when the rewards and risks have actually passed to the entity. Until then, the asset should not be recognised.

1.3.2 Second criterion: cost measured reliably

It is generally easy to measure the cost of an asset as the **transfer amount on purchase**, ie what was paid for it. **Self-constructed assets** can also be measured easily by adding together the purchase price of all the constituent parts (labour, material etc) paid to external parties.

1.4 Separate items

Most of the time assets will be identified individually, but this will not be the case for **smaller items**, such as tools, dies and moulds, which are sometimes classified as inventory and written off as an expense.

Major components or spare parts, however, should be recognised as property, plant and equipment.

For very **large and specialised items**, an apparently single asset should be broken down into its composite parts. This occurs where the different parts have different useful lives and different depreciation rates are applied to each part, eg an aircraft, where the body and engines are separated as they have different useful lives.

1.5 Safety and environmental equipment

When such assets as these are acquired they will qualify for recognition where they enable the entity to **obtain future economic benefits** from related assets in excess of those it would obtain otherwise. The recognition will only be to the extent that the carrying amount of the asset and related assets does not exceed the total recoverable amount of these assets.

1.6 Initial measurement

Once an item of property, plant and equipment qualifies for recognition as an asset, it will initially be **measured at cost**.

1.6.1 Components of cost

The standard lists the components of the cost of an item of property, plant and equipment.

- **Purchase price**, less any trade discount or rebate
- **Import duties** and non-refundable purchase taxes
- **Directly attributable costs** of bringing the asset to working condition for its intended use, eg:
    - The cost of site preparation
    - Initial delivery and handling costs
    - Installation costs
    - Testing
    - Professional fees (architects, engineers)
- Initial estimate of the unavoidable cost of dismantling and removing the asset and restoring the site on which it is located

The revised IAS 16 provides **additional guidance on directly attributable** costs included in the cost of an item of property, plant and equipment.

(a)   These costs bring the asset to the location and working conditions necessary for it to be capable of operating in the manner intended by management, including those costs to test whether the asset is functioning properly.

(b)   They are determined after deducting the net proceeds from selling any items produced when bringing the asset to its location and condition.

The revised standard also states that income and related expenses of operations that are **incidental** to the construction or development of an item of property, plant and equipment should be **recognised** in profit or loss.

The following costs **will not be part of the cost** of property, plant or equipment unless they can be attributed directly to the asset's acquisition, or bringing it into its working condition.

- Administration and other general overhead costs
- Start-up and similar pre-production costs
- Initial operating losses before the asset reaches planned performance

All of these will be recognised as an **expense** rather than an asset.

In the case of **self-constructed assets**, the same principles are applied as for acquired assets. If the entity makes similar assets during the normal course of business for sale externally, then the cost of the asset will be the cost of its production under IAS 2 *Inventories*. This also means that abnormal costs (wasted material, labour or other resources) are excluded from the cost of the asset. An example of a self-constructed asset is when a building company builds its own head office.

1.6.2 Exchanges of assets

The revised IAS 16 specifies that exchange of items of property, plant and equipment, regardless of whether the assets are similar, are measured at **fair value**, **unless the exchange transaction lacks commercial substance** or the fair value of neither of the assets exchanged can be **measured reliably**. If the acquired item is not measured at fair value, its cost is measured at the carrying amount of the asset given up.

Expenditure incurred in replacing or renewing a component of an item of property, plant and equipment must be **recognised in the carrying amount of the item**. The carrying amount of the replaced or renewed component must be derecognised. A similar approach is also applied when a separate component of an item of property, plant and equipment is identified in respect of a major inspection to enable the continued use of the item.

1.7 Measurement subsequent to initial recognition

The standard offers two possible treatments here, essentially a choice between keeping an asset recorded at **cost** or revaluing it to **fair value**.

(a) **Cost model.** Carry the asset at its cost less depreciation and any accumulated impairment loss.

(b) **Revaluation model.** Carry the asset at a revalued amount, being its fair value at the date of the revaluation less any subsequent accumulated depreciation and subsequent accumulated impairment losses. The revised IAS 16 makes clear that the **revaluation model is available only if the fair value of the item can be measured reliably**.

1.7.1 Revaluations

The **market value** of land and buildings usually represents fair value, assuming existing use and line of business. Such valuations are usually carried out by professionally qualified valuers.

In the case of **plant and equipment**, fair value can also be taken as **market value**. Where a market value is not available, however, depreciated replacement cost should be used. There may be no market value where types of plant and equipment are sold only rarely or because of their specialised nature (ie they would normally only be sold as part of an ongoing business).

The frequency of valuation depends on the **volatility of the fair values** of individual items of property, plant and equipment. The more volatile the fair value, the more frequently revaluations should be carried out. Where the current fair value is very different from the carrying value then a revaluation should be carried out.

Most importantly, when an item of property, plant and equipment is revalued, **the whole class of assets to which it belongs should be revalued.**

All the items within a class should be **revalued at the same time**, to prevent selective revaluation of certain assets and to avoid disclosing a mixture of costs and values from different dates in the financial statements. A rolling basis of revaluation is allowed if the revaluations are kept up to date and the revaluation of the whole class is completed in a short period of time.

How should any **increase in value** be treated when a revaluation takes place? The debit will be the increase in value in the statement of financial position, but what about the credit? IAS 16 requires the increase to be credited to a **revaluation surplus** (ie part of owners' equity), *unless* the increase is reversing a previous decrease which was recognised as an expense. To the extent that this offset is made, the increase is recognised as income; any excess is then taken to the revaluation surplus.

1.8 Example: revaluation surplus

Binkie Co has an item of land carried in its books at $13,000. Two years ago a slump in land values led the company to reduce the carrying value from $15,000. This was taken as an expense in the income statement. There has been a surge in land prices in the current year, however, and the land is now worth $20,000.

Account for the revaluation in the current year.

Solution

The double entry is:

DEBIT	Asset value (statement of financial position)	$7,000	
CREDIT	Income statement		$2,000
	Revaluation surplus		$5,000

Note: the credit to the revaluation surplus will be shown under 'other comprehensive income'.

The case is similar for a **decrease in value** on revaluation. Any decrease should be recognised as an expense, except where it offsets a previous increase taken as a revaluation surplus in owners' equity. Any decrease greater than the previous upwards increase in value must be taken as an expense in the profit or loss.

1.9 Example: revaluation decrease

Let us simply swap round the example given above. The original cost was $15,000, revalued upwards to $20,000 two years ago. The value has now fallen to $13,000.

Account for the decrease in value.

Solution

The double entry is:

DEBIT	Revaluation surplus	$5,000	
DEBIT	Income statement	$2,000	
CREDIT	Asset value (statement of financial position)		$7,000

There is a further complication when a **revalued asset is being depreciated**. As we have seen, an upward revaluation means that the depreciation charge will increase. Normally, a revaluation surplus is only realised when the asset is sold, but when it is being depreciated, part of that surplus is being realised as the asset is used. The amount of the surplus realised is the difference between depreciation charged on the revalued amount and the (lower) depreciation which would have been charged on the asset's original cost. **This amount can be transferred to retained (ie realised) earnings but *not* through profit or loss.**

1.10 Example: revaluation and depreciation

Crinckle Co bought an asset for $10,000 at the beginning of 20X6. It had a useful life of five years. On 1 January 20X8 the asset was revalued to $12,000. The expected useful life has remained unchanged (ie three years remain).

Account for the revaluation and state the treatment for depreciation from 20X8 onwards.

Solution

On 1 January 20X8 the carrying value of the asset is $10,000 − (2 × $10,000 ÷ 5) = $6,000. For the revaluation:

DEBIT	Asset value	$6,000	
CREDIT	Revaluation surplus		$6,000

The depreciation for the next three years will be $12,000 ÷ 3 = $4,000, compared to depreciation on cost of $10,000 ÷ 5 = $2,000. So each year, the extra $2,000 can be treated as part of the surplus which has become realised:

DEBIT	Revaluation surplus	$2,000	
CREDIT	Retained earnings		$2,000

This is a movement on owners' equity only, not an item in the income statement.

1.11 Depreciation

The standard states:

- The **depreciable amount** of an item of property, plant and equipment should be allocated on a systematic basis over its useful life.
- The **depreciation method** used should reflect the pattern in which the asset's economic benefits are consumed by the entity.
- The **depreciation charge** for each period should be recognised as an expense unless it is included in the carrying amount of another asset.

Land and buildings are dealt with separately even when they are acquired together because land normally has an unlimited life and is therefore not depreciated. In contrast buildings do have a limited life and must be depreciated. Any increase in the value of land on which a building is standing will have no impact on the determination of the building's useful life.

Depreciation is usually treated as an **expense**, but not where it is absorbed by the entity in the process of producing other assets. For example, depreciation of plant and machinery can be incurred in the production of goods for sale (inventory items). In such circumstances, the depreciation is included in the cost of the new assets produced.

1.11.1 Review of useful life

A review of the **useful life** of property, plant and equipment should be carried out **at least at each financial year end** and the depreciation charge for the current and future periods should be adjusted if expectations have changed significantly from previous estimates. Changes are changes in accounting estimates and are accounted for prospectively as adjustments to future depreciation.

1.11.2 Example: review of useful life

B Co acquired a non-current asset on 1 January 20X2 for $80,000. It had no residual value and a useful life of 10 years.

On 1 January 20X5 the total useful life was reviewed and revised to 7 years.

What will be the depreciation charge for 20X5?

Solution

	$
Original cost	80,000
Depreciation 20X3 – 20X4 (80,000 × 3/10)	(24,000)
Carrying amount at 1 December 20X5	56,000
Remaining life (7 – 3) =	4 years
Depreciation charge years 20X5 – 20X8 (56,000/4)	14,000

1.11.3 Review of depreciation method

The **depreciation method** should also be reviewed **at least at each financial year end** and, if there has been a significant change in the expected pattern of economic benefits from those assets, the method should be changed to suit this changed pattern. When such a change in depreciation method takes place the change should be accounted for as a **change in accounting estimate** and the depreciation charge for the current and future periods should be adjusted.

1.11.4 Impairment of asset values

An **impairment loss** should be treated in the same way as a **revaluation decrease** ie the decrease should be **recognised as an expense**. However, a revaluation decrease (or impairment loss) should be charged directly against any related revaluation surplus to the extent that the decrease does not exceed the amount held in the revaluation surplus in respect of that same asset.

A **reversal of an impairment** loss should be treated in the same way as a **revaluation increase**, ie a revaluation increase should be recognised as income to the extent that it reverses a revaluation decrease or an impairment loss of the same asset previously recognised as an expense.

1.12 Retirements and disposals

When an asset is permanently **withdrawn from use, or sold or scrapped**, and no future economic benefits are expected from its disposal, it should be withdrawn from the statement of financial position.

Gains or losses are the difference between the estimated net disposal proceeds and the carrying amount of the asset. They should be recognised as income or expense in profit or loss.

1.13 Derecognition

An entity is required to **derecognise the carrying amount** of an item of property, plant or equipment that it disposes of on the date the **criteria for the sale of goods** in IAS 18 *Revenue* would be met. This also applies to parts of an asset.

An entity cannot classify as revenue a gain it realises on the disposal of an item of property, plant and equipment.

1.14 Disclosure

The standard has a long list of disclosure requirements, for each class of property, plant and equipment.

(a) **Measurement bases** for determining the gross carrying amount (if more than one, the gross carrying amount for that basis in each category)

(b) **Depreciation methods** used

(c) **Useful lives** or depreciation rates used

(d) **Gross carrying amount** and accumulated depreciation (aggregated with accumulated impairment losses) at the beginning and end of the period

(e) **Reconciliation** of the carrying amount at the beginning and end of the period showing:

    (i)   Additions
    (ii)   Disposals
    (iii)   Acquisitions through business combinations (see Chapter 15)
    (iv)   Increases/decreases during the period from revaluations and from impairment losses
    (v)   Impairment losses recognised in profit or loss
    (vi)   Impairment losses reversed in profit or loss
    (vii)   Depreciation
    (viii) Net exchange differences (from translation of statements of foreign entity)
    (ix)   Any other movements.

The financial statements should also disclose the following.

(a) Any recoverable amounts of property, plant and equipment

(b) Existence and amounts of **restrictions on title**, and items pledged as security for liabilities

(c) Accounting policy for **the estimated costs of restoring the site**

(d) Amount of expenditures on account of **items in the course of construction**

(e) Amount of commitments to **acquisitions**

Revalued assets require further disclosures.

(a) Basis used to revalue the assets

(b) Effective date of the revaluation

(c) Whether an independent valuer was involved

(d) Nature of any indices used to determine replacement cost

(e) Carrying amount of each class of property, plant and equipment that would have been included in the financial statements had the assets been carried at cost less accumulated depreciation and accumulated impairment losses.

(f) Revaluation surplus, indicating the movement for the period and any restrictions on the distribution of the balance to shareholders.

The standard also **encourages disclosure** of additional information, which the users of financial statements may find useful.

(a)   The carrying amount of temporarily idle property, plant and equipment
(b)   The gross carrying amount of any fully depreciated property, plant and equipment that is still in use
(c)   The carrying amount of property, plant and equipment retired from active use and held for disposal
(d)   The fair value of property, plant and equipment when this is materially different from the carrying amount

The following format (with notional figures) is commonly used to disclose non-current assets movements.

	Total $	Land and buildings $	Plant and equipment $
Cost or valuation			
At 1 January 20X4	50,000	40,000	10,000
Revaluation surplus	12,000	12,000	–
Additions in year	4,000	–	4,000
Disposals in year	(1,000)	–	(1,000)
At 31 December 20X4	65,000	52,000	13,000
Depreciation			
At 1 January 20X4	16,000	10,000	6,000
Charge for year	4,000	1,000	3,000
Eliminated on disposals	(500)	–	(500)
At 31 December 20X4	19,500	11,000	8,500
Net book value			
At 31 December 20X4	45,500	41,000	4,500
At 1 January 20X4	34,000	30,000	4,000

Question   Non-current assets

(a)   In a statement of financial position prepared in accordance with IAS 16, what does the net book value (carrying value) represent?
(b)   In a set of financial statements prepared in accordance with IAS 16, is it correct to say that the net book value (carrying value) figure in a statement of financial position cannot be greater than the market (net realisable) value of the partially used asset as at the end of the reporting period? Explain your reasons for your answer.

Answer

(a)   In simple terms the net book value of an asset is the cost of an asset less the 'accumulated depreciation', that is, all depreciation charged so far. It should be emphasised that the main purpose of charging depreciation is to ensure that profits are fairly reported. Thus depreciation is concerned with the statement of comprehensive income rather than the statement of financial position. In consequence the net book value figure in the statement of financial position can be quite arbitrary. In particular, it does not necessarily bear any relation to the market value of an asset and is of little use for planning and decision making.

An obvious example of the disparity between net book value and market value is found in the case of buildings, which may be worth more than ten times as much as their net book value.

(b)   Net book value can in some circumstances be higher than market value (net realisable value). IAS 16 *Property, plant and equipment* states that the value of an asset cannot be greater than its 'recoverable amount'. However 'recoverable amount' as defined in IAS 16 is the amount recoverable from further use. This may be higher than the market value.

This makes sense if you think of a specialised machine which could not fetch much on the secondhand market but which will produce goods which can be sold at a profit for many years.

Exam focus point

Property and/or other non-current assets are likely to be tested as they have come up on a number of papers.

2 Depreciation accounting

FAST FORWARD

Where assets held by an entity have a **limited useful life** to that entity it is necessary to apportion the value of an asset over it's useful life.

2.1 Non-current assets

If an asset's life extends over more than one accounting period, it earns profits over more than one period. It is a **non-current asset**.

With the exception of land held on freehold or very long leasehold, **every non-current asset eventually wears out over time**. Machines, cars and other vehicles, fixtures and fittings, and even buildings do not last for ever. When a business acquires a non-current asset, it will have some idea about how long its useful life will be, and it might decide what to do with it.

(a)   Keep on using the non-current asset until it becomes **completely worn out**, useless, and worthless.

(b)   **Sell off** the non-current asset at the end of its useful life, either by selling it as a second-hand item or as scrap.

Since a non-current asset has a cost, and a limited useful life, and its value eventually declines, it follows that a charge should be made in profit or loss to reflect the use that is made of the asset by the business. This charge is called **depreciation**.

2.2 Scope

Depreciation accounting is governed by IAS 16 *Property, plant and equipment.* These are some of the IAS 16 definitions concerning depreciation.

Key terms

- **Depreciation** is the result of systematic allocation of the depreciable amount of an asset over its estimated useful life. Depreciation for the accounting period is charged to net profit or loss for the period either directly or indirectly.

- **Depreciable assets** are assets which:
  -     Are expected to be used during more than one accounting period
  -     Have a limited useful life
  -     Are held by an entity for use in the production or supply of goods and services, for rental to others, or for administrative purposes

- **Useful life** is one of two things.
  -     The period over which a depreciable asset is expected to be used by the entity, or
  -     The number of production or similar units expected to be obtained from the asset by the entity.

- **Depreciable amount** of a depreciable asset is the historical cost or other amount substituted for cost in the financial statements, less the estimated residual value.

(IAS 16)

An 'amount substituted for cost' will normally be a **current market value** after a revaluation has taken place.

2.3 Depreciation

IAS 16 requires the depreciable amount of a depreciable asset to be allocated on a **systematic basis** to each accounting period during the useful life of the asset. **Every part of an item of property, plant and equipment with a cost that is significant in relation to the total cost of the item must be depreciated separately**.

One way of defining depreciation is to describe it as a means of **spreading the cost** of a non-current asset over its useful life, and so matching the cost against the full period during which it earns profits for the business. Depreciation charges are an example of the application of the accrual assumption to calculate profits.

There are situations where, over a period, an asset has **increased in value**, ie its current value is greater than the carrying value in the financial statements. You might think that in such situations it would not be necessary to depreciate the asset. The standard states, however, that this is irrelevant, and that depreciation should still be charged to each accounting period, based on the depreciable amount, irrespective of a rise in value.

An entity is required to begin depreciating an item of property, plant and equipment when it is available for use and to continue depreciating it until it is derecognised even if it is idle during the period.

2.4 Useful life

The following factors should be considered when **estimating the useful life** of a depreciable asset.

- Expected **physical wear and tear**
- **Obsolescence**
- Legal or other **limits** on the use of the assets

Once decided, the useful life should be **reviewed at least every financial year end** and depreciation rates adjusted for the current and future periods if expectations vary significantly from the original estimates. The effect of the change should be disclosed in the accounting period in which the change takes place.

The assessment of useful life requires **judgement** based on previous experience with similar assets or classes of asset. When a completely new type of asset is acquired (ie through technological advancement or through use in producing a brand new product or service) it is still necessary to estimate useful life, even though the exercise will be much more difficult.

The standard also points out that the physical life of the asset might be longer than its useful life to the entity in question. One of the main factors to be taken into consideration is the **physical wear and tear** the asset is likely to endure. This will depend on various circumstances, including the number of shifts for which the asset will be used, the entity's repair and maintenance programme and so on. Other factors to be considered include obsolescence (due to technological advances/improvements in production/ reduction in demand for the product/service produced by the asset) and legal restrictions, eg length of a related lease.

2.5 Residual value

In most cases the residual value of an asset is **likely to be immaterial**. If it is likely to be of any significant value, that value must be estimated at the date of purchase or any subsequent revaluation. The amount of residual value should be estimated based on the current situation with other similar assets, used in the same way, which are now at the end of their useful lives. Any expected costs of disposal should be offset against the gross residual value.

2.6 Depreciation methods

Consistency is important. The depreciation method selected should be applied consistently from period to period unless altered circumstances justify a change. When the method *is* changed, the effect should be quantified and disclosed and the reason for the change should be stated.

Various methods of allocating depreciation to accounting periods are available, but whichever is chosen must be applied **consistently** (as required by IAS 1: see Chapter 1), to ensure comparability from period to period. Change of policy is not allowed simply because of the profitability situation of the entity.

You should be familiar with the various **accepted methods of allocating depreciation** and the relevant calculations and accounting treatments, which are revised in questions at the end of this section.

2.7 Disclosure

An accounting policy note should disclose the **valuation bases** used for determining the amounts at which depreciable assets are stated, along with the other accounting policies: see IAS 1.

IAS 16 also requires the following to be disclosed for each major class of depreciable asset.

- **Depreciation methods** used
- **Useful lives** or the depreciation rates used
- **Total depreciation** allocated for the period
- **Gross amount** of depreciable assets and the related accumulated depreciation

2.8 What is depreciation?

The need to depreciate non-current assets arises from the **accruals assumption**. If money is expended in purchasing an asset then the amount expended must at some time be charged against profits. If the asset is one which contributes to an entity's revenue over a number of accounting periods it would be inappropriate to charge any single period (eg the period in which the asset was acquired) with the whole of the expenditure. Instead, some method must be found of spreading the cost of the asset over its useful economic life.

This view of depreciation as a process of allocation of the cost of an asset over several accounting periods is the view adopted by IAS 16. It is worth mentioning here two **common misconceptions** about the purpose and effects of depreciation.

(a)   It is sometimes thought that the net book value (NBV) of an asset is equal to its net realisable value and that the object of charging depreciation is to **reflect the fall in value of an asset over its life**. This misconception is the basis of a common, but incorrect, argument which says that freehold properties (say) need not be depreciated in times when property values are rising. It is true that historical cost statements of financial position often give a misleading impression when a property's NBV is much below its market value, but in such a case it is open to a business to incorporate a revaluation into its books, or even to prepare its accounts based on current costs. This is a separate problem from that of allocating the property's cost over successive accounting periods.

(b)   Another misconception is that depreciation is provided **so that an asset can be replaced at the end of its useful life**. This is not the case.

(i)   If there is no intention of replacing the asset, it could then be argued that there is no need to provide for any depreciation at all.

(ii)   If prices are rising, the replacement cost of the asset will exceed the amount of depreciation provided.

The following questions are for revision purposes only.

A lorry bought for a business cost $17,000. It is expected to last for five years and then be sold for scrap for $2,000. Usage over the five years is expected to be:

Year 1	200 days
Year 2	100 days
Year 3	100 days
Year 4	150 days
Year 5	40 days

Required

Work out the depreciation to be charged each year under:

(a)   The straight line method
(b)   The reducing balance method (using a rate of 35%)
(c)   The machine hour method
(d)   The sum-of-the digits method

Answer

(a)   Under the straight line method, depreciation for each of the five years is:

$$\text{Annual depreciation} = \frac{\$(17,000 - 2,000)}{5} = \$3,000$$

(b)   Under the reducing balance method, depreciation for each of the five years is:

Year	Depreciation		
1	35% × $17,000	=	$5,950
2	35% × ($17,000 − $5,950) = 35% × $11,050	=	$3,868
3	35% × ($11,050 − $3,868) = 35% × $7,182	=	$2,514
4	35% × ($7,182 − $2,514) = 35% × $4,668	=	$1,634
5	Balance to bring book value down to $2,000 = $4,668 − $1,634 − $2,000	=	$1,034

(c)   Under the machine hour method, depreciation for each of the five years is calculated as follows.

Total usage (days) = 200 + 100 + 100 + 150 + 40 = 590 days

$$\text{Depreciation per day} = \frac{\$(17,000 - 2,000)}{590} = \$25.42$$

Year	Usage (days)	Depreciation ($) (days × $25.42)
1	200	5,084.00
2	100	2,542.00
3	100	2,542.00
4	150	3,813.00
5	40	1,016.80
		14,997.80

Note. The answer does not come to exactly $15,000 because of the rounding carried out at the 'depreciation per day' stage of the calculation.

(d)   The sum-of-the digits method begins by adding up the years of expected life. In this case, 5 + 4 + 3 + 2 + 1 = 15.

The depreciable amount of $15,000 will then be allocated as follows:

Year		
	1	15,000 × 5/15 = 5,000
	2	15,000 × 4/15 = 4,000
	3	15,000 × 3/15 = 3,000
	4	15,000 × 2/15 = 2,000
	5	15,000 × 1/15 = 1,000

Question

(a) What are the purposes of providing for depreciation?

(b) In what circumstances is the reducing balance method more appropriate than the straight-line method? Give reasons for your answer.

Answer

(a) The accounts of a business try to recognise that the cost of a non-current asset is gradually consumed as the asset wears out. This is done by gradually writing off the asset's cost to profit or loss over several accounting periods. This process is known as depreciation, and is an example of the accruals assumption. IAS 16 *Property, plant and equipment* requires that depreciation should be allocated on a systematic basis to each accounting period during the useful life of the asset.

With regard to the accrual principle, it is fair that the profits should be reduced by the depreciation charge; this is not an arbitrary exercise. Depreciation is not, as is sometimes supposed, an attempt to set aside funds to purchase new non-current assets when required. Depreciation is not generally provided on freehold land because it does not 'wear out' (unless it is held for mining etc).

(b) The reducing balance method of depreciation is used instead of the straight line method when it is considered fair to allocate a greater proportion of the total depreciable amount to the earlier years and a lower proportion to the later years on the assumption that the benefits obtained by the business from using the asset decline over time.

In favour of this method it may be argued that it links the depreciation charge to the costs of maintaining and running the asset. In the early years these costs are low and the depreciation charge is high, while in later years this is reversed.

Question

A business purchased two rivet-making machines on 1 January 20X5 at a cost of $15,000 each. Each had an estimated life of five years and a nil residual value. The straight line method of depreciation is used.

Owing to an unforeseen slump in market demand for rivets, the business decided to reduce its output of rivets, and switch to making other products instead. On 31 March 20X7, one rivet-making machine was sold (on credit) to a buyer for $8,000.

Later in the year, however, it was decided to abandon production of rivets altogether, and the second machine was sold on 1 December 20X7 for $2,500 cash.

Prepare the machinery account, provision for depreciation of machinery account and disposal of machinery account for the accounting year to 31 December 20X7.

Answer

MACHINERY ACCOUNT

		$			$
20X7			*20X7*		
1 Jan	Balance b/f	30,000	31 Mar	Disposal of machinery account	15,000
			1 Dec	Disposal of machinery account	15,000
		30,000			30,000

ACCUMULATED DEPRECIATION OF MACHINERY

		$			$
20X7			*20X7*		
31 Mar	Disposal of machinery account*	6,750	1 Jan	Balance b/f	12,000
1 Dec	Disposal of machinery account**	8,750	31 Dec	Income statement***	3,500
		15,500			15,500

*   Depreciation at date of disposal = $6,000 + $750
**   Depreciation at date of disposal = $6,000 + $2,750
***   Depreciation charge for the year = $750 + $2,750

DISPOSAL OF MACHINERY

		$			$
20X7			*20X7*		
31 Mar	Machinery account	15,000	31 Mar	Account receivable (sale price)	8,000
			31 Mar	Provision for depreciation	6,750
1 Dec	Machinery	15,000	1 Dec	Cash (sale price)	2,500
			1 Dec	Provision for depreciation	8,750
			31 Dec	Income statement (loss on disposal)	4,000
		30,000			30,000

You should be able to calculate that there was a loss on the first disposal of $250, and on the second disposal of $3,750, giving a total loss of $4,000.

Workings

1   At 1 January 20X7, accumulated depreciation on the machines will be:

$$2 \text{ machines} \times 2 \text{ years} \times \frac{\$15,000}{5} \text{ per machine pa} = \$12,000, \text{ or } \$6,000 \text{ per machine}$$

2   Monthly depreciation is $\frac{\$3,000}{12}$ = $250 per machine per month

3   The machines are disposed of in 20X7.

    (a)   On 31 March – after 3 months of the year. Depreciation for the year on the machine = 3 months × $250 = $750.

    (b)   On 1 December – after 11 months of the year. Depreciation for the year on the machine = 11 months × $250 = $2,750

3 IAS 20 Government grants

FAST FORWARD

It is common for entities to receive government grants for various purposes (grants may be called subsidies, premiums, etc). They may also receive other types of assistance which may be in many forms. The treatment of government grants is covered by IAS 20 *Accounting for government grants and disclosure of government assistance.*

3.1 Scope

IAS 20 does *not* cover the following situations.

- Accounting for government grants in financial statements reflecting the effects of **changing prices**
- Government assistance given in the form of **'tax breaks'**
- Government acting as **part-owner** of the entity

3.2 Definitions

These definitions are given by the standard.

- **Government.** Government, government agencies and similar bodies whether local, national or international.
- **Government assistance.** Action by government designed to provide an economic benefit specific to an entity or range of entities qualifying under certain criteria.
- **Government grants** Assistance by government in the form of transfers of resources to an entity in return for past or future compliance with certain conditions relating to the operating activities of the entity. They exclude those forms of government assistance which cannot reasonably have a value placed upon them and transactions with government which cannot be distinguished from the normal trading transactions of the entity.
- **Grants related to assets.** Government grants whose primary condition is that an entity qualifying for them should purchase, construct or otherwise acquire non-current assets. Subsidiary conditions may also be attached restricting the type or location of the assets or the periods during which they are to be acquired or held.
- **Grants related to income.** Government grants other than those related to assets.
- **Forgivable loans** Loans which the lender undertakes to waive repayment of under certain prescribed conditions.
- **Fair value** The amount for which an asset could be exchanged, or a liability settled, between knowledgeable, willing parties in an arm's length transaction.

You can see that there are many **different forms** of government assistance: both the type of assistance and the conditions attached to it will vary. Government assistance may have encouraged an entity to undertake something it otherwise would not have done.

How will the receipt of government assistance affect the financial statements?

(a)   An appropriate method must be found to account for any **resources transferred**.

(b)   The extent to which an entity has **benefited** from such assistance during the reporting period should be shown.

3.3 Government grants

An entity should not recognise government grants (including non-monetary grants at fair value) until it has **reasonable assurance** that:

- The entity will comply with any **conditions** attached to the grant
- The entity will **actually receive** the grant

Even if the grant has been received, this does not prove that the conditions attached to it have been or will be fulfilled.

It makes no difference in the treatment of the grant whether it is received in cash or given as a reduction in a liability to government, ie the **manner of receipt is irrelevant**.

Any related **contingency** should be recognised under IAS 37 Provisions, contingent liabilities and contingent assets, once the grant has been recognised.

In the case of a **forgivable loan** (as defined in key terms above) from government, it should be treated in the same way as a government grant when it is reasonably assured that the entity will meet the relevant terms for forgiveness.

3.3.1 Accounting treatment of government grants

There are two methods which could be used to account for government grants, and the arguments for each are given in IAS 20.

(a)   **Capital approach**: credit the grant directly to shareholders' interests.

(b)   **Income approach**: the grant is credited to the income statement over one or more periods.

Can you think of the different arguments used in support of each method?

Answer

The standard gives the following arguments in support of each method.

Capital approach

(a)   The grants are a **financing device**, so should go through the statement of financial position. In the statement of comprehensive income they would simply offset the expenses which they are financing. No repayment is expected by the Government, so the grants should be credited directly to shareholders' interests.

(b)   Grants are **not earned**, they are incentives without related costs, so it would be wrong to take them to profit or loss.

Income approach

(a)   The grants are **not received from shareholders** so should not be credited directly to shareholders' interests.

(b)   Grants are **not given or received for nothing**. They are earned by compliance with conditions and by meeting obligations. There are therefore associated costs with which the grant can be matched as these costs are being compensated by the grant.

(c)   Grants are an extension of **fiscal policies** and so as income taxes and other taxes are charged against income, so grants should be credited to income.

IAS 20 requires grants to be recognised under the **income approach**, ie grants are recognised as income over the relevant periods to match them with related costs which they have been received to compensate. This should be done on a systematic basis. **Grants should not, therefore, be credited directly to shareholders' interests.**

It would be against the accruals assumption to credit grants to income on a receipts basis, so a **systematic basis of matching** must be used. A receipts basis would only be acceptable if no other basis was available.

It will usually be easy to identify the **costs related to a government grant**, and thereby the period(s) in which the grant should be recognised as income, ie when the costs are incurred. Where grants are received in relation to a depreciating asset, the grant will be recognised over the periods in which the asset is depreciated *and* in the same proportions.

Arturo Co receives a government grant representing 50% of the cost of a depreciating asset which costs $40,000. How will the grant be recognised if Arturo Co depreciates the asset:

(a)   over four years straight line; or

(b)   at 40% reducing balance?

The residual value is nil. The useful life is four years.

The grant should be recognised in the same proportion as the depreciation.

(a)   Straight line

		Depreciation $	Grant income $
Year	1	10,000	5,000
	2	10,000	5,000
	3	10,000	5,000
	4	10,000	5,000

(b)   Reducing balance

		Depreciation $	Grant income $
Year	1	16,000	8,000
	2	9,600	4,800
	3	5,760	2,880
	4 (remainder)	8,640	4,320

In the case of **grants for non-depreciable assets**, certain obligations may need to be fulfilled, in which case the grant should be recognised as income over the periods in which the cost of meeting the obligation is incurred. For example, if a piece of land is granted on condition that a building is erected on it, then the grant should be recognised as income over the building's life.

There may be a **series of conditions** attached to a grant, in the nature of a package of financial aid. An entity must take care to identify precisely those conditions which give rise to costs which in turn determine the periods over which the grant will be earned. When appropriate, the grant may be split and the parts allocated on different bases.

An entity may receive a grant as compensation for expenses or losses which it has **already incurred**. Alternatively, a grant may be given to an entity simply to provide immediate financial support where no future related costs are expected. In cases such as these, the grant received should be recognised as income of the period in which it becomes receivable.

3.3.2 Non-monetary government grants

A non-monetary asset may be transferred by government to an entity as a grant, for example a piece of land, or other resources. The **fair value** of such an asset is usually assessed and this is used to account for both the asset and the grant. Alternatively, both may be valued at a nominal amount.

3.3.3 Presentation of grants related to assets

There are two choices here for how government grants related to assets (including non-monetary grants at fair value) should be shown in the statement of financial position.

(a)   Set up the grant as **deferred income.**
(b)   **Deduct the grant** in arriving at the **carrying amount** of the asset.

These are considered to be acceptable alternatives and we can look at an example showing both.
Example: accounting for grants related to assets

A company receives a 20% grant towards the cost of a new item of machinery, which cost $100,000. The machinery has an expected life of four years and a nil residual value. The expected profits of the company, before accounting for depreciation on the new machine or the grant, amount to $50,000 per annum in each year of the machinery's life.

Solution

The results of the company for the four years of the machine's life would be as follows.

(a)   *Reducing the cost of the asset*

	Year 1 $	Year 2 $	Year 3 $	Year 4 $	Total $
Profits					
Profit before depreciation	50,000	50,000	50,000	50,000	200,000
Depreciation*	20,000	20,000	20,000	20,000	80,000
Profit	30,000	30,000	30,000	30,000	120,000

*The depreciation charge on a straight line basis, for each year, is ¼ of $(100,000 − 20,000) = $20,000.

Statement of financial position at year end (extract)

	$	$	$	$
Non-current asset at cost	80,000	80,000	80,000	80,000
Depreciation	20,000	40,000	60,000	80,000
Net book value	60,000	40,000	20,000	–

(b)   *Treating the grant as deferred income*

	Year 1 $	Year 2 $	Year 3 $	Year 4 $	Total $
Profits					
Profit before grant & dep'n	50,000	50,000	50,000	50,000	200,000
Depreciation	(25,000)	(25,000)	(25,000)	(25,000)	(100,000)
Grant	5,000	5,000	5,000	5,000	20,000
Profit	30,000	30,000	30,000	30,000	120,000

Statement of financial position at year end (extract)

Non-current asset at cost	100,000	100,000	100,000	100,000
Depreciation	(25,000)	(50,000)	(75,000)	(100,000)
Net book value	75,000	50,000	25,000	–
Deferred income				
Government grant				
deferred income	15,000	10,000	5,000	–

Whichever of these methods is used, the **cash flows** in relation to the purchase of the asset and the receipt of the grant are often disclosed separately because of the significance of the movements in cash flow.

3.3.4 Presentation of grants related to income

These grants are a credit in profit or loss, but there is a choice in the method of disclosure.

(a)   Present as a **separate credit** or under a general heading, eg 'other income'

(b)   **Deduct from the related expense**

Some would argue that offsetting income and expenses in the statement of comprehensive income is not good practice. Others would say that the expenses would not have been incurred had the grant not been available, so offsetting the two is acceptable. Although both methods are acceptable, disclosure of the grant may be necessary for a **proper understanding** of the financial statements, particularly the effect on any item of income or expense which is required to be separately disclosed.

3.3.5 Repayment of government grants

If a grant must be repaid it should be accounted for as a **revision of an accounting estimate** (see IAS 8).

(a)   **Repayment of a grant related to income:** apply first against any unamortised deferred income set up in respect of the grant; any excess should be recognised immediately as an expense.

(b)   **Repayment of a grant related to an asset:** increase the carrying amount of the asset or reduce the deferred income balance by the amount repayable. The cumulative additional depreciation that would have been recognised to date in the absence of the grant should be immediately recognised as an expense.

It is possible that the circumstances surrounding repayment may require a review of the **asset value** and an impairment of the new carrying amount of the asset.

3.4 Government assistance

Some forms of government assistance are excluded from the definition of government grants.

(a)   Some forms of government assistance **cannot reasonably have a value placed on them**, eg free technical or marketing advice, provision of guarantees.

(b)   There are transactions with government which **cannot be distinguished from the entity's normal trading transactions**, eg government procurement policy resulting in a portion of the entity's sales. Any segregation would be arbitrary.

Disclosure of such assistance may be necessary because of its significance; its nature, extent and duration should be disclosed. Loans at low or zero interest rates are a form of government assistance, but the imputation of interest does not fully quantify the benefit received.

3.5 Disclosure

Disclosure is required of the following.

*   **Accounting policy** adopted, including method of presentation
*   **Nature and extent** of government grants recognised and other forms of assistance received
*   **Unfulfilled conditions and other contingencies** attached to recognised government assistance

3.6 SIC 10 Government assistance – no specific relation to operating activities

In some countries government assistance to entities may be aimed at encouragement or long-term support of business activities either in certain regions or industry sectors. Conditions to receive such assistance may not be specifically related to the operating activities of the entity. Examples of such assistance are transfers of resources by governments to entities which:

(a)   Operate in a particular industry
(b)   Continue operating in recently privatised industries
(c)   Start or continue to run their business in underdeveloped areas

The issue is whether such government assistance is a 'government grant' within the scope of IAS 20 and, therefore, should be accounted for in accordance with this Standard.

Government assistance to entities meets the definition of government grants in IAS 20, even if there are no conditions specifically relating to the operating activities of the entity other than the requirement to operate in certain regions or industry sectors. Such grants should therefore not be credited directly to equity.

4 IAS 40 Investment property

An entity may own land or a building **as an investment** rather than for use in the business. It may therefore generate cash flows largely independently of other assets which the entity holds. The treatment of investment property is covered by IAS 40.

4.1 Definitions

Consider the following definitions.

Key terms

> **Investment property** is property (land or a building – or part of a building – or both) held (by the owner or by the lessee under a finance lease) to earn rentals or for capital appreciation or both, rather than for:
>
> (a)   Use in the production or supply of goods or services or for administrative purposes, or
> (b)   Sale in the ordinary course of business
>
> **Owner-occupied property** is property held by the owner (or by the lessee under a finance lease) for use in the production or supply of goods or services or for administrative purposes.
>
> **Fair value** is the amount for which an asset could be exchanged between knowledgeable, willing parties in an arm's length transaction.
>
> **Cost** is the amount of cash or cash equivalents paid or the fair value of other consideration given to acquire an asset at the time of its acquisition or construction.
>
> **Carrying amount** is the amount at which an asset is recognised in the statement of financial position.
>
> A property interest that is held by a lessee under an **operating lease** may be classified and accounted for as an **investment property**, if and only if the property would otherwise meet the definition of an investment property and the lessee uses the IAS 40 **fair value model**. This classification is available on a property-by-property basis.

Examples of investment property include:

(a)   **Land held for long-term capital appreciation** rather than for short-term sale in the ordinary course of business

(b)   A **building** owned by the reporting entity (or held by the entity under a finance lease) and **leased out under an operating lease**

(c)   A building held by a **parent** and leased to a **subsidiary**. Note, however, that while this is regarded as an investment property in the individual parent company financial statements, in the **consolidated** financial statements this property will be regarded as owner-occupied (because it is occupied by the group) and will therefore be treated in accordance with IAS 16.

Question

Investment

Rich Co owns a piece of land. The directors have not yet decided whether to build a factory on it for use in its business or to keep it and sell it when its value has risen.

Would this be classified as an investment property under IAS 40?

Answer

Yes. If an entity has not determined that it will use the land either as an owner-occupied property or for short-term sale in the ordinary course of business, the land is considered to be held for capital appreciation.

4.2 IAS 40

IAS 40 *Investment property* was published in March 2000 and has recently been revised. Its objective is to prescribe the accounting treatment for investment property and related disclosure requirements.

The standard includes investment property held under a finance lease or leased out under an operating lease. However, the current IAS 40 does not deal with matters covered in IAS 17 *Leases*.

You now know what **is** an investment property under IAS 40. Below are examples of items that are **not investment property.**

Type of non-investment property	Applicable IAS
Property intended for sale in the ordinary course of business	IAS 2 *Inventories*
Property being constructed or developed on behalf of third parties	IAS 11 *Construction contracts*
Owner-occupied property	IAS 16 *Property, plant and equipment*
Property being constructed or developed for future use as investment property	IAS 16 until construction or development is complete, then treat as investment property

4.3 Recognition

Investment property should be recognised as an asset when **two conditions** are met.

(a)   It is **probable** that the **future economic benefits** that are associated with the investment property will **flow to the entity**.

(b)   The **cost** of the investment property can be **measured reliably**.

4.4 Initial measurement

An investment property should be measured initially at its **cost,** including transaction costs.

A property interest held under a lease and classified as an investment property shall be accounted for **as if it were a finance lease**. The asset is recognised at the lower of the fair value of the property and the present value of the minimum lease payments. An equivalent amount is recognised as a liability.

4.5 Measurement subsequent to initial recognition

IAS 40 requires an entity to **choose between two models.**

* The fair value model
* The cost model

Whatever policy it chooses should be applied to **all of its investment property**.

Where an entity chooses to classify a property held under an **operating lease** as an investment property, there is **no choice**. The **fair value model must be used** for **all the entity's investment property**, regardless of whether it is owned or leased.

4.5.1 Fair value model

Key terms

(a)   After initial recognition, an entity that chooses the **fair value model** should measure all of its investment property at fair value, except in the extremely rare cases where this cannot be measured reliably. In such cases it should apply the IAS 16 cost model.

(b)   A gain or loss arising from a change in the fair value of an investment property should be recognised in net profit or loss for the period in which it arises.

(c)   The fair value of investment property should reflect market conditions at the end of the reporting period.

This was the first time that the IASB has allowed a fair value model for non-financial assets. This is not the same as a revaluation, where increases in carrying amount above a cost-based measure are recognised as revaluation surplus. Under the fair-value model all changes in fair value are recognised in profit or loss.

The standard elaborates on **issues relating to fair value**.

(a)   Fair value assumes that an arm's length transaction has taken place between '**knowledgeable, willing parties**', ie both buyer and seller are reasonably informed about the nature and characteristics of the investment property.

(b)   A willing buyer is **motivated but not compelled** to buy. A willing seller is neither an over-eager nor a forced seller, nor one prepared to sell at any price or to hold out for a price not considered reasonable in the current market.

(c)   **Fair value is not the same as 'value in use'** as defined in IAS 36 *Impairment of assets*. Value in use reflects factors and knowledge specific to the entity, while fair value reflects factors and knowledge relevant to the market.

(d)   In determining fair value an entity **should not double count assets**. For example, elevators or air conditioning are often an integral part of a building and should be included in the investment property, rather than recognised separately.

(e)   In those rare cases where the **entity cannot determine the fair value of an investment property reliably**, the cost model in **IAS 16** must be applied until the investment property is disposed of. The **residual value must be assumed to be zero**.

4.5.2 Cost model

The cost model is the **cost model in IAS 16**. Investment property should be measured at **depreciated cost, less any accumulated impairment losses**. An entity that chooses the cost model should **disclose the fair value of its investment property**.

4.5.3 Changing models

Once the entity has chosen the fair value or cost model, it should apply it to all its investment property. It **should not change from one model to the other unless the change will result in a more appropriate presentation**. IAS 40 states that it is highly unlikely that a change from the fair value model to the cost model will result in a more appropriate presentation.

4.6 Transfers

Transfers to or from investment property should **only** be made **when there is a change in use**. For example, owner occupation commences so the investment property will be treated under IAS 16 as an owner-occupied property.

When there is a transfer from investment property carried at fair value to owner-occupied property or inventories, the property's cost for subsequent accounting under IAS 16 or IAS 2 should be its fair value at the date of change of use.

Conversely, an owner-occupied property may become an investment property and need to be carried at fair value. An entity should apply IAS 16 up to the date of change of use. It should treat any difference at that date between the carrying amount of the property under IAS 16 and its fair value as a revaluation under IAS 16.

4.7 Disposals

Derecognise (eliminate from the statement of financial position) an investment property on disposal or when it is permanently withdrawn from use and no future economic benefits are expected from its disposal.

Any **gain or loss** on disposal is the difference between the net disposal proceeds and the carrying amount of the asset. It should generally be **recognised as income or expense in profit or loss.**

Compensation from third parties for investment property that was impaired, lost or given up shall be recognised in profit or loss when the compensation becomes receivable.

4.8 Disclosure requirements

These relate to:

- Choice of fair value model or cost model
- Whether property interests held as operating leases are included in investment property
- Criteria for classification as investment property
- Assumptions in determining fair value
- Use of independent professional valuer (encouraged but not required)
- Rental income and expenses
- Any restrictions or obligations

4.8.1 Fair value model – additional disclosures

An entity that adopts this must also disclose a **reconciliation** of the carrying amount of the investment property at the beginning and end of the period.

4.8.2 Cost model – additional disclosures

These relate mainly to the depreciation method. In addition, an entity which adopts the cost model **must disclose the fair value** of the investment property.

4.9 Decision tree

The decision tree below summarises which IAS apply to various kinds of property.

Exam focus point

Learn this decision tree – it will help you tackle most of the problems you are likely to meet in the exam!

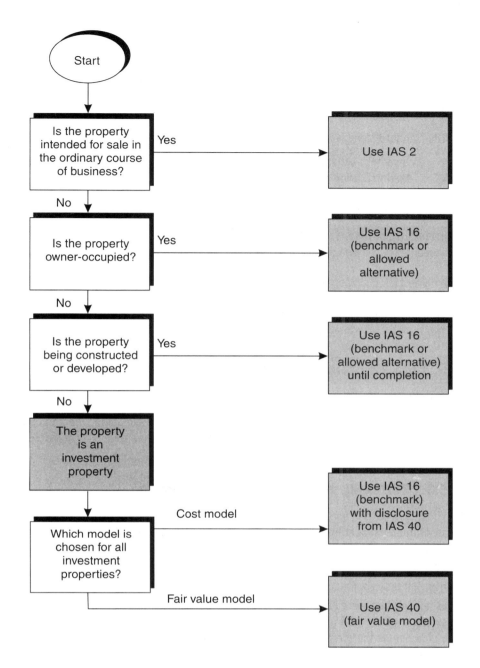

5 IAS 23 Borrowing costs

IAS 23 looks at the treatment of **borrowing costs**, particularly where the related borrowings are applied to the construction of certain assets. These are what are usually called 'self-constructed assets', where an entity builds its own inventory or non-current assets over a substantial period of time.

5.1 Definitions

Only two definitions are given by the standard.

Key terms

> **Borrowing costs**. Interest and other costs incurred by an entity in connection with the borrowing of funds.
>
> **Qualifying asset**. An asset that necessarily takes a substantial period of time to get ready for its intended use or sale.
> *(IAS 23)*

The standard lists what may be **included in borrowing costs**.

- Interest on bank overdrafts and short-term and long-term borrowings
- Amortisation of discounts or premiums relating to borrowings
- Amortisation of ancillary costs incurred in connection with the arrangement of borrowings
- Finance charges in respect of finance leases recognised in accordance with IAS 17 (See Chapter 15)

The standard also gives examples of qualifying assets.

- Inventories that require a substantial period of time to bring them to a saleable condition
- Manufacturing plants
- Power generation facilities
- Investment properties

Inventories produced in bulk over short periods and on a regular basis are **not qualifying assets**, nor are assets ready for sale or their intended use when purchased.

5.2 Benchmark treatment

Prior to the revision of IAS 23 the benchmark treatment was to recognise borrowing costs as an expense. **This benchmark/allowed alternative has now been removed**.

5.3 IAS 23 revised: capitalisation

Under the revised treatment, all eligible borrowing costs must be **capitalised**.

Only borrowing costs that are **directly attributable** to the acquisition, construction or production of a qualifying asset can be capitalised as part of the cost of that asset. The standard lays out the criteria for determining which borrowing costs are eligible for capitalisation.

5.3.1 Borrowing costs eligible for capitalisation

Those borrowing costs directly attributable to the acquisition, construction or production of a qualifying asset must be identified. These are the borrowing costs that **would have been avoided** had the expenditure on the qualifying asset not been made. This is obviously straightforward where funds have been borrowed for the financing of one particular asset.

Difficulties arise, however, where the entity uses a **range of debt instruments** to finance a wide range of assets, so that there is no direct relationship between particular borrowings and a specific asset. For example, all borrowings may be made centrally and then lent to different parts of the group or entity. Judgement is therefore required, particularly where further complications can arise (eg foreign currency loans).

Once the relevant borrowings are identified, which relate to a specific asset, then the **amount of borrowing costs available for capitalisation** will be the actual borrowing costs incurred on those borrowings during the period, *less* any investment income on the temporary investment of those borrowings. It would not be unusual for some or all of the funds to be invested before they are actually used on the qualifying asset.

Question   Capitalisation

On 1 January 20X6 Stremans Co borrowed $1.5m to finance the production of two assets, both of which were expected to take a year to build. Work started during 20X6. The loan facility was drawn down and incurred on 1 January 20X6, and was utilised as follows, with the remaining funds invested temporarily.

	Asset A	Asset B
	$'000	$'000
1 January 20X6	250	500
1 July 20X6	250	500

The loan rate was 9% and Stremans Co can invest surplus funds at 7%.

Required

Ignoring compound interest, calculate the borrowing costs which may be capitalised for each of the assets and consequently the cost of each asset as at 31 December 20X6.

		Asset A	Asset B
		$	$
Borrowing costs			
To 31 December 20X6	$500,000/$1,000,000 × 9%	45,000	90,000
Less investment income			
To 30 June 20X6	$250,000/$500,000 × 7% × 6/12	(8,750)	(17,500)
		36,250	72,500
Cost of assets			
Expenditure incurred		500,000	1,000,000
Borrowing costs		36,250	72,500
		536,250	1,072,500

In a situation where **borrowings are obtained generally**, but are applied in part to obtaining a qualifying asset, then the amount of borrowing costs eligible for capitalisation is found by applying the 'capitalisation rate' to the expenditure on the asset.

The **capitalisation rate** is the weighted average of the borrowing costs applicable to the entity's borrowings that are outstanding during the period, *excluding* borrowings made specifically to obtain a qualifying asset. However, there is a cap on the amount of borrowing costs calculated in this way: it must not exceed actual borrowing costs incurred.

Sometimes one overall weighted average can be calculated for a group or entity, but in some situations it may be more appropriate to use a weighted average for borrowing costs for **individual parts of the group or entity**.

Construction

Acruni Co had the following loans in place at the beginning and end of 20X6.

	1 January 20X6	31 December 20X6
	$m	$m
10% Bank loan repayable 20X8	120	120
9.5% Bank loan repayable 20X9	80	80
8.9% debenture repayable 20X7	–	150

The 8.9% debenture was issued to fund the construction of a qualifying asset (a piece of mining equipment), construction of which began on 1 July 20X6.

On 1 January 20X6, Acruni Co began construction of a qualifying asset, a piece of machinery for a hydro-electric plant, using existing borrowings. Expenditure drawn down for the construction was: $£30m on 1 January 20X6, $20m on 1 October 20X6.

Required

Calculate the borrowing costs that can be capitalised for the hydro-electric plant machine.

$$\text{Capitalisation rate = weighted average rate} = (10\% \times \frac{120}{120+80}) + (9.5\% \times \frac{80}{120+80}) = 9.8\%$$

$$\begin{aligned}\text{Borrowing costs} &= (\$30m \times 9.8\%) + (\$20m \times 9.8\% \times 3/12) \\ &= \$3.43m\end{aligned}$$

5.3.2 Carrying amount exceeds recoverable amount

A situation may arise whereby the carrying amount (or expected ultimate cost) of the qualifying asset exceeds its recoverable amount or net realisable value. In these cases, the carrying amount must be **written down or written off**, as required by other IASs. In certain circumstances (again as allowed by other IASs), these amounts may be written back in future periods.

5.3.3 Commencement of capitalisation

Three events or transactions must be taking place for capitalisation of borrowing costs to be started.

(a)   Expenditure on the asset is being incurred
(b)   Borrowing costs are being incurred
(c)   Activities are in progress that are necessary to prepare the asset for its intended use or sale

Expenditure must result in the payment of cash, transfer of other assets or assumption of interest-bearing liabilities. **Deductions from expenditure** will be made for any progress payments or grants received in connection with the asset. IAS 23 allows the **average carrying amount** of the asset during a period (including borrowing costs previously capitalised) to be used as a reasonable approximation of the expenditure to which the capitalisation rate is applied in the period. Presumably more exact calculations can be used.

Activities necessary to prepare the asset for its intended sale or use extend further than physical construction work. They encompass technical and administrative work prior to construction, eg obtaining permits. They do *not* include holding an asset when no production or development that changes the asset's condition is taking place, eg where land is held without any associated development activity.

5.3.4 Suspension of capitalisation

If active development is **interrupted for any extended periods**, capitalisation of borrowing costs should be suspended for those periods.

Suspension of capitalisation of borrowing costs is not necessary for **temporary delays** or for periods when substantial technical or administrative work is taking place.

5.3.5 Cessation of capitalisation

Once substantially all the activities necessary to prepare the qualifying asset for its intended use or sale are complete, then capitalisation of borrowing costs should cease. This will normally be when **physical construction of the asset is completed**, although minor modifications may still be outstanding.

The asset may be completed in **parts or stages**, where each part can be used while construction is still taking place on the other parts. Capitalisation of borrowing costs should cease for each part as it is completed. The example given by the standard is a business park consisting of several buildings.

5.3.6 Disclosure

The following should be disclosed in the financial statements in relation to borrowing costs.
(a)   Amount of borrowing costs **capitalised during the period**
(b)   **Capitalisation rate** used to determine the amount of borrowing costs eligible for capitalisation

Chapter Roundup

- IAS 16 covers all aspects of accounting for property, plant and equipment. This represents the bulk of items which are **'tangible' non-current assets**.

- Where assets held by an entity have a **limited useful life** it is necessary to apportion the value of an asset over its useful life.

- It is common for entities to receive government grants for various purposes. The treatment of these is covered by IAS 20 *Accounting for government grants and disclosure of government assistance.*

- An entity may own land or a building **as an investment** rather than for use in the business. It may therefore generate cash flows largely independently of other assets which the entity holds. The treatment of investment property is covered by IAS 40.

- IAS 23 looks at the treatment of **borrowing costs**, particularly where the related borrowings are applied to the construction of certain assets. These are what are usually called 'self-constructed assets,' where an entity builds its own inventory or non-current assets over a substantial period of time.

Quick Quiz

1 Define depreciation.
2 Which of the following elements can be included in the production cost of a non-current asset?
  (i)   Purchase price of raw materials
  (ii) Architect's fees
  (iii) Import duties
  (iv) Installation costs
3 Market value can usually be taken as fair value.

  True [ ]

  False [ ]

4 Investment properties must always be shown at fair value.

  True [ ]

  False [ ]

5 What is the correct treatment for property being constructed for future use as investment property?

1   See Para 2.2
2   All of them.
3   True
4   False. The cost model may be used, provided it is used consistently.
5   Use IAS 16 until construction is complete, then IAS 40.

Now try the questions below from the Exam Question Bank

Number	Level	Marks	Time
6	Examination	25	45 mins

Intangible assets

Topic list	Syllabus reference
1 IAS 38 Intangible assets	C3
2 Research and development costs	C3
3 Goodwill (IFRS 3)	C3

Introduction

We begin our examination of intangible non-current assets with a discussion of the IAS on the subject (**IAS 38**).

Goodwill and its treatment is a controversial area, as is the accounting for items similar to goodwill, such as brands. Goodwill is very important in **group accounts** and we will look at it again in Chapter 9.

Study guide

		Intellectual level
C	**Financial statements**	
3	**Intangible assets**	
(a)	discuss the nature and accounting treatment of internally generated and purchased intangibles.	2
(b)	distinguish between goodwill and other intangible assets.	2
(c)	describe the criteria for the initial recognition and measurement of intangible assets.	2
(d)	describe the subsequent accounting treatment, including the principle of impairment tests in relation to goodwill.	2
(e)	indicate why the value of purchase consideration for an investment may be less than the value of the acquired identifiable net assets and how the difference should be accounted for.	2
(f)	describe and apply the requirements of relevant accounting standards to research and development expenditure.	2

1 IAS 38 Intangible assets

FAST FORWARD

> Intangible assets are defined by IAS 38 as non-monetary assets without physical substance.

IAS 38 *Intangible assets* was originally published in September 1998. It has recently been revised to reflect changes introduced by IFRS 3 *Business combinations*.

1.1 The objectives of the standard

(a) To establish the criteria for when an intangible asset may or should be **recognised**
(b) To specify how intangible assets should be **measured**
(c) To specify the **disclosure requirements** for intangible assets

1.2 Definition of an intangible asset

The definition of an intangible asset is a key aspect of the standard, because the rules for deciding whether or not an intangible asset may be **recognised** in the accounts of an entity are based on the definition of what an intangible asset is.

Key term

An **intangible asset** is an identifiable non-monetary asset without physical substance The asset must be:

(a) controlled by the entity as a result of events in the past, and
(b) something from which the entity expects future economic benefits to flow.

Examples of items that might be considered as intangible assets include computer software, patents, copyrights, motion picture films, customer lists, franchises and fishing rights. An item should not be recognised as an intangible asset, however, unless it **fully meets the definition** in the standard. The guidelines go into great detail on this matter.

1.3 Intangible asset: must be identifiable

An intangible asset must be identifiable in order to distinguish it from goodwill. With non-physical items, there may be a problem with **'identifiability'**.

(a)   If an intangible asset is **acquired separately through purchase**, there may be a transfer of a legal right that would help to make an asset identifiable.

(b)   An intangible asset may be identifiable if it is **separable**, ie if it could be rented or sold separately. However, 'separability' is not an essential feature of an intangible asset.

1.4 Intangible asset: control by the entity

Another element of the definition of an intangible asset is that it must be under the control of the entity as a result of a past event. The entity must therefore be able to enjoy the future economic benefits from the asset, and prevent the access of others to those benefits. A **legally enforceable right** is evidence of such control, but is not always a *necessary* condition.

(a)   Control over **technical knowledge or know-how** only exists if it is protected by a **legal right**.

(b)   The skill of employees, arising out of the benefits of **training costs**, are most unlikely to be recognisable as an intangible asset, because an entity does not control the future actions of its staff.

(c)   Similarly, **market share and customer loyalty** cannot normally be intangible assets, since an entity cannot control the actions of its customers.

1.5 Intangible asset: expected future economic benefits

An item can only be recognised as an intangible asset if economic benefits are expected to flow in the future from ownership of the asset. Economic benefits may come from the **sale** of products or services, or from a **reduction in expenditures** (cost savings).

An intangible asset, when recognised initially, must be measured at **cost**. It should be recognised if, and only if **both** the following occur.

(a)   It is probable that the **future economic benefits** that are attributable to the asset will **flow to the entity**.

(b)   The **cost can be measured reliably**.

Management has to exercise its judgement in assessing the degree of certainty attached to the flow of economic benefits to the entity. External evidence is best.

(a)   If an intangible asset is **acquired separately**, its cost can usually be measured reliably as its purchase price (including incidental costs of purchase such as legal fees, and any costs incurred in getting the asset ready for use).

(b)   When an intangible asset is acquired as **part of a business combination** (ie an acquisition or takeover), the cost of the intangible asset is its fair value at the date of the acquisition.

IFRS 3 explains that the fair value of intangible assets acquired in business combinations can normally be measured with sufficient reliability to be **recognised separately** from goodwill.

Quoted market prices in an active market provide the most reliable estimate of the fair value of an intangible asset. If no active market exists for an intangible asset, its fair value is the amount that the entity would have paid for the asset, at the acquisition date, in an arm's length transaction between knowledgeable and willing parties, on the basis of the best information available. In determining this amount, an entity should consider the outcome of recent transactions for similar assets. There are techniques for estimating the fair values of unique intangible assets (such as brand names) and these may be used to measure an intangible asset acquired in a business combination.

In accordance with IAS 20, intangible assets acquired by way of government grant and the grant itself may be recorded initially either at cost (which may be zero) or fair value.

1.6 Exchanges of assets

If one intangible asset is exchanged for another, the cost of the intangible asset is measured at fair value unless:

(a)   The exchange transaction lacks commercial substance, or

(b)   The fair value of neither the asset received nor the asset given up can be measured reliably.

Otherwise, its cost is measured at the carrying amount of the asset given up.

1.7 Internally generated goodwill

Rule to Learn

Internally generated goodwill may **not** be recognised as an **asset**.

The standard deliberately precludes recognition of internally generated goodwill because it requires that, for initial recognition, the cost of the asset rather than its fair value should be capable of being measured reliably and that it should be identifiable and controlled. Thus you do not recognise an asset which is subjective and cannot be measured reliably.

2 Research and development costs

FAST FORWARD

Development costs can be recognised as an asset if they meet certain criteria.

2.1 Research

Research activities by definition do not meet the criteria for recognition under IAS 38. This is because, at the research stage of a project, it cannot be certain that future economic benefits will probably flow to the entity from the project. There is too much uncertainty about the likely success or otherwise of the project. **Research costs should therefore be written off as an expense as they are incurred.**

Examples of research costs

(a)   Activities aimed at obtaining new knowledge

(b)   The search for, evaluation and final selection of, applications of research findings or other knowledge

(c)   The search for alternatives for materials, devices, products, processes, systems or services

(d)   The formulation, design evaluation and final selection of possible alternatives for new or improved materials, devices, products, systems or services

2.2 Development

Development costs may qualify for recognition as intangible assets provided that the following strict criteria can be demonstrated.

(a)   The technical feasibility of completing the intangible asset so that it will be available for use or sale.

(b)   Its intention to complete the intangible asset and use or sell it.

(c)   Its ability to use or sell the intangible asset.

(d)   How the intangible asset will generate probable future economic benefits. Among other things, the entity should demonstrate the existence of a market for the output of the intangible asset or the intangible asset itself or, if it is to be used internally, the usefulness of the intangible asset.

(e)   Its ability to measure the expenditure attributable to the intangible asset during its development reliably.

In contrast with research costs development costs are incurred at a later stage in a project, and the probability of success should be more apparent. Examples of development costs include the following.

(a)   The design, construction and testing of pre-production or pre-use prototypes and models

(b)   The design of tools, jigs, moulds and dies involving new technology

(c) The design, construction and operation of a pilot plant that is not of a scale economically feasible for commercial production

(d) The design, construction and testing of a chosen alternative for new or improved materials, devices, products, processes, systems or services

2.3 Other internally generated intangible assets

The standard prohibits the recognition of internally generated brands, mastheads, publishing titles and customer lists and similar items as intangible assets. These all fail to meet one or more (in some cases all) the definition and recognition criteria and in some cases are probably indistinguishable from internally generated goodwill.

2.4 Cost of an internally generated intangible asset

FAST FORWARD

Intangible assets should be initially be measured at cost, but subsequently they can be carried at **cost** or at a **revalued amount**.

The costs allocated to an internally generated intangible asset should be only costs that can be directly attributed or allocated on a reasonable and consistent basis to creating, producing or preparing the asset for its intended use. The principles underlying the costs which may or may not be included are similar to those for other non-current assets and inventory.

The cost of an internally operated intangible asset is the sum of the expenditure incurred from the date when the intangible asset first meets the recognition criteria. If, as often happens, considerable costs have already been recognised as expenses before management could demonstrate that the criteria have been met, this earlier expenditure should not be retrospectively recognised at a later date as part of the cost of an intangible asset.

Question

Treatment

Doug Co is developing a new production process. During 20X3, expenditure incurred was $100,000, of which $90,000 was incurred before 1 December 20X3 and $10,000 between 1 December 20X3 and 31 December 20X3. Doug Co can demonstrate that, at 1 December 20X3, the production process met the criteria for recognition as an intangible asset. The recoverable amount of the know-how embodied in the process is estimated to be $50,000.

How should the expenditure be treated?

Answer

At the end of 20X3, the production process is recognised as an intangible asset at a cost of $10,000. This is the expenditure incurred since the date when the recognition criteria were met, that is 1 December 20X3. The $90,000 expenditure incurred before 1 December 20X3 is expensed, because the recognition criteria were not met. It will never form part of the cost of the production process recognised in the statement of financial position.

2.5 Recognition of an expense

All expenditure related to an intangible which does not meet the criteria for recognition either as an identifiable intangible asset or as goodwill arising on an acquisition should be **expensed as incurred**. The IAS gives examples of such expenditure.

- Start up costs
- Training costs
- Advertising costs
- Business relocation costs

Prepaid costs for services, for example advertising or marketing costs for campaigns that have been prepared but not launched, can still be recognised as a **prepayment**.

2.6 Measurement of intangible assets subsequent to initial recognition

The standard allows two methods of valuation for intangible assets after they have been first recognised.

Applying the **cost model**, an intangible asset should be **carried at its cost**, less any accumulated amortisation and less any accumulated impairment losses.

The **revaluation model** allows an intangible asset to be carried at a revalued amount, which is its **fair value** at the date of revaluation, less any subsequent accumulated amortisation and any subsequent accumulated impairment losses.

(a) The fair value must be able to be measured reliably with reference to an **active market** in that type of asset.

(b) The **entire class** of intangible assets of that type must be revalued at the same time (to prevent selective revaluations).

(c) If an intangible asset in a class of revalued intangible assets cannot be revalued because there is **no active market** for this asset, the asset should be carried at its **cost less any accumulated amortisation and impairment losses**.

(d) Revaluations should be made with such **regularity** that the carrying amount does not differ from that which would be determined using fair value at the end of the reporting period.

Point to note

> This treatment is not available for the initial recognition of intangible assets. This is because the cost of the asset must be reliably measured.

The guidelines state that there will not usually be an active market in an intangible asset; therefore the revaluation model will usually not be available. For example, although copyrights, publishing rights and film rights can be sold, each has a unique sale value. In such cases, revaluation to fair value would be inappropriate. A fair value might be obtainable however for assets such as fishing rights or quotas or taxi cab licences.

Where an intangible asset is revalued upwards to a fair value, the amount of the revaluation should be credited directly to equity under the heading of a **revaluation surplus**.

However, if a revaluation surplus is a **reversal of a revaluation decrease** that was previously charged against income, the increase can be recognised as income.

Where the carrying amount of an intangible asset is revalued downwards, the amount of the **downward revaluation** should be charged as an expense against income, unless the asset has previously been revalued upwards. A revaluation decrease should be first charged against any previous revaluation surplus in respect of that asset.

Question

Downward revaluation

An intangible asset is measured by a company at fair value. The asset was revalued by $400 in 20X3, and there is a revaluation surplus of $400 in the statement of financial position. At the end of 20X4, the asset is valued again, and a downward valuation of $500 is required.

Required

State the accounting treatment for the downward revaluation.

Answer

In this example, the downward valuation of $500 can first be set against the revaluation surplus of $400. The revaluation surplus will be reduced to 0 and a charge of $100 made as an expense in 20X4.

When the revaluation model is used, and an intangible asset is revalued upwards, the cumulative revaluation **surplus may be transferred to retained earnings** when the surplus is eventually realised. The surplus would be realised when the asset is disposed of. However, the surplus may also be realised over time as the **asset is used** by the entity. The amount of the surplus realised each year is the difference between the amortisation charge for the asset based on the revalued amount of the asset, and the amortisation that would be charged on the basis of the asset's historical cost. The realised surplus in such case should be transferred from revaluation surplus directly to retained earnings, and should not be taken through profit or loss.

2.7 Useful life

An entity should assess the useful life of an intangible asset, which may be **finite or indefinite**. An intangible asset has an indefinite useful life when there is **no foreseeable limit** to the period over which the asset is expected to generate net cash inflows for the entity.

Many factors are considered in determining the useful life of an intangible asset, including: expected usage; typical product life cycles; technical, technological, commercial or other types of obsolescence; the stability of the industry; expected actions by competitors; the level of maintenance expenditure required; and legal or similar limits on the use of the asset, such as the expiry dates of related leases. Computer software and many other intangible assets normally have short lives because they are susceptible to technological obsolescence. However, uncertainty does not justify choosing a life that is unrealistically short.

The useful life of an intangible asset that arises from **contractual or other legal rights** should not exceed the period of the rights, but may be shorter depending on the period over which the entity expects to use the asset.

2.8 Amortisation period and amortisation method

An intangible asset with a finite useful life should be amortised over its **expected useful life**.

(a) Amortisation should start when the asset is **available for use**.

(b) Amortisation should cease at the earlier of the date that the asset is classified **as held for sale** in accordance with IFRS 5 *Non-current assets held for sale and discontinued operations* and the date that the asset is **derecognised**.

(c) The amortisation method used should reflect the **pattern in which the asset's future economic benefits are consumed**. If such a pattern cannot be predicted reliably, the straight-line method should be used.

(d) The amortisation charge for each period should normally be recognised **in profit or loss**.

The **residual value** of an intangible asset with a finite useful life is **assumed to be zero** unless a third party is committed to buying the intangible asset at the end of its useful life or unless there is an active market for that type of asset (so that its expected residual value can be measured) and it is probable that there will be a market for the asset at the end of its useful life.

The amortisation period and the amortisation method used for an intangible asset with a finite useful life should be **reviewed at each financial year-end**.

2.9 Intangible assets with indefinite useful lives

An intangible asset with an indefinite useful life **should not be amortised**. (IAS 36 requires that such an asset is tested for impairment at least annually.)

The useful life of an intangible asset that is not being amortised should be **reviewed each year** to determine whether it is still appropriate to assess its useful life as indefinite. Reassessing the useful life of an intangible asset as finite rather than indefinite is an indicator that the asset may be impaired and therefore it should be tested for impairment.

Intangible assets could appear as part of the accounts preparation question or in Question 4 or 5. Make sure you know the capitalisation criteria.

Question

Intangible asset

It may be difficult to establish the useful life of an intangible asset, and judgement will be needed. Consider how to determine the useful life of a *purchased* brand name.

Answer

Factors to consider would include the following.

(a) Legal protection of the brand name and the control of the entity over the (illegal) use by others of the brand name (ie control over pirating)

(b) Age of the brand name

(c) Status or position of the brand in its particular market

(d) Ability of the management of the entity to manage the brand name and to measure activities that support the brand name (eg advertising and PR activities)

(e) Stability and geographical spread of the market in which the branded products are sold

(f) Pattern of benefits that the brand name is expected to generate over time

(g) Intention of the entity to use and promote the brand name over time (as evidenced perhaps by a business plan in which there will be substantial expenditure to promote the brand name)

2.10 Disposals/retirements of intangible assets

An intangible asset should be eliminated from the statement of financial position when it is disposed of or when there is no further expected economic benefit from its future use. On disposal the gain or loss arising from the **difference between the net disposal proceeds and the carrying amount** of the asset should be taken to profit or loss as a gain or loss on disposal (ie treated as income or expense).

2.11 Section summary

- An intangible asset should be recognised if, and only if, it is probable that future economic benefits will flow to the entity and the cost of the asset can be measured reliably.
- An asset is initially recognised at cost and subsequently carried either at cost or revalued amount.
- Costs that do not meet the recognition criteria should be expensed as incurred.
- An intangible asset with a finite useful life should be amortised over its useful life. An intangible asset with an indefinite useful life should not be amortised.

Question

R&D

As an aid to your revision, list the examples given in IAS 38 of activities that might be included in either research or development.

Answer

IAS 38 gives these examples.

Research

- Activities aimed at obtaining new knowledge

- The search for applications of research findings or other knowledge
- The search for product or process alternatives
- The formulation and design of possible new or improved product or process alternatives

Development

- The evaluation of product or process alternatives
- The design, construction and testing of pre-production prototypes and models
- The design of tools, jigs, moulds and dies involving new technology
- The design, construction and operation of a pilot plant that is not of a scale economically feasible for commercial production

3 Goodwill (IFRS 3)

Purchased goodwill arising on consolidation is retained in the statement of financial position as an intangible asset under IFRS 3. It must then be reviewed annually for impairment.

3.1 What is goodwill?

Goodwill is **created by good relationships** between a business and its customers.

(a) By building up a **reputation** (by word of mouth perhaps) for high quality products or high standards of service

(b) By **responding promptly and helpfully** to queries and complaints from customers

(c) Through the **personality of the staff** and their attitudes to customers

The value of goodwill to a business might be considerable. However, goodwill is not usually valued in the accounts of a business at all, and we should not normally expect to find an amount for goodwill in its statement of financial position. For example, the welcoming smile of the bar staff may contribute more to a bar's profits than the fact that a new electronic cash register has recently been acquired. Even so, whereas the cash register will be recorded in the accounts as a non-current asset, the value of staff would be ignored for accounting purposes.

On reflection, we might agree with this omission of goodwill from the accounts of a business.

(a) The goodwill is **inherent** in the business but it has not been paid for, and it does not have an 'objective' value. We can guess at what such goodwill is worth, but such guesswork would be a matter of individual opinion, and not based on hard facts.

(b) Goodwill **changes** from day to day. One act of bad customer relations might damage goodwill and one act of good relations might improve it. Staff with a favourable personality might retire or leave to find another job, to be replaced by staff who need time to find their feet in the job, etc. Since goodwill is continually changing in value, it cannot realistically be recorded in the accounts of the business.

3.2 Purchased goodwill

There is one exception to the general rule that goodwill has no objective valuation. This is **when a business is sold**. People wishing to set up in business have a choice of how to do it – they can either buy their own long-term assets and inventory and set up their business from scratch, or they can buy up an existing business from a proprietor willing to sell it. When a buyer purchases an existing business, he will have to purchase not only its long-term assets and inventory (and perhaps take over its accounts payable and receivable too) but also the goodwill of the business.

Purchased goodwill is shown in the statement of financial position because it has been paid for. It has no tangible substance, and so it is an **intangible non-current asset**

3.3 How is the value of purchased goodwill decided?

When a business is sold, there is likely to be some purchased goodwill in the selling price. But **how is the amount of this purchased goodwill decided**?

This is not really a problem for accountants, who must simply record the goodwill in the accounts of the new business. The value of the goodwill is a **matter for the purchaser and seller to agree upon in fixing the purchase/sale price**. However, two methods of valuation are worth mentioning here.

(a)   The seller and buyer agree on a price for the business **without specifically quantifying the goodwill**. The purchased goodwill will then be the difference between the price agreed and the value of the identifiable net assets in the books of the new business.

(b)   However, the calculation of goodwill often precedes the fixing of the purchase price and becomes a **central element of negotiation**. There are many ways of arriving at a value for goodwill and most of them are related to the profit record of the business in question.

No matter how goodwill is calculated within the total agreed purchase price, the goodwill shown by the purchaser in his accounts will be **the difference between the purchase consideration and his own valuation of the net assets acquired**. If A values his net assets at $40,000, goodwill is agreed at $21,000 and B agrees to pay $61,000 for the business but values the net assets at only $38,000, then the goodwill in B's books will be $61,000 − $38,000 = $23,000.

3.4 IFRS 3 Business combinations

IFRS 3 covers the accounting treatment of goodwill acquired in a business combination.

Key terms

> **Goodwill**. Future economic benefits arising from assets that are not capable of being individually identified and separately recognised.
> *(IFRS 3)*

Goodwill acquired in a business combination is **recognised as an asset** and is initially measured at **cost**. Cost is the excess of the cost of the combination over the acquirer's interest in the net fair value of the acquiree's identifiable assets, liabilities and contingent liabilities.

After initial recognition goodwill acquired in a business combination is measured **at cost less any accumulated impairment losses**. It is **not amortised**. Instead it is tested for impairment at least annually, in accordance with IAS 36 *Impairment of assets*.

Negative goodwill arises when the acquirer's interest in the net fair value of the acquiree's identifiable assets, liabilities and contingent liabilities exceeds the cost of the business combination. IFRS 3 refers to negative goodwill as the 'excess of acquirer's interest in the net fair value of acquiree's identifiable assets, liabilities and contingent liabilities over cost'.

Negative goodwill can arise as the result of **errors** in measuring the fair value of either the cost of the combination or the acquiree's identifiable net assets. It can also arise as the result of a **bargain purchase**.

Where there is negative goodwill, an entity should first **reassess** the amounts at which it has measured both the cost of the combination and the acquiree's identifiable net assets. This exercise should identify any errors.

Any negative goodwill remaining should be **recognised** immediately in profit or loss.

IFRS 3 requires extensive **disclosures**. These include a **reconciliation** of the carrying amount of goodwill at the beginning and end of the period, showing separately:

(a)   The gross amount and accumulated impairment losses at the beginning of the period
(b)   Additional goodwill recognised during the period
(c)   Impairment losses recognised during the period
(d)   Net exchange differences arising during the period, and
(e)   The gross amount and accumulated impairment losses at the end of the period

What are the main characteristics of goodwill which distinguish it from other intangible non-current assets? To what extent do you consider that these characteristics should affect the accounting treatment of goodwill? State your reasons.

Answer

Goodwill may be distinguished from other intangible non-current assets by reference to the following characteristics.

(a)   It is incapable of realisation separately from the business as a whole.

(b)   Its value has no reliable or predictable relationship to any costs which may have been incurred.

(c)   Its value arises from various intangible factors such as skilled employees, effective advertising or a strategic location. These indirect factors cannot be valued.

(d)   The value of goodwill may fluctuate widely according to internal and external circumstances over relatively short periods of time.

(e)   The assessment of the value of goodwill is highly subjective.

It could be argued that, because goodwill is so different from other intangible non-current assets it does not make sense to account for it in the same way. Thus the capitalisation and amortisation treatment would not be acceptable. Furthermore, because goodwill is so difficult to value, any valuation may be misleading, and it is best eliminated from the statement of financial position altogether. However, there are strong arguments for treating it like any other intangible non-current asset. This issue remains controversial.

Chapter Roundup

- **Intangible assets** are defined by **IAS 38** as non-monetary assets without physical substance. They must be:

  –   **Identifiable**
  –   **Controlled** as a result of a past event
  –   Able to provide **future economic benefits**

- Intangible assets should initially be measured at cost, but subsequently they can be carried at **cost or at a revalued amount**.

- **Internally-generated goodwill** cannot be recognised as an asset but other internally-generated assets may be, eg R & D.

- Purchased goodwill arising on consolidation is retained in the statement of financial position as an intangible asset under IFRS 3. It must then be reviewed annually for impairment.

- Purchased goodwill is shown in the statement of financial position because it has been paid for. It has no tangible substance and so it is an **intangible non-current asset**.

1   Intangible assets can only be recognised in a company's accounts if:

   •   It is probable that .... will flow to the entity
   •   The cost can be ....

2   What are the criteria which must be met before development expenditure can be deferred?

3   Start up costs must be expensed.

   True   ☐

   False   ☐

4   Peggy buys Phil's business for $30,000. The business assets are a bar valued at $20,000, inventories at $3,000 and receivables of $3,000. How much is goodwill valued at?

5   What method of accounting for goodwill arising on consolidation is required by IFRS 3?

6   How should negative goodwill be accounted for under IFRS 3?

Answers to Quick Quiz

1   Future economic benefits. Measured reliably.
2   See Para 2.2
3   True
4    $30,000 – $20,000 – $3,000 – $3,000 = $4,000
5   Cost less impairment losses
6   Recognised in profit or loss immediately

Impairment
of assets

Topic list	Syllabus reference
1 IAS 36 Impairment of assets	C8
2 Cash generating units	C8
3 Goodwill and impairment of assets	C8
4 Accounting treatment of an impairment loss	C8

Introduction

IAS 36 is a recent and important standard. Impairment rules apply to both tangible and intangible assets.

Study guide

		Intellectual level
8	**Impairment of assets**	
(a)	define an impairment loss.	2
(b)	identify the circumstances that may indicate impairments to assets.	2
(c)	describe what is meant by a cash generating unit.	2
(d)	state the basis on which impairment losses should be allocated, and allocate an impairment loss to the asserts of a cash generating unit.	2

1 IAS 36 Impairment of assets

FAST FORWARD

Impairment is determined by comparing the carrying amount of the asset with its recoverable amount. This is the higher of its **fair value less costs to sell** and its **value in use**.

There is an established principle that assets should not be carried at above their recoverable amount. An entity should write down the carrying value of an asset to its recoverable amount if the carrying value of an asset is not recoverable in full. IAS 36 was published in June 1998 and has recently been revised. It puts in place a detailed methodology for carrying out impairment reviews and related accounting treatments and disclosures.

1.1 Scope

IAS 36 applies to all tangible, intangible and financial assets except inventories, assets arising from construction contracts, deferred tax assets, assets arising under IAS 19 *Employee benefits* and financial assets within the scope of IAS 32 *Financial instruments: disclosure and presentation*. This is because those IASs already have rules for recognising and measuring impairment. Note also that IAS 36 does not apply to non-current assets held for sale, which are dealt with under IFRS 5 *Non-current assets held for sale and discontinued operations*

Key terms

> - **Impairment**: a fall in the value of an asset, so that its 'recoverable amount' is now less than its carrying value in the statement of financial position.
> - **Carrying amount**: is the net value at which the asset is included in the statement of financial position (ie after deducting accumulated depreciation and any impairment losses).
>
> *(IAS 36)*

The basic principle underlying IAS 36 is relatively straightforward. If an asset's value in the accounts is higher than its realistic value, measured as its 'recoverable amount', the asset is judged to have suffered an impairment loss. It should therefore be reduced in value, by the amount of the **impairment loss**. The amount of the impairment loss should be **written off against profit** immediately.

The main accounting issues to consider are therefore as follows.

(a) How is it possible to **identify when** an impairment loss may have occurred?
(b) How should the **recoverable amount** of the asset be measured?
(c) How should an 'impairment loss' be **reported in the accounts**?

1.2 Identifying a potentially impaired asset

An entity should assess at the end of each reporting period whether there are any indications of impairment to any assets. The concept of **materiality** applies, and only material impairment needs to be identified.

If there are indications of possible impairment, the entity is required to make a formal estimate of the **recoverable amount** of the assets concerned.

IAS 36 suggests how **indications of a possible impairment** of assets might be recognised. The suggestions are based largely on common sense.

(a) **External sources of information**

    (i) A fall in the asset's market value that is more significant than would normally be expected from passage of time over normal use.

    (ii) A significant change in the technological, market, legal or economic environment of the business in which the assets are employed.

    (iii) An increase in market interest rates or market rates of return on investments likely to affect the discount rate used in calculating value in use.

    (iv) The carrying amount of the entity's net assets being more than its market capitalisation.

(b) **Internal sources of information**: evidence of obsolescence or physical damage, adverse changes in the use to which the asset is put, or the asset's economic performance

Even if there are no indications of impairment, the following assets must **always** be tested for impairment annually.

(a) An intangible asset with an **indefinite useful life**

(b) **Goodwill** acquired in a business combination

1.3 Measuring the recoverable amount of the asset

What is an asset's recoverable amount?

Key term

> The **recoverable amount of an asset** should be measured as the *higher value* of:
>
> (a) the asset's fair value less costs to sell; and
> (b) its value in use. *(IAS 36)*

An asset's fair value less costs to sell is the amount net of selling costs that could be obtained from the sale of the asset. Selling costs include sales transaction costs, such as legal expenses.

(a) If there is **an active market** in the asset, the net selling price should be based on the **market value**, or on the price of recent transactions in similar assets.

(b) If there is **no active market** in the assets it might be possible to **estimate** a net selling price using best estimates of what 'knowledgeable, willing parties' might pay in an arm's length transaction.

Net selling price **cannot** be reduced, however, by including within selling costs any **restructuring or reorganisation expenses**, or any costs that have already been recognised in the accounts as liabilities.

The concept of 'value in use' is very important.

Key term

> The **value in use** of an asset is measured as the present value of estimated future cash flows (inflows minus outflows) generated by the asset, including its estimated net disposal value (if any) at the end of its expected useful life.

1.4 Recognition and measurement of an impairment loss

The rule for assets at historical cost is:

Rule to learn

If the recoverable amount of an asset is lower than the carrying amount, the carrying amount should be reduced by the difference (ie the impairment loss) which should be charged as an expense in profit or loss.

The rule for assets held at a revalued amount (such as property revalued under IAS 16) is:

Rule to learn

The impairment loss is to be treated as a revaluation decrease under the relevant IAS.

In practice this means:

- To the extent that there is a revaluation surplus held in respect of the asset, the impairment loss should be charged to revaluation surplus.
- Any excess should be charged to profit or loss.

2 Cash generating units

FAST FORWARD ▶▶ When it is not possible to calculate the recoverable amount of a single asset, then that of its **cash generating unit** should be measured instead.

2.1 Use of cash-generating unit

The IAS goes into quite a large amount of detail about the important concept of cash generating units. As a basic rule, the recoverable amount of an asset should be calculated for the **asset individually**. However, there will be occasions when it is not possible to estimate such a value for an individual asset, particularly in the calculation of value in use. This is because cash inflows and outflows cannot be attributed to the individual asset.

If it is not possible to calculate the recoverable amount for an individual asset, the recoverable amount of the asset's cash-generating unit should be measured instead.

Key term

> A **cash-generating unit** is the smallest identifiable group of assets for which independent cash flows can be identified and measured.

 Question | Cash-generating unit I

Can you think of some examples of how a cash-generating unit would be identified?

Answer

Here are two possibilities.

(a) A mining company owns a private railway that it uses to transport output from one of its mines. The railway now has no market value other than as scrap, and it is impossible to identify any separate cash inflows with the use of the railway itself. Consequently, if the mining company suspects an impairment in the value of the railway, it should treat the mine as a whole as a cash generating unit, and measure the recoverable amount of the mine as a whole.

(b)   A bus company has an arrangement with a town's authorities to run a bus service on four routes in the town. Separately identifiable assets are allocated to each of the bus routes, and cash inflows and outflows can be attributed to each individual route. Three routes are running at a profit and one is running at a loss. The bus company suspects that there is an impairment of assets on the loss-making route. However, the company will be unable to close the loss-making route, because it is under an obligation to operate all four routes, as part of its contract with the local authority. Consequently, the company should treat all four bus routes together as a cash generating unit, and calculate the recoverable amount for the unit as a whole.

Question   Cash-generating unit II

Minimart belongs to a retail store chain Maximart. Minimart makes all its retail purchases through Maximart's purchasing centre. Pricing, marketing, advertising and human resources policies (except for hiring Minimart's cashiers and salesmen) are decided by Maximart. Maximart also owns 5 other stores in the same city as Minimart (although in different neighbourhoods) and 20 other stores in other cities. All stores are managed in the same way as Minimart. Minimart and 4 other stores were purchased 5 years ago and goodwill was recognised.

What is the cash-generating unit for Minimart?

Answer

In identifying Minimart's cash-generating unit, an entity considers whether, for example:

(a)   Internal management reporting is organised to measure performance on a store-by-store basis.
(b)   The business is run on a store-by-store profit basis or on a region/city basis.

All Maximart's stores are in different neighbourhoods and probably have different customer bases. So, although Minimart is managed at a corporate level, Minimart generates cash inflows that are largely independent from those of Maximart's other stores. Therefore, it is likely that Minimart is a cash-generating unit.

If an active market exists for the output produced by the asset or a group of assets, this asset or group should be identified as a cash generating unit, even if some or all of the output is used internally.

Cash-generating units should be identified consistently from period to period for the same type of asset unless a change is justified.

The group of net assets less liabilities that are considered for impairment should be the same as those considered in the calculation of the recoverable amount. (For the treatment of goodwill and corporate assets see below.)

2.2 Example: Recoverable amount and carrying amount

Fourways Co is made up of four cash generating units. All four units are being tested for impairment.

(a)   Property, plant and equipment and separate intangibles would be allocated to be cash-generating units as far as possible.
(b)   Current assets such as inventories, receivables and prepayments would be allocated to the relevant cash-generating units.
(c)   Liabilities (eg payables) would be deducted from the net assets of the relevant cash-generating units.
(d)   The net figure for each cash-generating unit resulting from this exercise would be compared to the relevant recoverable amount, computed on the same basis.

3 Goodwill and the impairment of assets

3.1 Allocating goodwill to cash-generating units

Goodwill acquired in a business combination does not generate cash flows independently of other assets. It must be **allocated** to each of the acquirer's **cash-generating units** (or groups of cash-generating units) that are expected to benefit from the synergies of the combination. Each unit to which the goodwill is so allocated should:

(a)   Represent the **lowest level** within the entity at which the goodwill is monitored for internal management purposes

(b)   Not be **larger than a reporting segment** determined in accordance with IAS 14 *Segment reporting* (now IFRS 8 *Operating segments*).

It may be impractical to complete the allocation of goodwill before the first reporting date after a business combination, particularly if the acquirer is accounting for the combination for the first time using provisional values. The initial allocation of goodwill must be completed before the end of the first reporting period after the acquisition date.

3.2 Testing cash-generating units with goodwill for impairment

There are two situations to consider.

(a)   Where goodwill has been allocated to a cash-generating unit

(b)   Where it has not been possible to allocate goodwill to a specific cash-generating unit, but only to a group of units

A cash-generating unit to which goodwill has been allocated is tested for impairment annually. The **carrying amount** of the unit, including goodwill, is **compared with the recoverable amount**. If the carrying amount of the unit exceeds the recoverable amount, the entity must recognise an impairment loss.

Where goodwill relates to a cash-generating unit but has not been allocated to that unit, the unit is tested for impairment by **comparing its carrying amount** (excluding goodwill) **with its recoverable amount**. The entity must recognise an impairment loss if the carrying amount exceeds the recoverable amount.

The annual impairment test may be performed at any time during an accounting period, but must be performed at the **same time every year**.

3.3 Corporate assets

Corporate assets are group or divisional assets such as a head office building, computer equipment or a research centre. Essentially, corporate assets are assets that do not generate cash inflows independently from other assets, hence their carrying amount cannot be fully attributed to a cash-generating unit under review.

In testing a cash generating unit for impairment, an entity should identify all the corporate assets that relate to the cash-generating unit.

(a)   If a portion of the carrying amount of a corporate asset **can be allocated** to the unit on a reasonable and consistent basis, the entity compares the carrying amount of the unit (including the portion of the asset) with its recoverable amount.

(b)   If a portion of the carrying amount of a corporate asset **cannot be allocated** to the unit on a reasonable and consistent basis, the entity:

(i)   Compares the carrying amount of the unit (excluding the asset) with its recoverable amount and recognises any impairment loss

(ii)   Identifies the smallest group of cash-generating units that includes the cash-generating unit to which the asset belongs and to which a portion of the carrying amount of the asset can be allocated on a reasonable and consistent basis

(iii)   Compares the carrying amount of that group of cash-generating units (including the portion of the asset allocated to the group of units) with the recoverable amount of the group of units and recognises any impairment loss

4 Accounting treatment of an impairment loss

If, and only if, the recoverable amount of an asset is less than its carrying amount in the statement of financial position, an impairment loss has occurred. This loss should be **recognised immediately**.

(a)   The asset's **carrying amount** should be reduced to its recoverable amount in the statement of financial position.

(b)   The **impairment loss** should be recognised immediately in profit or loss (unless the asset has been revalued in which case the loss is treated as a revaluation decrease).

After reducing an asset to its recoverable amount, the **depreciation charge** on the asset should then be based on its new carrying amount, its estimated residual value (if any) and its estimated remaining useful life.

An impairment loss should be recognised for a **cash generating unit** if (and only if) the recoverable amount for the cash generating unit is less than the carrying amount in the statement of financial position for all the assets in the unit. When an impairment loss is recognised for a cash generating unit, the loss should be allocated between the assets in the unit in the following order.

(a)   First, to any assets that are obviously damaged or destroyed
(b)   Next, to the **goodwill** allocated to the cash generating unit
(c)   Then to all other assets in the cash-generating unit, on a **pro rata basis**

In allocating an impairment loss, the carrying amount of an asset should not be reduced below the highest of:

(a)   Its fair value less costs to sell
(b)   Its value in use (if determinable)
(c)   Zero

Any remaining amount of an impairment loss should be recognised as a liability if required by other IASs.

4.1 Example 1: impairment loss

A company that extracts natural gas and oil has a drilling platform in the Caspian Sea. It is required by legislation of the country concerned to remove and dismantle the platform at the end of its useful life. Accordingly, the company has included an amount in its accounts for removal and dismantling costs, and is depreciating this amount over the platform's expected life.

The company is carrying out an exercise to establish whether there has been an impairment of the platform.

(a)   Its carrying amount in the statement of financial position is $3m.

(b)   The company has received an offer of $2.8m for the platform from another oil company. The bidder would take over the responsibility (and costs) for dismantling and removing the platform at the end of its life.

(c)   The present value of the estimated cash flows from the platform's continued use is $3.3m (before adjusting for dismantling costs).

(d)   The carrying amount in the statement of financial position for the provision for dismantling and removal is currently $0.6m.

What should be the value of the drilling platform in the statement of financial position, and what, if anything, is the impairment loss?

Solution

Fair value less costs to sell	=	$2.8m
Value in use	=	PV of cash flows from use less the carrying amount of the provision/liability = $3.3m – $0.6m = $2.7m
Recoverable amount	=	Higher of these two amounts, ie $2.8m
Carrying value	=	$3m
Impairment loss	=	$0.2m

The carrying value should be reduced to $2.8m

4.2 Example 2: impairment loss

A company has acquired another business for $4.5m: tangible assets are valued at $4.0m and goodwill at $0.5m.

An asset with a carrying value of $1m is destroyed in a terrorist attack. The asset was not insured. The loss of the asset, without insurance, has prompted the company to assess whether there has been an impairment of assets in the acquired business and what the amount of any such loss is.

The recoverable amount of the business (a single cash generating unit) is measured as $3.1m.

Solution

There has been an impairment loss of $1.4m ($4.5m – $3.1m).

The impairment loss will be recognised in profit or loss. The loss will be allocated between the assets in the cash generating unit as follows.

(a)   A loss of $1m can be attributed directly to the uninsured asset that has been destroyed.
(b)   The remaining loss of $0.4m should be allocated to goodwill.

The carrying value of the assets will now be $3m for tangible assets and $0.1m for goodwill.

4.3 Reversal of an impairment loss

The annual assessment to determine whether there may have been some impairment should be **applied to all assets**, including assets that have already been impaired in the past.

In some cases, the recoverable amount of an asset that has previously been impaired might turn out to be **higher** than the asset's current carrying value. In other words, there might have been a reversal of some of the previous impairment loss.

(a)   The reversal of the impairment loss should be **recognised immediately** as income in profit or loss.
(b)   The carrying amount of the asset should be increased to its **new recoverable amount**.

An exception to this rule is for **goodwill**. An impairment loss for goodwill should not be reversed in a subsequent period.

Question

Reversal of impairment loss

A cash generating unit comprising a factory, plant and equipment etc and associated purchased goodwill becomes impaired because the product it makes is overtaken by a technologically more advanced model produced by a competitor. The recoverable amount of the cash generating unit falls to $60m, resulting in an impairment loss of $80m, allocated as follows.

	Carrying amounts before impairment $m	Carrying amounts after impairment $m
Goodwill	40	–
Patent (with no market value)	20	–
Tangible non-current assets (market value $60m)	80	60
Total	140	60

After three years, the entity makes a technological breakthrough of its own, and the recoverable amount of the cash generating unit increases to $90m. The carrying amount of the tangible non-current assets had the impairment not occurred would have been $70m.

Required

Calculate the reversal of the impairment loss.

Answer

The reversal of the impairment loss is recognised to the extent that it increases the carrying amount of the tangible non-current assets to what it would have been had the impairment not taken place, ie a reversal of the impairment loss of $10m is recognised and the tangible non-current assets written back to $70m. Reversal of the impairment is not recognised in relation to the goodwill and patent because the effect of the external event that caused the original impairment has not reversed – the original product is still overtaken by a more advanced model.

Exam focus point

An exam question may ask you to calculate and allocate an impairment loss. Make sure you know the order in which to allocate the loss.

4.4 Summary

The main aspects of IAS 36 to consider are:

- **Indications** of impairment of assets
- **Measuring recoverable amount**, as net selling price or value in use
- **Measuring value in use**
- **Cash generating units**
- **Accounting treatment** of an impairment loss, for individual assets and cash generating units
- **Reversal** of an impairment loss

Chapter Roundup

- Impairment is determined by comparing the carrying amount of the asset with its **recoverable amount**. This is the higher of its **fair value less costs to sell** and its **value in use**.

- When it is not possible to calculate the recoverable amount of a single asset, then that of its **cash generating unit** should be measured instead.

Quick Quiz

1   Define **recoverable amount** of an asset.
2   How is an impairment loss on a revalued asset treated?
3   How is an impairment loss allocated to the assets in a cash-generating unit?

Answers to Quick Quiz

1   Higher of **fair value less costs to sell** and **value in use**.

2   As a revaluation decrease.

3   In the following order: a) against any damaged or destroyed assets; then b) against goodwill; then c) against all other assets on a *pro rata* basis.

Now try the questions below from the Exam Question Bank

Number	Level	Marks	Time
8	Examination	15	27 mins

7

Reporting financial performance

Topic list	Syllabus reference
1 IAS 8 Accounting policies, changes in accounting estimates and errors	A2
2 Changes in accounting polices	A2
3 Errors	A2
4 IFRS 5 Non-current assets held for sale and discontinued operations	C11

Introduction

IAS 8 deals with accounting policies. It also looks at certain circumstances and transactions which require different treatment to normal profit or loss items.

IFRS 5 on assets held for sale and discontinued operations is an important standard which gives users additional information regarding the sources of the entity's profit and losses.

Study guide

		Intellectual level
A2	**A conceptual framework for financial reporting**	
(a)	distinguish between changes in accounting policies and changes in accounting estimates and describe how accounting standards apply the principle of comparability where an entity changes its accounting policies.	2
(b)	recognise and account for changes in accounting policies and the correction of prior period errors.	2
C11	**Financial statements**	
(a)	discuss the importance of identifying and reporting the results of discontinued operations.	2
(b)	define and account for non-current assets held for sale and discontinued operations.	2
(c)	indicate the circumstances where separate disclosure of material items of income and expense is required.	2

1 IAS 8 Accounting policies, changes in accounting estimates and errors

FAST FORWARD

IAS 8 deals with the treatment of changes in accounting estimates, changes in accounting policies and errors.

The standard was extensively revised in December 2003. The new title reflects the fact that the material on determining net profit or loss for the period has been transferred to IAS 1.

1.1 Definitions

The following definitions are given in the standard. Apart from the definition of accounting policies, most of the definitions are either new or heavily amended.

Key terms

- **Accounting policies** are the specific principles, bases, conventions, rules and practices adopted by an entity in preparing and presenting financial statements.

- A **change in accounting estimate** is an adjustment of the carrying amount of an asset or a liability or the amount of the periodic consumption of an asset, that results from the assessment of the present status of, and expected future benefits and obligations associated with, assets and liabilities. Changes in accounting estimates result from new information or new developments and, accordingly, are not corrections of errors.

- **Material**: as defined in the *Framework* (see Chapter 1 Section 5).

- **Prior period errors** are omissions from, and misstatements in, the entity's financial statements for one or more prior periods arising from a failure to use, or misuse of, reliable information that:

  - Was available when financial statements for those periods were authorised for issue, and
  - Could reasonably be expected to have been obtained and taken into account in the preparation and presentation of those financial statements.

  Such errors include the effects of mathematical mistakes, mistakes in applying accounting policies, oversights or misinterpretations of facts, and fraud.

- **Retrospective application** is applying a new accounting policy to transactions, other events and conditions as if that policy had always been applied.

- **Retrospective restatement** is correcting the recognition, measurement and disclosure of amounts of elements of financial statements as if a prior period error had never occurred.

- **Prospective application** of a change in accounting policy and of recognising the effect of a change in an accounting estimate, respectively, are:

  - Applying the new accounting policy to transactions, other events and conditions occurring after the date as at which the policy is changed; and
  - Recognising the effect of the change in the accounting estimate in the current and future periods affected by the change.

- **Impracticable** Applying a requirement is impracticable when the entity cannot apply it after making every reasonable effort to do so. It is impracticable to apply a change in an accounting policy retrospectively or to make a retrospective restatement to correct an error if one of the following apply.

  - The effects of the retrospective application or retrospective restatement are not determinable.
  - The retrospective application or retrospective restatement requires assumptions about what management's intent would have been in that period.
  - The retrospective application or retrospective restatement requires significant estimates of amounts and it is impossible to distinguish objectively information about those estimates that: provides evidence of circumstances that existed on the date(s) at which those amounts are to be recognised, measured or disclosed; and would have been available when the financial statements for that prior period were authorised for issue, from other information.

(IAS 8)

1.2 Accounting policies

Accounting policies are determined by **applying the relevant IFRS or IFRIC** and considering any relevant Implementation Guidance issued by the IASB for that IFRS/IFRIC.

Where there is no applicable IFRS or IFRIC management should use its **judgement** in developing and applying an accounting policy that results in information that is **relevant** and **reliable**. Management should refer to:

(a) The requirements and guidance in IFRSs and IFRICs dealing with **similar** and **related issues**
(b) The definitions, recognition criteria and measurement concepts for assets, liabilities and expenses in the **Framework**

Management may also consider the most recent pronouncements of **other standard setting bodies** that use a similar conceptual framework to develop standards, other accounting literature and accepted industry practices if these do not conflict with the sources above.

An entity must select and apply its accounting policies for a period **consistently** for similar transactions, other events and conditions, unless an IFRS or an IFRIC specifically requires or permits categorisation of items for which different policies may be appropriate. If an IFRS or an IFRIC requires or permits categorisation of items, an appropriate accounting policy must be selected and applied consistently to each category.

2 Changes in accounting policies

FAST FORWARD

Changes in accounting policy are applied **retrospectively**.

2.1 Introduction

The same accounting policies are usually adopted from period to period, to allow users to analyse trends over time in profit, cash flows and financial position. **Changes in accounting policy will therefore be rare** and should be made only if required by one of three things.

(a) By **statute**

(b) By an accounting standard setting body

(c) If the change will result in a **more appropriate presentation** of events or transactions in the financial statements of the entity

The standard highlights two types of event which do not constitute changes in accounting policy.

(a) Adopting an accounting policy for a **new type of transaction** or event not dealt with previously by the entity.

(b) Adopting a **new accounting policy** for a transaction or event which has not occurred in the past or which was not material.

In the case of tangible non-current assets, if a policy of revaluation is adopted for the first time then this is treated, not as a change of accounting policy under IAS 8, but as a revaluation under IAS 16 Property, plant and equipment (see Chapter 5). The following paragraphs do not therefore apply to a change in policy to adopt revaluations.

A change in accounting policy **must be applied retrospectively. Retrospective application** means that the new accounting policy is applied to transactions and events as if it had always been in use. In other words, at the earliest date such transactions or events occurred, the policy is applied from that date.

Prospective application is **no longer allowed** under the revised IAS 8 unless it is **impracticable** (see Key Terms) to determine the cumulative amount of charge.

2.2 Adoption of an IAS/IFRS

Where a new IAS or IFRS is adopted, IAS 8 requires any transitional provisions in the new IAS itself to be followed. If none are given in the IAS which is being adopted, then you should follow the general principles of IAS 8.

2.3 Other changes in accounting policy

IAS 8 requires **retrospective application**, unless it is **impracticable** to determine the cumulative amount of charge. Any resulting adjustment should be reported as an adjustment to the opening balance of retained earnings. Comparative information should be restated unless it is impracticable to do so.

This means that all comparative information must be restated **as if the new policy had always been in force**, with amounts relating to earlier periods reflected in an adjustment to opening reserves of the earliest period presented.

Prospective application is allowed only when it is impracticable to determine the cumulative effect of the change.

Certain **disclosures** are required when a change in accounting policy has a material effect on the current period or any prior period presented, or when it may have a material effect in subsequent periods.

(a) Reasons for the change

(b) Amount of the adjustment for the current period and for each period presented

(c) Amount of the adjustment relating to periods prior to those included in the comparative information

(d) The fact that comparative information has been restated or that it is impracticable to do so

An entity should also disclose information relevant to assessing the **impact of new IFRS** on the financial statements where these have **not yet come into force.**

2.4 Changes in accounting estimates

Changes in accounting estimate are **not** applied retrospectively..

Estimates arise in relation to business activities because of the **uncertainties inherent within them**. Judgements are made based on the most up to date information and the use of such estimates is a necessary part of the preparation of financial statements. It does not undermine their reliability. Here are some examples of accounting estimates.

(a)   A necessary **irrecoverable debt allowance**
(b)   **Useful lives** of depreciable assets
(c)   Provision for **obsolescence of inventory**

The rule here is that the **effect of a change in an accounting estimate** should be included in the determination of net profit or loss in one of:

(a)   The period of the change, if the change affects that period only
(b)   The period of the change and future periods, if the change affects both

Changes may occur in the circumstances which were in force at the time the estimate was calculated, or perhaps additional information or subsequent developments have come to light.

An example of a change in accounting estimate which affects only the **current period** is the bad debt estimate. However, a revision in the life over which an asset is depreciated would affect both the **current and future periods**, in the amount of the depreciation expense.

Reasonably enough, the effect of a change in an accounting estimate should be included in the **same expense classification** as was used previously for the estimate. This rule helps to ensure **consistency** between the financial statements of different periods.

The **materiality** of the change is also relevant. The nature and amount of a change in an accounting estimate that has a material effect in the current period (or which is expected to have a material effect in subsequent periods) should be disclosed. If it is not possible to quantify the amount, this impracticability should be disclosed.

3 Errors

Prior period errors must be corrected **retrospectively**.

3.1 Introduction

Errors discovered during a current period which **relate to a prior period** may arise through:

(a)   Mathematical mistakes
(b)   Mistakes in the application of accounting policies
(c)   Misinterpretation of facts
(d)   Oversights
(e)   Fraud

A more formal definition is given in the Key Terms in Paragraph 1.1.

Most of the time these errors can be **corrected through net profit or loss for the current period**. Where they are material prior period errors, however, this is not appropriate. The standard considers two possible treatments.

3.2 Accounting treatment

Prior period errors: correct retrospectively. There is no longer any allowed alternative treatment.

This involves:

(a) Either restating the comparative amounts for the prior period(s) in which the error occurred,

(b) Or, when the error occurred before the earliest prior period presented, restating the opening balances of assets, liabilities and equity for that period

so that the financial statements are presented **as if the error had never occurred**.

Only where it is **impracticable** to determine the cumulative effect of an error on prior periods can an entity correct an error **prospectively**.

Various **disclosures** are required.

(a) **Nature** of the prior period error

(b) For each prior period, to the extent practicable, the **amount** of the correction.

(i) For each financial statement line item affected

(ii) If IAS 33 applies, for basic and diluted earnings per share

(c) The amount of the correction at the **beginning of the earliest prior period** presented

(d) If **retrospective restatement is impracticable** for a particular prior period, the **circumstances** that led to the existence of that condition and a description of how and from when the error has been corrected. Subsequent periods need not repeat these disclosures

Exam focus point

> If you have to deal with a charge of accounting policy or an error in an accounts preparation question, remember to adjust the balance of retained earnings brought forward.

Question

Error

During 20X7 Global discovered that certain items had been included in inventory at 31 December 20X6, valued at $4.2m, which had in fact been sold before the year end. The following figures for 20X6 (as reported) and 20X7 (draft) are available.

	20X6	20X7 (draft)
	$'000	$'000
Sales	47,400	67,200
Cost of goods sold	(34,570)	(55,800)
Profit before taxation	12,830	11,400
Income taxes	(3,880)	(3,400)
Profit for the period	8,950	8,000

Retained earnings at 1 January 20X6 were $13m. The cost of goods sold for 20X7 includes the $4.2m error in opening inventory. The income tax rate was 30% for 20X6 and 20X7. No dividends have been declared or paid.

Required

Show the income statement for 20X7, with the 20X6 comparative, and retained earnings.

Answer

INCOME STATEMENT

	20X6	20X7
	$'000	$'000
Sales	47,400	67,200
Cost of goods sold (W1)	(38,770)	(51,600)
Profit before tax	8,630	15,600
Income tax (W2)	(2,620)	(4,660)
Profit for the year	6,010	10,940

RETAINED EARNINGS

	20X6	20X7
	$'000	$'000
Opening retained earnings		
As previously reported	13,000	21,950
Correction of prior period error (4,200 – 1,260)	–	(2,940)
As restated	13,000	19,010
Profit for the year	6,010	10,940
Closing retained earnings	19,010	29,950

Workings

1	Cost of goods sold	20X6	20X7
		$'000	$'000
	As stated in question	34,570	55,800
	Inventory adjustment	4,200	(4,200)
		38,770	51,600

2	Income tax	20X6	20X7
		$'000	$'000
	As stated in question	3,880	3,400
	Inventory adjustment (4,200 × 30%)	(1,260)	1,260
		2,620	4,660

4 IFRS 5 Non-current assets held for sale and discontinued operations

 FAST FORWARD

IFRS 5 requires assets 'held for sale' to be presented separately in the statement of financial position. It sets out the criteria for recognising a **discontinued operation**.

4.1 Background

IFRS 5 is the result of a short-term convergence project with the US Financial Accounting Standards Board (FASB). It replaces IAS 35 *Discontinuing operations*.

IFRS 5 requires assets and groups of assets that are 'held for sale' to be **presented separately** in the statement of financial position and the results of discontinued operations to be presented separately in the statement of comprehensive income. This is required so that users of financial statements will be better able to make **projections** about the financial position, profits and cash flows of the entity.

Key terms

> **Disposal group**: a group of assets to be disposed of, by sale or otherwise, together as a group in a single transaction, and liabilities directly associated with those assets that will be transferred in the transaction. (In practice a disposal group could be a subsidiary, a cash-generating unit or a single operation within an entity.) (IFRS 5)
>
> **Cash generating unit**: the smallest identifiable group of assets for which independent cash flows can be identified and measured

IFRS 5 does not apply to certain assets covered by other accounting standards:

(a) Deferred tax assets (IAS 12)

(b) Assets arising from employee benefits (IAS 19)

(c) Financial assets (IAS 39)

(d) Investment properties accounted for in accordance with the fair value model (IAS 40)

BPP
LEARNING MEDIA

(e) Agricultural and biological assets that are measured at fair value less estimated point of sale costs (IAS 41)

(f) Insurance contracts (IFRS 4)

4.2 Classification of assets held for sale

A non-current asset (or disposal group) should be classified as **held for sale** if its carrying amount will be recovered **principally through a sale transaction** rather than **through continuing use**. A number of detailed criteria must be met:

(a) The asset must be **available for immediate sale** in its present condition.

(b) Its sale must be **highly probable** (ie, significantly more likely than not).

For the sale to be highly probable, the following must apply.

(a) Management must be **committed** to a plan to sell the asset.

(b) There must be an active programme to **locate a buyer.**

(c) The asset must be marketed for sale at a **price that is reasonable** in relation to its current fair value.

(d) The sale should be expected to take place **within one year** from the date of classification.

(e) It is unlikely that significant changes to the plan will be made or that the plan will be withdrawn.

An asset (or disposal group) can still be classified as held for sale, even if the sale has not actually taken place within one year. However, the delay must have been **caused by events or circumstances beyond the entity's control** and there must be sufficient evidence that the entity is still committed to sell the asset or disposal group. Otherwise the entity must cease to classify the asset as held for sale.

If an entity acquires a disposal group (eg, a subsidiary) exclusively with a view to its subsequent disposal it can classify the asset as held for sale only if the sale is expected to take place within one year and it is highly probable that all the other criteria will be met within a short time (normally three months).

An asset that is to be **abandoned** should not be classified as held for sale. This is because its carrying amount will be recovered principally through continuing use. However, a disposal group to be abandoned may meet the definition of a discontinued operation and therefore separate disclosure may be required (see below).

Question	Held for sale

On 1 December 20X3, a company became committed to a plan to sell a manufacturing facility and has already found a potential buyer. The company does not intend to discontinue the operations currently carried out in the facility. At 31 December 20X3 there is a backlog of uncompleted customer orders. The company will not be able to transfer the facility to the buyer until after it ceases to operate the facility and has eliminated the backlog of uncompleted customer orders. This is not expected to occur until spring 20X4.

Required

Can the manufacturing facility be classified as 'held for sale' at 31 December 20X3?

Answer

The facility will not be transferred until the backlog of orders is completed; this demonstrates that the facility is not available for immediate sale in its present condition. The facility cannot be classified as 'held for sale' at 31 December 20X3. It must be treated in the same way as other items of property, plant and equipment: it should continue to be depreciated and should not be separately disclosed.

4.3 Measurement of assets held for sale

Fair value: the amount for which an asset could be exchanged, or a liability settled, between knowledgeable, willing parties in an arm's length transaction.

Costs to sell: the incremental costs directly attributable to the disposal of an asset (or disposal group), excluding finance costs and income tax expense.

Recoverable amount: the higher of an asset's fair value less costs to sell and its value in use.

Value in use: the present value of estimated future cash flows expected to arise from the continuing use of an asset and from its disposal at the end of its useful life.

A non-current asset (or disposal group) that is held for sale should be measured at the **lower of** its **carrying amount** and **fair value less costs to sell**. Fair value less costs to sell is equivalent to net realisable value.

An impairment loss should be recognised where fair value less costs to sell is lower than carrying amount. Note that this is an exception to the normal rule. IAS 36 Impairment of assets requires an entity to recognise an impairment loss only where an asset's recoverable amount is lower than its carrying value. Recoverable amount is defined as the higher of net realisable value and value in use. IAS 36 does not apply to assets held for sale.

Non-current assets held for sale **should not be depreciated**, even if they are still being used by the entity.

A non-current asset (or disposal group) that is **no longer classified as held for sale** (for example, because the sale has not taken place within one year) is measured at the **lower of**:

(a)   Its **carrying amount** before it was classified as held for sale, adjusted for any depreciation that would have been charged had the asset not been held for sale

(b)   Its **recoverable amount** at the date of the decision not to sell

4.4 Presenting discontinued operations

Discontinued operation: a component of an entity that has either been disposed of, or is classified as held for sale, and:

(a)   Represents a separate major line of business or geographical area of operations

(b)   Is part of a single co-ordinated plan to dispose of a separate major line of business or geographical area of operations, or

(c)   Is a subsidiary acquired exclusively with a view to resale.

Component of an entity: operations and cash flows that can be clearly distinguished, operationally and for financial reporting purposes, from the rest of the entity.

An entity should **present and disclose information** that enables users of the financial statements to evaluate the financial effects of **discontinued operations** and disposals of non-current assets or disposal groups.

An entity should disclose a **single amount** in the statement of comprehensive income comprising the total of:

(a)   The **post-tax profit or loss** of discontinued operations and

(b)   The post-tax gain or loss recognised on the **measurement to fair value less costs to sell** or on the disposal of the assets or disposal group(s) constituting the discontinued operation.

An entity should also disclose an **analysis** of this single amount into:

(a)   The revenue, expenses and pre-tax profit or loss of discontinued operations

(b)   The related income tax expense

(c) The gain or loss recognised on the measurement to fair value less costs to sell or on the disposal of the assets of the discontinued operation

(d) The related income tax expense

This may be presented either in the statement of comprehensive income or in the notes. If it is presented in the statement of comprehensive income it should be presented in a section identified as relating to discontinued operations, ie separately from continuing operations. This analysis is not required where the discontinued operation is a newly acquired subsidiary that has been classified as held for sale.

An entity should disclose the **net cash flows** attributable to the operating, investing and financing activities of discontinued operations. These disclosures may be presented either on the face of the cash flow statement or in the notes.

Gains and losses on the remeasurement of a disposal group that is not a discontinued operation but is held for sale should be included in profit or loss from continuing operations.

4.5 Illustration

The following illustration is taken from the implementation guidance to IFRS 5. Profit for the period from discontinued operations would be analysed in the notes.

XYZ GROUP
INCOME STATEMENT
FOR THE YEAR ENDED 31 DECEMBER 20X2

	20X2	20X1
	$'000	$'000
Continuing operations		
Revenue	X	X
Cost of sales	(X)	(X)
Gross profit	X	X
Other income	X	X
Distribution costs	(X)	(X)
Administrative expenses	(X)	(X)
Other expenses	(X)	(X)
Finance costs	(X)	(X)
Share of profit of associates	X	X
Profit before tax	X	X
Income tax expense	(X)	(X)
Profit for the year from continuing operations	X	X
Discontinued operations		
Profit for the year from discontinued operations	X	X
Profit for the year	X	X
Profit attributable to:		
Owners of the parent	X	X
Non-controlling interest	X	X
	X	X

Note that if there were items of 'other comprehensive income' this would be shown as a full 'statement of comprehensive income' as per the format in Chapter 3.

 Question   Closure

On 20 October 20X3 the directors of a parent company made a public announcement of plans to close a steel works. The closure means that the group will no longer carry out this type of operation, which until recently has represented about 10% of its total revenue. The works will be gradually shut down over a period of several months, with complete closure expected in July 20X4. At 31 December output had been significantly reduced and some redundancies had already taken place. The cash flows, revenues and expenses relating to the steel works can be clearly distinguished from those of the subsidiary's other operations.

Required

How should the closure be treated in the financial statements for the year ended 31 December 20X3?

Answer

Because the steel works is being closed, rather than sold, it cannot be classified as 'held for sale'. In addition, the steel works is not a discontinued operation. Although at 31 December 20X3 the group was firmly committed to the closure, this has not yet taken place nor can its assets be classified as held for sale, therefore the steel works must be included in continuing operations. Information about the planned closure could be disclosed in the notes to the financial statements.

4.6 Presentation of a non-current asset or disposal group classified as held for sale

Non-current assets and disposal groups classified as held for sale should be **presented separately** from other assets in the statement of financial position. The liabilities of a disposal group should be presented separately from other liabilities in the statement of financial position.

(a)   Assets and liabilities held for sale **should not be offset**.

(b)   The **major classes** of assets and liabilities held for sale should be **separately disclosed** either on the face of the statement of financial position or in the notes.

(c)   IFRS 5 requires non-current assets or disposal groups held for sale to be shown as a separate component of **current assets/current liabilities.**

For example (taken from standard)

ASSETS	
Non-current assets	
AAA	X
Current assets	
BBB	X
CCC	X
	X
Non-current assets classified as held for sale	X
	X
Total assets	X
EQUITY AND LIABILITIES	
Equity	
DDD	X
Non-current liabilities	
EEE	X
Current liabilities	
FFF	X
GGG	X
Liabilities directly associated with non-current assets classified as held for sale	X
	X
Total equity and liabilities	X

4.7 Additional disclosures

In the period in which a non-current asset (or disposal group) has been either classified as held for sale or sold the following should be disclosed.

(a) A **description** of the non-current asset (or disposal group)
(b) A description of the **facts and circumstances** of the disposal
(c) Any **gain or loss** recognised when the item was classified as held for sale

Where an asset previously classified as held for sale is **no longer held for sale**, the entity should disclose a description of the facts and circumstances leading to the decision and its effect on results.

Chapter Roundup

- IAS 8 deals with the treatment of changes in accounting estimates, changes in accounting policies and errors.

- Changes in accounting policy are applied **retrospectively**.

- Changes in accounting estimate are **not** applied retrospectively.

- Prior period errors must be corrected **retrospectively**.

- IFRS 5 requires assets 'held for sale' to be presented separately in the statement of financial position. It sets out the criteria for recognising a **discontinued operation**.

Quick Quiz

1 How should a prior period error be corrected under IAS 8?
2 Give three circumstances when a change in accounting policy might be required.
3 When can a non-current asset be classified as held for sale?
4 How should an asset held for sale be measured?
5 How does IFRS 5 define a discontinued operation?

Answers to Quick Quiz

1 By adjusting the opening balance of retained earnings.
2 (a) By statute
  (b) By the IASB
  (c) For a more appropriate presentation
3 See Para 4.2
4 See Para 4.3
5 See Para 4.4

Now try the questions below from the Exam Question Bank

Number	Level	Marks	Time
5	Examination	25	45 mins
7	Examination	15	27 mins

Introduction
to groups

Topic list	Syllabus reference
1 Group accounts	D1
2 IAS 27 Consolidated and separate financial statements	D1
3 Content of group accounts and group structure	D1
4 Group accounts: the related parties issue	D2

Introduction

Consolidation is an extremely important area of your Paper 7 syllabus.

The key to consolidation questions in the examination is to adopt a logical approach and to practise as many questions as possible.

In this chapter we will look at the major definitions in consolidation. These matters are fundamental to your comprehension of group accounts, so make sure you can understand them and then **learn them**.

IMPORTANT NOTE

The IASB has recently revised IFRS 3 *Business Combinations* and these revisions which affect group accounts will be examined in sittings from December 2008. in order to properly prepare for this exam, students must have the new Practice and Revision Kit which will be available in August.

The IFRS 3 revisions are covered in Chapter 9.

Study guide

		Intellectual level
D	**BUSINESS COMBINATIONS**	
1	**The concept and principles of a group**	
(a)	describe the concept of a group as a single economic unit.	2
(b)	explain and apply the definition of a subsidiary within relevant accounting standards.	2
(c)	describe why directors may not wish to consolidate a subsidiary and the circumstances where this is permitted.	2
(d)	explain the need for using coterminous year ends and uniform accounting policies when preparing consolidated financial statements.	2
2	**The concept of consolidated financial statements**	
(a)	explain the objective of consolidated financial statements.	2
(b)	indicate the effect that the related party relationship between a parent and subsidiary may have on the subsidiary's entity statements and the consolidated financial statements.	2

Exam guide

You will have a compulsory question on group accounts. Read this chapter carefully and refer back to it when needed.

1 Group accounts

FAST FORWARD

> Many large businesses consist of several companies controlled by one central or administrative company. Together these companies are called a **group**. The controlling company, called the parent or **holding company**, will own some or all of the shares in the other companies, called subsidiaries.

1.1 Introduction

There are many reasons for businesses to operate as groups; for the goodwill associated with the names of the subsidiaries, for tax or legal purposes and so forth. In many countries, company law requires that the results of a group should be presented as a whole. Unfortunately, it is not possible simply to add all the results together and this chapter and those following will teach you how to **consolidate** all the results of companies within a group.

In traditional accounting terminology, a **group of companies** consists of a **parent company** and one or more **subsidiary companies** which are controlled by the parent company.

1.2 Accounting standards

We will be looking at three accounting standards in this and the next three chapters.

- IAS 27 *Consolidated and separate financial statements*
- IFRS 3 *Business combinations*
- IAS 28 *Investments in associates*

These standards are all concerned with different aspects of group accounts, but there is some overlap between them, particularly between IFRS 3 and IAS 27.

In this and the next chapter we will concentrate on IAS 27, which covers the basic group definitions and consolidation procedures of a parent-subsidiary relationship. First of all, however, we will look at all the important definitions involved in group accounts, which **determine how to treat each particular type of investment** in group accounts.

1.3 Definitions

We will look at some of these definitions in more detail later, but they are useful here in that they give you an overview of all aspects of group accounts.

All the definitions relating to group accounts are extremely important. You must **learn them** and **understand** their meaning and application.

- **Control**. The power to govern the financial and operating policies of an entity so as to obtain benefits from its activities.   *(IFRS 3, IASs 27, 28)*

- **Subsidiary**. An entity that is controlled by another entity (known as the parent).   *(IFRS 3, IASs 27, 28)*

- **Parent**. An entity that has one or more subsidiaries.   *(IFRS 3, IAS 27)*

- **Group**. A parent and all its subsidiaries.   *(IAS 27)*

- **Associate**. An entity, including an unincorporated entity such as a partnership, in which an investor has significant influence and which is neither a subsidiary nor a joint venture of the investor.   *(IAS 28)*

- **Significant influence** is the power to participate in the financial and operating policy decisions of an investee or an economic activity but is not control or joint control over those policies.   *(IAS 28)*

We can summarise the different types of investment *and* the required accounting for them as follows.

Investment	Criteria	Required treatment in group accounts
Subsidiary	Control	Full consolidation
Associate	Significant influence	Equity accounting (see Chapter 11)
Investment which is none of the above	Asset held for accretion of wealth	As for single company accounts per IAS 39

1.4 Investments in subsidiaries

The important point here is **control**. In most cases, this will involve the holding company or parent owning a majority of the ordinary shares in the subsidiary (to which normal voting rights are attached). There are circumstances, however, when the parent may own only a minority of the voting power in the subsidiary, *but* the parent still has control.

IAS 27 states that control can usually be assumed to exist when the parent **owns more than half (ie over 50%) of the voting power** of an entity *unless* it can be clearly shown that **such ownership does not constitute control** (these situations will be very rare).

What about situations where this ownership criterion does not exist? IAS 27 lists the following situations where control exists, even when the parent owns only 50% or less of the voting power of an entity.

(a)   The parent has power over more than 50% of the voting rights by virtue of **agreement with other investors**

(b)   The parent has power to **govern the financial and operating policies** of the entity by statute or under an agreement

(c)   The parent has the power to **appoint or remove a majority of members of the board of directors** (or equivalent governing body)

(d)   The parent has power to cast a **majority of votes at meetings of the board of directors**

IAS 27 also states that a parent loses control when it loses the power to govern the financial and operating policies of an investee. Loss of control can occur without a change in ownership levels. This may happen if a subsidiary becomes subject to the control of a government, court administrator or regulator (for example, in bankruptcy).

Exam focus point

You should learn the contents of the above paragraph as you may be asked to apply them in the exam.

1.4.1 Accounting treatment in group accounts

IAS 27 requires a parent to present consolidated financial statements, in which the accounts of the parent and subsidiary (or subsidiaries) are combined and presented **as a single entity**.

1.5 Investments in associates

This type of investment is something less than a subsidiary, but more than a simple investment. The key criterion here is **significant influence**. This is defined as the 'power to participate', but *not* to 'control' (which would make the investment a subsidiary).

Significant influence can be determined by the holding of voting rights (usually attached to shares) in the entity. IAS 28 states that if an investor holds **20% or more** of the voting power of the investee, it can be presumed that the investor has significant influence over the investee, *unless* it can be clearly shown that this is not the case.

Significant influence can be presumed *not* to exist if the investor holds **less than 20%** of the voting power of the investee, unless it can be demonstrated otherwise.

The **existence of significant influence** is evidenced in one or more of the following ways.

(a)   Representation on the **board of directors** (or equivalent) of the investee
(b)   Participation in the **policy making process**
(c)   **Material transactions** between investor and investee
(d)   Interchange of management personnel
(e)   Provision of essential technical information

1.5.1 Accounting treatment in group accounts

IAS 28 requires the use of the **equity method** of accounting for investments in associates. This method will be explained in detail in Chapter 11.

 Question   Treatments

The section summary after this question will give an augmented version of the table given in Paragraph 1.3 above. Before you look at it, see if you can write out the table yourself.

1.6 Section summary

Investment	Criteria	Required treatment in group accounts
Subsidiary	Control (> 50% rule)	Full consolidation (IAS 27)
Associate	Significant influence (20%+ rule)	Equity accounting (IAS 28)
Investment which is none of the above	Asset held for accretion of wealth	As for single company accounts (IAS 39)

2 IAS 27 Consolidated and separate financial statements

FAST FORWARD ⟩⟩

IAS 27 requires a parent to present **consolidated** financial statements.

2.1 Introduction

Key term

> **Consolidated financial statements**. The financial statements of a group presented as those of a single economic entity. *(IAS 27)*

When a parent issues consolidated financial statements, it should consolidate **all subsidiaries**, both foreign and domestic.

2.2 Exemption from preparing group accounts

A parent **need not present** consolidated financial statements if and only if all of the following hold:

(a) The parent is itself a **wholly-owned subsidiary** or it is a **partially owned subsidiary** of another entity and its other owners, including those not otherwise entitled to vote, have been informed about, and do not object to, the parent not presenting consolidated financial statements

(b) Its securities are **not publicly traded**

(c) It is **not in the process of issuing securities** in public securities markets; and

(d) The **ultimate or intermediate parent** publishes consolidated financial statements that comply with International Financial Reporting Standards

A parent that does not present consolidated financial statements must comply with the IAS 27 rules on separate financial statements (discussed later in this section).

2.3 Potential voting rights

An entity may own share warrants, share call options, or other similar instruments that are **convertible into ordinary shares** in another entity. If these are exercised or converted they may give the entity voting power or reduce another party's voting power over the financial and operating policies of the other entity (potential voting rights). The **existence and effect** of potential voting rights, including potential voting rights held by another entity, should be considered when assessing whether an entity has control over another entity (and therefore has a subsidiary).

In assessing whether potential voting rights give rise to control, the entity examines all facts and circumstances that affect the rights (for example, terms and conditions), except the intention of management and the financial ability to exercise the rights or convert them into equity shares.

2.4 Exclusion of a subsidiary from consolidation

The rules on exclusion of subsidiaries from consolidation are necessarily strict, because this is a common method used by entities to manipulate their results. If a subsidiary which carries a large amount of debt can be excluded, then the gearing of the group as a whole will be improved. In other words, this is a way of taking debt **out of the statement of financial position**.

IAS 27 did originally allow a subsidiary to be excluded from consolidation where **control is intended to be temporary**. This exclusion was then removed by IFRS 5.

Subsidiaries held for sale are accounted for in accordance with IFRS 5 *Non-current assets held for sale and discontinued operations*.

It has been argued in the past that subsidiaries should be excluded from consolidation on the grounds of **dissimilar activities**, ie the activities of the subsidiary are so different to the activities of the other companies within the group that to include its results in the consolidation would be misleading. IAS 27 rejects this argument: exclusion on these grounds is not justified because better (relevant) information can be provided about such subsidiaries by consolidating their results and then giving additional information about the different business activities of the subsidiary.

The previous version of IAS 27 permitted exclusion where the subsidiary operates under **severe long-term restrictions** and these significantly impair its ability to transfer funds to the parent. This exclusion has now been **removed**. Control must actually be lost for exclusion to occur.

2.5 Different reporting dates

In most cases, all group companies will prepare accounts to the same reporting date. One or more subsidiaries may, however, prepare accounts to a different reporting date from the parent and the bulk of other subsidiaries in the group.

In such cases the subsidiary may prepare additional statements to the reporting date of the rest of the group, for consolidation purposes. If this is not possible, the subsidiary's accounts may still be used for the consolidation, *provided that* the gap between the reporting dates is **three months or less**.

Where a subsidiary's accounts are drawn up to a different accounting date, **adjustments should be made** for the effects of significant transactions or other events that occur between that date and the parent's reporting date.

2.6 Uniform accounting policies

Consolidated financial statements should be prepared using **the same accounting policies** for like transactions and other events in similar circumstances.

Adjustments must be made where members of a group use different accounting policies, so that their financial statements are suitable for consolidation.

2.7 Date of inclusion/exclusion

The results of subsidiary undertakings are included in the consolidated financial statements from:

(a)   the date of 'acquisition', ie the **date control passes to the parent**, to
(b)   the date of 'disposal', ie the **date control passes from the parent**.

Once an investment is no longer a subsidiary, it should be treated as an associate under IAS 28 (if applicable) or as an investment under IAS 39 (see Chapter 13).

2.8 Accounting for subsidiaries and associates in the parent's separate financial statements

A parent company will usually produce its own single company financial statements. In these statements, investments in subsidiaries and associates included in the consolidated financial statements should be *either*:

(a)   Accounted for at **cost**, *or*
(b)   In accordance with **IAS 39** (see Chapter 13).

Where subsidiaries are **classified as held for sale** in accordance with IFRS 5 they should be accounted for in accordance with IFRS 5 (see Chapter 4).

2.9 Disclosure

The disclosure requirements for **consolidated financial statements** are as follows.

(a)   **Summarised financial information** of **subsidiaries** that are **not consolidated**, either individually or in groups, including the amounts of total assets, total liabilities, revenues and profit or loss

(b) The nature of the **relationship** between the parent and a **subsidiary** of which the **parent** does **not own**, directly or indirectly through subsidiaries, **more than half of the voting power**

(c) For an investee of which more than half of the voting or potential voting power is owned, directly or indirectly through subsidiaries, but which, because of the absence of control, is not a subsidiary, the reasons **why** the **ownership** does **not constitute control**

(d) The reporting date of the financial statements of a subsidiary when such financial statements are used to prepare consolidated financial statements and are as of a reporting date or for a period that is different from that of the parent, and the **reason** for using a **different reporting date or different period**

(e) The nature and extent of any **restrictions** on the ability of subsidiaries to **transfer funds** to the parent in the form of cash dividends, repayment of loans or advances (ie borrowing arrangements, regulatory restraints etc)

Where a parent chooses to take advantage of the exemptions from preparing consolidated financial statements (see above) the **separate financial statements** must disclose:

(a) The fact that the financial statements are separate financial statements; that the exemption from consolidation has been used; the name and country of incorporation of the entity whose consolidated financial statements that comply with IFRSs have been published; and the address where those consolidated financial statements are obtainable

(b) A list of significant investments in subsidiaries, jointly controlled entities and associates, including the name, country of incorporation, proportion of ownership interest and, if different, proportion of voting power held

(c) A description of the method used to account for the investments listed under (b)

When a parent prepares separate financial statements in addition to consolidated financial statements, the separate financial statements must disclose:

(a) The fact that the statements are separate financial statements and the reasons why they have been prepared if not required by law

(b) Information about investments and the method used to account for them, as above.

2.10 Section summary

IAS 27 covers the basic rules and definitions of the parent-subsidiary relationship. You should learn:

- **Definitions**
- Rules for **exemption** from preparing consolidated financial statements
- **Disclosure**

3 Content of group accounts and group structure

FAST FORWARD

It is important to distinguish between the parent company individual accounts and the group accounts.

3.1 Introduction

The information contained in the individual statements of a parent company and each of its subsidiaries does not give a picture of the group's total activities. A **separate set of group statements** can be prepared from the individual ones. Remember that a group has no separate (legal) existence, except for accounting purposes.

Consolidated accounts are one form of group accounts which combines the information contained in the separate accounts of a holding company and its subsidiaries as if they were the accounts of a single entity. 'Group accounts' and 'consolidated accounts' are terms often used synonymously.

In simple terms a set of consolidated accounts is prepared by **adding together** the assets and liabilities of the parent company and each subsidiary. The **whole** of the assets and liabilities of each company are included, even though some subsidiaries may be only partly owned. The 'equity and liabilities' section of the statement of financial position will indicate how much of the net assets are attributable to the group and how much to outside investors in partly owned subsidiaries. These **outside investors** are known as the **non-controlling interest**.

Key term

> **Non-controlling interest**. The equity in a subsidiary not attributable, directly or indirectly, to a parent.
>
> *(IFRS 3, IAS 27)*

Non-controlling interest should be presented in the consolidated statement of financial position **within equity, separately from the parent shareholders' equity**.

Most parent companies present their own individual accounts and their group accounts in a single **package**. The package typically comprises the following.

- **Parent company financial statements**, which will include 'investments in subsidiary undertakings' as an asset in the statement of financial position, and income from subsidiaries (dividends) in the statement of comprehensive income
- **Consolidated statement of financial position**
- **Consolidated statement of comprehensive income** (or separate income statement)
- **Consolidated statement of cash flows**

It may not be necessary to publish all of the parent company's financial statements, depending on local or national regulations.

3.2 Group structure

With the difficulties of definition and disclosure dealt with, let us now look at group structures. The simplest are those in which a parent company has only a **direct interest** in the shares of its subsidiary companies. For example:

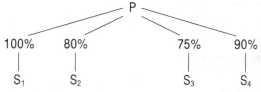

S_1 Co is a wholly owned subsidiary of P Co. S_2 Co, S_3 Co and S_4 Co are partly owned subsidiaries; a proportion of the shares in these companies is held by outside investors.

Often a parent will have **indirect holdings** in its subsidiary companies. This can lead to more complex group structures.

(a)

P Co owns 51% of the equity shares in S Co, which is therefore its subsidiary. S Co in its turn owns 51% of the equity shares in SS Co. SS Co is therefore a subsidiary of S Co and consequently a subsidiary of P Co. SS Co would describe S Co as its parent (or holding) company and P Co as its ultimate parent company.

Note that although P Co can control the assets and business of SS Co by virtue of the chain of control, its interest in the assets of SS Co is only 26%. This can be seen by considering a dividend of $100 paid by SS Co: as a 51% shareholder, S Co would receive $51; P Co would have an interest in 51% of this $51 = $26.01.

(b)

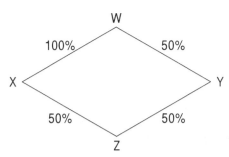

W Co owns 100% of the equity of X Co and 50% of the equity of Y Co. X Co and Y Co each own 50% of the equity of Z Co. Assume that:

(i)   W Co does not control the composition of Y Co's board, nor can it cast a majority of votes on the board

(ii)   W Co does not hold or control more than 50% of the **voting rights** in Y Co, either directly or by agreement with other investors

(iii)   W Co does not have the power to govern the financial or operating policies of Y Co by virtue of statute or an agreement

(iv)   None of the above apply to either X Co's or Y Co's holdings in Z Co

In other words, because W Co is not in co-operation with the holder(s) of the other 50% of the shares in Y Co, neither Y nor Z can be considered subsidiaries.

In that case:

(i)   X Co is a subsidiary of W Co
(ii)   Y Co is not a subsidiary of W Co
(iii)   Z Co is not a subsidiary of either X Co or Y Co. Consequently, it is not a subsidiary of W Co

If Z Co pays a dividend of $100, X Co and Y Co will each receive $50. The interest of W Co in this dividend is as follows.

	$
Through X Co (100% × $50)	50
Through Y Co (50% × $50)	25
	75

Although W Co has an interest in 75% of Z Co's assets, Z Co is not a subsidiary of W Co.

(c)

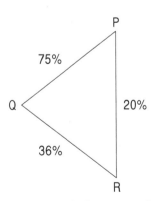

Q Co is a subsidiary of P Co. P Co therefore has indirect control over 36% of R Co's equity. P Co also has direct control over 20% of R Co's equity. R Co is therefore a subsidiary of P Co, although P Co's interest in R Co's assets is only 20% + (75% × 36%) = 47%.

Examples (b) and (c) illustrate an important point: in deciding whether a company A holds more than 50% of the equity (or equivalent) of an entity B it is necessary to aggregate:

- Shares (or equivalent) in B held directly by A
- Shares (or equivalent) in B held by entities which are subsidiaries of A

| Question | Consolidated accounts |

During the time until your examination you should obtain as many sets of the published accounts of large companies in your country as possible. Examine the accounting policies in relation to subsidiary and associated companies and consider how these policies are shown in the accounting and consolidation treatment. Consider the effect of any disposals during the year. Also, look at all the disclosures made relating to fair values, goodwill etc and match them to the disclosure requirements outlined in this chapter and in subsequent chapters on IFRS 3 and IAS 28.

Alternatively (or additionally) you should attempt to obtain such information from the financial press.

4 Group accounts: the related parties issue

FAST FORWARD

Parent companies and subsidiaries are **related parties** as per IAS 24. Bear in mind that this relationship can be exploited.

IAS 24 draws attention to the significance of related party relationships and transactions – that transactions between the parties may not be 'at arm's length' and that users of the accounts must be made aware of this, as it may affect their view of the financial statements.

4.1 Individual company accounts

The relationship between a parent and a subsidiary is the most obvious example of a related party relationship and it offers a number of opportunities for manipulating results. Some of these may be aimed at improving the parent's individual financial statements.

Any of the following could take place:

- The subsidiary sells goods to the parent company at an artificially low price. This increases parent company profit while reducing profit in the subsidiary, thus increasing profit available for distribution to parent company shareholders at the expense of the non-controlling interest.
- The parent sells goods to the subsidiary at an artificially high price. This has the same result as above.
- The subsidiary makes a loan to the parent at an artificially low rate of interest or the parent makes a loan to the subsidiary at an artificially high rate of interest. The loans will be cancelled on consolidation but the interest payments will transfer profits from the subsidiary to the parent.
- The parent can sell an asset to the subsidiary at an amount in excess of its carrying amount. This again serves to transfer profit (and cash) to the parent.

4.2 Consolidated accounts

The transactions above seek to improve the **individual** parent company accounts at the expense of the individual subsidiary accounts. Dividends are paid to shareholders on the basis of these individual company financial statements, not the consolidated financial statements.

The tightening up of the opportunities for excluding a subsidiary from consolidation under IAS 27 have reduced the opportunities for improving the appearance of the **consolidated** financial statements. Prior to this, a number of possibilities could be exploited:

- A group could obtain loans via a subsidiary, which was not then consolidated. The loan would not appear in the consolidated statement of financial position and group gearing (% of capital provided by loans) would appear lower than it actually was.

- Sale and leaseback transactions could be carried out in which assets were sold to a non-consolidated subsidiary and leased back under an operating lease. This enabled the asset and its associated borrowings to be removed from the statement of financial position.

4.3 Disposal of subsidiaries

While the situations above are all concerned with improving the appearance of the parent company or group financial statements at the expense of those of the subsidiary, there may be occasions where the **opposite** is the intention.

For instance, when a parent company has decided to dispose of its shares in a poorly-performing subsidiary, it may seek to enhance the results of that subsidiary for the purpose of selling at a profit. In this case, transactions such as those at 4.1 above may be undertaken in the other direction – to transfer profit from the **parent** to the **subsidiary**.

4.4 Effect on trading

Even where no related party transactions have taken place, the parent/subsidiary relationship can still affect how the parties do business. For instance if, prior to acquisition by the parent, the subsidiary had a major customer or supplier who was a competitor of the parent, that trading arrangement can be expected to cease. The subsidiary may itself have been a competitor of the parent, in which case it may now have had to withdraw from certain markets in favour of the parent.

Look out for any of these issues in a consolidated accounts question.

Chapter Roundup

- Many large businesses consist of several companies controlled by one central or administrative company. Together these companies are called a **group**. The controlling company, called the **parent** or **holding company** will own some or all of the shares in the other companies, called **subsidiaries**.

- IAS 27 requires a parent to present consolidated financial statements.

- It is important to distinguish between the parent company **individual accounts** and the **group accounts.**

- Parent companies and subsidiaries are **related parties** as per IAS 24. Bear in mind that this relationship can be exploited.

Quick Quiz

1 Define a 'subsidiary'.
2 When can control be assumed?
3 What accounting treatment does IAS 27 require of a parent company?
4 When is a parent exempted from preparing consolidated financial statements?
5 Under what circumstances should subsidiary undertakings be excluded from consolidation?
6 How should an investment in a subsidiary be accounted for in the separate financial statements of the parent?
7 What is a non-controlling interest?

1   An entity that is controlled by another entity.

2   When the parent owns more than half (ie over 50%) of the voting power of an entity, **unless** it can be clearly shown that such ownership does not constitute control.

3   The accounts of parent and subsidiary are combined and presented as a single entity.

4   When the parent is itself a wholly owned subsidiary, or a partially owned subsidiary and the non-controlling interests do not object.

5   Very rarely, if at all. See section 2.4.

6   (a)   At cost, or
     (b)   In accordance with IAS 39.

7   The equity in a subsidiary not attributable, directly or indirectly, to a parent.

The consolidated statement of financial position

Topic list	Syllabus reference
1 IAS 27 Summary of consolidation procedures	D1
2 Non-controlling interest	D3
3 Dividends paid by a subsidiary	D1
4 Goodwill arising on consolidation	D2
5 A technique of consolidation	D3
6 Intra-group trading	D1
7 Intra-group sales of non-current assets	D1
8 Summary: consolidated statement of financial position	D3
9 Acquisition of a subsidiary during its accounting period	D3
10 Dividends and pre-acquisition profits	D3
11 Fair values in acquisition accounting	D2

Introduction

This chapter introduces the **basic procedures** required in consolidation and gives a formal step plan for carrying out a statement of financial position consolidation. This step procedure should be useful to you as a starting guide for answering any question, but remember that you cannot rely on it to answer the question for you.

Each question must be approached and **answered on its own merits**. Examiners often put small extra or different problems in because, as they are always reminding students, it is not possible to 'rote-learn' consolidation.

The **method of consolidation** shown here uses schedules for workings (retained earnings, non-controlling interest etc) rather than the ledger accounts used in some other texts. This is because we believe that ledger accounts lead students to 'learn' the consolidation journals without thinking about what they are doing - always a dangerous practice in consolidation questions.

There are plenty of questions in this chapter - work through *all* of them carefully.

Study guide

D			BUSINESS COMBINATIONS	Intellectual level
1	(a)		explain why it is necessary to eliminate intra-group transactions.	2
2	(a)		describe and apply the required accounting treatment of consolidated goodwill.	2
	(b)		explain why it is necessary to use fair values for the consideration of an investment in a subsidiary together with the fair values of a subsidiary's identifiable assets and liabilities when preparing consolidated financial statements.	
3	(a)		prepare a consolidated statement of financial position for a simple group (parent and one subsidiary) dealing with pre and post acquisition profits, non-controlling interests and consolidated goodwill.	2
	(c)		explain and account for other reserves (eg. share premium and revaluation reserves).	1
	(d)		account for the effects (in the financial statements) of intra-group trading.	2
	(e)		account for the effects of fair value adjustments (including their effect on consolidated goodwill) to:	2
		(i)	depreciating and non-depreciating non-current assets	
		(ii)	inventory	
		(iii)	monetary liabilities	
		(iv)	assets and liabilities not included in the subsidiary's own statement of financial position, including contingent assets and liabilities.	
	(f)		account for goodwill impairment.	2

1 IAS 27 Summary of consolidation procedures

FAST FORWARD

> How are consolidated financial statements prepared? IAS 27 lays out the basic procedures and we will consider these in the rest of this chapter.

1.1 Basic procedure

The financial statements of a parent and its subsidiaries are **combined on a line-by-line basis** by adding together like items of assets, liabilities, equity, income and expenses.

The following steps are then taken, in order that the consolidated financial statements should **show financial information about the group as if it was a single entity**.

(a) The carrying amount of the parent's **investment in each subsidiary** and the parent's **portion of equity** of each subsidiary are **eliminated or cancelled**

(b) **Non-controlling interests in the net income of consolidated subsidiaries** are adjusted against group income, to arrive at the net income attributable to the owners of the parent

(c) **Non-controlling interests** in the net assets of consolidated subsidiaries should be presented separately in the consolidated statement of financial position

Other matters to be dealt with include the following.

(a) **Goodwill on consolidation** should be dealt with according to IFRS 3

(b) **Dividends paid** by a subsidiary must be accounted for

IAS 27 states that all intragroup balances and transactions, and the resulting **unrealised profits**, should be **eliminated in full**. **Unrealised losses** resulting from intragroup transactions should also be eliminated *unless* cost can be recovered. This will be explained later in this chapter.

1.2 Cancellation and part cancellation

The preparation of a consolidated statement of financial position, in a very simple form, consists of two procedures.

(a) Take the individual accounts of the parent company and each subsidiary and **cancel out items** which appear as an asset in one company and a liability in another.

(b) Add together all the uncancelled assets and liabilities throughout the group.

Items requiring cancellation may include the following.

(a) The asset **'shares in subsidiary companies'** which appears in the parent company's accounts will be matched with the liability 'share capital' in the subsidiaries' accounts.

(b) There may be **intra-group trading** within the group. For example, S Co may sell goods on credit to P Co. P Co would then be a receivable in the accounts of S Co, while S Co would be a payable in the accounts of P Co.

1.3 Example: cancellation

P Co regularly sells goods to its one subsidiary company, S Co, which it has owned since S Co's incorporation. The statement of financial position of the two companies on 31 December 20X6 are given below.

STATEMENT OF FINANCIAL POSITION AS AT 31 DECEMBER 20X6

	P Co $	S Co $
Assets		
Non-current assets		
Property, plant and equipment	35,000	45,000
Investment in 40,000 $1 shares in S Co at cost	40,000	
	75,000	
Current assets		
Inventories	16,000	12,000
Receivables: S Co	2,000	
Other	6,000	9,000
Cash at bank	1,000	
Total assets	100,000	66,000
Equity and liabilities		
Equity		
40,000 $1 ordinary shares		40,000
70,000 $1 ordinary shares	70,000	
Retained earnings	16,000	19,000
	86,000	59,000
Current liabilities		
Bank overdraft		3,000
Payables: P Co		2,000
Payables: Other	14,000	2,000
Total equity and liabilities	100,000	66,000

Required

Prepare the consolidated statement of financial position of P Co at 31 December 20X6.

Solution

The cancelling items are:

(a) P Co's asset 'investment in shares of S Co' ($40,000) cancels with S Co's liability 'share capital' ($40,000);

(b) P Co's asset 'receivables: S Co' ($2,000) cancels with S Co's liability 'payables: P Co' ($2,000).

The remaining assets and liabilities are added together to produce the following consolidated statement of financial position.

P CO

CONSOLIDATED STATEMENT OF FINANCIAL POSITION AS AT 31 DECEMBER 20X6

Assets	$	$
Non-current assets		
Property, plant and equipment		80,000
Current assets		
Inventories	28,000	
Receivables	15,000	
Cash at bank	1,000	
		44,000
Total assets		124,000
Equity and liabilities		
Equity		
70,000 $1 ordinary shares	70,000	
Retained earnings	35,000	
	105,000	
Current liabilities		
Bank overdraft	3,000	
Payables	16,000	
		19,000
Total equity and liabilities		124,000

Note the following.

(a) P Co's bank balance is **not netted off** with S Co's bank overdraft. To offset one against the other would be less informative and would conflict with the principle that assets and liabilities should not be netted off.

(b) The share capital in the consolidated statement of financial position is the **share capital of the parent company alone**. This must *always* be the case, no matter how complex the consolidation, because the share capital of subsidiary companies must *always* be a wholly cancelling item.

1.4 Part cancellation

An item may appear in the statements of financial position of a parent company and its subsidiary, but not at the same amounts.

(a) The parent company may have acquired **shares in the subsidiary** at a price **greater or less than their par value**. The asset will appear in the parent company's accounts at cost, while the liability will appear in the subsidiary's accounts at par value. This raises the issue of **goodwill**, which is dealt with later in this chapter.

(b) Even if the parent company acquired shares at par value, it **may not** have **acquired all the shares of the subsidiary** (so the subsidiary may be only partly owned). This raises the issue of **non-controlling interests**, which are also dealt with later in this chapter.

(c) The inter-company trading balances may be out of step because of **goods or cash in transit**.

(d) One company may have **issued loan stock** of which a **proportion only** is taken up by the other company.

The following question illustrates the techniques needed to deal with items (c) and (d) above. The procedure is to **cancel as far as possible**. The remaining uncancelled amounts will appear in the consolidated statement of financial position.

(a)   **Uncancelled loan stock** will appear as a **liability of the group**.

(b)   **Uncancelled balances on intra-group accounts** represent **goods or cash in transit**, which will appear in the consolidated statement of financial position.

Question	Cancellation

The statements of financial position of P Co and of its subsidiary S Co have been made up to 30 June. P Co has owned all the ordinary shares and 40% of the loan stock of S Co since its incorporation.

P CO
STATEMENT OF FINANCIAL POSITION AS AT 30 JUNE

	$	$
Assets		
Non-current assets		
Property, plant and equipment	120,000	
Investment in S Co, at cost		
80,000 ordinary shares of $1 each	80,000	
$20,000 of 12% loan stock in S Co	20,000	
		220,000
Current assets		
Inventories	50,000	
Receivables	40,000	
Current account with S Co	18,000	
Cash	4,000	
		112,000
Total assets		332,000
Equity and liabilities		
Equity		
Ordinary shares of $1 each, fully paid	100,000	
Retained earnings	95,000	
		195,000
Non-current liabilities		
10% loan stock		75,000
Current liabilities		
Payables	47,000	
Taxation	15,000	
		62,000
Total equity and liabilities		332,000

S CO
STATEMENT OF FINANCIAL POSITION AS AT 30 JUNE

	$	$
Assets		
Property, plant and equipment		100,000
Current assets		
Inventories	60,000	
Receivables	30,000	
Cash	6,000	
		96,000
Total assets		196,000

	$	$
Equity and liabilities		
Equity		
80,000 ordinary shares of $1 each, fully paid	80,000	
Retained earnings	28,000	
		108,000
Non-current liabilities		
12% loan stock		50,000
Current liabilities		
Payables	16,000	
Taxation	10,000	
Current account with P Co	12,000	
		38,000
Total equity and liabilities		196,000

The difference on current account arises because of goods in transit.

Required

Prepare the consolidated statement of financial position of P Co.

Answer

P CO
CONSOLIDATED STATEMENT OF FINANCIAL POSITION AS AT 30 JUNE

	$	$
Assets		
Non-current assets		
Property, plant and equipment (120,000 + 100,000)		220,000
Current assets		
Inventories (50,000 + 60,000)	110,000	
Goods in transit (18,000 – 12,000)	6,000	
Receivables (40,000 + 30,000)	70,000	
Cash (4,000 + 6,000)	10,000	
		196,000
Total assets		416,000
Equity and liabilities		
Equity		
Ordinary shares of $1 each, fully paid (parent)	100,000	
Retained earnings (95,000 + 28,000)	123,000	
		223,000
Non-current liabilities		
10% loan stock	75,000	
12% loan stock (50,000 × 60%)	30,000	
		105,000
Current liabilities		
Payables (47,000 + 16,000)	63,000	
Taxation (15,000 + 10,000)	25,000	
		88,000
Total equity and liabilities		416,000

Note especially how:

(a)   The uncancelled loan stock in S Co becomes a liability of the group
(b)   The goods in transit is the difference between the current accounts ($18,000 – $12,000)
(c)   The investment in S Co's shares is cancelled against S Co's share capital

2 Non-controlling interests

In the consolidated statement of financial position it is necessary to distinguish non-controlling interests from those net assets attributable to the group and financed by shareholders' equity.

2.1 Introduction

It was mentioned earlier that the total assets and liabilities of subsidiary companies are included in the consolidated statement of financial position, even in the case of subsidiaries which are only partly owned. A proportion of the net assets of such subsidiaries in fact belongs to investors from outside the group (**non-controlling interests**).

IFRS allows two alternative ways of calculating non-controlling interest in the group statement of financial position. Non-controlling interest can be valued at:

(a) Its proportionate share of the fair value of the subsidiary's net assets; or
(b) Full (or fair) value (usually based on the market value of the shares held by the non-controlling interest).

You are required to be able to apply both of these methods in F7. The exam question will tell you which method to use. If you are required to use the 'full (or fair) value' method, then you will be given the share price or told what the fair value of the non-controlling interest is.

The following example shows non-controlling interest calculated at its proportionate share of the subsidiary's net assets.

2.2 Example: non-controlling interest

P Co has owned 75% of the share capital of S Co since the date of S Co's incorporation. Their latest statements of financial position are given below.

P CO
STATEMENT OF FINANCIAL POSITION

	$	$
Assets		
Non-current assets		
Property, plant and equipment	50,000	
30,000 $1 ordinary shares in S Co at cost	30,000	
		80,000
Current assets		45,000
Total assets		125,000
Equity and liabilities		
Equity		
80,000 $1 ordinary shares	80,000	
Retained earnings	25,000	
		105,000
Current liabilities		20,000
Total equity and liabilities		125,000

S CO
STATEMENT OF FINANCIAL POSITION

	$	$
Assets		
Property, plant and equipment		35,000
Current assets		35,000
Total assets		70,000

	$	$
Equity and liabilities		
Equity		
40,000 $1 ordinary shares	40,000	
Retained earnings	10,000	
		50,000
Current liabilities		20,000
Total equity and liabilities		70,000

Required

Prepare the consolidated statement of financial position.

Solution

All of S Co's net assets are consolidated despite the fact that the company is only 75% owned. The amount of net assets attributable to non-controlling interests is calculated as follows.

	$
Non-controlling share of share capital (25% × $40,000)	10,000
Non-controlling share of retained earnings (25% × $10,000)	2,500
	12,500

Of S Co's share capital of $40,000, $10,000 is included in the figure for non-controlling interest, while $30,000 is cancelled with P Co's asset 'investment in S Co'.

The consolidated statement of financial position can now be prepared.

P GROUP
CONSOLIDATED STATEMENT OF FINANCIAL POSITION

	$	$
Assets		
Property, plant and equipment		85,000
Current assets		80,000
Total assets		165,000
Equity and liabilities		
Equity attributable to owners of the parent		
Share capital	80,000	
Retained earnings $(25,000 + (75% × $10,000))	32,500	
		112,500
Non-controlling interest		12,500
		125,000
Current liabilities		40,000
Total equity and liabilities		165,000

2.3 Procedure

(a) Aggregate the assets and liabilities in the statement of financial position ie 100% P + 100% S irrespective of how much P actually owns.

This shows the amount of net assets **controlled** by the group.

(b) Share capital is that of the parent only.

(c) Calculate the non-controlling interest share of the subsidiary's net assets (share capital plus reserves).

(d) Balance of subsidiary's reserves are consolidated (after cancelling any intra-group items).

Set out below are the draft statement of financial position of P Co and its subsidiary S Co. You are required to prepare the consolidated statement of financial position. The non-controlling interest is valued at its proportional share of the fair value of the subsidiary's net assets.

P CO

	$	$
Assets		
Non-current assets		
Property, plant and equipment		31,000
Investment in S Co		
12,000 $1 ordinary shares at cost	12,000	
$8,000 10% loan stock at cost	8,000	
		20,000
		51,000
Current assets		21,000
Total assets		72,000
Equity and liabilities		
Equity		
Ordinary shares of $1 each	40,000	
Retained earnings	22,000	
		62,000
Current liabilities		10,000
Total equity and liabilities		72,000

S CO

	$	$
Assets		
Property, plant and equipment		34,000
Current assets		32,000
Total assets		66,000
Equity and liabilities		
Equity		
Ordinary shares of $1 each	20,000	
Revaluation surplus	6,000	
Retained earnings	4,000	
		30,000
Non-current liabilities		
10% loan stock		26,000
Current liabilities		10,000
Total equity and liabilities		66,000

Answer

The group structure is:

P Co

60%

S Co

Partly cancelling items are the components of P Co's investment in S Co, ie ordinary shares, loan stock. Non-controlling shareholders have an interest in 40% (8,000/20,000) of S Co's ordinary shares, including reserves.

You should now aggregate the assets and liabilities and produce workings for non-controlling interest, revaluation surplus and retained earnings as follows.

Workings

1   *Non-controlling interest*

		$
S Co's net assets (66,000 – 36,000)		30,000
× 40%		12,000

2   *Revaluation surplus*

	$
P Co	–
Share of S Co's revaluation surplus (60% × 6,000)	3,600
	3,600

3   *Retained earnings*

	$
P Co	22,000
Share of S Co's retained earnings (60% × 4,000)	2,400
	24,400

The results of the workings are now used to construct the consolidated statement of financial position.

P GROUP
CONSOLIDATED STATEMENT OF FINANCIAL POSITION

	$	$
Assets		
Property, plant and equipment		65,000
Current assets		53,000
Total assets		118,000
Equity and liabilities		
Equity attributable to owners of the parent		
Ordinary shares of $1 each	40,000	
Revaluation surplus (W2)	3,600	
Retained earnings (W3)	24,400	
		68,000
Non-controlling interest (W1)		12,000
		80,000
Non-current liabilities		
10% loan stock (26,000 – 8,000)		18,000
Current liabilities		20,000
Total equity and liabilities		118,000

Notes

(a)   S Co is a subsidiary of P Co because P Co owns 60% of its ordinary capital.

(b)   As always, the share capital in the consolidated statement of financial position is that of the parent company alone. The share capital in S Co's statement of financial position was partly cancelled against the investment shown in P Co's balance sheet, while the uncancelled portion was credited to non-controlling interest.

(c)   The figure for non-controlling interest comprises the interest of outside investors in the share capital and reserves of the subsidiary. The uncancelled portion of S Co's loan stock is not shown as part of non-controlling interest but is disclosed separately as a liability of the group.

3 Dividends paid by a subsidiary

When a subsidiary company pays a **dividend** during the year the accounting treatment is not difficult. Suppose S Co, a 60% subsidiary of P Co, pays a dividend of $1,000 on the last day of its accounting period. Its total reserves before paying the dividend stood at $5,000.

(a) $400 of the dividend is paid to non-controlling shareholders. The cash leaves the group and will not appear anywhere in the consolidated statement of financial position.

(b) The parent company receives $600 of the dividend, debiting cash and crediting profit or loss. This will be cancelled on consolidation.

(c) The remaining balance of retained earnings in S Co's statement of financial position ($4,000) will be consolidated in the normal way. The group's share (60% × $4,000 = $2,400) will be included in group retained earnings in the statement of financial position; the non-controlling interest share (40% × $4,000 = $1,600) is credited to the non-controlling interest account in the statement of financial position.

However, the situation is more complicated when a subsidiary pays a dividend shortly after acquisition and some of that dividend is deemed to been paid from pre-acquisition profits. This situation is considered in Section 10.

4 Goodwill arising on consolidation

In the examples we have looked at so far the cost of shares acquired by the parent company has always been equal to the par value of those shares. This is seldom the case in practice and we must now consider some more complicated examples.

4.1 Accounting

To begin with, **we will examine the entries made by the parent company in its own statement of financial position when it acquires shares.**

When a company P Co wishes to **purchase shares** in a company S Co it must pay the previous owners of those shares. The most obvious form of payment would be in **cash**. Suppose P Co purchases all 40,000 $1 shares in S Co and pays $60,000 cash to the previous shareholders in consideration. The entries in P Co's books would be:

DEBIT   Investment in S Co at cost $60,000
CREDIT   Bank $60,000

However, the previous shareholders might be prepared to accept some other form of consideration. For example, they might accept an agreed number of **shares** in P Co. P Co would then issue new shares in the agreed number and allot them to the former shareholders of S Co. This kind of deal might be attractive to P Co since it avoids the need for a heavy cash outlay. The former shareholders of S Co would retain an indirect interest in that company's profitability via their new holding in its parent company.

Continuing the example, suppose the shareholders of S Co agreed to accept one $1 ordinary share in P Co for every two $1 ordinary shares in S Co. P Co would then need to issue and allot 20,000 new $1 shares. How would this transaction be recorded in the books of P Co?

The simplest method would be as follows.

DEBIT   Investment in S Co $20,000
CREDIT   Share capital $20,000

However, if the 40,000 $1 shares acquired in S Co are thought to have a value of $60,000 this would be misleading. The former shareholders of S Co have presumably agreed to accept 20,000 shares in P Co because they consider each of those shares to have a value of $3. This view of the matter suggests the following method of recording the transaction in P Co's books.

DEBIT	Investment in S Co	$60,000	
CREDIT	Share capital		$20,000
	Share premium account		$40,000

The second method is the one which should normally be used in preparing consolidated accounts.

The amount which P Co records in its books as the cost of its investment in S Co may be more or less than the book value of the assets it acquires. Suppose that S Co in the previous example has nil reserves and nil liabilities, so that its share capital of $40,000 is balanced by tangible assets with a book value of $40,000. For simplicity, assume that the book value of S Co's assets is the same as their market or fair value.

Now when the directors of P Co agree to pay $60,000 for a 100% investment in S Co they must believe that, in addition to its tangible assets of $40,000, S Co must also have intangible assets worth $20,000. This amount of $20,000 paid over and above the value of the tangible assets acquired is called **goodwill arising on consolidation** (sometimes **premium on acquisition**).

Following the normal cancellation procedure the $40,000 share capital in S Co's statement of financial position could be cancelled against $40,000 of the 'investment in S Co' in the statement of financial position of P Co. This would leave a $20,000 debit uncancelled in the parent company's accounts and this $20,000 would appear in the consolidated statement of financial position under the caption 'Intangible non-current assets: goodwill arising on consolidation'.

4.2 Goodwill and pre-acquisition profits

Up to now we have assumed that S Co had nil retained earnings when its shares were purchased by P Co. Assuming instead that S Co had earned profits of $8,000 in the period before acquisition, its statement of financial position just before the purchase would look as follows.

	$
Total assets	48,000
Share capital	40,000
Retained earnings	8,000
	48,000

If P Co now purchases all the shares in S Co it will acquire total assets worth $48,000 at a cost of $60,000. Clearly in this case S Co's intangible assets (goodwill) are being valued at $12,000. It should be apparent that any earnings retained by the subsidiary **prior to its acquisition** by the parent company must be **incorporated in the cancellation** process so as to arrive at a figure for goodwill arising on consolidation. In other words, not only S Co's share capital, but also its **pre-acquisition** retained earnings, must be cancelled against the asset 'investment in S Co' in the accounts of the parent company. The uncancelled balance of $12,000 appears in the consolidated statement of financial position.

The consequence of this is that **any pre-acquisition retained earnings of a subsidiary company are not aggregated with the parent company's retained earnings** in the consolidated statement of financial position. The figure of consolidated retained earnings comprises the retained earnings of the parent company plus the **post-acquisition retained earnings only of subsidiary companies**. The post-acquisition retained earnings are simply retained earnings now *less* retained earnings at acquisition.

4.3 Example: goodwill and pre-acquisition profits

Sing Co acquired the ordinary shares of Wing Co on 31 March when the draft statements of financial position of each company were as follows.

SING CO
STATEMENT OF FINANCIAL POSITION AS AT 31 MARCH

	$
Assets	
Non-current assets	
Investment in 50,000 shares of Wing Co at cost	80,000
Current assets	40,000
Total assets	120,000
Equity and liabilities	
Equity	
Ordinary shares	75,000
Retained earnings	45,000
Total equity and liabilities	120,000

WING CO
STATEMENT OF FINANCIAL POSITION AS AT 31 MARCH

	$
Current assets	60,000
Equity	
50,000 ordinary shares of $1 each	50,000
Retained earnings	10,000
	60,000

Prepare the consolidated statement of financial position as at 31 March.

Solution

The technique to adopt here is to produce a new working: 'Goodwill'. A proforma working is set out below.

Goodwill

	$	$
Consideration transferred		X
Non-controlling interest at acquisition		X
Net assets acquired as represented by:		X
Ordinary share capital	X	
Share premium	X	
Retained earnings on acquisition	X	
		(X)
Goodwill		X

Applying this to our example the working will look like this.

	$	$
Consideration transferred		80,000
Non-controlling interest		-
Net assets acquired as represented by:		80,000
Ordinary share capital	50,000	
Retained earnings on acquisition	10,000	
		(60,000)
Goodwill		20,000

SING CO
CONSOLIDATED STATEMENT OF FINANCIAL POSITION AS AT 31 MARCH

	$
Assets	
Non-current assets	
Goodwill arising on consolidation	20,000
Current assets	100,000
	120,000

Equity

Ordinary shares	75,000
Retained earnings	45,000
	120,000

4.4 Goodwill and non-controlling interest

Not let us look at what would happen if Sing Co had obtained less than 100% of the shares of Wing Co.

If Sing Co had paid $80,000 for 40,000 shares in Wing Co, the goodwill working would be as follows:

	$
Consideration transferred	80,000
Non-controlling interest (60,000 × 20%)	12,000
Net assets acquired	(60,000)
Goodwill	32,000

The goodwill has been increased by the non-controlling interest – Sing Co has paid the same amount but acquired a smaller shareholding.

Note: Work out the net assets and **then** the non-controlling interest.

4.5 Non-controlling interest at fair value

IFRS 3 (revised) gives entities the option of valuing non-controlling interest at fair value. The thinking behind this is that the non-controlling interest, in purchasing their shares, also purchased goodwill in the subsidiary, and that the traditional method of consolidation does not show this goodwill.

IFRS 3 revised suggests that the closest approximation to fair value will be the market price of the shares held by non-controlling shareholders just before acquisition by the parent.

Continuing our example above, we will assume that the market price of the shares was $1.25. The goodwill calculation will then be as follows:

	$
Consideration transferred	80,000
Non-controlling interest (10,000 × $1.25)	12,500
Net assets at acquisition	(60,000)
Goodwill	32,500

Goodwill is $500 higher than goodwill calculated measuring non-controlling interest at its share of the net assets of the subsidiary. This $500 represents the **goodwill attributable to the non-controlling interest**.

4.6 Non-controlling interest at year end

Where the option is used to value non-controlling interest at fair value, this applies only to **non-controlling interest at acquisition**. At the year end, the non-controlling interest is measured at its share of the subsidiary's year end net assets, subject to adjustments for intra-group trading which we will cover later in this chapter.

However, **where the fair value option has been used**, goodwill at the year end will include the additional goodwill attributable to the non-controlling interest, in the example above $500. The other side of the entry is to **add the goodwill onto the non-controlling interest at the year end**.

This is illustrated in the following worked example.

4.7 Worked example

P acquired 75% of the shares in S on 1 January 2007 when S had retained earnings of $15,000. The market price of S's shares just before the date of acquisition was $1.60. P values non-controlling interest at fair value. Goodwill is not impaired.

The statements of financial position of P and S at 31 December 20X7 were as follows:

	P	S
	$	$
Property, plant and equipment	60,000	50,000
Shares in S	68,000	–
Current assets	128,000	50,000
	52,000	35,000
	180,000	85,000
Share capital – $1 shares	100,000	50,000
Retained earnings	70,000	25,000
	170,000	75,000
Current liabilities	10,000	10,000
	180,000	85,000

Prepare the consolidated statement of financial position of the P Group.

4.8 Solution

CONSOLIDATED STATEMENT OF FINANCIAL POSITION

	$
Assets	
Property plant and equipment (60,000 + 50,000)	110,000
Goodwill (W1)	23,000
Current assets (52,000 + 35,000)	87,000
Total assets	220,000
Equity and liabilities	
Equity attributable to the owners of P	
Share capital	100,000
Retained earnings (W2)	77,500
	177,500
Non-controlling interest (W3)	22,500
Total equity	200,000
Current liabilities (10,000 + 10,000)	20,000
	220,000

Workings

1. *Goodwill*

	$
Consideration transferred	68,000
Non-controlling interest at acquisition (12,500 shares @ $1.60)	20,000
Net assets of S at acquisition (50,000 + 15,000)	(65,000)
Goodwill (parent and non-controlling interest)	23,000
Non-controlling interest at fair value (as above)	20,000
Non-controlling share of net assets at acquisition (65,000 × 25%)	(16,250)
Goodwill attributable to non-controlling interest	3,750

2. *Retained earnings*

	P	S
	$	$
Per statement of financial position	70,000	25,000
Less pre- acquisition		(15,000)
		10,000
Group share of S (10,000 × 75%)	7,500	
Group retained earnings	77,500	

3.   *Non-controlling interest at year end*

	$
Share of net assets of S (75,000 × 25%)	18,750
Goodwill (W1)	3,750
	22,500

4.9 Effect of non-controlling interest at fair value

You can see from the above example that the use of the fair value option increases goodwill and non-controlling interest by the same amount. That amount represents goodwill attributable to the shares held by non-controlling shareholders. It is not necessarily proportionate to the goodwill attributed to the parent. The parent may have paid more to acquire a controlling interest. If non-controlling interest was valued under the usual method (share of net assets) goodwill and non-controlling interest in the example above would be as follows:

W1 Goodwill

	$
Considered transferred	68,000
Non-controlling interest ((50,000 + 15,000) × 25%)	16,250
Net assets of S at acquisition (50,000 + 15,000)	(65,000)
	19,250

W3 Non-controlling interest at year end

	$
Share of net assets of S (75,000 × 25%)	18,750

Compare these with goodwill and non-controlling interest in the solution above and you will see that both have been reduced by $3,750 – the goodwill attributable to the non-controlling interest. So whether non-controlling interest is valued at share of net assets or at fair value, the statement of financial position will still balance.

Exam focus point

> The option to value non-controlling interest at fair value is introduced by the revised IFRS 3, but it is just an **option**. Companies can choose to adopt it or to continue to value non-controlling interest at share of net assets. In the exam, unless you are directed to apply the fair value option, you should value non-controlling interest at share of net assets. It is likely that the examiner will specifically tell you this. If you are required to use the fair value option, the examiner has stated that there are three possible options:
>
> 1)   You may be given the share price of the subsidiary just before acquisition.
> 2)   You may be told that the non-controlling interest is valued at a certain amount.
> 3)   You may be given the amount of goodwill attributable to the non-controlling interest. In this case you would calculate goodwill and non-controlling interest under the traditional method and then add the goodwill to both of them.
>
> **In the exam**, the consolidation question will tell you which method of use. It will state either:
>
> 'It is the group policy to value the non-controlling interest at full (or fair) value;' or
>
> 'It is the group policy to value the non-controlling interest at its proportionate share of the (fair value of the) subsidiary's identifiable net assets'.

4.10 Impairment of goodwill

Goodwill arising on consolidation is subjected to an annual impairment review and impairment may be expressed as an amount or as a percentage. The double entry to write off the impairment is:
DR Group retained earnings   CR Goodwill.

However, when non-controlling interest is valued at **fair value** the goodwill in the statement of financial position includes goodwill attributable to the non-controlling interest. In this case the double entry will reflect the non-controlling interest proportion based on their shareholding as follows:

DEBIT Group retained earnings   CREDIT Goodwill
DEBIT Non-controlling interest

In our solution above in 4.8 the non-controlling interest holds 25%. If the goodwill of $23,000 was impaired by 20% the double entry for this would be:

	$		$
DEBIT Retained earnings	3,450	CREDIT Goodwill	4,600
DEBIT Non-controlling interest	1,150		

Non-controlling interest at the year end would then be $21,350.

4.11 Gain on a bargain purchase

Goodwill arising on consolidation is one form of **purchased goodwill**, and is governed by IFRS 3. As explained in an earlier chapter IFRS 3 requires that goodwill arising on consolidation should **be capitalised in the consolidated statement of financial position** and **reviewed for impairment every year**.

Goodwill arising on consolidation is the difference between the cost of an acquisition and the value of the subsidiary's net assets acquired. This difference can be **negative**: the aggregate of the fair values of the separable net assets acquired may **exceed** what the parent company paid for them. IFRS 3 refers to this as a 'bargain purchase'. In this situation:

(a)   An entity should first **re-assess** the amounts at which it has measured both the cost of the combination and the acquiree's identifiable net assets. This exercise should **identify any errors.**

(b)   Any **excess remaining** should be **recognised immediately in profit or loss**.

4.12 Forms of consideration

The consideration paid by the parent for the shares in the subsidiary can take different forms and this will affect the calculation of goodwill. Here are some examples:

4.12.1 Contingent consideration

The parent acquired 60% of the subsidiary's $100m share capital on 1 Jan 20X6 for a cash payment of $150m and a further payment of $50m on 31 March 20X7 if the subsidiary's post acquisition profits have exceeded an agreed figure by that date.

In the financial statements for the year to 31 December 20X6 $50m will be added to the cost of the combination, discounted as appropriate.

IFRS 3 requires the acquisition-date **fair value** of contingent consideration to be recognised as part of the consideration for the acquiree. In an examination question students will be told the acquisition-date fair value or told how to calculate it.

The acquirer may be required to pay contingent consideration in the form of equity or of a debt instrument or cash. A debt instrument should be presented as under IAS 32. Contingent consideration can also be an asset, if the consideration has already been transferred and the acquirer has the right to return of some of it, if certain considerations are met.

Note: The previous version of IFRS 3 only required contingent consideration to be recognised if it was **probable** that it would become payable. IFRS 3 revised dispenses with this requirement – **all contingent consideration is now recognised**. It is possible that the fair value of the contingent consideration may change after the acquisition date. If this is due to additional information obtained that affects the position at acquisition date goodwill should be remeasured. If the change is due to events after the acquisition date (such as a higher earnings target has been met, so more is payable) it should be accounted for under IAS 39 if the consideration is in the form of a financial instrument (such as loan notes) or under IAS 37 as an increase in a provision if it is cash. Any equity instrument is not remeasured.

4.12.2 Deferred consideration

The parent acquired 75% of the subsidiary's 80m $1 shares on 1 Jan 20X6. It paid $3.50 per share and agreed to pay a further $108m on 1 Jan 20X8.

The parent company's cost of capital is 8%.

In the financial statements for the year to 31 December 20X6 the cost of the combination will be as follows:

	$m
80m shares × 75% × $3.50	210
Deferred consideration:	
$108m × 1/1.08	100
Total consideration	310

At 31 December 20X7, the cost of the combination will be unchanged but $8 will be charged to finance costs, being the unwinding of the discount on the deferred consideration.

4.12.3 Share exchange

The parent has acquired 12,000 $1 shares in the subsidiary by issuing 5 of its own $1 shares for every 4 shares in the subsidiary. The market value of the parent company's shares is $6.

Cost of the combination:

	$
12,000 × 5/4 × $6	90,000

Note that this is credited to the share capital and share premium of the parent company as follows:

	DR	CR
Investment in subsidiary	90,000	
Share capital ($12,000 × 5/4)		15,000
Share premium ($12,000 × 5/4 × 5)		75,000

4.12.4 Expenses and issue costs

Expenses of the combination, such as lawyers and accountants fees are written off as incurred. However, IFRS 3 requires that the costs of issuing equity are treated as a deduction from the proceeds of the equity issue. Share issue costs will therefore be debited to the share premium account. Issue costs of financial instruments are deducted from the proceeds of the financial instrument.

4.13 Adjustments to goodwill

At the date of acquisition the parent recognises the assets, liabilities and contingent liabilities of the subsidiary at their fair value at the date when control is acquired. It may be that some of these assets or liabilities had not previously been recognised by the acquiree.

For instance, the subsidiary may have tax losses brought forward, but had not recognised these as an asset because it could not foresee future profits against which they could be offset. If it now appears that taxable profits will be forthcoming, the deferred tax asset can be recognised.

An entity has acquired a 60% interest in another entity which has brought forward tax losses unutilised of $200,000. The tax losses can now be utilised.

The adjustment will be:

	DR	CR
Deferred tax (subsidiary)	200,000	
Goodwill		200,000

5 A technique of consolidation

FAST FORWARD

We have now looked at the topics of cancellation, non-controlling interests and goodwill arising on consolidation. It is time to set out an approach to be used in tackling **consolidated statements of financial position**.

1   Aggregate the assets and liabilities on the statement of financial position. Cancel common items.
2   Calculate goodwill.
3   Calculate non-controlling interest.
4   Calculate retained earnings.

Question   Consolidated statement of financial position

The draft statements of financial position of Ping Co and Pong Co on 30 June 20X4 were as follows.

PING CO
STATEMENT OF FINANCIAL POSITION AS AT 30 JUNE 20X4

	$	$
Assets		
Non-current assets		
Property, plant and equipment	50,000	
20,000 ordinary shares in Pong Co at cost	30,000	
		80,000
Current assets		
Inventory	3,000	
Receivables	16,000	
Cash	2,000	
		21,000
Total assets		101,000
Equity and liabilities		
Equity		
Ordinary shares of $1 each	45,000	
Revaluation surplus	12,000	
Retained earnings	26,000	
		83,000
Current liabilities		
Owed to Pong Co	8,000	
Trade payables	10,000	
		18,000
Total equity and liabilities		101,000

PONG CO
STATEMENT OF FINANCIAL POSITION AS AT 30 JUNE 20X4

	$	$
Assets		
Property, plant and equipment		40,000
Current assets		
Inventory	8,000	
Owed by Ping Co	10,000	
Receivables	7,000	
		25,000
Total assets		65,000
Equity and liabilities		
Equity		
Ordinary shares of $1 each	25,000	
Revaluation surplus	5,000	
Retained earnings	28,000	
		58,000
Current liabilities		
Trade payables		7,000
Total equity and liabilities		65,000

Ping Co acquired its investment in Pong Co on 1 July 20X1 when the retained earnings of Pong Co stood at $6,000. There have been no changes in the share capital or revaluation surplus of Pong Co since that date. At 30 June 20X4 Pong Co had invoiced Ping Co for goods to the value of $2,000 which had not been received by Ping Co.

There is no impairment of goodwill. It is group policy to value non-controlling interest at its proportionate share of the subsidiary's identifiable net assets.

Prepare the consolidated statement of financial position of Ping Co as at 30 June 20X4.

Answer

1   **Agree current accounts.**

Ping Co has goods in transit of $2,000 making its total inventory $3,000 + $2,000 = $5,000 and its liability to Pong Co $8,000 + $2,000 = $10,000.

Cancel common items: these are the current accounts between the two companies of $10,000 each.

2   **Calculate goodwill.**

Goodwill

	$	$
Consideration transferred		30,000
Non-controlling interest (W3)		7,200
		37,200
Net assets acquired as represented by:		
Ordinary share capital	25,000	
Revaluation surplus on acquisition	5,000	
Retained earnings on acquisition	6,000	
		(36,000)
Goodwill		1,200

This goodwill must be capitalised in the consolidated statement of financial position.

3   **Calculate non-controlling interest**

(a)   *at acquisition*

	$
Pong Co's net assets (W2)	36,000
× 20%	7,200

(b)   *at year end*

	$
Pong Co's net assets (65,000 − 7,000)	58,000
× 20%	11,600

4   **Calculate consolidated reserves.**

Consolidated revaluation surplus

	$
Ping Co	12,000
Share of Pong Co's post acquisition revaluation surplus	−
	12,000

Consolidated retained earnings

	Ping	Pong
	$	$
Retained earnings per question	26,000	28,000
Less pre-acquisition		(6,000)
		22,000
Share of Pong: 80% × $22,000	17,600	
	43,600	

5   Prepare the consolidated statement of financial position.

PING CO
CONSOLIDATED STATEMENT OF FINANCIAL POSITION AS AT 30 JUNE 20X4

	$	$
Assets		
Non-current assets		
Property, plant and equipment ($50,000 + $40,000)		90,000
Intangible asset: goodwill		1,200
Current assets		
Inventories ($5,000 + $8,000)	13,000	
Receivables ($16,000 + $7,000)	23,000	
Cash	2,000	
		38,000
Total assets		129,200
Equity and liabilities		
Equity		
Ordinary shares of $1 each	45,000	
Revaluation surplus	12,000	
Retained earnings	43,600	
		100,600
Non-controlling interest		11,600
		112,200
Current liabilities		
Trade payables ($10,000 + $7,000)		17,000
Total equity and liabilities		129,200

5.1 Non-controlling interest at fair value

Now we will look at how the answer to the question above would appear if the non-controlling interest was at fair value. We will take a share price of $1.50. The non-controlling interest would become:

	$
5,000 shares at $1.50	7,500

Now let us look at how this affects the goodwill calculation:

	$
Consideration transferred	30,000
Non-controlling interest	7,500
Net assets of Pong Co	(36,000)
Goodwill	1,500

The non-controlling interest at acquisition has increased by $300 (7,500 – 7,200) and the goodwill has increased by the same amount (1,500 – 1,200). If the share price were $1.25, the non-controlling interest would be $6,250, a reduction of $950 from the original value of $7,200 and the goodwill would be (30,000 + 6,250 – 36,000 = 250) – a reduction of $950 from the original value of $1,200.

Note: In this text, unless stated otherwise, non-controlling interest is valued at share of fair value of net assets.

Exam focus point

A consolidated statement of financial position will come up as regularly as clockwork. There will nearly always be an adjustment for intra-group trading, which we look at next.

6 Intra-group trading

We have already come across cases where one company in a group engages in trading with another group company.

6.1 Unrealised profit

Any receivable/payable balances outstanding between the companies are cancelled on consolidation. No further problem arises if all such intra-group transactions are **undertaken at cost**, without any mark-up for profit.

However, each company in a group is a separate trading entity and may wish to treat other group companies in the same way as any other customer. In this case, a company (say A Co) may buy goods at one price and sell them at a higher price to another group company (B Co). The accounts of A Co will quite properly include the profit earned on sales to B Co; and similarly B Co's statement of financial position will include inventories at their cost to B Co, ie at the amount at which they were purchased from A Co.

This gives rise to two problems.

(a)   Although A Co makes a profit as soon as it sells goods to B Co, the group does not make a sale or achieve a profit until an outside customer buys the goods from B Co.

(b)   Any purchases from A Co which remain unsold by B Co at the year end will be included in B Co's inventory. Their value in the statement of financial position will be their cost to B Co, which is not the same as their cost to the group.

The objective of consolidated accounts is to present the financial position of several connected companies as that of a single entity, the group. This means that **in a consolidated statement of financial position the only profits recognised should be those earned by the group** in providing goods or services to outsiders; and similarly, inventory in the consolidated statement of financial position should be valued at cost to the group.

Suppose that a holding company P Co buys goods for $1,600 and sells them to a wholly owned subsidiary S Co for $2,000. The goods are in S Co's inventory at the year end and appear in S Co's statement of financial position at $2,000. In this case, P Co will record a profit of $400 in its individual accounts, but from the group's point of view the figures are:

Cost	$1,600
External sales	nil
Closing inventory at cost	$1,600
Profit/loss	nil

If we add together the figures for retained earnings and inventory in the individual statements of financial position of P Co and S Co the resulting figures for consolidated retained earnings and consolidated inventory will each be overstated by $400. A **consolidation adjustment** is therefore necessary as follows.

DEBIT   Group retained earnings
CREDIT   Group inventory (statement of financial position)

with the amount of **profit unrealised** by the group.

P Co acquired all the shares in S Co one year ago when the reserves of S Co stood at $10,000. Draft statements of financial position for each company are as follows.

	P Co $	P Co $	S Co $	S Co $
Assets				
Non-current assets				
Property, plant and equipment	80,000			40,000
Investment in S Co at cost	46,000			
		126,000		
Current assets		40,000		30,000
Total assets		166,000		70,000
Equity and liabilities				
Equity				
Ordinary shares of $1 each	100,000		30,000	
Retained earnings	45,000		22,000	
		145,000		52,000
Current liabilities		21,000		18,000
Total equity and liabilities		166,000		70,000

During the year S Co sold goods to P Co for $50,000, the profit to S Co being 20% of selling price. At the end of the reporting period, $15,000 of these goods remained unsold in the inventories of P Co. At the same date, P Co owed S Co $12,000 for goods bought and this debt is included in the trade payables of P Co and the receivables of S Co. The goodwill arising on consolidation has been impaired. The amount of the impairment is $1,500.

Required

Prepare a draft consolidated statement of financial position for P Co.

Answer

1 Goodwill

	$	$
Consideration transferred		46,000
Non-controlling interest		-
Net assets acquired as represented by		
Share capital	30,000	
Retained earnings	10,000	
		(40,000)
Goodwill		6,000

2 Retained earnings

	P Co $	S Co $
Retained earnings per question	45,000	22,000
Unrealised profit: 20% × $15,000	(3,000)	
	42,000	
Pre-acquisition		(10,000)
		12,000
Share of S Co	12,000	
Goodwill impairment loss	(1,500)	
	52,500	

P CO
CONSOLIDATED STATEMENT OF FINANCIAL POSITION

	$	$
Assets		
Non-current assets		
Property, plant and equipment	120,000	
Goodwill (6,000 – 1,500)	4,500	
		124,500
Current assets (W1)		55,000
Total assets		179,500
Equity and liabilities		
Equity		
Ordinary shares of $1 each	100,000	
Retained earnings	52,500	
		152,500
Current liabilities (W2)		27,000
Total equity and liabilities		179,500

Workings

1 *Current assets*

	$	$
In P Co's statement of financial position		40,000
In S Co's statement of financial position	30,000	
Less S Co's current account with P Co cancelled	(12,000)	
		18,000
		58,000
Less unrealised profit excluded from inventory valuation		(3,000)
		55,000

2 *Current liabilities*

	$
In P Co's statement of financial position	21,000
Less P Co's current account with S Co cancelled	(12,000)
	9,000
In S Co's statement of financial position	18,000
	27,000

6.2 Non-controlling interests in unrealised intra-group profits

A further problem occurs where a subsidiary company which is **not wholly owned is involved in intra-group trading** within the group. If a subsidiary S Co is 75% owned and sells goods to the parent company for $16,000 cost plus $4,000 profit, ie for $20,000 and if these items are unsold by P Co at the end of the reporting period, the 'unrealised' profit of $4,000 earned by S Co and charged to P Co will be partly owned by the non-controlling interest of S Co. As far as the non-controlling interest of S Co is concerned, their share (25% of $4,000) amounting to $1,000 of profit on the sale of goods would appear to have been fully realised. It is only the group that has not yet made a profit on the sale.

There are three different possibilities as regards the treatment of these intra-group profits.

(a)   Remove only the group's share of the profit loading

(b)   **Remove the whole profit loading, charging the non-controlling interest with their proportion**

(c)   Remove the whole of the profit without charging the non-controlling interest (to reduce group retained earnings by the whole profit loading)

The method given under (b) is usually considered best practice and the double entry is therefore as follows.

DEBIT	Group retained earnings
DEBIT	Non-controlling interest
CREDIT	Group inventory (statement of financial position)

6.3 Example: non-controlling interests and intra-group profits

P Co has owned 75% of the shares of S Co since the incorporation of that company. During the year to 31 December 20X2, S Co sold goods costing $16,000 to P Co at a price of $20,000 and these goods were still unsold by P Co at the end of the year. Draft statements of financial position of each company at 31 December 20X2 were as follows.

	P Co		S Co	
Assets	$	$	$	$
Non-current assets				
Property, plant and equipment	125,000		120,000	
Investment: 75,000 shares in S Co at cost	75,000		–	
		200,000		120,000
Current assets				
Inventories	50,000		48,000	
Trade receivables	20,000		16,000	
		70,000		64,000
Total assets		270,000		184,000
Equity and liabilities				
Equity				
Ordinary shares of $1 each fully paid	80,000		100,000	
Retained earnings	150,000		60,000	
		230,000		160,000
Current liabilities		40,000		24,000
Total equity and liabilities		270,000		184,000

Required

Prepare the consolidated statement of financial position of P Co at 31 December 20X2. It is the group policy to value the non-controlling interest at its proportionate share of the subsidiary's net assets.

Solution

The profit earned by S Co but unrealised by the group is $4,000 of which $3,000 (75%) is attributable to the group and $1,000 (25%) to the non-controlling interest. Remove the whole of the profit loading, charging the non-controlling interest with their proportion.

	P Co	S Co
	$	$
Retained earnings		
Per question	150,000	60,000
Less unrealised profit		(4,000)
		56,000
Share of S Co: $56,000 × 75%	42,000	
	192,000	
Non-controlling interest		
S Co's net assets (184,000 – 24,000)		160,000
Unrealised profit		(4,000)
		156,000
× 25%		39,000

P CO
CONSOLIDATED STATEMENT OF FINANCIAL POSITION AS AT 31 DECEMBER 20X2

	$	$
Assets		
Property, plant and equipment		245,000
Current assets		
Inventories $(50,000 + 48,000 – 4,000)$	94,000	
Trade receivables	36,000	
		130,000
Total assets		375,000
Equity and liabilities		
Equity		
Ordinary shares of $1 each	80,000	
Retained earnings	192,000	
		272,000
Non-controlling interest		39,000
		311,000
Current liabilities		64,000
Total equity and liabilities		375,000

7 Intra-group sales of non-current assets

 FAST FORWARD

As well as engaging in trading activities with each other, group companies may on occasion wish to **transfer non-current assets**.

7.1 Accounting treatment

In their individual accounts the companies concerned will treat the transfer just like a sale between unconnected parties: the selling company will record a profit or loss on sale, while the purchasing company will record the asset at the amount paid to acquire it, and will use that amount as the basis for calculating depreciation.

On consolidation, the usual **'group entity' principle applies**. The consolidated statement of financial position must show assets at their cost to the group, and any depreciation charged must be based on that cost. Two consolidation adjustments will usually be needed to achieve this.

(a) An adjustment to alter retained earnings and non-current assets cost so as to remove any element of unrealised profit or loss. This is similar to the adjustment required in respect of unrealised profit in inventory.

(b) An adjustment to alter retained earnings and accumulated depreciation is made so that consolidated depreciation is based on the asset's cost to the group.

In practice, these steps are combined so that the retained earnings of the entity making the unrealised profit are debited with the unrealised profit less the additional depreciation.

The double entry is as follows.

(a) Sale by parent

DEBIT Group retained earnings
CREDIT Non-current assets

with the profit on disposal, less the additional depreciation.

(b) Sale by subsidiary

DEBIT Group retained earnings (P's share of S)
DEBIT Non-controlling interest (NCI's share of S)
CREDIT Non-current assets

with the profit on disposal, less additional depreciation

7.2 Example: intra-group sale of non-current assets

P Co owns 60% of S Co and on 1 January 20X1 S Co sells plant costing $10,000 to P Co for $12,500. The companies make up accounts to 31 December 20X1 and the balances on their retained earnings at that date are:

P Co   after charging depreciation of 10% on plant $27,000

S Co   including profit on sale of plant $18,000

Required

Show the working for consolidated retained earnings.

Solution

Retained earnings

	P Co $	S Co $
Per question	27,000	18,000
Disposal of plant		
Profit		(2,500)
Depreciation: 10% × $2,500		250
		15,750
Share of S Ltd: $15,750 × 60%	9,450	
	36,450	

Notes

1 The non-controlling interest in the retained earnings of S Co is 40% × $15,750 = $6,300.

2 The asset is written down to cost and depreciation on the 'profit' element is removed. The group profit for the year is thus reduced by a net (($2,500 − $250) × 60%) = $1,350.

8 Summary: consolidated statement of financial position

Purpose	To show the net assets which P controls and the ownership of those assets.
Net assets	Always 100% P plus 100% S providing P holds a majority of voting rights.
Share capital	P only.
Reason	Simply reporting to the parent company's shareholders in another form.
Retained earnings	100% P plus group share of post-acquisition retained earnings of S less consolidation adjustments.
Reason	To show the extent to which the group actually owns total assets less liabilities.
Non-controlling interest	NCI share of S's consolidated net assets, or valuation at fair value.
Reason	To show the equity in a subsidiary not attributable to the parent.

9 Acquisition of a subsidiary during its accounting period

When a parent company acquires a subsidiary during its accounting period the only accounting entries made at the time will be those recording the **cost of acquisition in the parent company's books**.

9.1 Accounting problem

As we have already seen, at the end of the accounting year it will be necessary to prepare consolidated accounts.

The subsidiary company's accounts to be consolidated will show the subsidiary's profit or loss for the whole year. For consolidation purposes, however, it will be necessary to distinguish between:

(a)   Profits earned before acquisition
(b)   Profits earned after acquisition

In practice, a subsidiary company's profit may not accrue evenly over the year; for example, the subsidiary might be engaged in a trade, such as toy sales, with marked seasonal fluctuations. Nevertheless, the assumption can be made that **profits accrue evenly** whenever it is impracticable to arrive at an accurate split of pre– and post-acquisition profits.

Once the amount of pre-acquisition profit has been established the appropriate consolidation workings (goodwill, retained earnings) can be produced.

Bear in mind that in calculating **non-controlling interests** at the year end, the distinction between pre– and post-acquisition profits is irrelevant. The non-controlling shareholders are simply credited with their share of the subsidiary's total net assets at the end of the reporting period.

It is worthwhile to summarise what happens on consolidation to the retained earnings figures extracted from a subsidiary's statement of financial position. Suppose the accounts of S Co, a 60% subsidiary of P Co, show retained earnings of $20,000 at the end of the reporting period, of which $14,000 were earned prior to acquisition. The figure of $20,000 will appear in the consolidated statement of financial position as follows.

	$
Non-controlling interests working: their share of total retained earnings at the end of the reporting period (40% × $20,000)	8,000
Goodwill working: group share of pre-acquisition retained earnings (60% × $14,000)	8,400
Consolidated retained earnings working: group share of post-acquisition retained earnings (60% × $6,000)	3,600
	20,000

Question	Acquisition

Hinge Co acquired 80% of the ordinary shares of Singe Co on 1 April 20X5. On 31 December 20X4 Singe Co's accounts showed a share premium account of $4,000 and retained earnings of $15,000. The statements of financial position of the two companies at 31 December 20X5 are set out below. Neither company has paid any dividends during the year. Non-controlling interest should be valued at its proportionate share of net assets.

You are required to prepare the consolidated statement of financial position of Hinge Co at 31 December 20X5. There has been no impairment of goodwill.

HINGE CO
STATEMENT OF FINANCIAL POSITION AS AT 31 DECEMBER 20X5

	$	$
Assets		
Non-current assets		
Property, plant and equipment	32,000	
16,000 ordinary shares of 50c each in Singe Co	50,000	
		82,000
Current assets		85,000
Total assets		167,000
Equity and liabilities		
Equity		
Ordinary shares of $1 each	100,000	
Share premium account	7,000	
Retained earnings	40,000	
		147,000
Current liabilities		20,000
Total equity and liabilities		167,000

SINGE CO
STATEMENT OF FINANCIAL POSITION AS AT 31 DECEMBER 20X5

	$	$
Assets		
Property, plant and equipment		30,000
Current assets		43,000
Total assets		73,000
Equity and liabilities		
Equity		
20,000 ordinary shares of 50c each	10,000	
Share premium account	4,000	
Retained earnings	39,000	
		53,000
Current liabilities		20,000
Total equity and liabilities		73,000

Answer

Singe Co has made a profit of $24,000 ($39,000 – $15,000) for the year. In the absence of any direction to the contrary, this should be assumed to have arisen evenly over the year; $6,000 in the three months to 31 March and $18,000 in the nine months after acquisition. The company's pre-acquisition retained earnings are therefore as follows.

	$
Balance at 31 December 20X4	15,000
Profit for three months to 31 March 20X5	6,000
Pre-acquisition retained earnings	21,000

The balance of $4,000 on share premium account is all pre-acquisition.

The consolidation workings can now be drawn up.

1 Goodwill

	$	$
Consideration transferred		50,000
Non-controlling interest (W2)		7,000
Net assets acquired		57,000
represented by		
Ordinary share capital	10,000	
Retained earnings (pre-acquisition)	21,000	
Share premium	4,000	
		(35,000)
Goodwill		22,000

2 Non-controlling interest at acquisition

	$	$
Share capital	10,000	
Share premium	4,000	
Retained earnings 31.12.X4	15,000	
Earnings 3 months to 31.03.X5	6,000	
		35,000
NCI 20%		7,000

3 Non-controlling interest at reporting date

	$
Singe Co net assets (73,000 – 20,000)	53,000
× 20%	10,600

4 Retained earnings

	Hinge Co $	Singe Co $
Per question	40,000	39,000
Pre-acquisition (see above)		(21,000)
		18,000
Share of Singe: $18,000 × 80%	14,400	
	54,400	

5 Share premium account

	$
Hinge Co	7,000
Share of Singe Co's post-acquisition share premium	–
	7,000

HINGE CO
CONSOLIDATED STATEMENT OF FINANCIAL POSITION AS AT 31 DECEMBER 20X5

	$	$
Assets		
Property, plant and equipment		62,000
Goodwill (W1)		22,000
Current assets		128,000
Total assets		212,000
Equity and liabilities		
Equity		
Ordinary shares of $1 each	100,000	
Reserves		
Share premium account (W5)	7,000	
Retained earnings (W4)	54,400	
		161,400
Non-controlling interest (W3)		10,600
		172,000
Current liabilities		40,000
Total equity and liabilities		212,000

9.2 Example: pre-acquisition losses of a subsidiary

As an illustration of the entries arising when a subsidiary has pre-acquisition *losses*, suppose P Co acquired all 50,000 $1 ordinary shares in S Co for $20,000 on 1 January 20X1 when there was a debit balance of $35,000 on S Co's retained earnings. In the years 20X1 to 20X4 S Co makes profits of $40,000 in total, leaving a credit balance of $5,000 on retained earnings at 31 December 20X4. P Co's retained earnings at the same date are $70,000.

Solution

The consolidation workings would appear as follows.

1   *Goodwill*

		$	$
Consideration transferred			20,000
Net assets acquired			
as represented by			
Ordinary share capital		50,000	
Retained earnings		(35,000)	
			(15,000)
Goodwill			5,000

2   *Retained earnings*

	P Co	S Co
	$	$
At the end of the reporting period	70,000	5,000
Pre-acquisition loss		35,000
		40,000
S Co – share of post-acquisition retained earnings		
(40,000 × 100%)	40,000	
	110,000	

10 Dividends and pre-acquisition profits

FAST FORWARD

A further problem in consolidation occurs when a subsidiary pays out **a dividend soon after acquisition**.

10.1 Pre-acquisition profits

The parent company, as a member of the subsidiary, is entitled to its share of the dividends paid but it is necessary to decide whether or not these dividends come out of the pre-acquisition profits of the subsidiary.

If the dividends come from **post-acquisition** profits there is no problem. The holding company simply **credits** the relevant amount to its **own statement of comprehensive income**, as with any other dividend income. The dividend received by the parent and paid by the subsidiary are then cancelled upon consolidation. The double entry is quite different, however, if the dividend is paid from **pre-acquisition profits**, being as follows.

DEBIT	Cash
CREDIT	Investment in subsidiary

Where the dividend is paid from pre-acquisition profits, it **reduces** the cost of the parent company's investment.

10.2 Is the dividend paid from pre-acquisition profits?

We need next to consider how it is decided whether a dividend is paid from pre-acquisition profits. The simplest example is where a parent acquires a subsidiary on the first day of an accounting period and the dividend was in respect of the previous accounting period. Clearly, the dividend was paid from profits earned in the period before acquisition.

The position is less straightforward if shares are acquired **during the subsidiary's accounting period**. The usual method of dealing with this is by **time-apportionment.**

Example

P acquires a 60% interest in S on 1 September 20X0. S's year end is 31 December. On 10 January 20X1 S pays a dividend of $10,000 in respect of 20X0. P's share of the dividend is $6,000. However, as it relates to the year of acquisition, $2,000 ($6,000 \times ^4/_{12}$ is treated as being from post-acquisition profits and $4,000 ($6,000 \times ^8/_{12}$) is treated as being from pre-acquisition profits.

Why do we make this distinction? If we consider the situation of a holding company deciding whether to invest in a subsidiary, we can see the significance of a dividend paid from pre-acquisition profits. If the prospective subsidiary's financial statements disclose that it proposes to pay a dividend in the near future, the prospective holding company knows that if it invests in the shares some of its investment will be returned to it very soon. Also, a dividend paid out of pre-acquisition cannot be regarded as a return on the company's investment because it relates to the period before the investment was made. So we treat it as what it effectively is – a reduction in the cost of the investment.

Example

To continue the example of P and S above, P has paid $175,000 for its 60% shareholding in S. At the date of acquisition S had share capital of $100,000 and retained earnings of $70,000.

In 20X1 S pays a $10,000 dividend of which P receives $6,000. $4,000 is deemed to be from pre-acquisition profits. The goodwill calculation at 31 December 20X1 is as follows:

	$	$
Consideration transferred		175,000
Less pre-acquisition dividend		(4,000)
		171,000
Non-controlling interest (170,000 × 40%)		68,000
		239,000
Net assets acquired:		
Share capital	100,000	
Retained earnings	70,000	
		(170,000)
Goodwill		69,000

11 Fair values in acquisition accounting

FAST FORWARD
> Fair values are very important in calculating goodwill.

11.1 Goodwill

To understand the importance of fair values in the acquisition of a subsidiary consider again what we mean by goodwill.

Key term

> **Goodwill.** Any excess of the consideration transferred over the acquirer's interest in the fair value of the identifiable assets and liabilities acquired as at the date of the exchange transaction.

The **statement of financial position of a subsidiary company** at the date it is acquired may not be a guide to the fair value of its net assets. For example, the market value of a freehold building may have risen greatly since it was acquired, but it may appear in the statement of financial position at historical cost less accumulated depreciation.

11.2 What is fair value?

Fair value is defined as follows by IFRS 3 and various other standards – it is an important definition.

Key term

> **Fair value.** The amount for which an asset could be exchanged, or a liability settled, between knowledgeable, willing parties in an arm's length transaction.

We will look at the requirements of IFRS 3 regarding fair value in more detail below. First let us look at some practical matters.

11.3 Fair value adjustment calculations

Until now we have calculated goodwill as the difference between the consideration transferred and the **book value** of net assets acquired by the group. If this calculation is to comply with the definition above we must ensure that the book value of the subsidiary's net assets is the same as their **fair value**.

There are two possible ways of achieving this.

(a) The **subsidiary company** might **incorporate any necessary revaluations** in its own books of account. In this case, we can proceed directly to the consolidation, taking asset values and reserves figures straight from the subsidiary company's statement of financial position.

(b) The **revaluations** may be made as a **consolidation adjustment without being incorporated** in the subsidiary company's books. In this case, we must make the necessary adjustments to the subsidiary's statement of financial position as a working. Only then can we proceed to the consolidation.

Note. Remember that when depreciating assets are revalued there may be a corresponding alteration in the amount of depreciation charged and accumulated.

11.4 Example: fair value adjustments

P Co acquired 75% of the ordinary shares of S Co on 1 September 20X5. At that date the fair value of S Co's non-current assets was $23,000 greater than their net book value, and the balance of retained earnings was $21,000. The statements of financial position of both companies at 31 August 20X6 are given below. S Co has not incorporated any revaluation in its books of account.

P CO
STATEMENT OF FINANCIAL POSITION AS AT 31 AUGUST 20X6

	$	$
Assets		
Non-current assets		
Property, plant and equipment	63,000	
Investment in S Co at cost	51,000	
		114,000
Current assets		82,000
Total assets		196,000
Equity and liabilities		
Equity		
Ordinary shares of $1 each	80,000	
Retained earnings	96,000	
		176,000
Current liabilities		20,000
Total equity and liabilities		196,000

S CO
STATEMENT OF FINANCIAL POSITION AS AT 31 AUGUST 20X6

	$	$
Assets		
Property, plant and equipment		28,000
Current assets		43,000
Total assets		71,000
Equity and liabilities		
Equity		
Ordinary shares of $1 each	20,000	
Retained earnings	41,000	
		61,000
Current liabilities		10,000
Total equity and liabilities		71,000

If S Co had revalued its non-current assets at 1 September 20X5, an addition of $3,000 would have been made to the depreciation charged for 20X5/X6.

Required

Prepare P Co's consolidated statement of financial position as at 31 August 20X6. Non-controlling interest is to be valued at its proportionate share of the fair value of the subsidiary's identifiable net assets.

Solution

P CO CONSOLIDATED STATEMENT OF FINANCIAL POSITION AS AT 31 AUGUST 20X6

	$	$
Non-current assets		
Property, plant and equipment $(63,000 + 48,000)*$	111,000	
Goodwill (W1)	3,000	
		114,000
Current assets		125,000
		239,000
Equity and liabilities		
Equity		
Ordinary shares of $1 each	80,000	
Retained earnings (W3)	108,750	
		188,750
Non-controlling interest (W2)		20,250
		209,000
Current liabilities		30,000
		239,000

* (28,000 + 23,000 – 3,000)

1 *Goodwill*

	$	$
Consideration transferred		51,000
Non-controlling interest (64,000 × 25%)		16,000
		67,000
Net assets acquired as represented by		
Ordinary share capital	20,000	
Retained earnings	21,000	
Fair value adjustment	23,000	
		(64,000)
Goodwill		3,000

2   *Non-controlling interest at reporting date*

	$
S Co's net assets (71,000 – 10,000)	61,000
Fair value adjustment (23,000 – 3,000)	20,000
	81,000
× 25%	20,250

3   *Retained earnings*

	P Co $	S Co $
Per question	96,000	41,000
Pre acquisition profits		(21,000)
Depreciation adjustment		(3,000)
Post acquisition S Co		17,000
Group share in S Co		
($17,000 × 75%)	12,750	
Group retained earnings	108,750	

Question
Fair value

An asset is recorded in S Co's books at its historical cost of $4,000. On 1 January 20X5 P Co bought 80% of S Co's equity. Its directors attributed a fair value of $3,000 to the asset as at that date. It had been depreciated for two years out of an expected life of four years on the straight line basis. There was no expected residual value. On 30 June 20X5 the asset was sold for $2,600. What is the profit or loss on disposal of this asset to be recorded in S Co's accounts and in P Co's consolidated accounts for the year ended 31 December 20X5?

Answer

S Co: NBV at disposal (at historical cost) = $4,000 × 1½/4 = $1,500
        ∴ Profit on disposal = $1,100 (depreciation charge for the year = $500)

P Co: NBV at disposal (at fair value) = $3,000 × 1½/2 = $2,250
        ∴ Profit on disposal for consolidation = $350 (depreciation for the year = $750).

The non-controlling interest would be credited with 20% of both the profit on disposal and the depreciation charge as part of the one line entry in the consolidated income statement .

11.5 IFRS 3 Fair values

IFRS 3 sets out **general principles** for arriving at the fair values of a subsidiary's assets and liabilities. The acquirer should recognise the acquiree's identifiable assets, liabilities and contingent liabilities at the acquisition date only if they satisfy the following criteria.

(a)   In the case of an **asset** other than an intangible asset, it is **probable** that any associated **future economic benefits** will flow to the acquirer, and its fair value can be **measured reliably.**

(b)   In the case of a **liability** other than a contingent liability, it is probable that an **outflow** of resources embodying economic benefits will be required to settle the obligation, and its fair value can be **measured reliably.**

(c)   In the case of an **intangible asset** or a **contingent liability**, its fair value can be **measured reliably.**

The acquiree's identifiable assets and liabilities might include assets and liabilities **not previously recognised** in the acquiree's financial statements. For example, a tax benefit arising from the acquiree's tax losses that was not recognised by the acquiree may be recognised by the group if the acquirer has future taxable profits against which the unrecognised tax benefit can be applied.

11.5.1 Restructuring and future losses

An acquirer **should not recognise liabilities for future losses** or other costs expected to be incurred as a result of the business combination.

IFRS 3 explains that a plan to restructure a subsidiary following an acquisition is not a present obligation of the acquiree at the acquisition date. Neither does it meet the definition of a contingent liability. Therefore an acquirer **should not recognise a liability for** such **a restructuring plan** as part of allocating the cost of the combination unless the subsidiary was already committed to the plan before the acquisition.

This **prevents creative accounting**. An acquirer cannot set up a provision for restructuring or future losses of a subsidiary and then release this to the profit or loss in subsequent periods in order to reduce losses or smooth profits.

11.5.2 Intangible assets

The acquiree may have **intangible assets**, such as development expenditure. These can be recognised separately from goodwill only if they are **identifiable**. An intangible asset is identifiable only if it:

(a)   Is **separable**, ie capable of being separated or divided from the entity and sold, transferred, or exchanged, either individually or together with a related contract, asset or liability, or

(b)   Arises from contractual or other legal rights

11.5.3 Contingent liabilities

Contingent liabilities of the acquirer are **recognised** if their **fair value can be measured reliably**. This is a departure from the normal rules in IAS 37; contingent liabilities are not normally recognised, but only disclosed.

After their initial recognition, the acquirer should measure contingent liabilities that are recognised separately at the higher of:

(a)   The amount that would be recognised in accordance with IAS 37

(b)   The amount initially recognised

11.5.4 Cost of a business combination

The general principle is that the acquirer should measure the cost of a business combination as the total of the **fair values**, at the date of exchange, **of assets given**, liabilities incurred or assumed, and equity instruments issued by the acquirer, in exchange for control of the acquiree.

Sometimes all or part of the cost of an acquisition is deferred (ie, does not become payable immediately). The fair value of any deferred consideration is determined by **discounting** the amounts payable to their **present value** at the date of exchange.

Where equity instruments (eg, ordinary shares) of a quoted entity form part of the cost of a combination, the **published price** at the date of exchange normally provides the best evidence of the instrument's fair value and except in rare circumstances this should be used.

Future losses or other costs expected to be incurred as a result of a combination should not be included in the cost of the combination.

Costs **attributable** to the combination, for example professional fees and administrative costs, should not be included: they are recognised as an expense when incurred. **Costs of issuing debt instruments and equity shares** are covered by IAS 32 *Financial instruments: presentation*, which states that such costs should **reduce the proceeds from the debt issue or the equity issue**.

On 1 September 20X7 Tyzo Co acquired 6 million $1 shares in Kono Co at $2.00 per share. At that date Kono Co produced the following interim financial statements.

	$m		$m
Property, plant and equipment		Trade payables	3.2
(note 1)	16.0	Taxation	0.6
Inventories (note 2)	4.0	Bank overdraft	3.9
Receivables	2.9	Long-term loans	4.0
Cash in hand	1.2	Share capital ($1 shares)	8.0
		Retained earnings	4.4
	24.1		24.1

Notes

1   The following information relates to the property, plant and equipment of Kono Co at 1 September 20X7.

	$m
Gross replacement cost	28.4
Net replacement cost (gross replacement cost less depreciation)	16.6
Economic value	18.0
Net realisable value	8.0

2   The inventories of Kono Co which were shown in the interim financial statements are raw materials at cost to Kono Co of $4 million. They would have cost $4.2 million to replace at 1 September 20X7.

3   On 1 September 20X7 Tyzo Co took a decision to rationalise the group so as to integrate Kono Co. The costs of the rationalisation were estimated to total $3.0 million and the process was due to start on 1 March 20X8. No provision for these costs has been made in the financial statements given above.

Required

Compute the goodwill on consolidation of Kono Co that will be included in the consolidated financial statements of the Tyzo Co group for the year ended 31 December 20X7, explaining your treatment of the items mentioned above. You should refer to the provisions of relevant accounting standards.

Answer

Goodwill on consolidation of Kono Co

	$m	$m
Consideration ($2.00 × 6m)		12.0
Non-controlling interest (13.2 × 25%)		3.3
		15.3
Fair value of net assets acquired		
Share capital	8.0	
Pre-acquisition reserves	4.4	
Fair value adjustments		
Property, plant and equipment (16.6 – 16.0)	0.6	
Inventories (4.2 – 4.0)	0.2	
		(13.2)
Goodwill		2.1

Notes on treatment

(a)   Share capital and pre-acquisition profits represent the book value of the net assets of Kono Co at the date of acquisition. Adjustments are then required to this book value in order to give the fair value of the net assets at the date of acquisition. For short-term monetary items, fair value is their carrying value on acquisition.

(b) IFRS 3 states that the fair value of property, plant and equipment should be determined by market value or, if information on a market price is not available (as is the case here), then by reference to depreciated replacement cost, reflecting normal business practice. The net replacement cost (ie $16.6m) represents the gross replacement cost less depreciation based on that amount, and so further adjustment for extra depreciation is unnecessary.

(c) IFRS 3 also states that raw materials should be valued at replacement cost. In this case that amount is $4.2m.

(d) The rationalisation costs cannot be reported in pre-acquisition results under IFRS 3 as they are not a liability of Kono Co at the acquisition date.

11.5.5 Example: cost of a business combination

Rather than pay cash for Kono Co's shares, Tyzo has funded the acquisition by issuing 4.5m of its own shares to Kono Co's shareholders.

Tyzo's shares have a market value of $3. The costs of the share issue amounted to $500,000 and Tyzo paid a total of $750,000 to lawyers and accountants to carry out the combination.

Calculate the goodwill.

Solution

	$
Consideration:	
Share issue (4.5m × $3)	13.5
Non-controlling interest (as above)	3.3
	16.8
Net assets acquired (as above)	(13.2)
Goodwill	3.6

Note. The share issue costs are debited to share premium and the $750,000 expenses are written off.

11.6 Goodwill arising on acquisition

Goodwill should be carried in the statement of financial position at **cost less any accumulated impairment losses**. Refer back to paragraph 4.10 for more detail on this.

- This chapter has covered the mechanics of preparing simple **consolidated statements of financial position**. In particular, procedures have been described for dealing with:

  - Cancellation
  - Calculation of non-controlling interests
  - Calculation of goodwill arising on consolidation

- A **seven-stage drill** has been described and exemplified in a comprehensive example.

- The stages are as follows.

  - Update the draft statements of financial position to take account of any dividend paid but not accounted for

  - Agree intra-group current accounts by adjusting for items in transit

  - Cancel items common to both statements of financial position

  - Non-controlling interests

  - Goodwill

  - Retained earnings

  - Consolidated statement of financial position

- We have examined the consolidation adjustments necessary when group companies **trade with or sell non-current assets to each other**.

  - The guiding principle is that the consolidated statement of financial position must show assets at their cost to the group.

  - Any profit arising on intra-group transactions must be eliminated from the group retained earnings unless and until it is realised by a sale outside the group.

- It is important that you have a clear understanding of the material in this chapter before you move on to more complicated aspects of consolidation.

- In this chapter we have looked at certain problems involved in distinguishing between **pre-acquisition** and **post-acquisition profits** of subsidiary companies.

- When a subsidiary is acquired **during its accounting period**, its **pre-acquisition profits** will include a **proportion of its total profits** for the accounting period.

- In the absence of information to the contrary, the profits earned during the period may be assumed to have **accrued evenly** and should be allocated accordingly.

- **Dividends** paid by a subsidiary to its parent company may only be **credited to profit or loss in the parent's financial statements** to the extent that they are paid from **post-acquisition profits**.

- **Dividends** received by the parent company **from pre-acquisition profits** should be credited to 'investment in subsidiary' account and treated as **reducing the cost of the shares** acquired.

- **Goodwill arising on consolidation** is the difference between the consideration transferred plus the non-controlling interest and the fair value of the identifiable assets and liabilities acquired.

- **Goodwill** should be calculated **after revaluing** the subsidiary company's assets to fair value.

- If the subsidiary does not incorporate the revaluation in its own accounts, it should be done as a **consolidation adjustment**.

- The accounting requirements and disclosures of the **fair value exercise** are covered by **IFRS 3**.

1   Chicken Co owns 80% of Egg Co. Egg Co sells goods to Chicken Co at cost plus 50%. The total invoiced sales to Chicken Co by Egg Co in the year ended 31 December 20X9 were $900,000 and, of these sales, goods which had been invoiced at $60,000 were held in inventory by Chicken Co at 31 December 20X9. What is the reduction in aggregate group gross profit?

2   Major Co, which makes up its accounts to 31 December, has an 80% owned subsidiary Minor Co. Minor Co sells goods to Major Co at a mark-up on cost of 33.33%. At 31 December 20X8, Major had $12,000 of such goods in its inventory and at 31 December 20X9 had $15,000 of such goods in its inventory.

      What is the amount by which the consolidated profit attributable to Major Co's shareholders should be adjusted in respect of the above?

      Ignore taxation

      A $1,000 Debit
      B $800 Credit
      C $750 Credit
      D $600 Debit

3   What are the components making up the figure of non-controlling interest in a consolidated statement of financial position?

4   Goodwill is always positive. True or false?

5   A parent company can assume that, for a subsidiary acquired during its accounting period, profits accrue evenly during the year. True or false?

6   What entries are made in the workings to record the pre-acquisition profits of a subsidiary?

7   What entries are made in the parent company's accounts to record a dividend received from a subsidiary's pre-acquisition profits?

8   Describe the requirement of IFRS 3 in relation to the revaluation of a subsidiary company's assets to fair value at the acquisition date.

9   What guidelines are given by IFRS 3 in relation to valuing land and buildings fairly?

Answers to Quick Quiz

1     $60,000 \times \dfrac{50}{150} = \$20,000$

2   D $(15,000 - 12,000) \times \dfrac{33.3}{133.3} \times 80\%$

3   The non-controlling interests' share of ordinary shares, reserves and retained earnings *or* the market value of their shares.

4   False. Goodwill can be negative if the purchaser has 'got a bargain'.

5   Not necessarily – the examiner will advise you on this.

6   See Para 4.2

7   DEBIT   Cash
      CREDIT   Investment in subsidiary

8   See para 11.5

9   Market value is the best guideline.

Now try the question below from the Exam Question Bank

Number	Level	Marks	Time
9	Examination	15	27 mins
10	Examination	15	27 mins

10

The consolidated income statement

Topic list	Syllabus reference
1 The consolidated income statement	D3
2 The consolidated statement of comprehensive income	D3

Introduction

This chapter deals with the consolidated income statement and the consolidated statement of comprehensive income.

Most of the consolidation adjustments will involve the **income statement**, so that is the focus of this chapter.

Study guide

		Intellectual level
D	**BUSINESS COMBINATIONS**	
3	(b) prepare a consolidated income statement and consolidated statement of comprehensive income for simple group dealing with an acquisition in the period and non-controlling interest.	2

1 The consolidated income statement

FAST FORWARD
> The source of the consolidated income statement is the individual accounts of the separate companies in the group.

1.1 Consolidation procedure

It is customary in practice to prepare a working paper (known as a **consolidation schedule**) on which the individual income statements are set out side by side and totalled to form the basis of the consolidated income statement.

Exam focus point

> In an examination it is very much quicker not to do this. Use workings to show the calculation of complex figures such as the non-controlling interest and show the derivation of others on the face of the income statement, as shown in our examples.

FAST FORWARD
> In the consolidated income statement non-controlling interest is brought in as a one-line adjustment at the end of the income statement.

1.2 Simple example: consolidated income statement

P Co acquired 75% of the ordinary shares of S Co on that company's incorporation in 20X3. The summarised income statements and movement on retained earnings of the two companies for the year ending 31 December 20X6 are set out below.

	P Co $	S Co $
Sales revenue	75,000	38,000
Cost of sales	30,000	20,000
Gross profit	45,000	18,000
Administrative expenses	14,000	8,000
Profit before tax	31,000	10,000
Income tax expense	10,000	2,000
Profit for the year	21,000	8,000

Note: Movement on retained earnings

Retained earnings brought forward	87,000	17,000
Profit for the year	21,000	8,000
Retained earnings carried forward	108,000	25,000

Required

Prepare the consolidated income statement and extract from the statement of changes in equity showing retained earnings and non-controlling interest.

Solution

P CO
CONSOLIDATED INCOME STATEMENT
FOR THE YEAR ENDED 31 DECEMBER 20X6

	$
Sales revenue (75 + 38)	113,000
Cost of sales (30 + 20)	50,000
Gross profit	63,000
Administrative expenses (14 + 8)	22,000
Profit before tax	41,000
Income tax expense	12,000
Profit for the year	29,000
Profit attributable to:	
Owners of the parent	27,000
Non-controlling interest ($8,000 × 25%)	2,000
	29,000

STATEMENT OF CHANGES IN EQUITY (EXTRACT)

	Retained Earnings $	Non-controlling Interest $	Total Equity $
Balance b/f	99,750	4,250	104,000
Profit for the year	27,000	2,000	29,000
	126,750	6,250	133,000

Notice how the non-controlling interest is dealt with.

(a) Down to the line **'profit for the year'** the **whole** of S Co's results is included without reference to group share or non-controlling share. A **one-line adjustment** is then inserted to deduct the non-controlling share of S Co's profit.

(b) The non-controlling share ($4,250) of S Co's retained earnings brought forward (17,000 × 25%) is **excluded** from group retained earnings. This means that the carried forward figure of $126,750 is the figure which would appear in the statement of financial position for group retained earnings.

This last point may be clearer if we construct the working for group retained earnings.

Group retained earnings

	P Co $	S Co $
At balance sheet date	108,000	25,000
Less pre-acquisition retained earnings		–
		25,000
S Co – share of post acquisition retained earnings (25,000 × 75%)	18,750	
	126,750	

The non-controlling share of S Co's retained earnings comprises the non-controlling interest in the $17,000 profits brought forward plus the non-controlling interest ($2,000) in $8,000 retained profits for the year.

Notice that a consolidated income statement **links up** with a consolidated statement of financial position exactly as in the case of an individual company's accounts: the figure of retained earnings carried forward at the bottom of the income statement appears as the figure for retained earnings in the statement of financial position.

We will now look at the complications introduced by **inter-company trading**, **inter-company dividends** and **pre-acquisition profits** in the subsidiary.

1.3 Intra-group trading

Intra-group sales and purchases are eliminated from the consolidated income statement.

Like the consolidated statement of financial position, the consolidated income statement should deal with the results of the group as those of a single entity. When one company in a group sells goods to another an identical amount is added to the sales revenue of the first company and to the cost of sales of the second. Yet as far as the entity's dealings with outsiders are concerned no sale has taken place.

The consolidated figures for sales revenue and cost of sales should represent **sales to**, and **purchases from, outsiders**. An adjustment is therefore necessary to reduce the sales revenue and cost of sales figures by the value of intra-group sales during the year.

We have also seen in an earlier chapter that any unrealised profits on intra-group trading should be excluded from the figure for group profits. This will occur whenever goods sold at a profit within the group remain in the inventory of the purchasing company at the year end. The best way to deal with this is to **calculate the unrealised profit on unsold inventories at the year end and reduce consolidated gross profit by this amount**. Cost of sales will be the balancing figure.

1.4 Example: intra-group trading

Suppose in our earlier example that S Co had recorded sales of $5,000 to P Co during 20X6. S Co had purchased these goods from outside suppliers at a cost of $3,000. One half of the goods remained in P Co's inventory at 31 December 20X6. Prepare the revised consolidated income statement.

Solution

The consolidated income statement for the year ended 31 December 20X6 would now be as follows.

	$
Sales revenue (75 + 38 − 5)	108,000
Cost of sales (30 + 20 − 5 + 1*)	(46,000)
Gross profit (45 + 18 − 1*)	62,000
Administrative expenses	(22,000)
Profit before taxation	40,000
Income tax expense	(12,000)
Profit for the year	28,000
Profit attributable to :	
Owners of the parent	26,250
Non-controlling interest	1,750
	28,000

Note:

Retained earnings brought forward	99,750
Profit for the year	26,250
Retained earnings carried forward	126,000

*Unrealised profit: ½ × ($5,000 − $3,000)

An adjustment will be made for the unrealised profit against the inventory figure in the consolidated statement of financial position.

1.5 Intra-group dividends

In our example so far we have assumed that S Co retains all of its after-tax profit. It may be, however, that S Co distributes some of its profits as dividends. As before, the **non-controlling interest** in the subsidiary's profit should be calculated immediately after the figure of after-tax profit. For this purpose, no account need be taken of how much of the non-controlling interest is to be distributed by S Co as dividend.

Note that group retained earnings are only adjusted for dividends paid to the parent company shareholders. Dividends paid by the subsidiary to the parent are cancelled on consolidation and dividends paid to the non-controlling interest are replaced by the allocation to the non-controlling interest of their share of the profit for the year of the subsidiary.

1.6 Pre-acquisition profits

FAST FORWARD

Only the **post acquisition** profits of the subsidiary are brought into the consolidated income statement.

As explained above, the figure for retained earnings carried forward must be the same as the figure for retained earnings in the consolidated statement of financial position. We have seen in previous chapters that retained earnings in the consolidated statement of financial position comprise:

(a) The **whole of the parent company's** retained earnings

(b) A **proportion of the subsidiary company's** retained earnings. The proportion is the **group's share of post-acquisition retained earnings** in the subsidiary. From the total retained earnings of the subsidiary we must therefore **exclude** both the **non-controlling share** of total retained earnings and the **group's share of pre-acquisition** retained earnings.

A **similar procedure is necessary in the consolidated income statement** if it is to link up with the consolidated statement of financial position. Previous examples have shown how the non-controlling share of profits is excluded in the income statement. Their share of profits for the year is deducted from profit after tax, while the figure for profits brought forward in the consolidation schedule includes only the group's proportion of the subsidiary's profits.

In the same way, when considering examples which include pre-acquisition profits in a subsidiary, the figure for profits brought forward should include only the group's share of the post-acquisition retained profits. If the subsidiary is **acquired during the accounting year**, it is therefore necessary to apportion its profit for the year between pre-acquisition and post-acquisition elements. The part year method is used.

With the part-year method, the entire income statement of the subsidiary is split between pre-acquisition and post-acquisition proportions. Only the post-acquisition figures are included in the consolidated income statement.

Question

Acquisition

P Co acquired 60% of the equity of S Co on 1 April 20X5. The income statements of the two companies for the year ended 31 December 20X5 are set out below.

	P Co	S Co	S Co ($^9/_{12}$)
	$	$	$
Sales revenue	170,000	80,000	60,000
Cost of sales	65,000	36,000	27,000
Gross profit	105,000	44,000	33,000
Other income – dividend received S Co	3,600		
Administrative expenses	43,000	12,000	9,000
Profit before tax	65,600	32,000	24,000
Income tax expense	23,000	8,000	6,000
Profit for the year	42,600	24,000	18,000
Note			
Dividends (paid 31 December)	12,000	6,000	
Profit retained	30,600	18,000	
Retained earnings brought forward	81,000	40,000	
Retained earnings carried forward	111,600	58,000	

Prepare the consolidated income statement and retained earnings extract from the statement of changes in equity.

Answer

The shares in S Co were acquired three months into the year. Only the post-acquisition proportion (9/12ths) of S Co's income statement is included in the consolidated income statement. This is shown above for convenience.

**P CO CONSOLIDATED INCOME STATEMENT
FOR THE YEAR ENDED 31 DECEMBER 20X5**

	$
Sales revenue (170 + 60)	230,000
Cost of sales (65 + 27)	(92,000)
Gross profit	138,000
Administrative expenses (43 + 9)	(52,000)
Profit before tax	86,000
Income tax expense (23 + 6)	(29,000)
Profit for the year	57,000
Profit attributable to:	
Owners of the parent	49,800
Non-controlling interest (18 × 40%)	7,200
	57,000

STATEMENT OF CHANGES IN EQUITY	*Retained earnings*
	$
Balance brought forward*	81,000
Dividend paid (P)	(12,000)
Total comprehensive income for the year	49,800
Balance carried forward	118,800

* All of S Co's profits brought forward are pre-acquisition.

 ## Question

The following information relates to Brodick Co and its subsidiary Lamlash Co for the year to 30 April 20X7.

	Brodick Co	Lamlash Co
	$'000	$'000
Sales revenue	1,100	500
Cost of sales	(630)	(300)
Gross profit	470	200
Administrative expenses	(105)	(150)
Dividend from Lamlash Co	24	–
Profit before tax	389	50
Income tax expense	(65)	(10)
Profit for the year	324	40
Note		
Dividends paid	200	30
Profit retained	124	10
Retained earnings brought forward	460	106
Retained earnings carried forward	584	116

Additional information

(a) The issued share capital of the group was as follows.

    Brodick Co : 5,000,000 ordinary shares of $1 each.
    Lamlash Co : 1,000,000 ordinary shares of $1 each.

(b) Brodick Co purchased 80% of the issued share capital of Lamlash Co in 20X0. At that time, the revenue reserves of Lamlash amounted to $56,000.

Required

Insofar as the information permits, prepare the Brodick group consolidated income statement for the year to 30 April 20X7 in accordance with IASs, and the extract from the statement of changes in equity showing retained earnings.

Answer

BRODICK GROUP
CONSOLIDATED INCOME STATEMENT
FOR THE YEAR TO 30 APRIL 20X7

	$'000
Sales revenue (1,100 + 500)	1,600
Cost of sales (630 + 300)	(930)
Gross profit	670
Administrative expenses (105 + 150)	(255)
Profit before tax	415
Income tax expense (65 + 10)	(75)
Profit for the year	340

Profit attributable to:

	$
Owners of the parent	332
Non-controlling interest	8
	340

STATEMENT OF CHANGES IN EQUITY	Retained earnings
	$
Balance brought forward (W2)	500
Dividend paid (parent)	(200)
Total comprehensive income for the year	332
Balance carried forward	632

Workings

1   *Non-controlling interests*

	$'000
In Lamlash (20% × 40)	8

2   *Retained earnings brought forward*

	Brodick Co	Lamlash Co
	$'000	$'000
Per question	460	106
Less pre-aqn		(56)
		50
Share of Lamlash: 80% × 50	40	
	500	

1.7 Section summary

The table below summarises the main points about the consolidated income statement.

Purpose	To show the results of the group for an accounting period as if it were a single entity.
Sales revenue to profit for year	100% P + 100% S (excluding adjustments for inter-company transactions).
Reason	To show the results of the group which were controlled by the parent company.
Intra-group sales	Strip out inter-company activity from both sales revenue and cost of sales.
Unrealised profit on intra-group sales	(a) Goods sold by P. Increase cost of sales by unrealised profit. (b) Goods sold by S. Increase cost of sales by full amount of unrealised profit and decrease non-controlling interest by their share of unrealised profit.
Depreciation	If the value of S's non-current assets have been subjected to a fair value uplift then any additional depreciation must be charged in the consolidated income statement. The non-controlling interest will need to be adjusted for their share.
Transfer of non-current assets	Expenses must be increased by any profit on the transfer and reduced by any additional depreciation arising from the increased carrying value of the asset.

Non-controlling interests	S's profit after tax (PAT) X
	Less: * unrealised profit (X)
	         * profit on disposal of non-current assets (X)
	         additional depreciation following FV uplift (X)
	Add: ** additional depreciation following disposal of non-current assets X
	                          X
	NCI% X
	
	* Only applicable if sales of goods and non-current assets made by subsidiary.
	** Only applicable if sale of non-current assets made by subsidiary.

Reason	To show the extent to which profits generated through P's control are in fact owned by other parties.
Reserves carried forward	As per the calculations for the statement of financial position.

2 The consolidated statement of comprehensive income

FAST FORWARD

The consolidated statement of comprehensive income is produced using the consolidated income statement as a basis.

The only items of other comprehensive income that are included in your syllabus are revaluation gains and losses, so a consolidated statement of comprehensive income will be easy to produce once you have done the income statement.

We will take the last question and add an item of comprehensive income to illustrate this.

2.1 Example: Consolidated statement of comprehensive income

The consolidated income statement of the Brodrick Group is as in the answer to the last question. In addition, Lamlash made a $200,000 revaluation gain on one of its properties during the year.

2.2 Solution

BRODRICK GROUP
CONSOLIDATED STATEMENT OF COMPREHENSIVE INCOME FOR THE YEAR TO 30 APRIL 20X7

	$'000
Sales revenue	1,600
Cost of sales	(930)
Gross profit	670
Administrative expenses	(255)
Profit before tax	415
Income tax expense	(75)
Profit for the year	340
Other comprehensive income:	
Gain on property revaluation	200
Total comprehensive income for the year	540
Profit attributable to:	
Owners of the parent	332
Non-controlling interest	8
	340
Total comprehensive income attributable to:	
Owners of the parent (332 + (200 × 80%))	492
Non-controlling interest (8 + (200 × 20%))	48
	540

2.3 Consolidated statement of comprehensive income (separate statement)

If we were using the two-statement format (as explained in Chapter 3) we would produce a separate income statement and statement of comprehensive income.

2.4 Example: Statement of comprehensive income

BRODRICK GROUP
CONSOLIDATED STATEMENT OF COMPREHENSIVE INCOME

Profit for the year	340
Other comprehensive income:	
Gain on property revaluation	200
Total comprehensive income for the year	540
Total comprehensive income attributable to:	
Owners of the parent (332 + (200 × 80%))	492
Non-controlling interest (8 + (200 × 20%)	48
	540

2.5 Consolidated statement of changes in equity

These amounts would appear in the consolidated statement of changes in equity as follows:

	Retained earnings $'000	Revaluation surplus $'000	Total $'000	Non-controlling interest $'000	Total $'000
Total comprehensive income for the year	332	160	492	48	540

Chapter Roundup

- The source of the consolidated income statement is the individual accounts of the separate companies in the group.

- In the consolidated income statement non-controlling interest is brought in as a one-line adjustment after 'profit for the year'.

- Intra-group sales and purchases are eliminated from the consolidated income statement.

- Only the **post acquisition** profits of the subsidiary are brought into the consolidated income statement.

- The consolidated statement of comprehensive income is produced using the consolidated income statement as a basis.

Quick Quiz

1   Where does unrealised profit on intra-group trading appear in the income statement?
2   At the beginning of the year a 75% subsidiary transfers a non-current asset to the parent for $500,000. It's carrying value was $400,000 and it has 4 years of useful life left. How is this accounted for at the end of the year in the consolidated income statement?

Answers to Quick Quiz

1   As a deduction from consolidated gross profit.
2

	$
Unrealised profit	100,000
Additional depreciation (100 ÷ 4)	(25,000)
Net charge to income statement	75,000

	DR $	CR $
Non-current asset		100,000
Additional depreciation	25,000	
Group profit (75%)	56,250	
Non-controlling interest (25%)	18,750	
	100,000	100,000

Now try the questions below from the Exam Question Bank

Number	Level	Marks	Time
11	Examination	25	45 mins
12	Examination	15	27 mins
13	–	20	36 mins

11

Accounting for associates

Introduction

In this chapter we deal with the treatment of associates in the consolidated financial statements. As the group's share of profit in the associate appears in the income statement section, we have concentrated on the separate income statement.

Study guide

D	Business combinations	Intellectual level
3	(a) define an associate and explain the principle and reasoning for the use of equity accounting.	2
	(b) prepare consolidated financial statements to include a single subsidiary and an associate.	2

1 Accounting for associates

FAST FORWARD

This is covered by IAS 28 *Investments in associates*. The investing company does not have control, as it does with a subsidiary, but it does have **significant influence**.

1.1 Definitions

We looked at some of the important definitions in Chapter 8; these are repeated here with some additional important terms.

Key terms

- **Associate**. An entity, including an unincorporated entity such as a partnership, over which an investor has significant influence and which is neither a subsidiary nor an interest in a joint venture.
- **Significant influence** is the power to participate in the financial and operating policy decisions of the investee but is not control or joint control over those policies.
- **Equity method**. A method of accounting whereby the investment is initially recorded at cost and adjusted thereafter for the post-acquisition change in the investor's share of net assets of the investee. The profit or loss of the investor includes the investor's share of the profit or loss of the investee.

We have already looked at how the **status** of an investment in an associate should be determined. Go back to Section 1 of Chapter 8 to revise it. (Note that, as for an investment in a subsidiary, any **potential voting rights** should be taken into account in assessing whether the investor has **significant influence** over the investee.)

IAS 28 requires all investments in associates to be accounted for in the consolidated accounts using the equity method, *unless* the investment is classified as 'held for sale' in accordance with IFRS 5 in which case it should be accounted for under IFRS 5 (see Chapter 7), or the exemption in the paragraph below applies.

An investor is exempt from applying the equity method if:

(a)   It is a parent exempt from preparing consolidated financial statements under IAS 27, or

(b)   All of the following apply:

(i)   The investor is a **wholly-owned subsidiary** or it is a **partially owned subsidiary** of another entity and its other owners, including those not otherwise entitled to vote, have been informed about, and do not object to, the investor not applying the equity method;

(ii)   The investor's securities are **not publicly traded**

(iii)   It is **not in the process of issuing securities** in public securities markets; and

(iv)   The **ultimate or intermediate parent** publishes consolidated financial statements that comply with International Financial Reporting Standards.

The revised version of IAS 28 **no longer allows** an investment in an associate to be excluded from equity accounting when an investee operates under severe long-term restrictions that significantly impair its ability to transfer funds to the investor. Significant influence must be lost before the equity method ceases to be applicable.

The use of the equity method should be **discontinued** from the date that the investor **ceases to have significant influence.**

From that date, the investor shall account for the investment in accordance with IAS 39 *Financial instruments: recognition and measurement*. The carrying amount of the investment at the date that it ceases to be an associate shall be regarded as its cost on initial measurement as a financial asset under IAS 39.

1.2 Separate financial statements of the investor

If an investor **issues consolidated financial statements** (because it has subsidiaries), an investment in an associate should be *either:*

(a)   Accounted for at **cost**, or
(b)   In accordance with **IAS 39** (at fair value)

in its separate financial statements.

If an investor that does *not* **issue consolidated financial statements** (ie it has no subsidiaries) but has an investment in an associate this should similarly be included in the financial statements of the investor either at cost, or in accordance with IAS 39 (see Chapter 14).

2 The equity method

2.1 Application of the equity method: consolidated accounts

Many of the procedures required to apply the equity method are the same as are required for full consolidation. In particular, **intra-group unrealised profits** must be excluded.

Goodwill is calculated as the difference (positive or negative) between the cost of acquisition and the investor's share of the fair values of the net identifiable assets of the associate. This should be treated as required by IFRS 3 (see Chapter 10).

2.1.1 Consolidated income statement

The basic principle is that the investing company (X Co) should take account of its **share of the earnings** of the associate, Y Co, whether or not Y Co distributes the earnings as dividends. X Co achieves this by adding to consolidated profit the group's share of Y Co's profit after tax.

Notice the difference between this treatment and the **consolidation** of a subsidiary company's results. If Y Co were a subsidiary X Co would take credit for the whole of its sales revenue, cost of sales etc and would then make a one-line adjustment to remove any non-controlling share.

Under equity accounting, the associate's sales revenue, cost of sales and so on are *not* **amalgamated** with those of the group. Instead the group share only of the associate's profit before tax and tax charge for the year is added to the corresponding lines of the parent company and its subsidiaries.

2.1.2 Consolidated statement of financial position

A figure for **investment in associates** is shown which at the time of the acquisition must be stated at cost. This amount will increase (decrease) each year by the amount of the group's share of the associated company's profit (loss) for the year.

2.2 Example: associate

P Co, a company with subsidiaries, acquires 25,000 of the 100,000 $1 ordinary shares in A Co for $60,000 on 1 January 20X8. In the year to 31 December 20X8, A Co earns profits after tax of $24,000, from which it pays a dividend of $6,000.

How will A Co's results be accounted for in the individual and consolidated accounts of P Co for the year ended 31 December 20X8?

Solution

In the **individual accounts** of P Co, the investment will be recorded on 1 January 20X8 at cost. Unless there is an impairment in the value of the investment (see below), this amount will remain in the individual statement of financial position of P Co permanently. The only entry in P Co's individual income statement will be to record dividends received. For the year ended 31 December 20X8, P Co will:

DEBIT	Cash	$1,500	
CREDIT	Income from shares in associates		$1,500

In the **consolidated accounts** of P Co equity accounting principles will be used to account for the investment in A Co. Consolidated profit after tax will include the group's share of A Co's profit after tax (25% × $24,000 = $6,000). To the extent that this has been distributed as dividend, it is already included in P Co's individual accounts and will automatically be brought into the consolidated results. That part of the group's share of profit in the associate which has not been distributed as dividend ($4,500) will be brought into consolidation by the following adjustment.

DEBIT	Investment in associates	$4,500	
CREDIT	Income from shares in associates		$4,500

The asset 'Investment in associates' is then stated at $64,500, being cost plus the group share of post-acquisition retained profits.

3 Income statement and statement of financial position

3.1 Consolidated income statement

FAST FORWARD

In the **consolidated income statement** the investing group takes credit for its **share of the after-tax profits** of associates whether or not they are distributed as dividends.

A **consolidation schedule** may be used to prepare the consolidated income statement of a group with associates. The treatment of associates' profits in the following example should be studied carefully.

3.2 Illustration

The following **consolidation schedule** relates to the P Co group, consisting of the parent company, an 80% owned subsidiary (S Co) and an associate (A Co) in which the group has a 30% interest.

CONSOLIDATION SCHEDULE

	Group $'000	P Co $'000	S Co $'000	A Co $'000
Sales revenue	1,400	600	800	300
Cost of sales	770	370	400	120
Gross profit	630	230	400	180
Administrative expenses	290	110	180	80
	340	120	220	100
Interest receivable	30	30	–	–
	370	150	220	100
Interest payable	(20)	–	(20)	–
Share of profit of associate ((100 – 43) × 30%)	17	–	–	–
	367	150	200	100
Income tax expense				
Group	(145)	(55)	(90)	
Associate		–	–	(43)
Profit for the year	222	95	110	57
Non-controlling interest (110× 20%)	(22)	–	(22)	–
	200	95	88	57
Inter-company dividends	–	20	(18)	(2)
Group profit	200	115	70	55

Note the following

(a)   Group sales revenue, group gross profit and costs such as depreciation etc exclude the sales revenue, gross profit and costs etc of associated companies.

(b)   The group share of the associated company profits is credited to the group income statement. If the associated company has been acquired during the year, it would be necessary to deduct the pre-acquisition profits (remembering to allow for tax on current year profits).

(c)   The non-controlling interest will only ever apply to subsidiary companies.

3.3 Pro-forma consolidated income statement

The following is a **suggested layout** (using the figures given in the illustration above) for the consolidated income statement for a company having subsidiaries as well as associated companies.

	$'000
Sales revenue	1,400
Cost of sales	770
Gross profit	630
Administrative expenses	290
	340
Other income: interest receivable	30
	370
Finance costs	(20)
	350
Share of profit of associate (30 – 13)	17
Profit before taxation	367
Income tax expense	(145)
Profit for the year	222
Profit attributable to:	
Owners of the parent	200
Non-controlling interest	22
	222

3.4 Consolidated statement of financial position

FAST FORWARD

In the consolidated statement of financial position the investment in associates should be shown as:

- Cost of the investment in the associate; plus
- Group share of post acquisition profits; less
- Any amounts paid out as dividends; less
- Any amount written off the investment

As explained earlier, the consolidated statement of financial position will contain an **asset 'Investment in associates'**. The amount at which this asset is stated will be its original cost plus the group's share of any **profits earned since acquisition** which have not been distributed as dividends.

3.5 Example: consolidated statement of financial position

On 1 January 20X6 the net tangible assets of A Co amount to $220,000, financed by 100,000 $1 ordinary shares and revenue reserves of $120,000. P Co, a company with subsidiaries, acquires 30,000 of the shares in A Co for $75,000. During the year ended 31 December 20X6 A Co's profit after tax is $30,000, from which dividends of $12,000 are paid.

Show how P Co's investment in A Co would appear in the consolidated statement of financial position at 31 December 20X6.

Solution

CONSOLIDATED STATEMENT OF FINANCIAL POSITION
AS AT 31 DECEMBER 20X6 (extract)

	$
Non-current assets	
Investment in associated company	
Cost	75,000
Group share of post-acquisition retained profits	
(30% × $18,000)	5,400
	80,400

Question	Associate I

Set out below are the draft accounts of Parent Co and its subsidiaries and of Associate Co. Parent Co acquired 40% of the equity capital of Associate Co three years ago when the latter's reserves stood at $40,000.

SUMMARISED STATEMENTS OF FINANCIAL POSITION

	Parent Co & subsidiaries $'000	Associate Co $'000
Tangible non-current assets	220	170
Investment in Associate at cost	60	–
Loan to Associate Co	20	–
Current assets	100	50
Loan from Parent Co	–	(20)
	400	200
Share capital ($1 shares)	250	100
Retained earnings	150	100
	400	200

SUMMARISED INCOME STATEMENTS

	Parent Co & subsidiaries $'000	Associate Co $'000
Net profit	95	80
Taxation	35	30
	60	50

You are required to prepare the summarised consolidated accounts of Parent Co.

Notes

(1)   Assume that the associate's assets/liabilities are stated at fair value.
(2)   Assume that there are no non-controlling interests in the subsidiary companies.

Answer	

PARENT CO
CONSOLIDATED INCOME STATEMENT

	$'000
Net profit	95
Share of profits of associated company (80 × 40%)	32
Profit before tax	127
Taxation (35 + (30 × 40%) note (a))	47
Profit attributable to the members of Parent Co	80

Notes

(a) The note to the tax charge would disclose that $12,000 is the share of Associate's tax.

(b) The accounts should disclose the amount of the profit attributable to the members of Parent Co which has been dealt with in that company's own accounts. In this example there is insufficient information to do this.

PARENT CO
CONSOLIDATED STATEMENT OF FINANCIAL POSITION

	$'000
Assets	
Tangible non-current assets	220
Interest in associated company (see note)	104
Current assets	100
Total assets	424
Equity and liabilities	
Share capital	250
Retained earnings (W1)	174
Total equity and liabilities	424

Note

	$'000
Interest in associate	
Cost of investment	60
Share of post-acquisition retained earnings (W1)	24
Loan to associate	20
	104

Workings

1

Retained earnings	Parent & Subsidiaries $'000	Associate $'000
Per question	150	100
Pre-acquisition		40
Post-acquisition		60
Group share in associate		
($60 × 40%)	24	
Group retained earnings	174	

 Question | *Associate II*

Alfred Co bought a 25% shareholding on 31 December 20X8 in Grimbald Co at a cost of $38,000.

During the year to 31 December 20X9 Grimbald Co made a profit before tax of $82,000 and the taxation charge on the year's profits was $32,000. A dividend of $20,000 was paid on 31 December out of these profits.

Calculate the entries for the associate which would appear in the consolidated accounts of the Alfred group, in accordance with the requirements of IAS 28.

Answer

CONSOLIDATED INCOME STATEMENT

	$
Group share of profit of associate (82,000 × 25%)	20,500
Less taxation (32,000 × 25%)	(8,000)
Share of profit of associate	12,500

CONSOLIDATED STATEMENT OF FINANCIAL POSITION

	$
Interest in associate	45,500

Working

	$
Cost of investment	38,000
Share of post-acquisition retained earnings ((82,000 – 32,000 – 20,000) × 25%)	7,500
	45,500

The following points are also relevant and are similar to a parent-subsidiary consolidation situation.

(a) Use financial statements drawn up to the **same reporting date.**

(b) If this is impracticable, adjust the financial statements for **significant transactions/ events** in the intervening period. The difference between the reporting date of the associate and that of the investor must be no more than three months.

(c) Use **uniform accounting policies** for like transactions and events in similar circumstances, adjusting the associate's statements to reflect group policies if necessary.

3.6 'Upstream' and 'downstream' transactions

'Upstream' transactions are, for example, sales of assets from an associate to the investor. 'Downstream' transactions are, for example, sales of assets from the investor to an associate.

Profits and losses resulting from 'upstream' and 'downstream' transactions between an investor (including its consolidated subsidiaries) and an associate are eliminated to the extent of the investor's interest in the associate. This is very similar to the procedure for eliminating intra-group transactions between a parent and a subsidiary. The important thing to remember is that **only the group's share is eliminated**.

3.7 Example: downstream transaction

A Co, a parent with subsidiaries, holds 25% of the equity shares in B Co. During the year, A Co makes sales of $1,000,000 to B Co at cost plus a 25% mark-up. At the year-end, B Co has all these goods still in inventories.

Solution

A Co has made an unrealised profit of $200,000 (1,000,000 × 25/125) on its sales to the associate. The group's share (25%) of this must be eliminated:

DEBIT	Cost of sales (consolidated income statement)	$50,000
CREDIT	Investment in associate (consolidated statement of financial position)	$50,000

Because the sale was made to the associate, the group's share of the unsold inventory forms part of the investment in the associate at the year-end. If the associate had made the sale to the parent, the adjustment would have been:

DEBIT	Cost of sales (consolidated income statement)	$50,000	
CREDIT	Inventories (consolidated statement of financial position)		$50,000

The group's share of the revenue must also be eliminated from the consolidated income statement.

DEBIT	Revenue (25% × 1,000,000)	$250,000	
CREDIT	Cost of sales		$250,000

3.8 Associate's losses

When the equity method is being used and the investor's share of losses of the associate equals or exceeds its interest in the associate, the investor should **discontinue** including its share of further losses. The investment is reported at nil value. The interest in the associate is normally the carrying amount of the investment in the associate, but it also includes any other long-term interests, for example, long term receivables or loans.

After the investor's interest is reduced to nil, **additional losses** should only be recognised where the investor has incurred obligations or made payments on behalf of the associate (for example, if it has guaranteed amounts owed to third parties by the associate).

3.9 Impairment losses

IAS 39 sets out a list of indications that a financial asset (including an associate) may have become impaired. Any impairment loss is recognised in accordance with IAS 36 *Impairment of assets* for each associate individually.

In the case of an associate, any impairment loss will be deducted from the carrying value in the statement of financial position.

The working would be as follows.

	$
Cost of investment	X
Share of post-acquisition retained earnings	X
	X
Impairment loss	(X)
Interest in associate	X

Exam focus point

It is not unusual in the exam to have both an associate and a subsidiary to account for in a consolidation.

Question   Consolidated statement of financial position

The statements of financial position of J Co and its investee companies, P Co and S Co, at 31 December 20X5 are shown below.

STATEMENTS OF FINANCIAL POSITION AS AT 31 DECEMBER 20X5

	J Co $'000	P Co $'000	S Co $'000
Non-current assets			
Freehold property	1,950	1,250	500
Plant and machinery	795	375	285
Investments	1,500	–	–
	4,245	1,625	785
Current assets			
Inventory	575	300	265
Trade receivables	330	290	370
Cash	50	120	20
	955	710	655
Total assets	5,200	2,335	1,440

	J Co $'000	P Co $'000	S Co $'000
Equity and liabilities			
Equity			
Share capital – $1 shares	2,000	1,000	750
Retained earnings	1,460	885	390
	3,460	1,885	1,140
Non-current liabilities			
12% loan stock	500	100	
Current liabilities			
Trade payables	680	350	300
Bank overdraft	560	–	–
	1,240	350	300
Total equity and liabilities	5,200	2,335	1,440

Additional information

(a) J Co acquired 600,000 ordinary shares in P Co on 1 January 20X0 for $1,000,000 when the retained earnings of P Co were $200,000.

(b) At the date of acquisition of P Co, the fair value of its freehold property was considered to be $400,000 greater than its value in P Co's statement of financial position. P Co had acquired the property in January 20W0 and the buildings element (comprising 50% of the total value) is depreciated on cost over 50 years.

(c) J Co acquired 225,000 ordinary shares in S Co on 1 January 20X4 for $500,000 when the retained earnings of S Co were $150,000.

(d) P Co manufactures a component used by both J Co and S Co. Transfers are made by P Co at cost plus 25%. J Co held $100,000 inventory of these components at 31 December 20X5 and S Co held $80,000 at the same date.

(e) The goodwill in P Co is impaired and should be fully written off. An impairment loss of $92,000 is to be recognised on the investment in S Co.

Required

Prepare, in a format suitable for inclusion in the annual report of the J Group, the consolidated statement of financial position at 31 December 20X5.

Answer

J GROUP CONSOLIDATED STATEMENT OF FINANCIAL POSITION AS AT 31 DECEMBER 20X5

	$'000
Non-current assets	
Freehold property (W2)	3,570.00
Plant and machinery (795 + 375)	1,170.00
Investment in associate (W8)	475.20
	5,215.20
Current assets	
Inventory (W3)	855.00
Receivables (W4)	620.00
Cash (50 + 120)	170.00
	1,645.00
Total assets	6,860.20

	$'000
Equity and liabilities	
Equity	
Share capital	2,000.00
Retained earnings (W9)	1,778.12
	3,778.12
Non-controlling interest (W6)	892.08
	4,670.20
Non-current liabilities	
12% loan stock (500 + 100)	600.00
Current liabilities (W5)	1,590.00
Total equity and liabilities	6,860.20

Workings

1 *Group structure*

```
                          J
  1.1.X0          60% /     \ 30%      1.1.X4
(6 years ago)        /       \      (2 years ago)
                    P         S
```

2 *Freehold property*

	$'000
J Co	1,950
P Co	1,250
Fair value adjustment	400
Additional depreciation (400 × 50% ÷ 40) × 6 years (20X0-20X5)	(30)
	3,570

3 *Inventory*

	$'000
J Co	575
P Co	300
PUP (100 × $^{25}/_{125}$)	(20)
	855

4 *Receivables*

	$'000
J Co	330
P Co	290
	620

5 *Current liabilities*

		$'000
J Co:	bank overdraft	560
	trade payables	680
P Co:	trade payables	350
		1,590

6 *Non-controlling interest at reporting date*

	$'000
Net assets of P Co	1,885.0
Fair value adjustment (W11)	370.0
Less PUP: sales to J Co	(20.0)
sales to S Co (80 × $^{25}/_{125}$ × 30%)	(4.8)
	2,230.2
Non-controlling interest (40%)	892.08

7   Goodwill

		$'000	$'000
P Co			
Consideration transferred			1,000
Non-controlling interest at acquisition (1,600 × 40%)			640
Net assets acquired			
Share capital		1,000	
Retained earnings		200	
Fair value adjustment		400	
			(1,600)
Goodwill at acquisition			40
Impairment loss			(40)
			0

8   Investment in associate

	$'000
Cost of investment	500.00
Share of post-acquisition profit (390 − 150) × 30%	72.00
Less PUP	(4.80)
Less impairment loss	(92.00)
	475.20

9   Retained earnings

	J $'000	P $'000	S $'000
Retained earnings per question	1,460.0	885.0	390.0
Adjustments			
Unrealised profit (W10)		(24.8)	
Fair value adjustments (W11)		(30.0)	
		830.2	390.0
Less pre-acquisition reserves		(200.0)	(150.0)
	1,460.0	630.2	240.0
P: 60% × 630.2	378.1		
S: 30% × 240	72.0		
Less impairment losses : P	(40.0)		
S	(92.0)		
	1,778.1		

10   Unrealised profit (PUP)

	$'000
On sales to J (parent co) 100 × 25/125	20.0
On sales to S (associate) 80 × 25/125 × 30%	4.8
	24.8

11   Fair value adjustments

	Difference at acquisition $'000	Difference now $'000
Property	400	400
Additional depreciation: 200 × 6/40	–	(30)
	400	370

∴ Charge $30,000 to retained earnings

Chapter Roundup

- IAS 28 requires that, in consolidated accounts, **associates** should be accounted for using **equity accounting principles**.

- In the **consolidated income statement** the investing group takes credit for its **share of the after-tax profits** of associates, whether or not they are distributed as dividends.

- In the **consolidated statement of financial position**, the investment in associates should be shown as:

    - **Cost of the investment in the associate**; plus
    - Group share of post-acquisition profits; less
    - Any amounts paid out as dividends and any amounts written off.

Quick Quiz

1   Barley Co has owned 100% of the issued share capital of Oats Co for many years. Barley Co sells goods to Oats Co at cost plus 20%. The following information is available for the year:

Revenue   – Barley Co $460,000
                – Oats Co $120,000

During the year Barley Co sold goods to Oats Co for $60,000 of which $18,000 were still held in inventory by Oats at the year end.

At what amount should revenue appear in the consolidated income statement?

2   Horace Co acquired 75% of the ordinary share capital of Sylvia Co several years ago. The income statement of Sylvia Co for the year ended 28 February 20X0 showed the following:

	$
Profit on ordinary activities after tax	4,000
Ordinary dividend	(2,000)
	2,000

What is the non-controlling interest in the consolidated income statement of Horace Co for the year ended 28 February 20X0?

3   Saroti Co owns 70% of the ordinary shares of Macari Co. An extract from Macari Co's income statement is as follows:

	$
Profit after tax	10,000
Ordinary dividend paid	(5,000)
Retained profit	5,000

What amount for non-controlling interest should be shown in the consolidated income statement of Saroti Co?

4   Define an associate.

5   How should associates be accounted for in the separate financial statements of the investor?

6   What is the effect of the equity method on the consolidated income statement and statement of financial position?

Answers to Quick Quiz

1   Revenue: 460 + 120 – 60 = $520,000

2   25% × $4,000 = $1,000

3   30% × $10,000 = $3,000

4   An entity in which an investor has a significant influence, but which is not a subsidiary or a joint venture of the investor.

5   Either at cost or in accordance with IAS 39.

6   (a)   *Income statement.* Investing company includes its share of the earnings of the associate, by adding its share of profit after tax.

            (b)   *Statement of financial position.* Investment in associates is initially included in assets at cost. This will increase or decrease each year according to whether the associated company makes a profit or loss.

Now try the questions below from the Exam Question Bank

Number	Level	Marks	Time
14	Examination	25	45 mins

12

Inventories and construction contracts

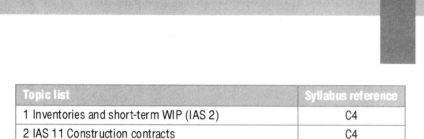

Topic list	Syllabus reference
1 Inventories and short-term WIP (IAS 2)	C4
2 IAS 11 Construction contracts	C4

Introduction

You have encountered inventory and its valuation in your earlier studies. Inventory and short-term work-in-progress valuation has a direct impact on a company's gross profit and it is usually a material item in any company's accounts. This is therefore an important subject area. If you have any doubts about accounting for inventories and methods of inventory valuation you would be advised to go back to your earlier study material and revise this topic.

Section 1 of this chapter goes over some of this ground again, concentrating on the effect of IAS 2. Section 2 goes on to discuss a new area, construction contracts, which are effectively long-term work in progress. You should find this topic fairly logical as long as you work through the examples and question carefully.

Study guide

		Intellectual level
4	**Inventory**	
	(a) describe and apply the principles of inventory valuation.	2
	(b) define a construction contract and discuss the role of accounting concepts in the recognition of profit.	2
	(c) describe the acceptable methods of determining the stage (percentage) of completion of a contract.	2
	(d) prepare financial statement extracts for construction contracts.	2

Exam guide

The **pilot paper** contained a question on construction contracts. They are a good test of double entry. The examiner is likely to test them regularly, if only because they do not feature at Paper P2.

1 Inventories and short-term WIP (IAS 2)

FAST FORWARD Most of this is revision. However you should be aware that the use of LIFO is prohibited under the revised IAS 2.

1.1 Introduction

In most businesses the value put on inventory is an important factor in the determination of profit. Inventory valuation is, however, a highly subjective exercise and consequently there is a wide variety of different methods used in practice.

1.2 IAS 2 (revised) Inventories

IAS 2 was revised in December 2003. It lays out the required accounting treatment for inventories (sometimes called stocks) under the historical cost system. The major area of contention is the cost **value of inventory** to be recorded. This is recognised as an asset of the entity until the related revenues are recognised (ie the item is sold) at which point the inventory is recognised as an expense (ie cost of sales). Part or all of the cost of inventories may also be expensed if a write-down to **net realisable value** is necessary. The revised IAS also provides guidance on the cost formulas that are used to assign costs to inventories.

In other words, the fundamental accounting assumption of **accruals** requires costs to be matched with associated revenues. In order to achieve this, costs incurred for goods which remain unsold at the year end must be carried forward in the statement of financial position and matched against future revenues.

1.3 Scope

The following items are **excluded** from the scope of the standard.

* Work in progress under **construction contracts** (covered by IAS 11 *Construction contracts*, see Section 2)
* **Financial instruments** (ie shares, bonds)
* **Biological assets**

Certain inventories are exempt from the standard's **measurement rules**, ie those held by:

* Producers of **agricultural and forest products**
* **Commodity-broker traders**

1.4 Definitions

The standard gives the following important definitions.

- **Inventories** are assets:
    - held for sale in the ordinary course of business;
    - in the process of production for such sale; or
    - in the form of materials or supplies to be consumed in the production process or in the rendering of services.
- **Net realisable value** is the estimated selling price in the ordinary course of business less the estimated costs of completion and the estimated costs necessary to make the sale.
- **Fair value** is the amount for which an asset could be exchanged or a liability settled between knowledgeable, willing parties in an arm's length transaction. (*IAS 2*)

Inventories can **include** any of the following.

- **Goods purchased and held for resale**, eg goods held for sale by a retailer, or land and buildings held for resale
- **Finished goods** produced
- **Work in progress** being produced
- Materials and supplies awaiting use in the production process (**raw materials**)

1.5 Measurement of inventories

The standard states that '**Inventories should be measured at the lower of cost and net realisable value**.'

This is a very important rule and you will be expected to apply it in the exam.

1.6 Cost of inventories

The cost of inventories will consist of all costs of:

- **Purchase**
- **Costs of conversion**
- **Other costs** incurred in bringing the inventories to their **present location and condition**

1.6.1 Costs of purchase

The standard lists the following as comprising the costs of purchase of inventories:

- **Purchase price** *plus*
- **Import duties** and other taxes *plus*
- Transport, handling and any other cost **directly attributable** to the acquisition of finished goods, services and materials *less*
- **Trade discounts**, rebates and other similar amounts

1.6.2 Costs of conversion

Costs of conversion of inventories consist of two main parts.

(a) Costs **directly related** to the units of production, eg direct materials, direct labour
(b) Fixed and variable **production overheads** that are incurred in converting materials into finished goods, allocated on a systematic basis.

You may have come across the terms 'fixed production overheads' or 'variable production overheads' elsewhere in your studies. The standard defines them as follows.

- **Fixed production overheads** are those indirect costs of production that remain relatively constant regardless of the volume of production, eg the cost of factory management and administration.

- **Variable production overheads** are those indirect costs of production that vary directly, or nearly directly, with the volume of production, eg indirect materials and labour. *(IAS 2)*

The standard emphasises that fixed production overheads must be allocated to items of inventory on the basis of the **normal capacity of the production facilities**. This is an important point.

(a) **Normal capacity** is the expected achievable production based on the average over several periods/seasons, under normal circumstances.

(b) The above figure should take account of the capacity lost through **planned maintenance**.

(c) If it approximates to the normal level of activity then the **actual level of production** can be used.

(d) **Low production** or **idle plant** will *not* result in a higher fixed overhead allocation to each unit.

(e) **Unallocated overheads** must be recognised as an expense in the period in which they were incurred.

(f) When production is **abnormally high**, the fixed production overhead allocated to each unit will be reduced, so avoiding inventories being stated at more than cost.

(g) The allocation of variable production overheads to each unit is based on the **actual use** of production facilities.

1.6.3 Other costs

Any other costs should only be recognised if they are incurred in bringing the inventories to their **present location and condition**.

The standard lists types of cost which **would not be included** in cost of inventories. Instead, they should be recognised as an **expense** in the period they are incurred.

(a) **Abnormal amounts** of wasted materials, labour or other production costs

(b) **Storage costs** (except costs which are necessary in the production process before a further production stage)

(c) **Administrative overheads** not incurred to bring inventories to their present location and conditions

(d) **Selling costs**

1.6.4 Techniques for the measurement of cost

Two techniques are mentioned by the standard, both of which produce results which **approximate to cost**, and so both of which may be used for convenience.

(a) **Standard costs** are set up to take account of normal production values: amount of raw materials used, labour time etc. They are reviewed and revised on a regular basis.

(b) **Retail method**: this is often used in the retail industry where there is a large turnover of inventory items, which nevertheless have similar profit margins. The only practical method of inventory valuation may be to take the total selling price of inventories and deduct an overall average profit margin, thus reducing the value to an approximation of cost. The percentage will take account of reduced price lines. Sometimes different percentages are applied on a department basis.

1.7 Cost formulas

Cost of inventories should be assigned by **specific identification** of their individual costs for:

(a) Items that are **not ordinarily interchangeable**

(b) Goods or services produced and segregated for **specific projects**

Specific costs should be attributed to individual items of inventory when they are segregated for a specific project, but not where inventories consist of a large number of interchangeable (ie identical or very similar) items. In the latter case the rule is as specified below.

1.7.1 Interchangeable items

You should be familiar with these methods from your Paper 1.1 studies. Under the weighted average cost method, a recalculation can be made after each purchase, **or alternatively only at the period end**.

1.8 Net realisable value (NRV)

As a general rule assets should not be carried at amounts greater than those expected to be realised from their sale or use. In the case of inventories this amount could fall below cost when items are **damaged or become obsolete**, or where the **costs to completion have increased** in order to make the sale.

In fact we can identify the principal situations in which **NRV is likely to be less than cost**, ie where there has been:

(a)   An **increase in costs** or a **fall in selling price**
(b)   A **physical deterioration** in the condition of inventory
(c)   **Obsolescence** of products
(d)   A decision as part of the company's marketing strategy to manufacture and sell products at a **loss**
(e)   **Errors in production or purchasing**

A write down of inventories would normally take place on an item by item basis, but similar or related items may be **grouped together**. This grouping together is acceptable for, say, items in the same product line, but it is not acceptable to write down inventories based on a whole classification (eg finished goods) or a whole business.

The assessment of NRV should take place **at the same time** as estimates are made of selling price, using the most reliable information available. Fluctuations of price or cost should be taken into account if they relate directly to **events after the reporting period,** which confirm conditions existing at the end of the period.

The reasons why inventory is held must also be taken into account. Some inventory, for example, may be held to satisfy a firm contract and its NRV will therefore be the **contract price**. Any additional inventory of the same type held at the period end will, in contrast, be assessed according to general sales prices when NRV is estimated.

Net realisable value must be reassessed at the end of each period and compared again with cost. If the NRV has risen for inventories held over the end of more than one period, then the previous write down must be **reversed** to the extent that the inventory is then valued at the lower of cost and the new NRV. This may be possible when selling prices have fallen in the past and then risen again.

On occasion a write down to NRV may be of such size, incidence or nature that it must be **disclosed separately**.

1.9 Recognition as an expense

The following treatment is required **when inventories are sold**.

(a)   The **carrying amount** is recognised as an expense in the period in which the related revenue is recognised
(b)   The amount of any **write-down of inventories** to NRV and all losses of inventories are recognised as an expense in the period the write-down or loss occurs
(c)   The amount of any **reversal of any write-down of inventories**, arising from an increase in NRV, is recognised as a reduction in the amount of inventories recognised as an expense in the period in which the reversal occurs

You are the accountant at Water Pumps Co, and you have been asked to calculate the valuation of the company's inventory at cost at its year end of 30 April 20X5.

Water Pumps manufactures a range of pumps. The pumps are assembled from components bought by Water Pumps (the company does not manufacture any parts).

The company does not use a standard costing system, and work in progress and finished goods are valued as follows.

(a)   Material costs are determined from the product specification, which lists the components required to make a pump.

(b)   The company produces a range of pumps. Employees record the hours spent on assembling each type of pump, this information is input into the payroll system which prints the total hours spent each week assembling each type of pump. All employees assembling pumps are paid at the same rate and there is no overtime.

(c)   Overheads are added to the inventory value in accordance with IAS 2 *Inventories*. The financial accounting records are used to determine the overhead cost, and this is applied as a percentage based on the direct labour cost.

For direct labour costs, you have agreed that the labour expended for a unit in work in progress is half that of a completed unit.

The draft accounts show the following materials and direct labour costs in inventory.

	Raw materials	Work in progress	Finished goods
Materials ($)	74,786	85,692	152,693
Direct labour ($)		13,072	46,584

The costs incurred in April, as recorded in the financial accounting records, were as follows.

	$
Direct labour	61,320
Selling costs	43,550
Depreciation and finance costs of production machines	4,490
Distribution costs	6,570
Factory manager's wage	2,560
Other production overheads	24,820
Purchasing and accounting costs relating to production	5,450
Other accounting costs	7,130
Other administration overheads	24,770

For your calculations assume that all work in progress and finished goods were produced in April 20X5 and that the company was operating at a normal level of activity.

Required

Calculate the value of overheads which should be added to work in progress and finished goods in accordance with IAS 2 *Inventories*.

Note. You should include details and a description of your workings and all figures should be calculated to the nearest $.

Calculation of overheads for inventories

Production overheads are as follows.

	$
Depreciation/finance costs	4,490
Factory manager's wage	2,560
Other production overheads	24,820
Accounting/purchasing costs	5,450
	37,320

Direct labour = $61,320

∴ Production overhead rate = $\dfrac{37,320}{61,320}$ = 60.86%

Inventory valuation

	Raw materials $	WIP $	Finished goods $	Total $
Materials	74,786	85,692	152,693	313,171
Direct labour	–	13,072	46,584	59,656
Production overhead (at 60.86% of labour)	–	7,956	28,351	36,307
	74,786	106,720	227,628	409,134

1.10 Consistency – different cost formulas for inventories

IAS 2 allows two cost formulas (FIFO or weighted average cost) for inventories that are ordinarily interchangeable or are not produced and segregated for specific projects. The issue is whether an entity may use different cost formulas for different types of inventories.

IAS 2 provides that an entity should use **the same cost formula for all inventories having similar nature and use to the entity.** For inventories with different nature or use (for example, certain commodities used in one business segment and the same type of commodities used in another business segment), different cost formulas may be justified. A difference in geographical location of inventories (and in the respective tax rules), by itself, is not sufficient to justify the use of different cost formulas.

2 IAS 11 Construction contracts

 FAST FORWARD

Sales revenue on a construction contract is normally based upon stage of completion.

2.1 Introduction

Imagine that you are the accountant at a construction company. Your company is building a large tower block that will house offices, under a contract with an investment company. It will take three years to build the block and over that time you will obviously have to pay for building materials, wages of workers on the building, architects' fees and so on. You will receive periodic payments from the investment company at various predetermined stages of the construction. How do you decide, in each of the three years, **what to include as income and expenditure** for the contract in the statement of comprehensive income?

This is the problem tackled by IAS 11 *Construction contracts*.

2.2 Example: construction contract

A numerical example might help to illustrate the problem. Suppose that a contract is started on 1 January 20X5, with an estimated completion date of 31 December 20X6. The final contract price is $1,500,000. In the first year, to 31 December 20X5:

(a)   Costs incurred amounted to $600,000.

(b)   Half the work on the contract was completed.

(c)   Certificates of work completed have been issued, to the value of $750,000. (*Note*. It is usual, in a construction contract, for a qualified person such as an architect or engineer to inspect the work completed, and if it is satisfactory, to issue certificates. This will then be the notification to the customer that progress payments are now due to the contractor. Progress payments are commonly the amount of valuation on the work certificates issued, minus a precautionary retention of 10%).

(d)   It is estimated with reasonable certainty that further costs to completion in 20X6 will be $600,000.

What is the contract profit in 20X5, and what entries would be made for the contract at 31 December 20X5 if:

(a)   Profits are deferred until the completion of the contract?

(b)   A proportion of the estimated revenue and profit is credited to profit or loss in 20X5?

Solution

(a)   If profits were deferred until the completion of the contract in 20X6, the revenue and profit recognised on the contract in 20X5 would be nil, and the value of work in progress on 31 December 20X5 would be $600,000. IAS 11 takes the view that this policy is unreasonable, because in 20X6, the total profit of $300,000 would be recorded. Since the contract revenues are earned throughout 20X5 and 20X6, a profit of nil in 20X5 and $300,000 in 20X6 would be contrary to the accruals concept of accounting.

(b)   **It is fairer to recognise revenue and profit throughout the duration of the contract.**

As at 31 December 20X5 revenue of $750,000 should be matched with cost of sales of $600,000 in the statement of comprehensive income, leaving an attributable profit for 20X5 of $150,000.

The only entry in the statement of financial position as at 31 December 20X5 is a receivable of $750,000 recognising that the company is owed this amount for work done to date. No balance remains for work in progress, the whole $600,000 having been recognised in cost of sales.

2.3 What is a construction contract?

A contract which needs IAS 11 treatment does not have to last for a period of more than one year. The main point is that the contract activity **starts in one financial period and ends in another**, thus creating the problem: to which of two or more periods should contract income and costs be allocated? In fact the definition given in the IAS of a construction contract is very straightforward.

Key term

> **Construction contract.** A contract specifically negotiated for the construction of an asset or a combination of assets that are closely interrelated or interdependent in terms of their design, technology and function or their ultimate purpose or use. *(IAS 11)*

The standard differentiates between fixed price contracts and cost plus contracts.

Key terms

> - **Fixed price contract.** A contract in which the contractor agrees to a fixed contract price, or a fixed rate per unit of output, which in some cases is subject to cost escalation clauses.
> - **Cost plus contract.** A construction contract in which the contractor is reimbursed for allowable or otherwise defined costs, plus a percentage of these costs or a fixed fee.

Construction contracts may involve the building of one asset, eg a bridge, or a series of interrelated assets eg an oil refinery. They may also include **rendering of services** (eg architects) or restoring or demolishing an asset.

2.4 Combining and segmenting construction contracts

The standard lays out the factors which determine whether the construction of a **series of assets** under one contract should be treated as several contracts.

- **Separate proposals** are submitted for each asset
- **Separate negotiations** are undertaken for each asset; the customer can accept/reject each individually
- **Identifiable costs and revenues** can be separated for each asset

There are also circumstances where a **group of contracts** should be treated as **one single construction contract**.

- The group of contracts are negotiated as a **single package**
- Contracts are **closely interrelated**, with an overall profit margin
- The contracts are performed **concurrently** or **in a single sequence**

2.5 Contract revenue

Contract revenue will be the **amount specified in the contract**, subject to variations in the contract work, incentive payments and claims *if* these will probably give rise to revenue and *if* they can be reliably measured. The result is that contract revenue is measured at the **fair value** of received or receivable revenue.

The standard elaborates on the types of uncertainty, which depend on the outcome of future events, that affect the **measurement of contract revenue**.

- An **agreed variation** (increase/decrease)
- **Cost escalation clauses** in a fixed price contract (increase)
- **Penalties** imposed due to delays by the contractor (decrease)
- **Number of units** varies in a contract for fixed prices per unit (increase/decrease)

In the case of any variation, claim or incentive payment, two factors should be assessed to determine whether contract revenue should be recognised.

- Whether it is **probable** that the customer will accept the variation/claim, or that the contract is sufficiently advanced that the performance criteria will be met
- Whether the amount of the revenue can be **measured reliably**

2.6 Contract costs

Contract costs consist of:

- Costs relating **directly** to the contract
- Costs attributable to general contract activity which can be **allocated** to the contract, such as insurance, cost of design and technical assistance not directly related to a specific contract and construction overheads
- Any other costs which can be **charged to the customer** under the contract, which may include general administration costs and development costs

Costs that **relate directly** to a specific contract include the following.

- **Site labour costs**, including site supervision
- Costs of **materials** used in construction
- **Depreciation** of plant and equipment used on the contract
- Costs of **moving** plant, equipment and materials to and from the contract site

- Costs of **hiring** plant and equipment
- Costs of **design and technical assistance** that are directly related to the contract
- Estimated costs of **rectification and guarantee work**, including expected warranty costs
- **Claims from third parties**

General contract activity costs should be **allocated systematically and rationally**, and all costs with similar characteristics should be treated **consistently**. The allocation should be based on the **normal level** of construction activity. Borrowing costs may be attributed in this way (see IAS 23: Chapter 10).

Some costs **cannot be attributed** to contract activity and so the following should be **excluded** from construction contract costs.

- **General administration costs** (unless reimbursement is specified in the contract)
- **Selling costs**
- **R&D** (unless reimbursement is specified in the contract)
- **Depreciation** of idle plant and equipment not used on any particular contract

2.7 Recognition of contract revenue and expenses

Revenue and costs associated with a contract should be recognised according to the stage of completion of the contract at the end of the reporting period, but *only when* the **outcome of the activity can be estimated reliably**. If a loss is predicted on a contract, then it should be recognised immediately. This is often known as the **percentage of completion method**.

A reliable estimate of the outcome of a construction contract can only be made when **certain conditions** have been met, and these conditions will be different for fixed price and cost plus contracts.

- **Fixed price contracts**

  - Probable that economic benefits of the contract will flow to the entity
  - Total contract revenue can be reliably measured
  - Stage of completion at the period end and costs to complete the contract can be reliably measured
  - Costs attributable to the contract can be identified clearly and be reliably measured (actual costs can be compared to previous estimates)

- **Cost plus contracts**

  - Probable that economic benefits of the contract will flow to the entity
  - Costs attributable to the contract (whether or not reimbursable) can be identified clearly and be reliably measured

The **percentage of completion method** is an application of the accruals assumption. Contract revenue is matched to the contract costs incurred in reaching the stage of completion, so revenue, costs and profit are attributed to the proportion of work completed.

We can **summarise** the treatment as follows.

- Recognise **contract revenue** as revenue in the accounting periods in which the work is performed
- Recognise **contract costs** as an expense in the accounting period in which the work to which they relate is performed
- Any **expected excess** of total contract costs over total contract revenue should be recognised as an expense immediately
- Any costs incurred which relate to **future activity** should be recognised as an asset if it is probable that they will be recovered (often called contract work in progress, ie amounts due from the customer)
- Where amounts have been recognised as contract revenue, but their **collectability** from the customer becomes doubtful, such amounts should be recognised as an expense, not a deduction from revenue

2.8 When can reliable estimates be made?

IAS 11 only allows contract revenue and costs to be recognised when the outcome of the contract can be predicted, ie when it is probable that the economic benefits attached to the contract will flow to the entity. IAS 11 states that this can only be when a contract has been agreed which establishes the following.

- The **enforceable rights** of each party in respect of the asset to be constructed
- The **consideration** that is to be exchanged
- **Terms and manner of settlement**

In addition, the entity should have an **effective internal financial budgeting and reporting system**, in order to review and revise the estimates of contract revenue and costs as the contract progresses.

2.9 Determining the stage of completion

How should you decide on the stage of completion of any contract? The standard lists several methods.

- **Proportion of contract costs incurred** for work carried out to date
- **Surveys** of work carried out
- **Physical proportion** of the contract work completed

2.10 Example: stage of completion

Centrepoint Co have a fixed price contract to build a tower block. The initial amount of revenue agreed is $220m. At the beginning of the contract on 1 January 20X6 our initial estimate of the contract costs is $200m. At the end of 20X6 our estimate of the total costs has risen to $202m.

During 20X7 the customer agrees to a variation which increases expected revenue from the contract by $5m and causes additional costs of $3m. At the end of 20X7 there are materials stored on site for use during the following period which cost $2.5m.

We have decided to determine the stage of completion of the contract by calculating the proportion that contract costs incurred for work to date bear to the latest estimated total contract costs. The contract costs incurred at the end of each year were 20X6: $52.52m, 20X7: $154.2m (including materials in store), 20X8 $205m.

Required

Calculate the stage of completion for each year of the contract and show how revenues, costs and profits will be recognised in each year.

Solution

We can summarise the financial data for each year end during the construction period as follows.

	20X6 $'000	20X7 $'000	20X8 $'000
Initial amount of revenue agreed in the contract	220,000	220,000	220,000
Variation	–	5,000	5,000
Total contract revenue	220,000	225,000	225,000
Contract costs incurred to date	52,520	154,200	205,000
Contract costs to complete	149,480	50,800	–
Total estimated contract costs	202,000	205,000	205,000
Estimated profit	18,000	20,000	20,000
Stage of completion	26.0%	74.0%	100.0%

The stage of completion has been calculated using the formula:

$$\frac{\text{Contract costs incurred to date}}{\text{Total estimated contract costs}}$$

The stage of completion in 20X7 is calculated by deducting the $2.5m of materials held for the following period from the costs incurred up to that year end, ie $154.2m − $2.5m = $151.7m. $151.7m/$205m = 74%.

Revenue, expenses and profit will be recognised in profit or loss as follows.

		To date $'000	Recognised in prior years $'000	Recognised in current year $'000
20X6	Revenue ($220m × 26%)	57,200		
	Costs ($202m × 26%)	52,520		
		4,680		
20X7	Revenue ($225m × 74%)	166,500	57,200	109,300
	Costs ($205m × 74%)	151,700	52,520	99,180
		14,800	4,680	10,120
20X8	Revenue ($225m × 100%)	225,000	166,500	58,500
	Costs ($205m × 100%)	205,000	151,700	53,300
		20,000	14,800	5,200

You can see from the above example that, when the stage of completion is determined using the contract costs incurred to date, only contract costs reflecting the work to date should be included in costs incurred to date.

- Exclude costs relating to **future activity**, eg cost of materials delivered but not yet used
- Exclude payments made to subcontractors **in advance** of work performed

2.11 Outcome of the contract cannot be reliably estimated

When the contract's outcome cannot be reliably estimated the following treatment should be followed.

- Only recognise revenue to the extent of contract costs incurred which are expected to be **recoverable**
- Recognise contract costs as an **expense** in the period they are incurred

This **no profit/no loss approach** reflects the situation near the beginning of a contract, ie the outcome cannot be reliably estimated, but it is likely that costs will be recovered.

Contract costs which **cannot be recovered** should be recognised as an expense straight away. IAS 11 lists the following situations where this might occur.

- The contract is **not fully enforceable**, ie its validity is seriously questioned
- The completion of the contract is subject to the outcome of **pending litigation or legislation**
- The contract relates to properties which will probably be **expropriated or condemned**
- The customer is **unable to meet its obligations** under the contract
- The contractor **cannot complete** the contract or in any other way meet its obligations under the contract

Where these **uncertainties cease to exist,** contract revenue and costs should be recognised as normal, ie by reference to the stage of completion.

2.12 Recognition of expected losses

Any loss on a contract should be **recognised as soon as it is foreseen**. The loss will be the amount by which total expected contract revenue is exceeded by total expected contract costs. The loss amount is not affected by whether work has started on the contract, the stage of completion of the work or profits on other contracts (unless they are related contracts treated as a single contract).

2.13 Changes in estimates

The effect of any change in the estimate of contract revenue or costs or the outcome of a contract should be accounted for as a **change in accounting estimate** under IAS 8 *Accounting policies, changes in accounting estimates and errors.*

2.14 Example: changes in estimates

The example below shows the effect of a change in estimate of costs on the figures that appear in the statement of comprehensive income and statement of financial position.

Battersby Co enters into a three-year contract.

Estimated revenue = $20,000
Estimated total cost = $16,000.

However, during Year 2, management revises its estimate of total costs incurred and thus the outcome of the contract. As a result, during Year 2, a loss is recognised on the contract for the year, even though the contract will still be profitable overall.

	Year 1 $	Year 2 $	Year 3 $
Estimated revenue	20,000	20,000	20,000
Estimated total cost	16,000	18,000	18,000
Estimated total profit	4,000	2,000	2,000
Cost incurred to date	$8,000	$13,500	$18,000
Percentage of completion	50%	75%	100%
Recognised profit/(loss) for year	$2,000	($500)	$500
Cumulative recognised profit	$2,000	$1,500	$2,000

Progress billings of $8,000, $8,000 and $4,000 are made on the last day of each year and are received in the first month of the following year. The asset at the end of each year is:

	Year 1 $	Year 2 $	Year 3 $
Costs incurred	8,000	13,500	18,000
Recognised profits	2,000	2,000	2,500
(Recognised losses)		(500)	(500)
(Progress billings)	(8,000)	(16,000)	(20,000)
Amount recognised as an asset/(liability)	2,000	(1,000)	0

In addition, at each year end, the entity recognises a trade receivable for the amount outstanding at the end of the year of $8,000, $8,000 and $4,000.

2.15 Section summary

In valuing long-term contracts and the other disclosures required under IAS 11, an organised approach is essential. The following suggested method breaks the process down into five logical steps.

Step 1   **Compare the contract value** and the **total costs** expected to be incurred on the contract. If a loss is foreseen (that is, if the costs to date plus estimated costs to completion exceed the contract value) then it must be charged against profits. If a loss has already been charged in previous years, then only the difference between the loss as previously and currently estimated need be charged.

Step 2   Using the percentage completed to date (or other formula given in the question), calculate sales revenue **attributable** to the contract for the period (for example percentage complete × total contract value, less of course, revenue taken in previous periods).

Step 3 **Calculate the cost of sales** on the contract for the period.

	$
Total contract costs × percentage complete (or follow instructions in question)	X
Less any costs charged in previous periods	(X)
	X
Add foreseeable losses in full (not previously charged)	X
Cost of sales on contract for the period	X

Step 4 **Deduct the cost of sales** for the period as calculated above (including any foreseeable loss) from the sales revenue calculated at step 2 to give profit (loss) recognised for the period.

Step 5 **Calculate amounts due to/from** customers as per the working on the previous page.

	$
Contract costs incurred to date	X
Recognised profits/(losses) to date	X
	X
Progress billings to date	(X)
Amounts due from/(to) customers	X

Note: This represents unbilled revenue. Unpaid billed revenue will be shown under trade receivables.

2.16 Summary of accounting treatment

The following summarises the accounting treatment for long-term contracts – **make sure that you understand it.**

2.16.1 Statement of comprehensive income (income statement)

(a) **Revenue and costs**

(i) Sales revenue and associated costs should be recorded in the income statement section as the contract activity progresses.

(ii) Include an appropriate proportion of total contract value as sales revenue in the income statement.

(iii) The costs incurred in reaching that stage of completion are matched with this sales revenue, resulting in the reporting of results which can be attributed to the proportion of work completed.

(iv) Sales revenue is the value of work carried out to date.

(b) **Profit recognised in the contract**

(i) It must reflect the proportion of work carried out.

(ii) It should take into account any known inequalities in profitability in the various stages of a contract.

2.16.2 Statement of financial position

(a) **Inventories**

	$
Costs to date	X
Plus recognised profits	(X)
	X
Less recognised losses	(X)
	X
Less progress billings	(X)
Amount due from customers	X

(b)   **Receivables**

	$
Unpaid progress billings	X

(c)   **Payables**. Where (a) gives a net 'amount due to customers' this amount should be included in payables under 'payments on account'.

Question   Construction contract

The main business of Santolina Co is construction contracts. At the end of September 20X3 there is an uncompleted contract on the books, details of which are as follows.

CONTRACT B

Date commenced	1.4.X1
Expected completion date	23.12.X3
	$
Final contract price	290,000
Costs to 30.9.X3	210,450
Value of work certified to 30.9.X3	230,000
Progress billings to 30.9.X3	210,000
Cash received to 30.9.X3	194,000
Estimated costs to completion at 30.9.X3	20,600

Required

Prepare calculations showing the amount to be included in the statement of financial position at 30 September 20X3 in respect of the above contract.

Answer

Contract B is a construction contract and will be included in the statement of financial position at cost plus attributable profit less progress billings.

The estimated final profit is:

	$
Final contract price	290,000
Less: costs to date	(210,450)
estimated future costs	(20,600)
Estimated final profit	58,950

The attributable profit is found as follows.

$$\text{Estimated final profit} \times \frac{\text{Work certified}}{\text{Total contract price}}$$

$$\$58,950 \times \frac{230,000}{290,000}$$

Attributable profit = $46,753

Long-term contract work in progress

CONTRACT B

	$
Costs to date	210,450
Attributable profit	46,753
	257,203
Progress billings	(210,000)
Amount due from customers	47,203
Trade receivables	16,000

Exam focus point

A question is more likely to be set on construction contracts than on inventory, simply because inventory is tested at the lower level.

Question

IAS 11 calculations

Haggrun Co has two contracts in progress, the details of which are as follows.

	Happy (profitable)	Grumpy (loss-making)
	$'000	$'000
Total contract price	300	300
Costs incurred to date	90	150
Estimated costs to completion	135	225
Progress payments invoiced and received	116	116

Required

Show extracts from the statement of comprehensive income and the statement of financial position for each contract, assuming they are both:

(a)   40% complete; and
(b)   36% complete.

Answer

Happy contract

(a)   *40% complete*

$'000

Statement of comprehensive income
	$'000
Revenue (300 × 40%)	120
Cost of sales ((90+ 135) × 40%)	(90)
Profit to date (W)	30

Working

Profit to date

	$'000
Total contract price	300
Costs to date	(90)
Cost to completion	(135)
Total expected profit	75
Profit to date (75 × 40%)	30

Statement of financial position

	$'000
Costs to date	90
Profit recognised to date	30
Progress billings	(116)
Amount due from customers	4

(b)   *36% complete*

$'000

Statement of comprehensive income
	$'000
Revenue (300 × 36%)	108
Cost of sales (((90 + 135) × 36%))	(81)
Profit to date (75 × 36%)	27

	$'000
Statement of financial position	
Costs to date	90
Profit recognised to date	27
Progress billings	(116)
Amount due from customers	1

Grumpy contract

(a) *40% complete*

	$'000
Statement of comprehensive income	
Revenue (300 × 40%)	120
Cost of sales*	(195)
Foreseeable loss (W)	(75)

Working

	$'000
Total contract revenue	300
Costs to date	(150)
Costs to complete	(225)
Foreseeable loss	(75)

Statement of financial position	
Costs to date	150
Foreseeable loss	(75)
Progress billings	(116)
Amounts due to customers	(41)

	$'000
* Costs to date (150 + 225) × 40%	150
Forseeable loss (75) × 60%**	45
	195

** The other 40% is taken into account in costs to date. We make this adjustment to bring in the **whole** of the foreseeable loss.

(b) *36% complete*

	$'000
Statement of comprehensive income	
Revenue (300 × 36%)	108
Cost of sales*	(183)
Foreseeable loss	(75)

Statement of financial position	
Costs to date	150
Foreseeable loss	(75)
Progress billings	(116)
Amount due to customers	(41)

	$'000
* Costs to date (150 + 225) × 36%	135
Forseeable loss (75) × 64%**	48
	183

Chapter roundup

- IAS 2 *Inventories* requires that the statement of financial position should show **inventories** classified in a manner appropriate to the entity. Common **classifications** are:

  Merchandise
  Production supplies
  Materials
  Work in progress
  Finished goods

- The use of **LIFO** is **prohibited** under the revised IAS 2.

- Full details are required of inventory carried at **NRV** as well as the reversal of any previous write down.

- The rules for calculating accounting entries on **construction contracts** can be summarised as follows.

  - Sales revenue is based upon the stage of completion.
  - Calculate profit to date and cost of sales is a balancing figure.
  - Foreseeable losses are recognised immediately.
  - The financial position amount (amounts due from/(to) customers) is calculated as:

Costs to date	X
Profits (losses) to date	X
Progress billings	(X)
	X

Quick quiz

1 Net realisable value = Selling price **less** .... **less** ....

2 Which inventory costing method is allowed under IAS 2?

  (a) FIFO
  (b) LIFO

3 Any expected loss on a construction contract must be recognised, in full, in the year it was identified.

  True ☐

  False ☐

4 List the five steps to be taken when valuing construction contracts.

5 Which items in the statement of comprehensive income and statement of financial position are potentially affected by construction contracts?

Answers to quick quiz

1 Net realisable value = selling price costs to completion **less** costs necessary to make the sale.

2 (a) FIFO. LIFO is not allowed.

3 True

4 See paragraph 2.17

5 Statement of comprehensive income: revenue and cost of sales.
  Statement of financial position: inventories, receivables, payables

Now try the question below from the Exam Question Bank

Number	Level	Marks	Time
15	Examination	15	27 mins
16	Examination	15	27 mins

13

Provisions, contingent liabilities and contingent assets

Topic list	Syllabus reference
1 Provisions	C7
2 Provisions for restructuring	C7
3 Contingent liabilities and contingent assets	C7

Introduction

You will have met this standard in your earlier studies. However, you will be asked in more detail about IAS 37 for Paper 7.

Study guide

			Intellectual level
C7	**Provisions, contingent liabilities and contingent assets**		
	(a)	explain why an accounting standard on provisions is necessary	2
	(b)	distinguish between legal and constructive obligations.	2
	(c)	state when provisions may and may not be made and demonstrate how they should be accounted for.	2
	(d)	explain how provisions should be measured.	1
	(e)	define contingent assets and liabilities and describe their accounting treatment.	2
	(f)	identify and account for:	2
		(i) warranties/guarantees	
		(ii) onerous contracts	
		(iii) environmental and similar provisions	
		(iv) provisions for future repairs or refurbishments	

1 Provisions

FAST FORWARD

Under IAS 37 a provision should be recognised when:

- An entity has a **present obligation**, legal or constructive
- It is probable that a **transfer of resources embodying economic benefits** will be required to settle it
- A reliable estimate can be made of its amount.

1.1 Objective

IAS 37 *Provisions, contingent liabilities and contingent assets* aims to ensure that appropriate **recognition criteria** and **measurement bases** are applied to provisions, contingent liabilities and contingent assets and that **sufficient information** is disclosed in the **notes** to the financial statements to enable users to understand their nature, timing and amount.

1.2 Provisions

Before IAS 37, there was no accounting standard dealing with provisions. Companies wanting to show their results in the most favourable light used to make large 'one off' provisions in years where a high level of underlying profits was generated. These provisions, often known as 'big bath' provisions, were then available to shield expenditure in future years when perhaps the underlying profits were not as good.

In other words, provisions were used for profit smoothing. Profit smoothing is misleading.

Important

> The key aim of IAS 37 is to ensure that **provisions are made only** where there are valid grounds for them.

IAS 37 views a provision as a liability.

Key terms

> A **provision** is a **liability** of uncertain timing or amount.
>
> A **liability** is a present obligation of the entity arising from past events , the settlement of which is expected to result in an outflow from the entity of resources embodying economic benefits.   *(IAS 37)*

The IAS distinguishes provisions from other liabilities such as trade creditors and accruals. This is on the basis that for a provision there is **uncertainty** about the timing or amount of the future expenditure. Whilst uncertainty is clearly present in the case of certain accruals the uncertainty is generally much less than for provisions.

1.3 Recognition

IAS 37 states that a provision should be **recognised** as a liability in the financial statements when:

- An entity has a **present obligation** (legal or constructive) as a result of a past event
- It is probable that an **outflow of resources embodying economic benefits** will be required to settle the obligation
- A **reliable estimate** can be made of the amount of the obligation

1.4 Meaning of obligation

It is fairly clear what a legal obligation is. However, you may not know what a **constructive obligation** is.

Key term

> IAS 37 defines a **constructive obligation** as
>
> 'An obligation that derives from an entity's actions where:
>
> - by an established pattern of past practice, published policies or a sufficiently specific current statement the entity has indicated to other parties that it will accept certain responsibilities; and
> - as a result, the entity has created a valid expectation on the part of those other parties that it will discharge those responsibilities.'

1.4.1 Probable transfer of resources

For the purpose of the IAS, a transfer of resources embodying economic benefits is regarded as **'probable'** if the event is **more likely than not** to occur. This appears to indicate a probability of more than 50%. However, the standard makes it clear that where there is a number of similar obligations the probability should be based on considering the population as a whole, rather than one single item.

1.4.2 Example: transfer of resources

If a company has entered into a warranty obligation then the probability of transfer of resources embodying economic benefits may well be extremely small in respect of one specific item. However, when considering the population as a whole the probability of some transfer of resources is quite likely to be much higher. If there is a **greater than 50% probability** of some transfer of economic benefits then a **provision** should be made for the **expected amount**.

1.4.3 Measurement of provisions

Important

> The amount recognised as a provision should be the best estimate of the expenditure required to settle the present obligation at the end of the reporting period.

The estimates will be determined by the **judgement** of the entity's management supplemented by the experience of similar transactions.

Allowance is made for **uncertainty**. Where the provision being measured involves a large population of items, the obligation is estimated by weighting all possible outcomes by their associated probabilities, ie **expected value**.

Parker Co sells goods with a warranty under which customers are covered for the cost of repairs of any manufacturing defect that becomes apparent within the first six months of purchase. The company's past experience and future expectations indicate the following pattern of likely repairs.

% of goods sold	Defects	Cost of repairs if all items suffered from these defects $m
75	None	–
20	Minor	1.0
5	Major	4.0

What is the provision required?

Answer

The cost is found using 'expected values' (75% × $nil) + (20% × $1.0m) + (5% × $4.0m) = $400,000.

Where the effect of the **time value of money** is material, the amount of a provision should be the **present value** of the expenditure required to settle the obligation. An appropriate **discount** rate should be used.

The discount rate should be a pre-tax rate that reflects current market assessments of the time value of money. The discount rate(s) should not reflect risks for which future cash flow estimates have been adjusted.

Example

A company knows that when it ceases a certain operation in 5 years time it will have to pay environmental cleanup costs of $5m.

The provision to be made now will be the present value of $5m in 5 years time.

The relevant discount rate in this case is 10%.

Therefore a provision will be made for:

	$
$5m × 0.62092*	3,104,600

* The discount rate for 5 yeas at 10%.

The following year the provision will be:

	$
$5m × 0.68301	3,415,050
	310,540

The increase in the second year of $310,450 will be charged to profit or loss. It is referred to as the **unwinding** of the discount. This is accounted for as a finance cost.

1.4.4 Future events

Future events which are reasonably expected to occur (eg new legislation, changes in technology) may affect the amount required to settle the entity's obligation and should be taken into account.

1.4.5 Expected disposal of assets

Gains from the expected disposal of assets should not be taken into account in measuring a provision.

1.4.6 Reimbursements

Some or all of the expenditure needed to settle a provision may be expected to be recovered from a third party. If so, the reimbursement should be recognised only when it is virtually certain that reimbursement will be received if the entity settles the obligation.

- The reimbursement should be treated as a separate asset, and the amount recognised should not be greater than the provision itself.
- The provision and the amount recognised for reimbursement may be netted off in profit or loss.

1.4.7 Changes in provisions

Provisions should be reviewed at the end of each reporting period and adjusted to reflect the current best estimate. If it is no longer probable that a transfer of resources will be required to settle the obligation, the provision should be reversed.

1.4.8 Use of provisions

A provision should be used only for expenditures for which the provision was originally recognised. Setting expenditures against a provision that was originally recognised for another purpose would conceal the impact of two different events.

1.4.9 Future operating losses

Provisions should not be recognised for future operating losses. They do not meet the definition of a liability and the general recognition criteria set out in the standard.

1.4.10 Onerous contracts

If an entity has a contract that is onerous, the present obligation under the contract **should be recognised and measured** as a provision. An example might be vacant leasehold property. The entity is under an obligation to maintain the property but is receiving no income from it.

Key term

> An **onerous contract** is a contract entered into with another party under which the unavoidable costs of fulfilling the terms of the contract exceed any revenues expected to be received from the goods or services supplied or purchased directly or indirectly under the contract and where the entity would have to compensate the other party if it did not fulfil the terms of the contract.

1.5 Examples of possible provisions

It is easier to see what IAS 37 is driving at if you look at examples of those items which are possible provisions under this standard. Some of these we have already touched on.

(a) **Warranties**. These are argued to be genuine provisions as on past experience it is probable, ie more likely than not, that some claims will emerge. The provision must be estimated, however, on the basis of the class as a whole and not on individual claims. There is a clear legal obligation in this case.

(b) **Major repairs**. In the past it has been quite popular for companies to provide for expenditure on a major overhaul to be accrued gradually over the intervening years between overhauls. Under IAS 37 this is no longer possible as IAS 37 would argue that this is a mere intention to carry out repairs, not an obligation. The entity can always sell the asset in the meantime. The only solution is to treat major assets such as aircraft, ships, furnaces etc as a series of smaller assets where each part is depreciated over shorter lives. Thus any major overhaul may be argued to be replacement and therefore capital rather than revenue expenditure.

(c) **Self insurance**. A number of companies have created a provision for self insurance based on the expected cost of making good fire damage etc instead of paying premiums to an insurance company. Under IAS 37 this provision is no longer justifiable as the entity has no obligation until a fire or accident occurs. No obligation exists until that time.

(d) **Environmental contamination**. If the company has an environmental policy such that other parties would expect the company to clean up any contamination or if the company has broken current environmental legislation then a provision for environmental damage must be made.

(e) **Decommissioning or abandonment costs**. When an oil company initially purchases an oilfield it is put under a legal obligation to decommission the site at the end of its life. Prior to IAS 37 most oil companies set up the provision gradually over the life of the field so that no one year would be unduly burdened with the cost.

IAS 37, however, insists that a legal obligation exists on the initial expenditure on the field and therefore a liability exists immediately. This would appear to result in a large charge to profit and loss in the first year of operation of the field. However, the IAS takes the view that the cost of purchasing the field in the first place is not only the cost of the field itself but also the costs of putting it right again. Thus all the costs of decommissioning may be capitalised.

(f) **Restructuring**. This is considered in detail below.

Exam focus point

These examples are the sort of situation you may get in the exam.

2 Provisions for restructuring

FAST FORWARD

One of the main purposes of IAS 37 was to target abuses of provisions for restructuring. Accordingly, IAS 37 lays down **strict criteria** to determine when such a provision can be made.

Key term

IAS 37 defines a **restructuring** as:

A programme that is planned and is controlled by management and materially changes one of two things.

- The scope of a business undertaken by an entity
- The manner in which that business is conducted

The IAS gives the following **examples** of events that may fall under the definition of restructuring.

- The **sale or termination** of a line of business
- The **closure of business locations** in a country or region or the **relocation** of business activities from one country region to another
- **Changes in management structure**, for example, the elimination of a layer of management
- **Fundamental reorganisations** that have a material effect on the **nature and focus** of the entity's operations

The question is whether or not an entity has an obligation – legal or constructive – at the end of the reporting period. For this to be the case:

- An entity must have a **detailed formal plan** for the restructuring
- It must have **raised a valid expectation** in those affected that it will carry out the restructuring by starting to implement that plan or announcing its main features to those affected by it

Important

A mere management decision is not normally sufficient. Management decisions may sometimes trigger off recognition, but only if earlier events such as negotiations with employee representatives and other interested parties have been concluded subject only to management approval.

Where the restructuring involves the **sale of an operation** then IAS 37 states that no obligation arises until the entity has entered into a **binding sale agreement**. This is because until this has occurred the entity will be able to change its mind and withdraw from the sale even if its intentions have been announced publicly.

2.1 Costs to be included within a restructuring provision

The IAS states that a restructuring provision should include only the **direct expenditures** arising from the restructuring, which are those that are both:

- **Necessarily entailed** by the restructuring; and
- Not associated with the **ongoing activities** of the entity.

The following costs should specifically **not** be included within a restructuring provision.

- **Retraining** or relocating continuing staff
- **Marketing**
- **Investment in new systems** and distribution networks

2.2 Disclosure

Disclosures for provisions fall into two parts.

- Disclosure of details of the **change in carrying value** of a provision from the beginning to the end of the year
- Disclosure of the **background** to the making of the provision and the uncertainties affecting its outcome

Question
Provision

In which of the following circumstances might a provision be recognised?

(a)   On 13 December 20X9 the board of an entity decided to close down a division. The accounting date of the company is 31 December. Before 31 December 20X9 the decision was not communicated to any of those affected and no other steps were taken to implement the decision.

(b)   The board agreed a detailed closure plan on 20 December 20X9 and details were given to customers and employees.

(c)   A company is obliged to incur clean up costs for environmental damage (that has already been caused).

(d)   A company intends to carry out future expenditure to operate in a particular way in the future.

Answer

(a)   No provision would be recognised as the decision has not been communicated.

(b)   A provision would be made in the 20X9 financial statements.

(c)   A provision for such costs is appropriate.

(d)   No present obligation exists and under IAS 37 no provision would be appropriate. This is because the entity could avoid the future expenditure by its future actions, maybe by changing its method of operation.

3 Contingent liabilities and contingent assets

FAST FORWARD

An entity should not **recognise** a contingent asset or liability, but they should be **disclosed**.

Now you understand provisions it will be easier to understand contingent assets and liabilities.

> IAS 37 defines a **contingent liability** as:
>
> - A possible obligation that arises from past events and whose existence will be confirmed only by the occurrence or non-occurrence of one or more uncertain future events not wholly within the control of the entity; or
> - A present obligation that arises from past events but is not recognised because:
>   - It is not probable that an outflow of resources embodying economic benefits will be required to settle the obligation; or
>   - The amount of the obligation cannot be measured with sufficient reliability.

As a rule of thumb, probable means more than 50% likely. If an obligation is probable, it is not a contingent liability – instead, a provision is needed.

3.1 Treatment of contingent liabilities

Contingent liabilities **should not be recognised in financial statements** but they **should be disclosed**. The required disclosures are:

- A brief description of the nature of the contingent liability
- An estimate of its financial effect
- An indication of the uncertainties that exist
- The possibility of any reimbursement

3.2 Contingent assets

> IAS 37 defines a **contingent asset** as:
>
> A possible asset that arises from past events and whose existence will be confirmed by the occurrence or non-occurrence of one or more uncertain future events not wholly within control of the entity.

A contingent asset must not be recognised. Only when the realisation of the related economic benefits is **virtually certain** should recognition take place. At that point, **the asset is no longer a contingent asset**!

3.3 Disclosure

3.3.1 Disclosure: contingent liabilities

A **brief description** must be provided of all material contingent liabilities unless they are likely to be remote. In addition, provide

- An estimate of their **financial effect**
- Details of **any uncertainties**
- The possibility of any reimbursement

3.3.2 Disclosure: contingent assets

Contingent assets must only be disclosed in the notes if they are **probable**. In that case a brief description of the contingent asset should be provided along with an estimate of its likely financial effect.

3.4 'Let out'

IAS 37 permits reporting entities to avoid disclosure requirements relating to provisions, contingent liabilities and contingent assets if they would be expected to **seriously prejudice** the position of the entity in dispute with other parties. However, this should only be employed in **extremely rare** cases. Details of the general nature of the provision/contingencies must still be provided, together with an explanation of why it has not been disclosed.

3.5 Flow chart

You must practise the questions below to get the hang of IAS 37. But first, study the flow chart, taken from IAS 37, which is a good summary of its requirements concerning provisions and contingent liabilities.

Exam focus point

> If you learn this flow chart you should be able to deal with most questions you are likely to meet in an exam.

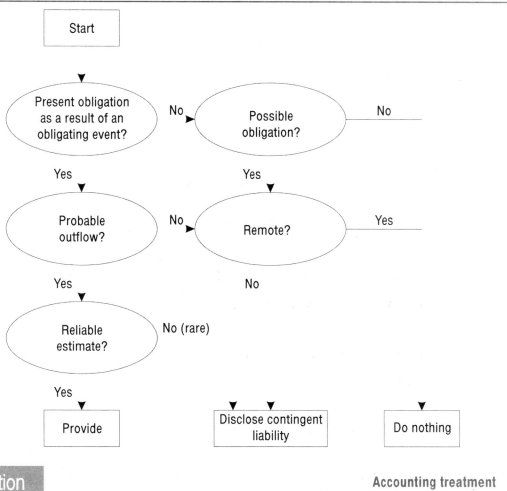

Question

Accounting treatment

During 20X0 Smack Co gives a guarantee of certain borrowings of Pony Co, whose financial condition at that time is sound. During 20X1, the financial condition of Pony Co deteriorates and at 30 June 20X1 Pony Co files for protection from its creditors.

What accounting treatment is required:

(a)   At 31 December 20X0?
(b)   At 31 December 20X1?

Answer

(a)   *At 31 December 20X0*

There is a present obligation as a result of a past obligating event. The obligating event is the giving of the guarantee, which gives rise to a legal obligation. However, at 31 December 20X0 no transfer of resources is probable in settlement of the obligation.

No provision is recognised. The guarantee is disclosed as a contingent liability unless the probability of any transfer is regarded as remote.

(b) *At 31 December 20X1*

As above, there is a present obligation as a result of a past obligating event, namely the giving of the guarantee.

At 31 December 20X1 it is probable that a transfer of resources will be required to settle the obligation. A provision is therefore recognised for the best estimate of the obligation.

Question
Recognition of provision

Warren Co gives warranties at the time of sale to purchasers of its products. Under the terms of the warranty the manufacturer undertakes to make good, by repair or replacement, manufacturing defects that become apparent within a period of three years from the date of the sale. Should a provision be recognised?

Answer

Warren Co **cannot avoid** the cost of repairing or replacing all items of product that manifest manufacturing defects in respect of which warranties are given before the end of the reporting period, and a provision for the cost of this should therefore be made.

Warren Co is obliged to repair or replace items that fail within the entire warranty period. Therefore, in respect of **this year's sales**, the obligation provided for at the end of the reporting period should be the cost of making good items for which defects have been notified but not yet processed, **plus** an estimate of costs in respect of the other items sold for which there is sufficient evidence that manufacturing defects **will** manifest themselves during their remaining periods of warranty cover.

Question
Accounting treatment

After a wedding in 20X0 ten people died, possibly as a result of food poisoning from products sold by Callow Co. Legal proceedings are started seeking damages from Callow but it disputes liability. Up to the date of approval of the financial statements for the year to 31 December 20X0, Callow's lawyers advise that it is probable that it will not be found liable. However, when Callow prepares the financial statements for the year to 31 December 20X1 its lawyers advise that, owing to developments in the case, it is probable that it will be found liable.

What is the required accounting treatment:

(a) At 31 December 20X0?
(b) At 31 December 20X1?

Answer

(a) *At 31 December 20X0*

On the basis of the evidence available when the financial statements were approved, there is no obligation as a result of past events. No provision is recognised. The matter is disclosed as a contingent liability unless the probability of any transfer is regarded as remote.

(b) *At 31 December 20X1*

On the basis of the evidence available, there is a present obligation. A transfer of resources in settlement is probable.

A provision is recognised for the best estimate of the amount needed to settle the present obligation.

3.6 Section summary

- The objective of IAS 37 is to ensure that appropriate recognition criteria and measurement bases are applied to provisions and contingencies and that sufficient information is disclosed.
- The IAS seeks to ensure that provisions are **only recognised** when a **measurable obligation** exists. It includes detailed rules that can be used to ascertain when an obligation exists and how to measure the obligation.
- The standard attempts to **eliminate** the **'profit smoothing'** which has gone on before it was issued.

Chapter Roundup

- Under **IAS 37**, a **provision** should be recognised
  - When an entity has a **present obligation**, legal or constructive
  - It is probable that a **transfer of resources embodying economic benefits** will be required to settle it
  - A **reliable estimate** can be made of its amount

- One the main purposes of IAS 37 was to target abuses of provisions for restructuring. Accordingly, IAS 37 lays down **strict criteria** to determine when such a provision can be made.

- An entity **should not recognise a contingent asset or liability**, but they **should be disclosed**.

Quick Quiz

1   A provision is a .... of .... timing or amount.
2   A programme is undertaken by management which converts the previously wholly owned chain of restaurants they ran into franchises. Is this restructuring?
3   Define contingent asset and contingent liability.
4   How should decommissioning costs on an oilfield be accounted for under IAS 37?
5   'Provisions for major overhauls should be accrued for over the period between overhauls'. Is this correct?

Answers to Quick Quiz

1   Liability of uncertain timing or amount
2   Yes. The manner in which the business is conducted has changed
3   Refer to paragraphs 3.1 and 3.2
4   They should be capitalised as part of the initial expenditure on the oilfield.
5   No. It is not correct. See paragraph 1.5.

Now try the questions below from the Exam Question Bank

Number	Level	Marks	Time
17	Examination	25	45 mins

14

Financial assets and liabilities

Topic list	Syllabus reference
1 Financial instruments	C5
2 Presentation of financial instruments	C5
3 Disclosure of financial instruments	C5
4 Recognition of financial instruments	C5
5 Measurement of financial instruments	C5

Introduction

IAS 32: *Financial instruments: presentation,* IAS 39: *Financial instruments: recognition and measurement* and IFRS 7: *Financial instruments: disclosure* are very topical standards. IAS 32 and IAS 39 were introduced to regulate the accounting treatment of financial instruments, especially derivatives which had previously been 'off balance sheet'.

Study guide

			Intellectual level
C5	**Financial assets and financial liabilities**		
	(a)	explain the need for an accounting standard on financial instruments.	1
	(b)	define financial instruments in terms of financial assets and financial liabilities.	1
	(c)	indicate for the following categories of financial instruments how they should be measured and how any gains and losses from subsequent measurement should be treated in the financial statements:	1
		(i) fair value through profit and loss	
		(ii) held to maturity (use of amortised cost, interest to income)	
		(iii) available for sale (carried at fair value with changes to equity, but dividends to income)	
		(iv) loans and receivables	
	(d)	distinguish between debt and equity capital.	2
	(e)	apply the requirements of relevant accounting standards to the issue and finance costs of:	2
		(i) equity	
		(ii) redeemable preference shares and debt instruments with no conversion rights (principle of amortised cost)	
		(iii) convertible debt	

Exam guide

Financial instruments are generally tested as part of a question rather than as a full question.

1 Financial instruments

 FAST FORWARD

Financial instruments can be very complex, particularly derivative instruments.

1.1 Introduction

If you read the financial press you will probably be aware of **rapid international expansion** in the use of financial instruments. These vary from straightforward, traditional instruments, eg bonds, through to various forms of so-called 'derivative instruments'.

We can perhaps summarise the reasons why a project on accounting for financial instruments was considered necessary as follows.

(a)   The **significant growth of financial instruments** over recent years has outstripped the development of guidance for their accounting.

(b)   The topic is of **international concern**, other national standard-setters are involved as well as the IASB.

(c)   There have been recent **high-profile disasters** involving derivatives (eg Barings) which, while not caused by accounting failures, have raised questions about accounting and disclosure practices.

Three accounting standards deal with financial instruments:

(a)   IAS 32 *Financial instruments:* **presentation**, which deals with:

   (i)   The classification of financial instruments between liabilities and equity
   (ii)   Presentation of certain compound instruments (instruments combining debt and equity)

(b)   IAS 39 Financial instruments: recognition and measurement, which deals with:

   (i)   Recognition and derecognition
   (ii)   The measurement of financial instruments
   (iii)   Hedge accounting (not in your syllabus)

(c)   IFRS 7 *Financial instruments: disclosure*

1.2 Definitions

The most important definitions are common to both standards.

- **Financial instrument.** Any contract that gives rise to both a financial asset of one entity and a financial liability or equity instrument of another entity.

- **Financial asset.** Any asset that is:

   (a)   cash
   (b)   an equity instrument of another entity
   (c)   a contractual right to receive cash or another financial asset from another entity; or to exchange financial instruments with another entity under conditions that are potentially favourable to the entity

- **Financial liability.** Any liability that is:

   (a)   a contractual obligation:

      (i)   to deliver cash or another financial asset to another entity, or
      (ii)   to exchange financial instruments with another entity under conditions that are potentially unfavourable

- **Equity instrument.** Any contract that evidences a residual interest in the assets of an entity after deducting all of its liabilities.

- **Fair value** is the amount for which an asset could be exchanged, or a liability settled, between knowledgeable, willing parties in an arm's length transaction.   *(IAS 32 and IAS 39)*

These definitions are very important – so learn them.

We should clarify some points arising from these definitions. Firstly, one or two terms above should be themselves defined.

(a)   A '**contract**' need not be in writing, but it must comprise an agreement that has 'clear economic consequences' and which the parties to it cannot avoid, usually because the agreement is enforceable in law.

(b)   An '**entity**' here could be an individual, partnership, incorporated body or government agency.

The definitions of **financial assets** and **financial liabilities** may seem rather circular, referring as they do to the terms financial asset and financial instrument. The point is that there may be a chain of contractual rights and obligations, but it will lead ultimately to the receipt or payment of cash *or* the acquisition or issue of an equity instrument.

Examples of **financial assets** include:

(a) Trade receivables
(b) Options
(c) Shares (when held as an investment)

Examples of **financial liabilities** include:

(a) Trade payables
(b) Debenture loans payable
(c) Redeemable preference (non-equity) shares

IAS 32 makes it clear that the following items are *not* financial instruments.

(a) **Physical assets**, eg inventories, property, plant and equipment, leased assets and **intangible assets** (patents, trademarks etc)
(b) **Prepaid expenses**, deferred revenue and most warranty obligations
(c) Liabilities or assets that are **not contractual** in nature

Question

Definitions

Can you give the reasons why physical assets and prepaid expenses do not qualify as financial instruments?

Answer

Refer to the definitions of financial assets and liabilities given above.

(a) **Physical assets**: control of these creates an opportunity to generate an inflow of cash or other assets, but it does not give rise to a present right to receive cash or other financial assets.
(b) **Prepaid expenses, etc**: the future economic benefit is the receipt of goods/services rather than the right to receive cash or other financial assets.

Contingent rights and obligations meet the definition of financial assets and financial liabilities respectively, even though many do not qualify for recognition in financial statements. This is because the contractual rights or obligations exist because of a past transaction or event (eg assumption of a guarantee).

1.3 Section summary

* Three accounting standards are relevant:

    - **IAS 32**: Financial instruments: Presentation
    - **IAS 39**: Financial instruments: Recognition and measurement
    - **IFRS 7**: Financial instruments: Disclosure

* The definitions of **financial asset, financial liability** and **equity instrument** are fundamental to IAS 32 and IAS 39.

2 Presentation of financial instruments

FAST FORWARD

The objective of IAS 32 is to help users understand how financial instruments may have affected the entity's financial position, financial performance and cash flows.

2.1 Scope

IAS 32 should be applied in the presentation and disclosure of **all types of financial instruments**.

Certain items are **excluded** for example subsidiaries, associates and joint ventures, pensions and insurance contracts.

2.2 Liabilities and equity

The main thrust of IAS 32 is that financial instruments should be presented according to their **substance, not merely their legal form**. In particular, entities which issue financial instruments should classify them (or their component parts) as **either financial liabilities, or equity**.

The classification of a financial instrument as a liability or as equity depends on the following.

- The **substance of the contractual arrangement** on initial recognition
- The definitions of a **financial liability** and an **equity instrument**

How should a **financial liability be distinguished from an equity instrument**? The critical feature of a **liability** is an **obligation** to transfer economic benefit. Therefore a financial instrument is a financial liability if there is a **contractual obligation** on the issuer either to deliver cash or another financial asset to the holder or to exchange another financial instrument with the holder under potentially unfavourable conditions to the issuer.

Where the above critical feature is *not* met, then the financial instrument is an **equity instrument**. IAS 32 explains that although the holder of an equity instrument may be entitled to a *pro rata* share of any distributions out of equity, the issuer does *not* have a contractual obligation to make such a distribution. For instance, a company is not obliged to pay a dividend to its ordinary shareholders. Although substance and legal form are often **consistent with each other**, this is not always the case. In particular, a financial instrument may have the legal form of equity, but in substance it is in fact a liability. Other instruments may combine features of both equity instruments and financial liabilities.

For example, many entities issue **preference shares** which must be **redeemed** by the issuer for a fixed (or determinable) amount at a fixed (or determinable) future date. Alternatively, the holder may have the right to require the issuer to redeem the shares at or after a certain date for a fixed amount. In such cases, the issuer has an **obligation**. Therefore the instrument is a **financial liability** and should be classified as such.

The distinction between redeemable and non-redeemable preference shares is important. Most preference shares are redeemable and are therefore classified as a **financial liability**. Expect to see this in your exam.

2.3 Compound financial instruments

Some financial instruments contain both a liability and an equity element. In such cases, IAS 32 requires the component parts of the instrument to be **classified separately**, according to the substance of the contractual arrangement and the definitions of a financial liability and an equity instrument.

One of the most common types of compound instrument is **convertible debt**. This creates a primary financial liability of the issuer and grants an option to the holder of the instrument to convert it into an equity instrument (usually ordinary shares) of the issuer. This is the economic equivalent of the issue of conventional debt plus a warrant to acquire shares in the future.

Although in theory there are several possible ways of calculating the split, IAS 32 requires the following method:

(a)   Calculate the value for the liability component.
(b)   Deduct this from the instrument as a whole to leave a residual value for the equity component.

The reasoning behind this approach is that an entity's equity is its residual interest in its assets amount after deducting all its liabilities.

The **sum of the carrying amounts** assigned to liability and equity will always be equal to the carrying amount that would be ascribed to the instrument **as a whole**.

2.4 Example: valuation of compound instruments

Rathbone Co issues 2,000 convertible bonds at the start of 20X2. The bonds have a three year term, and are issued at par with a face value of $1,000 per bond, giving total proceeds of $2,000,000. Interest is payable annually in arrears at a nominal annual interest rate of 6%. Each bond is convertible at any time up to maturity into 250 ordinary shares.

When the bonds are issued, the prevailing market interest rate for similar debt without conversion options is 9%.

Required

What is the value of the equity component in the bond?

Solution

The liability component is valued first, and the **difference** between the proceeds of the bond issue and the fair value of the liability is assigned to the **equity component**. The present value of the liability component is calculated using a discount rate of 9%, the market interest rate for similar bonds having no conversion rights, as shown.

	$
Present value of the principal: $2,000,000 payable at the end of three years ($2m × 0.772)*	1,544,367
Present value of the interest: $120,000 payable annually in arrears for three years ($120,000 × 2.5313)*	303,755
Total liability component	1,848,122
Equity component (balancing figure)	151,878
Proceeds of the bond issue	2,000,000

* These figures can be obtained from discount and annuity tables or simply calculated arithmetically as follows.

		$
Principal		
$2,000,000 discounted at 9% over 3 years:		
2,000,000 ÷ 1.09 ÷ 1.09 ÷ 1.09		1,544,367
Interest		
Year 1 120,000 ÷ 1.09	110,091	
Year 2 110,091 ÷ 1.09	101,002	
Year 3 101,002 ÷ 1.09	92,662	
		303,755
Value of liability component		1,848,122
Equity component (balancing figure		151,878
Proceeds of bond issue		2,000,000

The split between the liability and equity components remains the same throughout the term of the instrument, even if there are changes in the **likelihood of the option being exercised**. This is because it is not always possible to predict how a holder will behave. The issuer continues to have an obligation to make future payments until conversion, maturity of the instrument or some other relevant transaction takes place.

2.5 Interest, dividends, losses and gains

As well as looking at presentation in the statement of financial position, IAS 32 considers how financial instruments affect the income statement or statement of comprehensive income (and movements in equity). The treatment varies according to whether interest, dividends, losses or gains relate to a **financial liability** or an **equity instrument**.

(a) Interest, dividends, losses and gains relating to a financial instrument (or component part) classified as a **financial liability** should be recognised as **income or expense** in profit or loss.

(b)   Distributions to holders of a financial instrument classified as an **equity instrument** (dividends to ordinary shareholders) should be **debited directly to equity** by the issuer. These will appear in the statement of changes in equity.

(c)   **Transaction costs** of an equity transaction shall be accounted for as a **deduction from equity** usually debited to the share premium account (unless they are directly attributable to the acquisition of a business, in which case they are expensed in the period under IFRS 3).

2.6 Section summary

- Issuers of financial instruments must classify them as **liabilities** or **equity**
- The **substance** of the financial instrument is more important than its **legal form**
- The **critical feature of a financial liability** is the contractual obligation to deliver cash or another financial asset
- **Compound instruments** are split into equity and liability parts and presented accordingly
- **Interest, dividends, losses and gains** are treated according to whether they relate to a financial liability or an equity instrument

3 Disclosure of financial instruments

One of the main purposes of IAS 32 is to provide full and useful disclosures relating to financial instruments. IFRS 7 revises, enhances and replaces the disclosures in IAS 32.

3.1 IFRS 7

As well as specific monetary disclosures, **narrative commentary** by issuers is encouraged by the Standard. This will enable users to understand management's attitude to risk, whatever the current transactions involving financial instruments are at the period end.

The standard does not prescribe the **format or location** for disclosure of information. A combination of narrative descriptions and specific quantified data should be given, as appropriate.

The **level of detail** required is a matter of judgement. Where a large number of very similar financial instrument transactions are undertaken, these may be grouped together. Conversely, a single significant transaction may require full disclosure.

Classes of instruments will be grouped together by management in a manner appropriate to the information to be disclosed.

Exam focus point

> The examiner has indicated that he will not set questions about the **financial risks** of financial instruments.

4 Recognition of financial instruments

IAS 39 *Financial instruments: Recognition and measurement* establishes principles for recognising and measuring financial assets and financial liabilities.

4.1 Scope

IAS 39 applies to **all entities** and to **all types of financial instruments except** those specifically excluded, for example investments in subsidiaries, associates and joint ventures.

4.2 Initial recognition

A financial asset or financial liability should be recognised in the statement of financial position when the reporting entity becomes a party to the contractual provisions of the instrument.

Notice that this is **different** from the recognition criteria in the *Framework* and in most other standards. Items are normally recognised when there is a probable inflow or outflow of resources and the item has a cost or value that can be measured reliably.

4.3 Derecognition

Derecognition is the removal of a previously recognised financial instrument from an entity's statement of financial position.

An entity should derecognise a **financial asset** when:

(a)   the **contractual rights** to the cash flows from the financial asset **expire**; or

(b)   it transfers substantially all the risks and rewards of ownership of the financial asset to another party.

Exam focus point

> The principle here is that of **substance over form**.

An entity should derecognise a **financial liability** when it is **extinguished** – ie, when the obligation specified in the contract is discharged or cancelled or expires.

It is possible for only **part** of a financial asset or liability to be derecognised. This is allowed if the part comprises:

(a)   only specifically identified cash flows; or

(b)   only a fully proportionate (pro rata) share of the total cash flows.

For example, if an entity holds a bond it has the right to two separate sets of cash inflows: those relating to the principal and those relating to the interest. It could sell the right to receive the interest to another party while retaining the right to receive the principal.

On derecognition, the amount to be included in net profit or loss for the period is calculated as follows:

	$	$
Carrying amount of asset/liability (or the portion of asset/liability) transferred		X
Less: Proceeds received/paid	X	
Any cumulative gain or loss reported in equity	X	
	(X)	
Difference to net profit/loss		X

Where only part of a financial asset is derecognised, the carrying amount of the asset should be allocated between the part retained and the part transferred based on their relative fair values on the date of transfer. A gain or loss should be recognised based on the proceeds for the portion transferred.

4.4 Section summary

- All financial assets and liabilities should be recognised in the statement of financial position, including derivatives.
- Financial assets should be derecognised when the rights to the cash flows from the asset expire or where substantially all the risks and rewards of ownership are transferred to another party.
- Financial liabilities should be derecognised when they are extinguished.

5 Measurement of financial instruments

All financial assets should be initially measured at cost.

5.1 Initial measurement

Financial instruments are initially measured at the **fair value** of the consideration given or received (ie, **cost**) **plus** (in most cases) **transaction costs** that are **directly attributable** to the acquisition or issue of the financial instrument.

The **exception** to this rule is where a financial instrument is designated as **at fair value through profit or loss** (this term is explained below). In this case, **transaction costs** are **not** added to fair value at initial recognition.

The fair value of the consideration is normally the transaction price or market prices. If market prices are not reliable, the fair value may be **estimated** using a valuation technique (for example, by discounting cash flows).

5.2 Subsequent measurement

For the purposes of measuring a financial asset held subsequent to initial recognition, IAS 39 classifies financial assets into four categories defined here.

Key terms

> A **financial asset or liability at fair value through profit or loss** meets either of the following conditions:
>
> (a)   It is classified as held for trading. A financial instrument is classified as held for trading if it is:
>
>   (i)   acquired or incurred principally for the purpose of selling or repurchasing it in the near term;
>
>   (ii)   part of a portfolio of identified financial instruments that are managed together and for which there is evidence of a recent actual pattern of short-term profit-taking
>
> **Key terms**
>
> (b)   Upon initial recognition it is **designated** by the entity as at fair value through profit or loss.
>
> **Held-to-maturity investments** are non-derivative financial assets with fixed or determinable payments and fixed maturity that an entity has the positive intent and ability to hold to maturity.
>
> **Loans and receivables** are non-derivative financial assets with fixed or determinable payments that are not quoted in an active market.
>
> **Available-for-sale financial assets** are those financial assets that are not:
>
> (a)   loans and receivables originated by the entity,
> (b)   held-to-maturity investments, or
> (c)   financial assets at fair value through profit or loss.   *(IAS 39)*

After initial recognition, all financial assets should be **remeasured to fair value**, without any deduction for transaction costs that may be incurred on sale or other disposal, except for:

(a)   **Loans and receivables**
(b)   **Held to maturity investments**
(c)   Investments in **equity instruments** that do not have a quoted market price in an active market and whose **fair value cannot be reliably measured**

Loans and receivables and **held to maturity investments** should be measured at **amortised cost** using the **effective interest method**.

> **Amortised cost of a financial asset or financial liability** is the amount at which the financial asset or liability is measured at initial recognition minus principal repayments, plus or minus the cumulative amortisation of any difference between that initial amount and the maturity amount, and minus any write-down for impairment or uncollectability.
>
> The **effective interest method** is a method of calculating the amortised cost of a financial instrument and of allocating the interest income or interest expense over the relevant period.
>
> The **effective interest rate** is the rate that exactly discounts estimated future cash payments or receipts through the expected life of the financial instrument to the net carrying amount. *(IAS 39)*

5.3 Example: amortised cost

On 1 January 20X1 Abacus Co purchases a debt instrument for its fair value of $1,000. The debt instrument is due to mature on 31 December 20X5. The instrument has a principal amount of $1,250 and the instrument carries fixed interest at 4.72% that is paid annually.
How should Abacus Co account for the debt instrument over its five year term?

Solution

Abacus Co will receive interest of $59 (1,250 × 4.72%) each year and $1,250 when the instrument matures.

Abacus must allocate the discount of $250 and the interest receivable over the five year term at a constant rate on the carrying amount of the debt. To do this, it must apply the effective interest rate of 10%. The following table shows the allocation over the years:

Year	Amortised cost at beginning of year	Income statement: Interest income for year (@10%)	Interest received during year (cash inflow)	Amortised cost at end of year
	$	$	$	$
20X1	1,000	100	(59)	1,041
20X2	1,041	104	(59)	1,086
20X3	1,086	109	(59)	1,136
20X4	1,136	113	(59)	1,190
20X5	1,190	119	(1,250+59)	–

Each year the carrying amount of the financial asset is increased by the interest income for the year and reduced by the interest actually received during the year.

Investments whose **fair value cannot be reliably measured** should be measured at **cost**.

5.4 Classification

There is a certain amount of flexibility in that **any** financial instrument can be designated as at fair value through profit or loss. However, this is a **once and for all choice** and has to be made on initial recognition. Once a financial instrument has been classified in this way it **cannot be reclassified**, even if it would otherwise be possible to measure it at cost or amortised cost.

In contrast, it is quite difficult for an entity **not** to remeasure financial instruments to fair value.

For a financial instrument to be held to maturity it must meet several extremely narrow criteria. The entity must have a **positive intent** and a **demonstrated ability** to hold the investment to maturity. These conditions are not met if:

(a)   The entity intends to hold the financial asset for an undefined period

(b)   The entity stands ready to sell the financial asset in response to changes in interest rates or risks, liquidity needs and similar factors (unless these situations could not possibly have been reasonably anticipated)

(c) The issuer has the right to settle the financial asset at an amount significantly below its amortised cost (because this right will almost certainly be exercised)

(d) It does not have the financial resources available to continue to finance the investment until maturity

(e) It is subject to an existing legal or other constraint that could frustrate its intention to hold the financial asset to maturity

In addition, an **equity** instrument is **unlikely** to meet the criteria for classification as held to maturity.

If an entity can no longer hold an investment to maturity, it is no longer appropriate to use amortised cost and the asset must be re-measured to fair value. **All** remaining held-to-maturity investments must also be re-measured to fair value and classified as available-for-sale (see above).

5.5 Subsequent measurement of financial liabilities

After initial recognition, all financial liabilities should be measured at **amortised cost**, with the exception of financial liabilities at fair value through profit or loss. These should be measured at **fair value**, but where the fair value **is not capable of reliable measurement**, they should be measured at **cost**.

Question

Bond

Galaxy Co issues a bond for $503,778 on 1 January 20X2. No interest is payable on the bond, but it will be held to maturity and redeemed on 31 December 20X4 for $600,000. The bond has **not** been designated as at fair value through profit or loss. The effective interest rate is 6%.

Required

Calculate the charge to the income statement of Galaxy Co for the year ended 31 December 20X2 and the balance outstanding at 31 December 20X2.

Answer

The bond is a 'deep discount' bond and is a financial liability of Galaxy Co. It is measured at amortised cost. Although there is no interest as such, the difference between the initial cost of the bond and the price at which it will be redeemed is a finance cost. This must be allocated over the term of the bond at a constant rate on the carrying amount. This is done by applying the effective interest rate.

The charge to the income statement is $30,226 (503,778 × 6%)

The balance outstanding at 31 December 20X2 is $534,004 (503,778 + 30,226)

5.6 Gains and losses

Instruments at **fair value through profit or loss**: gains and losses are recognised **in profit or loss** (ie, in the income statement).

Available for sale financial assets: gains and losses are recognised **directly in equity** through the statement of comprehensive income. When the asset is derecognised the cumulative gain or loss previously recognised in equity should be recognised in profit or loss.

Financial instruments carried at **amortised cost**: gains and losses are recognised **in profit and loss** as a result of the amortisation process and when the asset is derecognised.

5.7 Impairment and uncollectability of financial assets

At each balance sheet date, an entity should assess whether there is any objective evidence that a financial asset or group of assets is impaired.

Where there is objective evidence of impairment, the entity should **determine the amount** of any impairment loss.

5.7.1 Financial assets carried at amortised cost

The impairment loss is the **difference** between the asset's **carrying amount** and its **recoverable amount**. The asset's recoverable amount is the present value of estimated future cash flows, discounted at the financial instrument's **original** effective interest rate.

The amount of the loss should be **recognised in profit or loss.**

5.7.2 Financial assets carried at cost

Unquoted equity instruments are carried at cost if their fair value cannot be reliably measured. The impairment loss is the difference between the asset's **carrying amount** and the **present value of estimated future cash flows**, discounted at the current market rate of return for a similar financial instrument. Such impairment losses cannot be reversed.

5.7.3 Available for sale financial assets

Available for sale financial assets are carried at fair value and gains and losses are recognised directly in equity. Any impairment loss on an available for sale financial asset should be **removed from equity** and **recognised in net profit or loss for the period** even though the financial asset has not been derecognised.

The impairment loss is the difference between its **acquisition cost** (net of any principal repayment and amortisation) and **current fair value** (for equity instruments) or recoverable amount (for debt instruments), less any impairment loss on that asset previously recognised in profit or loss.

5.8 Section summary

- On initial recognition, financial instruments are measured at **cost**.
- Subsequent measurement depends on how a financial asset is **classified**.
- Financial assets at **fair value through profit or loss** are measured at **fair value**; gains and losses are recognised in **profit or loss**.
- **Available for sale** assets are measured at **fair value**; gains and losses are taken to **equity**.
- **Loans and receivables** and **held to maturity** investments are measured at **amortised cost**; gains and losses are recognised in **profit or loss**.
- Financial **liabilities** are normally measured at **amortised cost**, unless they have been classified as at fair value through profit or loss.

- The important definitions to learn are:
    - **Financial asset**
    - **Financial liability**
    - **Equity instrument**

- Financial instruments must be classified as **liabilities** or **equity** according to their **substance**.

- The critical feature of a financial liability is the **contractual obligation to deliver cash** or another financial asset.

- **Compound instruments** are split into **equity** and **liability** components and presented in the statement of financial position accordingly

- Most **preference shares** are **redeemable** and classified as **liabilities**.

- IAS 39 states that **all financial assets and liabilities** should be **recognised in the statement of financial position, including derivatives**.

- **Financial assets** should **initially** be measured at **cost = the fair value** of the consideration paid.

- Subsequently they should be **re-measured to fair value** except for

    - Loans and receivables not held for trading
    - Other **held-to-maturity investments**
    - Investments in **equity instruments** whose value **cannot be reliably measured**

Quick Quiz

1 Which issues are dealt with by IAS 32?
2 Define the following.
   (a)   Financial asset
   (b)   Financial liability
   (c)   Equity instrument
3 What is the critical feature used to identify a financial liability?
4 How should compound instruments be classified by the issuer?
5 When should a financial asset be de-recognised?
6 How are financial instruments initially measured?
7 After initial recognition, all financial liabilities should be measured at amortised cost. True or false?
8 Where should redeemable preference shares appear in the statement of financial position?

Answers to Quick Quiz

1   Classification between liabilities and equity; presentation; disclosure
2   See Key Terms, paragraph 1.2
3   The contractual obligation to deliver cash or another financial asset to the holder
4   By calculating the present value of the liability component and then deducting this from the instrument as a whole to leave a residual value for the equity component.
5   Financial assets should be derecognised when the rights to the cash flows from the asset expire or where substantially all the risks and rewards of ownership are transferred to another party.
6   At cost
7   False. See paragraph 5.5
8   Under non-current liabilities (not equity).

Now try the questions below from the Exam Question Bank

Number	Level	Marks	Time
21	–	10	18 mins

15

The legal versus the commercial view of accounting

Topic list	Syllabus reference
1 Off-balance sheet finance explained	A4
2 Substance over form	A4
3 The IASB Framework	A4
4 Common forms of off-balance sheet finance	A4
5 Revenue recognition	A3

Introduction

This is a very topical area and has been for some time. Companies (and other entities) have in the past used the **legal form** of a transaction to determine its accounting treatment, when in fact the **substance** of the transaction has been very different. We will look at the question of **substance over form** and the kind of transactions undertaken by entities trying to avoid reporting true substance in Sections 1 and 2.

The main weapon in tackling these abuses is the IASB's *Framework for the Preparation and Presentation of Financial Statements* because it applies **general definitions** to the elements that make up financial statements. We will look at how this works in Section 3.

Study guide

		Intellectual level
A	**CONCEPTUAL FRAMEWORK FOR FINANCIAL REPORTING**	
3	(a) demonstrate the role of the principle of substance over form in relation to recognising sales revenue.	2
4	**The legal versus the commercial view of accounting**	
	(a) explain the importance of recording the commercial substance rather than the legal form of transactions – give examples where recording the legal form of transactions may be misleading.	2
	(b) describe the features which may indicate that the substance of transactions differs from their legal form.	2
	(c) apply the principle of substance over form to the recognition and derecognition of assets and liabilities.	2
	(d) recognise the substance of transactions in general, and specifically account for the following types of transactions:	2
	(i) goods sold on sale or return/consignment inventory	
	(ii) sale and repurchase/leaseback agreements	
	(iii) factoring of receivables.	

Exam guide

Although there is no IFRS on this subject comparable to the UK's FRS 5 *Reporting the substance of transactions,* the examiner is likely to set a question on this area as he sets both the UK and the international variants.

1 Off-balance sheet finance explained

Key term

> **Off-balance sheet finance** is the funding or refinancing of a company's operations in such a way that, under legal requirements and traditional accounting conventions, some or all of the finance may not be shown in its statement of financial position.

'Off-balance sheet transactions' are transactions which meet the above objective. These transactions may involve the **removal of assets** from the statement of financial position, as well as liabilities, and they are also likely to have a significant impact on profit or loss.

1.1 Why off balance sheet finance exists

Why might company managers wish to enter into such transactions?

(a) In some countries, companies traditionally have a lower level of gearing than companies in other countries. Off balance sheet finance is used to **keep gearing low**, probably because of the views of analysts and brokers.

(b) A company may need to keep its gearing down in order to stay within the terms of **loan covenants** imposed by lenders.

(c) A quoted company with high borrowings is often expected (by analysts and others) to declare a **rights issue** in order to reduce gearing. This has an adverse effect on a company's share price and so off-balance sheet financing is used to reduce gearing *and* the expectation of a rights issue.

(d) Analysts' short term views are a problem for companies **developing assets** which are not producing income during the development stage. Such companies will match the borrowings associated with such developing assets, along with the assets themselves, off-balance sheet. They are brought back into the statement of financial position once income is being generated by the assets. This process keeps return on capital employed higher than it would have been during the development stage.

(e) In the past, groups of companies have excluded **subsidiaries** from consolidation in an off-balance sheet transaction because they carry out completely different types of business and have different characteristics. The usual example is a leasing company (in say a retail group) which has a high level of gearing. This exclusion is now disallowed.

You can see from this brief list of reasons that the overriding motivation is to avoid **misinterpretation**. In other words, the company does not trust the analysts or other users to understand the reasons for a transaction and so avoids any effect such transactions might have by taking them off-balance sheet. Unfortunately, the position of the company is then misstated and the user of the accounts is misled.

You must understand that not all forms of 'off-balance sheet finance' are undertaken for cosmetic or accounting reasons. Some transactions are carried out to **limit or isolate risk**, to reduce interest costs and so on. In other words, these transactions are in the best interests of the company, not merely a cosmetic repackaging of figures which would normally appear in the statement of financial position.

1.2 The off balance sheet finance problem

The result of the use of increasingly sophisticated off-balance sheet finance transactions is a situation where the users of financial statements do not have a proper or clear view of the **state of the company's affairs**. The disclosures required by national company law and accounting standards did not in the past provide sufficient rules for disclosure of off balance sheet finance transactions and so very little of the true nature of the transaction was exposed.

Whatever the purpose of such transactions, **insufficient disclosure** creates a problem. This problem has been debated over the years by the accountancy profession and other interested parties and some progress has been made (see the later sections of this chapter). However, company collapses during recessions have often revealed much higher borrowings than originally thought, because part of the borrowing was off balance sheet.

The main argument used for banning off-balance sheet finance is that the true **substance** of the transactions should be shown, not merely the **legal form**, particularly when it is exacerbated by poor disclosure.

2 Substance over form

Key term

Substance over form. The principle that transactions and other events are accounted for and presented in accordance with their substance and economic reality and not merely their legal form. *(Framework)*

This is a very important concept. It is used to **determine accounting treatment** in financial statements through accounting standards and so prevent off balance sheet transactions. The following paragraphs give examples of where the principle of substance over form is enforced in various accounting standards.

2.1 IAS 17 Leases

In IAS 17, there is an explicit requirement that if the lessor transfers substantially all the **risks and rewards of ownership** to the lessee then, even though the legal title has not necessarily passed, the item being leased should be shown as an asset in the statement of financial position of the lessee and the amount due to the lessor should be shown as a liability. (This will be covered in Chapter 16.)

2.2 IAS 24 Related party disclosures

IAS 24 requires financial statements to disclose fully any material transactions undertaken with a related party by the reporting entity, **regardless of any price charged**.

2.3 IAS 11 Construction contracts

In IAS 11 there is a requirement to account for **attributable profits** on construction contracts under the accruals convention. However, there may be a problem with realisation, since it is arguable whether we should account for profit which, although attributable to the work done, may not have yet been invoiced to the customer. It is argued that the convention of substance over form is applied to justify ignoring the strict legal position.

2.4 IAS 27 Consolidated and separate financial statements

This is perhaps the most important area of off balance sheet finance which has been prevented by the application of the substance over form concept. The use of **quasi-subsidiaries** was very common in the 1980s. These may be defined as follows.

Key term

> A **quasi-subsidiary** of a reporting entity is a company, trust, partnership or other vehicle that, though not fulfilling the definition of a subsidiary, is directly or indirectly controlled by the reporting entity and gives rise to benefits for that entity that are in substance no different from those that would arise were the vehicle a subsidiary.

IAS 27 contains a definition of a subsidiary based on **control** rather than just ownership rights, thus substantially reducing the effectiveness of this method of off-balance sheet finance. IAS 27 defines control of another entity as follows:

Key term

> **Control** is the power to govern the financial and operating policies of an entity so as to obtain benefit from its activities.
> *(IAS 27)*

The IAS goes on to state that control exists when:

(a) The parent has a **majority of the voting rights** in the subsidiary (possibly **by agreement** with other members), *or*

(b) The parent can appoint or remove a **majority of the board** of the subsidiary, *or*

(c) The parent can **direct the operating and financial policies** through a statute or agreement, *or*

(d) The parent can cast the **majority of votes** at a board meeting of directors (or equivalent).

The main effects of this definition on the use of quasi-subsidiaries were as follows.

(a) The use of 'voting rights' rather than 'equity shares' prevents the use of **company structures** which give the benefits of ownership to one class of shareholder without the appearance of doing so, eg a company has 100 'A' shares with 10 votes each and 900 'B' shares with one vote each.

(b) The right to appoint or remove a majority of the board now means those directors who control a majority of the voting rights at board meetings. This prevents control through **differential voting rights** at board meetings.

IAS 27 therefore **curtailed drastically** the use of quasi-subsidiaries for off balance sheet finance. More complex schemes are likely to be curtailed by the IASB's *Framework* and by various other standards (see below).

You may also hear the term **creative accounting** used in the context of reporting the substance of transactions. This can be defined simply as the manipulation of figures for a desired result. Remember, however, that it is very rare for a company, its directors or employees to manipulate results for the purpose of fraud. The major consideration is usually the effect the results will have on the company's share price. Some areas open to abuse (although some of these loopholes have been closed) are given below and you should by now understand how these can distort a company results.

(a) Income recognition and cut-off

(b) Impairment of purchased goodwill

(c) Manipulation of reserves

(d) Revaluations and depreciation

(e)   Window dressing – transactions undertaken, eg. loans repaid just before the year end and then reversed in the following period.

(f)   Changes in accounting policy

Articles on creative accounting appear fairly regularly in *Student Accountant*. Although often based on UK accounting, most of the points can be applied to international accounting.

Question   Creative accounting

Creative accounting, off balance sheet finance and related matters (in particular how ratio analysis can be used to discover these practices) often come up in articles in the financial press. Find a library, preferably a good technical library, which can provide you with copies of back issues of such newspapers or journals and look for articles on creative accounting.

3 The IASB Framework

As noted above, the IASB Framework states that accounting for items according to substance and economic reality and not merely legal form is a key determinant of reliable information.

(a)   For the majority of transactions there is **no difference** between the two and therefore no issue.

(b)   For other transactions **substance and form diverge** and the choice of treatment can give different results due to non-recognition of an asset or liability even though benefits or obligations result.

Full disclosure is not enough: all transactions must be **accounted for** correctly, with full disclosure of related details as necessary to give the user of accounts a full understanding of the transactions.

3.1 Relationship to IASs

The interaction of the Framework **with other standards** is also an important issue. Whichever rules are the more specific should be applied, given that IASs should be consistent with the Framework. Leasing provides a good example: straightforward leases which fall squarely within the terms of IAS 17 should be accounted for without any need to refer to the Framework, but where their terms are more complex, or the lease is only one element in a larger series of transactions, then the Framework comes into play. In addition, the Framework implicitly requires that its general principle of substance over form should apply in the application of other existing rules.

3.2 Basic principles

How else does the Framework enforce the substance over form rule? Its main method is to define the elements of financial statements and therefore to give rules for their recognition. The key considerations are whether a transaction has **given rise to new assets and liabilities**, and whether it has **changed any existing assets and liabilities**.

The characteristics of transactions whose substance is not readily apparent are as follows.

(a)   The **legal title** to an item is separated from the ability to enjoy the principal benefits, and the exposure to the main risks associated with it.

(b)   The transaction is **linked to one or more others** so that the commercial effect of the transaction cannot be understood without reference to the complete series.

(c)   The transaction includes **one or more options**, under such terms that it makes it highly likely that the option(s) will be exercised.

3.3 Definitions

These are perhaps the most important definitions.

Key terms

- An **asset** is a resource controlled by the entity as a result of past events and from which future economic benefits are expected to flow to the entity.

- A **liability** is a present obligation of the entity arising from past events, the settlement of which is expected to result in an outflow from the entity of resources embodying economic benefits.

(Framework)

Identification of **who has the risks** relating to an asset will generally indicate **who has the benefits** and hence **who has the asset**. If an entity is in certain circumstances unable to avoid an **outflow of benefits**, this will provide evidence that it has a liability.

The definitions given in the IASB Framework of income and expenses are not as important as those of assets and liabilities. This is because income and expenses are **described in terms of changes in assets and liabilities**, ie they are secondary definitions.

Key terms

- **Income** is increases in economic benefits during the accounting period in the form of inflows or enhancements of assets or decreases of liabilities that result in increases in equity, other than those relating to contributions from equity participants.

- **Expenses** are decreases in economic benefits during the accounting period in the form of outflows or depletions of assets or incurrences of liabilities that result in decreases in equity, other than those relating to distributions to equity participants.

(Framework)

The real importance, then, is the way the Framework defines assets and liabilities. This forces entities to acknowledge their assets and liabilities regardless of the legal status.

It is not sufficient, however, that the asset or liability fulfils the above definitions; it must also satisfy **recognition criteria** in order to be shown in an entity's accounts.

3.4 Recognition

Key term

Recognition is the process of incorporating in the statement of financial position or statement of comprehensive income an item that meets the definition of an element and satisfies the criteria for recognition set out below. It involves the depiction of the item in words and by a monetary amount and the inclusion of that amount in the statement of financial position or statement of comprehensive income totals.

The next key question is deciding **when** something which satisfies the definition of an asset or liability has to be recognised in the statement of financial position. Where a transaction results in an item that meets the definition of an asset or liability, that item should be recognised in the statement of financial position if:

(a)   it is **probable that a future inflow or outflow** of benefit to or from the entity will occur, and

(b)   the item can be **measured at a monetary amount with sufficient reliability.**

This effectively prevents entities abusing the definitions of the elements by recognising items that are vague in terms of likelihood of occurrence and measurability. If this were not in force, entities could **manipulate the financial statements** in various ways, eg recognising assets when the likely future economic benefits cannot yet be determined.

Probability is assessed based on the situation at the end of the reporting period. For example, it is usually expected that some customers of an entity will not pay what they owe. The expected level of non-payment is based on past experience and the receivables asset is reduced by a percentage (the general bad debt provision).

Measurement must be reliable, but it does not preclude the use of **reasonable estimates**, which is an essential part of the financial statement preparation.

Even if something does not qualify for recognition now, it may meet the criteria **at a later date**.

3.5 Other standards

The Framework provides the general guidance for reporting the substance of transactions and preventing off balance sheet finance. The IASB has developed guidance for specific transactions. These were mentioned in Section 2 and they are covered in various parts of this text. You should consider the particular off balance sheet finance problem they tackle as you study them.

- IAS 17 Leases (see Chapter 15)
- IAS 32 Financial instruments (see Chapter 13)
- IAS 27 Consolidated and separate financial statements (see Chapter 7)
- IAS 24 Related party disclosures (see Chapter 7)
- IAS 18 Revenue (see Section 5)

3.6 Section summary

Important points to remember from the Framework are:

- **Substance over form**
- Definitions of **assets** and **liabilities**
- Definition of **recognition**
- **Criteria** for recognition

4 Common forms of off-balance sheet finance

FAST FORWARD

How does the theory of the *Framework* **apply in practice**, to real transactions? The rest of this section looks at some complex transactions that occur frequently in practice.

We will consider how the principles of the *Framework* would be applied to these transactions.

- Consignment inventory
- Sale and repurchase agreements/sale and leaseback agreements
- Factoring of receivables/debts

4.1 Consignment inventory

Consignment inventory is an arrangement where inventory is held by one party (say a distributor) but is owned by another party (for example a manufacturer or a finance company). Consignment inventory is common in the motor trade and is similar to goods sold on a 'sale or return' basis.

To identify the correct treatment, it is necessary to identify the point at which the distributor or dealer acquired the benefits of the asset (the inventory) rather than the point at which legal title was acquired. If the manufacturer has the right to require the return of the inventory, and if that right is likely to be exercised, then the inventory is *not* an asset of the dealer. If the dealer is rarely required to return the inventory, then this part of the transaction will have little commercial effect in practice and should be ignored for accounting purposes. The potential liability would need to be disclosed in the accounts.

4.1.1 Summary of indications of asset status

The following analysis summarises the range of possibilities in such a transaction.

Indications that the inventory is *not an asset* of the dealer at delivery	Indications that the inventory *is an asset* of the dealer at delivery
Manufacturer can require dealer to **return inventory** (or transfer inventory to another dealer) without compensation.	Manufacturer cannot require dealer to **return or transfer inventory**.
Penalty paid by the dealer to prevent returns/transfers of inventory at the manufacturer's request.	**Financial incentives** given to persuade dealer to transfer inventory at manufacturer's request.
Dealer has unfettered **right to return inventory** to the manufacturer without penalty and actually exercises the right in practice.	Dealer has **no right to return inventory** or is commercially compelled not to exercise its right of return.
Manufacturer bears **obsolescence risk**, eg: • obsolete inventory is returned to the manufacturer without penalty, or • financial incentives given by manufacturer to prevent inventory being returned to it (eg on a model change or if it becomes obsolete).	Dealer bears **obsolescence risk**, eg: • penalty charged if dealer returns inventory to manufacturer, or • obsolete inventory cannot be returned to the manufacturer and no compensation is paid by manufacturer for losses due to obsolescence.
Inventory **transfer price** charged by manufacturer is based on manufacturer's list price at date of transfer of legal title.	Inventory **transfer price** charged by manufacturer is based on manufacturer's list price at date of delivery.
Manufacturer bears **slow movement risk**, eg: transfer price set independently of time for which dealer holds inventory, and there is no deposit.	Dealer bears **slow movement risk**, eg: • dealer is effectively charged interest as transfer price or other payments to manufacturer vary with time for which dealer holds inventory, or • dealer makes a substantial interest-free deposit that varies with the levels of inventory held.

4.1.2 Required accounting

The following apply where it is concluded that the inventory **is in substance an asset** of the dealer.

(a)   The inventory should be recognised as such in the dealer's statement of financial position, together with a corresponding liability to the manufacturer.

(b)   Any deposit should be deducted from the liability and the excess classified as a trade payable.

Where it is concluded that the inventory is **not in substance an asset** of the dealer, the following apply.

(a)   The inventory should not be included in the dealer's statement of financial position until the transfer of risks and rewards has crystallised.

(b)   Any deposit should be included under 'other receivables'.

 Question   Recognition

Daley Motors Co owns a number of car dealerships throughout a geographical area. The terms of the arrangement between the dealerships and the manufacturer are as follows.

(a)   Legal title passes when the cars are either used by Daley Co for demonstration purposes or sold to a third party.

(b)   The dealer has the right to return vehicles to the manufacturer without penalty. (Daley Co has rarely exercised this right in the past.)

(c)   The transfer price is based on the manufacturer's list price at the date of delivery.

(d)   Daley Co makes a substantial interest-free deposit based on the number of cars held.

Should the asset and liability be recognised by Daley Co at the date of delivery?

Answer

(a) Legal form is irrelevant
(b) Yes: only because rarely exercised (otherwise 'no')
(c) Yes
(d) Yes: the dealership is effectively forgoing the interest which could be earned on the cash sum

4.2 Sale and repurchase agreements

These are arrangements under which the company sells an asset to another person on terms that allow the company to **repurchase the asset** in certain circumstances. A common example is the sale and repurchase of maturing whisky inventories. The key question is whether the transaction is a **straightforward sale**, or whether it is, in effect, a **secured loan**. It is necessary to look at the arrangement to determine who has the rights to the economic benefits that the asset generates, and the terms on which the asset is to be repurchased.

If the seller has the right to the benefits of the **use of the asset**, and the repurchase terms are such that the **repurchase is likely** to take place, the transaction should be accounted for as a **loan**.

4.2.1 Summary of indications of the sale of the asset

The following summary is helpful.

Indications of *sale* of original asset to buyer (nevertheless, the seller may retain a different asset)	Indications of *no sale* of original asset to buyer (secured loan)
	Sale price does not equal **market value** at date of sale.
No commitment for **seller to repurchase** asset, eg call option where there is a real possibility the option will fail to be exercised.	Commitment for **seller to repurchase** asset, eg: • put and call option with the same exercise price • either a put or a call option with no genuine commercial possibility that the option will fail to be exercised, or • seller requires asset back to use in its business, or asset is in effect the only source of seller's future sales
Risk of **changes in asset value** borne by buyer such that buyer does not receive solely a lender's return, eg both sale and repurchase price equal market value at date of sale/repurchase.	Risk of **changes in asset value** borne by seller such that buyer receives solely a lender's return, eg: • repurchase price equals sale price plus costs plus interest • original purchase price adjusted retrospectively to pass variations in the value of the asset to the seller • seller provides residual value guarantee to buyer or subordinated debt to protect buyer from falls in the value of the asset

Indications of *sale* of original asset to buyer (nevertheless, the seller may retain a different asset)	Indications of *no sale* of original asset to buyer (secured loan)
Nature of the asset is such that it will be used over the life of the agreement, and seller has no rights to **determine its use**. Seller has no rights to determine asset's development or future sale.	Seller retains right to **determine asset's use**, development or sale, or rights to profits therefrom.

4.2.2 Required accounting

Where the substance of the transaction is that of a **secured loan**:

(a)   The seller should continue to recognise the original asset and record the proceeds received from the buyer as a liability.

(b)   Interest, however designated, should be accrued.

(c)   The carrying amount of the asset should be reviewed for impairment and written down if necessary.

4.2.3 Sale and leaseback transactions

A sale and leaseback transaction involves the sale of an asset and the leasing back of the same asset. The lease payment and the sale price are usually negotiated as a package.

The accounting treatment depends upon the type of lease involved. If the transaction results in a **finance lease**, then it is in substance a loan from the lessor to the lessee (the lessee has sold the asset and then leased it back), with the asset as security. In this case, any 'profit' on the sale should not be recognised as such, but should be deferred and amortised over the lease term.

If the transaction results in an **operating lease** and the transaction has been conducted at fair value, then it can be regarded as a normal sale transaction. The asset is derecognised and any profit on the sale is recognised. The operating lease instalments are treated as lease payments, rather than repayments of capital plus interest.

This will become clearer when you have covered Chapter 16 and you may want to return to it at that point.

Question	Recognition and sales proceeds

A construction company, Mecanto Co, agrees to sell to Hamlows Bank some of the land within its landbank. The terms of the sale are as follows.

(a)   The sales price is to be at open market value.

(b)   Mecanto Co has the right to develop the land on the basis that it will pay all the outgoings on the land plus an annual fee of 5% of the purchase price.

(c)   Mecanto has the option to buy back the land at any time within the next five years. The repurchase price is based on:

   (i)   original purchase price
   (ii)   expenses relating to the purchase
   (iii)   an interest charge of base rate + 2%
   (iv)   less amounts received from Mecanto by Hamlows

(d)   At the end of five years Hamlows Bank may offer the land for sale generally. Any shortfall on the proceeds relative to the agreed purchase price agreed with Mecanto has to be settled by Mecanto in cash.

Should the asset continue to be recognised by Mecanto Co and the sales proceeds treated as a loan?

(a)   No: the sales price is as for an arm's length transaction.

(b)   Yes: Mecanto has control over the asset.
        Yes: Mecanto has to pay a fee based on cash received.

(c)   Yes: interest is charged on the proceeds paid by Mecanto.
        Yes: the repurchase price is based on the lender's return

(d)   Yes: options ensure that Mecanto bears all the risk (both favourable and unfavourable) of changes in the market value of the land.

In this case the evidence overwhelmingly suggests that Mecanto has obtained a loan from Hamlows using the land as security. So the asset should continue to be recognised and the sales proceeds should be treated as a loan.

4.3 Factoring of receivables/debts

Where debts or receivables are factored, the original creditor **sells the debts to the factor**. The sales price may be fixed at the outset or may be adjusted later. It is also common for the factor to offer a credit facility that allows the seller to draw upon a proportion of the amounts owed.

In order to determine the correct accounting treatment it is necessary to consider whether the benefit of the debts has been passed on to the factor, or whether the factor is, in effect, providing a loan on the security of the receivable balances. If the seller has to **pay interest** on the difference between the amounts advanced to him and the amounts that the factor has received, and if the seller bears the **risks of non-payment** by the debtor, then the indications would be that the transaction is, in effect, a loan.

4.3.1 Summary of indications of appropriate treatment

The following is a summary of indicators of the appropriate treatment.

Indications the debts are *not an asset* of the seller	Indications that the debts are an *asset* of the seller
Transfer is for a single non-returnable fixed sum.	Finance cost varies with speed of collection of debts, eg: • by adjustment to consideration for original transfer, or • subsequent transfers priced to recover costs of earlier transfers.
There is no recourse to the seller for losses.	There is full recourse to the seller for losses.
Factor is paid all amounts received from the factored debts (and no more). Seller has no rights to further sums from the factor.	Seller is required to repay amounts received from the factor on or before a set date, regardless of timing or amounts of collections from debtors.

4.3.2 Required accounting

Where the seller has retained no significant benefits and risks relating to the debts and has no obligation to repay amounts received from the factors, the receivables should be removed from its statement of financial position and no liability shown in respect of the proceeds received from the factor. A profit or loss should be recognised, calculated as the difference between the carrying amount of the debts and the proceeds received.

Where the seller does retain significant benefits and risks, a gross asset (equivalent in amount to the gross amount of the receivables) should be shown in the statement of financial position of the seller within assets, and a corresponding liability in respect of the proceeds received from the factor should be shown within liabilities. The interest element of the factor's charges should be recognised as it accrues and included in profit or loss with other interest charges. Other factoring costs should be similarly accrued.

5 Revenue recognition

Revenue recognition is straightforward in most business transactions, but some situations are more complicated and some give opportunities for manipulation.

5.1 Introduction

Accruals accounting is based on the **matching of costs with the revenue they generate**. It is crucially important under this convention that we can establish the point at which revenue may be recognised so that the correct treatment can be applied to the related costs. For example, the costs of producing an item of finished goods should be carried as an asset in the statement of financial position until such time as it is sold; they should then be written off as a charge to the trading account. Which of these two treatments should be applied cannot be decided until it is clear at what moment the sale of the item takes place.

The decision has a **direct impact on profit** since under the prudence concept it would be unacceptable to recognise the profit on sale until a sale had taken place in accordance with the criteria of revenue recognition.

Revenue is generally recognised as **earned at the point of sale**, because at that point four criteria will generally have been met.

- The product or service has been **provided to the buyer**.
- The buyer has **recognised his liability** to pay for the goods or services provided. The converse of this is that the seller has recognised that ownership of goods has passed from himself to the buyer.
- The buyer has indicated his **willingness to hand over cash** or other assets in settlement of his liability.
- The **monetary value** of the goods or services has been established.

At earlier points in the business cycle there will not in general be **firm evidence** that the above criteria will be met. Until work on a product is complete, there is a risk that some flaw in the manufacturing process will necessitate its writing off; even when the product is complete there is no guarantee that it will find a buyer.

At later points in the business cycle, for example when cash is received for the sale, the recognition of revenue may occur in a period later than that in which the related costs were charged. Revenue recognition would then depend on fortuitous circumstances, such as the cash flow of a company's customers, and might fluctuate misleadingly from one period to another.

However, there are times when revenue is **recognised at other times than at the completion of a sale**. For example, in the recognition of profit on long-term construction contracts. Under IAS 11 *Construction contracts* (see Chapter 11) contract revenue and contract costs associated with the construction contract should be recognised as revenue and expenses respectively by reference to the stage of completion of the contract activity at the end of the reporting period.

(a)   Owing to the length of time taken to complete such contracts, to defer taking profit into account until completion may result in the statement of comprehensive income reflecting, not so much a fair view of the activity of the company during the year, but rather the results relating to contracts which have been completed by the year end.

(b)   Revenue in this case is recognised when production on, say, a section of the total contract is complete, even though no sale can be made until the whole is complete.

5.2 IAS 18 Revenue

IAS 18 governs the recognition of revenue in specific (common) types of transaction. Generally, recognition should be when it is probable that **future economic benefits** will flow to the entity and when these benefits can be **measured reliably**.

Income, as defined by the IASB's *Framework* document (see paragraph 3.3), includes both revenues and gains. Revenue is income arising in the ordinary course of an entity's activities and it may be called different names, such as sales, fees, interest, dividends or royalties.

5.3 Scope

IAS 18 covers the revenue from specific types of transaction or events.

- **Sale of goods** (manufactured products and items purchased for resale)
- **Rendering of services**
- Use by others of entity assets yielding **interest, royalties and dividends**

Interest, royalties and dividends are included as income because they arise from the use of an entity's assets by other parties.

Key terms

> **Interest** is the charge for the use of cash or cash equivalents or amounts due to the entity.
>
> **Royalties** are charges for the use of non-current assets of the entity, eg patents, computer software and trademarks.
>
> **Dividends** are distributions of profit to holders of equity investments, in proportion with their holdings, of each relevant class of capital.

The standard specifically **excludes** various types of revenue arising from leases, insurance contracts, changes in value of financial instruments or other current assets, natural increases in agricultural assets and mineral ore extraction.

5.4 Definitions

The following definitions are given in the standard.

Key terms

> **Revenue** is the gross inflow of economic benefits during the period arising in the course of the ordinary activities of an entity when those inflows result in increases in equity, other than increases relating to contributions from equity participants.
>
> **Fair value** is the amount for which an asset could be exchanged, or a liability settled, between knowledgeable, willing parties in an arm's length transaction. *(IAS 18)*

Revenue **does not include** sales taxes, value added taxes or goods and service taxes which are only collected for third parties, because these do not represent an economic benefit flowing to the entity. The same is true for revenues collected by an agent on behalf of a principal. Revenue for the agent is only the commission received for acting as agent.

5.5 Measurement of revenue

When a transaction takes place, the amount of revenue is usually decided by the **agreement of the buyer and seller**. The revenue is actually measured, however, as the **fair value of the consideration received**, which will take account of any trade discounts and volume rebates.

5.6 Identification of the transaction

Normally, each transaction can be looked at **as a whole**. Sometimes, however, transactions are more complicated, and it is necessary to break a transaction down into its **component parts**. For example, a sale may include the transfer of goods and the provision of future servicing, the revenue for which should be deferred over the period the service is performed.

At the other end of the scale, **seemingly separate transactions must be considered together** if apart they lose their commercial meaning. An example would be to sell an asset with an agreement to buy it back at a later date. The second transaction cancels the first and so both must be considered together. We looked at sale and repurchase in paragraph 4.2.

5.7 Sale of goods

Revenue from the sale of goods should only be recognised when *all* these conditions are satisfied.

(a)   The entity has transferred the **significant risks and rewards** of ownership of the goods to the buyer

(b)   The entity has **no continuing managerial involvement** to the degree usually associated with ownership, and no longer has effective control over the goods sold

(c)   The amount of revenue can be **measured reliably**

(d)   It is probable that the **economic benefits** associated with the transaction will flow to the entity

(e)   The **costs incurred** in respect of the transaction can be measured reliably

The transfer of risks and rewards can only be decided by examining each transaction. Mainly, the transfer occurs at the same time as either the **transfer of legal title**, or the **passing of possession** to the buyer – this is what happens when you buy something in a shop.

If **significant risks and rewards remain with the seller**, then the transaction is *not* a sale and revenue cannot be recognised, for example if the receipt of the revenue from a particular sale depends on the buyer receiving revenue from his own sale of the goods.

It is possible for the seller to retain only an **'insignificant' risk of ownership** and for the sale and revenue to be recognised. The main example here is where the seller retains title only to ensure collection of what is owed on the goods. This is a common commercial situation, and when it arises the revenue should be recognised on the date of sale.

The probability of the entity receiving the revenue arising from a transaction must be assessed. It may only become probable that the economic benefits will be received when an uncertainty is removed, for example government permission for funds to be received from another country. Only when the uncertainty is removed should the revenue be recognised. This is in contrast with the situation where revenue has already been recognised but where the **collectability of the cash** is brought into doubt. Where recovery has ceased to be probable, the amount should be recognised as an expense, *not* an adjustment of the revenue previously recognised. These points also refer to services and interest, royalties and dividends below.

Matching should take place, ie the revenue and expenses relating to the same transaction should be recognised at the same time. It is usually easy to estimate expenses at the date of sale (eg warranty costs, shipment costs, etc). Where they cannot be estimated reliably, then revenue cannot be recognised; any consideration which has already been received is treated as a liability.

5.8 Example

A washing machine sells for $500 with a one-year warranty. The dealer knows from experience that 15% of these machines develop a fault in the first year and that the average cost of repair is $100. He sells 200 machines. How does he account for this sale?

Solution

He will recognise revenue of $100,000 ($500 × 200) and an associated expense of $3,000 ($100 × 200 × 15%).

5.9 Servicing fees included in the price

The sales price of a product may include an identifiable amount for subsequent servicing. In this case, that amount is deferred and recognised as revenue over the period during which the service is performed. The amount deferred must cover the cost of those services together with a reasonable profit on those services.

5.10 Example

A computerised accountancy package is sold with one year's after sales support. The cost of providing support to one customer for one year is calculated to be $50. The company has an expected return of 15%. The product is sold for $350. How is this sale accounted for?

Solution

$57.50 (50 + (50 × 15%)) will be treated as deferred income and recognised over the course of the year.

The remaining $292.50 will be treated as revenue.

5.11 Rendering of services

When the outcome of a transaction involving the rendering of services can be estimated reliably, the associated revenue should be recognised by reference to the **stage of completion of the transaction** at the end of the reporting period. The outcome of a transaction can be estimated reliably when *all* these conditions are satisfied.

(a)   The amount of revenue can be **measured reliably**

(b)   It is probable that the **economic benefits** associated with the transaction will flow to the entity

(c)   The **stage of completion** of the transaction at the end of the reporting period can be measured reliably

(d)   The **costs incurred** for the transaction and the costs to complete the transaction can be measured reliably

The parties to the transaction will normally have to agree the following before an entity can make reliable estimates.

(a)   Each party's **enforceable rights** regarding the service to be provided and received by the parties

(b)   The **consideration** to be exchanged

(c)   The **manner and terms of settlement**

There are various methods of determining the stage of completion of a transaction, but for practical purposes, when services are performed by an indeterminate number of acts over a period of time, revenue should be recognised on a **straight line basis** over the period, unless there is evidence for the use of a more appropriate method. If one act is of more significance than the others, then the significant act should be carried out *before* revenue is recognised.

In uncertain situations, when the outcome of the transaction involving the rendering of services cannot be estimated reliably, the standard recommends a **no loss/no gain approach**. Revenue is recognised only to the extent of the expenses recognised that are recoverable.

This is particularly likely during the **early stages of a transaction**, but it is still probable that the entity will recover the costs incurred. So the revenue recognised in such a period will be equal to the expenses incurred, with no profit.

Obviously, if the costs are not likely to be reimbursed, then they must be recognised as an expense immediately. **When the uncertainties cease to exist**, revenue should be recognised as laid out in the first paragraph of this section.

5.12 Interest, royalties and dividends

When others use the entity's assets yielding interest, royalties and dividends, the revenue should be recognised on the bases set out below when:

(a)   it is probable that the **economic benefits** associated with the transaction will flow to the entity; and

(b)   the amount of the revenue can be **measured reliably**.

The revenue is recognised on the following bases.

(a)   **Interest** is recognised on a time proportion basis that takes into account the effective yield on the asset

(b)   **Royalties** are recognised on an accruals basis in accordance with the substance of the relevant agreement

(c)   **Dividends** are recognised when the shareholder's right to receive payment is established

It is unlikely that you would be asked about anything as complex as this in the exam, but you should be aware of the basic requirements of the standard. The **effective yield** on an asset mentioned above is the rate of interest required to discount the stream of future cash receipts expected over the life of the asset to equate to the initial carrying amount of the asset.

Royalties are usually recognised on the same basis that they accrue **under the relevant agreement**. Sometimes the true substance of the agreement may require some other systematic and rational method of recognition.

Once again, the points made above about **probability and collectability** on sale of goods also apply here.

5.13 Disclosure

The following items should be disclosed.

(a)   The **accounting policies** adopted for the recognition of revenue, including the methods used to determine the stage of completion of transactions involving the rendering of services

(b)   The amount of each **significant category of revenue** recognised during the period including revenue arising from:

　　　(i)   The sale of goods
　　　(ii)   The rendering of services
　　　(iii)   Interest
　　　(iv)   Royalties
　　　(v)   Dividends

(c)   The amount of revenue arising from **exchanges of goods or services** included in each significant category of revenue

Any **contingent gains or losses**, such as those relating to warranty costs, claims or penalties should be treated according to IAS 37 *Provisions, contingent liabilities and contingent assets* (covered in Chapter 12).

Question	Recognition

Given that prudence is the main consideration, discuss under what circumstances, if any, revenue might be recognised at the following stages of a sale.

(a)   Goods are acquired by the business which it confidently expects to resell very quickly.
(b)   A customer places a firm order for goods.
(c)   Goods are delivered to the customer.
(d)   The customer is invoiced for goods.
(e)   The customer pays for the goods.
(f)   The customer's cheque in payment for the goods has been cleared by the bank.

(a)   A sale must never be recognised before the goods have even been ordered by a customer. There is no certainty about the value of the sale, nor when it will take place, even if it is virtually certain that goods will be sold.

(b)   A sale must never be recognised when the customer places an order. Even though the order will be for a specific quantity of goods at a specific price, it is not yet certain that the sale transaction will go through. The customer may cancel the order, the supplier might be unable to deliver the goods as ordered or it may be decided that the customer is not a good credit risk.

(c)   A sale will be recognised when delivery of the goods is made only when:

   (i)   the sale is for cash, and so the cash is received at the same time; or
   (ii)   the sale is on credit and the customer accepts delivery (eg by signing a delivery note).

(d)   The critical event for a credit sale is usually the despatch of an invoice to the customer. There is then a legally enforceable debt, payable on specified terms, for a completed sale transaction.

(e)   The critical event for a cash sale is when delivery takes place and when cash is received; both take place at the same time.

   It would be too cautious or 'prudent' to await cash payment for a credit sale transaction before recognising the sale, unless the customer is a high credit risk and there is a serious doubt about his ability or intention to pay.

(f)   It would again be over-cautious to wait for clearance of the customer's cheques before recognising sales revenue. Such a precaution would only be justified in cases where there is a very high risk of the bank refusing to honour the cheque.

Chapter Roundup

- The subject of **off-balance sheet finance** is a complex one which has plagued the accountancy profession. In practice, off-balance sheet finance schemes are often very sophisticated and these are beyond the range of this syllabus.

- Make sure that you have memorised the definitions for **assets and liabilities** (and income and expenses) and the criteria for their **recognition** given in the IASB's *Framework*.

- We have looked at some of the **major types** of off-balance sheet finance, including factoring, sale and leaseback and consignment inventory.

- Revenue recognition is straightforward in most business transactions, but some situations are more complicated and give some opportunities for manipulation.

Quick Quiz

1   Why do companies want to use off-balance sheet finance?
2   How does the *Framework* describe substance over form?
3   What is a quasi subsidiary?
4   How has the use of quasi subsidiaries been curtailed?
5   What are the common features of transactions whose substance is not readily apparent?
6   When should a transaction be recognised?

1 The overriding motivation is to avoid misinterpretation. However the result is that users are misled.

2 The principle that transactions and other events are accounted for and presented in accordance with their substance and economic reality rather than merely their legal form.

3 An entity that does not fulfil the definition of a subsidiary but is directly or indirectly controlled by the reporting entity and gives rise to benefits that are in substance no different from those arising if it were a subsidiary.

4 By IAS 27 – the definition of a subsidiary based on **control** rather than ownership.

5 (a) The legal title is separated from the ability to enjoy benefits.

   (b) The transaction is linked to others so that the commercial effect cannot be understood without reference to the complete series.

   (c) The transaction includes one or more options under such terms that it is likely the option(s) will be exercised.

6 When it is probable that a future inflow or outflow of economic benefit to the entity will occur and the item can be measured in monetary terms with sufficient reliability.

Now try the questions below from the Exam Question Bank

Number	Level	Marks	Time
18	Examination	25	45 mins
19	Examination	25	45 mins

Leasing

Introduction

Leasing transactions are extremely common so this is an important practical subject. **Lease accounting is regulated by IAS 17**, which was introduced because of abuses in the use of lease accounting by companies.

These companies effectively 'owned' an asset and 'owed' a debt for its purchase, but showed neither the asset nor the liability in the statement of financial position because they were not required to do so. This is called **'off-balance sheet finance'**, as explained in Chapter 15.

Study guide

			Intellectual level
6	**Leases**		
(a)	explain why recording the legal form of a finance lease can be misleading to users (referring to the commercial substance of such leases).		2
(b)	describe and apply the method of determining a lease type (ie. an operating or finance lease).		2
(c)	discuss the effect on the financial statements of a finance lease being incorrectly treated as an operating lease.		2
(d)	account for assets financed by finance leases in the records of the lessee.		2
(e)	account for operating leases in the records of the lessee.		2

Exam guide

You are quite likely to meet a finance lease in a consolidation or accounts preparation question.

1 Types of lease

FAST FORWARD

A finance lease is a means of acquiring the long-term use of an asset whereas an operating lease is a short-term rental agreement. Substance over form is important in distinguishing between them.

1.1 What is a lease?

Where goods are acquired other than on immediate cash terms, arrangements have to be made in respect of the future payments on those goods. In the simplest case of **credit sales**, the purchaser is allowed a period of time (say one month) to settle the outstanding amount and the normal accounting procedure in respect of receivables/payables will be adopted. However, in recent years there has been considerable growth in leasing agreements (some types of lease are called **hire purchase agreements** in some countries).

IAS 17 *Leases* standardises the accounting treatment and disclosure of assets held under lease.

In a leasing transaction there is a **contract** between the lessor and the lessee for the hire of an asset. The lessor retains legal ownership but conveys to the lessee the right to use the asset for an agreed period of time in return for specified rentals. IAS 17 defines a lease and recognises two types.

Key terms

> **Lease.** An agreement whereby the lessor conveys to the lessee in return for rent the right to use an asset for an agreed period of time.
>
> **Finance lease.** A lease that transfers substantially all the risks and rewards incident to ownership of an asset. Title may or may not eventually be transferred.
>
> **Operating lease.** A lease other than a finance lease. *(IAS 17)*

A **finance lease** may be a **hire purchase agreement**. (The difference is that under a hire purchase agreement the customer eventually, after paying an agreed number of instalments, becomes entitled to exercise an option to purchase the asset. Under other leasing agreements, ownership remains forever with the lessor.)

In this chapter the **user** of an asset will often be referred to simply as the **lessee**, and the **supplier** as the **lessor**. You should bear in mind that identical requirements apply in the case of hirers and vendors respectively under hire purchase agreements.

To expand on the definition above, a finance lease should be presumed if at the inception of a lease the **present value of the minimum lease payments** is approximately equal to the **fair value of the leased asset**.

The present value should be calculated by using the **interest rate implicit in the lease**.

Key terms

> - **Minimum lease payments.** The payments over the lease term that the lessee is or can be required to make.
>
> - **Interest rate implicit in the lease**.
>
>   The discount rate that, at the inception of the lease, causes the aggregate present value of
>
>   (a)   the minimum lease payments, and
>   (b)   the unguaranteed residual value
>
>   to be equal to the sum of
>
>   (a)   the fair value of the leased asset, and
>   (b)   any initial direct costs.
>
> - **Lease term.** The non-cancellable period for which the lessee has contracted to lease the asset together with any further terms for which the lessee has the option to continue to lease the asset, with or without further payment, when at the inception of the lease it is reasonably certain that the lessee will exercise the option.

Note that in an exam question you will be given the interest rate implicit in the lease.

1.2 Accounting for operating leases

Operating leases do not really pose an accounting problem. The lessee pays amounts periodically to the lessor and these are **charged to the income statement**.

Where the lessee is offered an incentive such as a **rent-free period** or **cashback incentive**, this is effectively a **discount**, which will be spread over the period of the operating lease in accordance with the accruals principle. For instance, if a company entered into a 4-year operating lease but was not required to make any payments until year 2, the total payments to be made over years 2-4 should be charged evenly over years 1-4.

Where a cashback incentive is received, the total amount payable over the lease term, less the cashback, should be charged evenly over the term of the lease. This can be done by crediting the cashback received to deferred income and releasing it to profit or loss over the lease term.

1.3 Accounting for finance leases

For assets held under **finance leases or hire purchase** this accounting treatment would not disclose the reality of the situation. If a **lessor** leases out an asset on a finance lease, the asset will probably never be seen on his premises or used in his business again. It would be inappropriate for a lessor to record such an asset as a non-current asset. In reality, what he owns is a **stream of cash flows receivable** from the lessee. **The asset is an amount receivable rather than a non-current asset.**

Similarly, a **lessee** may use a finance lease to fund the 'acquisition' of a major asset which he will then use in his business perhaps for many years. **The substance of the transaction is that he has acquired a non-current asset**, and this is reflected in the accounting treatment prescribed by IAS 17, even though in law the lessee never becomes the owner of the asset.

The following summary diagram should help you when deciding whether a lease is an operating lease or a finance lease.

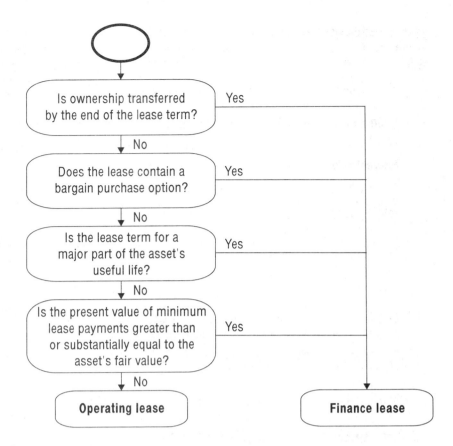

1.4 Land and buildings

Under IAS 17 the land and buildings elements of a lease of land and buildings are considered separately for the purposes of lease classification.

A lease of land is normally treated as an operating lease, unless title is expected to pass at the end of the lease term. A lease of buildings will be treated as a finance lease if it satisfies the requirements in paragraph 1.1 above. The minimum lease payments are allocated between the land and buildings elements in proportion to the relative fair values of the leasehold interests in the land and the buildings. If the value of the land is immaterial, classification will be according to the buildings.

If payments cannot be reliably allocated, the entire lease is classified as a finance lease, unless both elements are operating leases, in which case the entire lease is classified as an operating lease.

1.5 Example

A business has taken out a new lease on a factory building. The value of the building is $5m and the lease is for 5 years with annual payments of $500,000. The factory was constructed on waste ground which is valued at $400,000.

Solution

The value of the land is not material in this case, so the lease will be based on the building. The minimum lease payments do not amount to 90% of the fair value of the building, so the whole lease will be treated as an operating lease.

2 Lessees

FAST FORWARD

You must learn the accounting and disclosure requirements for lessees under finance leases and operating leases.

2.1 Accounting treatment

IAS 17 requires that, when an asset changes hands under a **finance lease, lessor and lessee should account for the transaction as though it were a credit sale**. In the lessee's books therefore:

DEBIT   Asset account
CREDIT   Lessor (liability) account

The amount to be recorded in this way is the **lower of** the **fair value** and the **present value** of the **minimum lease payments**.

IAS 17 states that it is not appropriate to show liabilities for leased assets as deductions from the leased assets. A distinction should be made between **current and non-current** lease liabilities, if the entity makes this distinction for other liabilities.

The asset should be **depreciated** (on the bases set out in IASs 16 and 38) over the shorter of:

* The lease term
* The asset's useful life

If there is reasonable certainty of eventual ownership of the asset, then it should be depreciated over its useful life.

2.2 Apportionment of rental payments

When the lessee makes a rental payment it will comprise two elements.

(a)   An **interest charge** on the finance provided by the lessor. This proportion of each payment is interest payable in the statement of comprehensive income of the lessee.

(b)   A repayment of part of the **capital cost** of the asset. In the lessee's books this proportion of each rental payment must be debited to the lessor's account to reduce the outstanding liability.

The accounting problem is to decide what proportion of each instalment paid by the lessee represents interest, and what proportion represents a repayment of the capital advanced by the lessor. There are two usual apportionment methods:

* The **actuarial method**
* The **sum-of-the-digits method**

<table>
<tr><td>**Exam focus point**</td><td>An examination question would always make it clear which method should be used. In theory, the aim is that the finance charge should reduce over the lease term in line with the outstanding liability. The examiner will not examine the **sum-of-the-digits method.**</td></tr>
</table>

The **actuarial method** is the best and most scientific method. It derives from the common-sense assumption that the interest charged by a lessor company will equal the rate of return desired by the company, multiplied by the amount of capital it has invested.

(a)   At the beginning of the lease the capital invested is equal to the fair value of the asset (less any initial deposit paid by the lessee).

(b)   This amount reduces as each instalment is paid. It follows that the interest accruing is greatest in the early part of the lease term, and gradually reduces as capital is repaid. In this section, we will look at a simple example of the actuarial method.

2.3 Example

On 1 January 20X0 Bacchus Co, wine merchants, buys a small bottling and labelling machine from Silenus Co under a finance lease. The cash price of the machine was $7,710 while the amount to be paid was $10,000. The agreement required the immediate payment of a $2,000 deposit with the balance being settled in four equal annual instalments commencing on 31 December 20X0. The charge of $2,290 represents interest of 15% per annum, calculated on the remaining balance of the liability during each accounting period. Depreciation on the plant is to be provided for at the rate of 20% per annum on a straight line basis assuming a residual value of nil.

Solution

Interest is calculated as 15% of the outstanding *capital* balance at the beginning of each year. The outstanding capital balance reduces each year by the capital element comprised in each instalment. The outstanding capital balance at 1 January 20X0 is $5,710 ($7,710 fair value less $2,000 deposit).

	$
Balance 1 January 20X0	5,710
Interest 15%	856
Instalment 31 December 20X0	(2,000)
Balance outstanding 31 December 20X0	4,566
Interest 15%	685
Instalment 31 December 20X1	(2,000)
Balance outstanding 31 December 20X1	3,251
Interest 15%	488
Instalment 31 December 20X2	(2,000)
Balance outstanding 31 December 20X2	1,739
Interest 15%	261
Instalment 31 December 20X3	(2,000)
	–

Note

You will not be required to do this whole calculation in an exam. You will probably have to calculate the first few instalments in order to obtain figures for current and non-current liabilities (as in Section 2.5).

2.4 Disclosure requirements for lessees

IAS 17 (revised) requires the following disclosures by lessees in respect of finance leases:

- The **net carrying amount** at the end of the reporting period for each class of asset

- A **reconciliation** between the total of minimum lease payments at the end of the reporting period, and their present value. In addition, an entity should disclose the total of minimum lease payments at the end of the reporting period, and their present value, for each of the following periods:

    - Not later than one year
    - Later than one year and not later than five years
    - Later than five years

2.5 Example: lessee disclosures

These disclosure requirements will be illustrated for Bacchus Co (above example). We will assume that Bacchus Co makes up its accounts to 31 December and uses the actuarial method to apportion finance charges.

Solution

The company's accounts for the first year of the lease, the year ended 31 December 20X0, would include the information given below.

STATEMENT OF FINANCIAL POSITION AS AT 31 DECEMBER 20X0 (EXTRACTS)

	$	$
Non-current assets		
Assets held under finance leases		
Plant and machinery at cost	7,710	
Less accumulated depreciation (20% × $7,710)	1,542	
		6,168
Non-current liabilities		
Obligations under finance leases		
(Balance at 31 December 20X1)		3,251
Current liabilities		
Obligations under finance leases (4,566 − 3,251)		1,315

(Notice that only the outstanding **capital** element is disclosed under liabilities, ie the total of the minimum lease payments with future finance charges separately deducted.)

INCOME STATEMENT/STATEMENT OF COMPREHENSIVE INCOME
FOR THE YEAR ENDED 31 DECEMBER 20X0 (EXTRACT)

	$
Interest payable and similar charges	
Interest on finance leases	856

2.6 Example: 6-monthly payments

Now let us see what would change if Bacchus was not required to pay a deposit but had to pay $1,250 every 6 months for 4 years. We will use the same interest rate and calculate the amounts for the first year's financial statements.

	$
Balance 1 January 20X0	7,710
Interest to 30 June 20X0 (7,710 × 15% × 6/12)	478
Instalment paid 30 June 20X0	(1,250)
Balance 30 June 20X0	7,038
Interest to 31 December 20X0 (7,038 × 15% × 6/12)	528
Instalment paid 31 December 20X0	(1,250)
Balance 31 December 20X0	6,316
Interest to 30 June 20X1 (6,316 × 15% × 6/12)	478
Instalment paid 30 June 20X1	(1,250)
Balance 30 June 20X1	5,544
Interest to 31 December 20X0 (5,544 × 15% × 6/12)	416
Instalment paid 31 December 20X1	(1,250)
Balance 31 December 20X1	4,710

Financial statement extracts at 31 December 20X0:

	$
Non-current assets (as above)	6,168
Non-current liabilities	
Obligations under finance leases	4,710
Current liabilities	
Obligations under finance leases (6,316 − 4,710)	1,606
Income statement: interest payable (578 + 528)	1,106

2.7 Operating leases: disclosures

For **operating leases** the disclosures are as follows.

The total of future minimum lease payments under non-cancellable operating leases for each of the following periods:

(a)   Not later than one year
(b)   Later than one year and not later than five years
(c)   Later than five years

2.8 Summary

The following diagram gives a useful summary of the **accounting treatment for a finance lease by a lessee.**

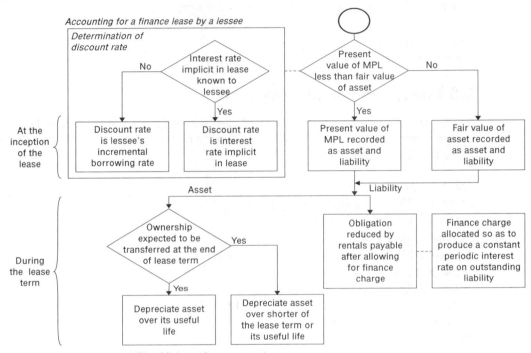

MPL = Minimum lease payments

Chapter Roundup

- A finance lease is a means of acquiring the long-term use of an asset whereas an operating lease is a short-term rental agreement. Substance over form is important in distinguishing between them.

- Under **finance leases**:

  –   Assets acquired should be capitalised
  –   Interest element of instalments should be charged against profit.

- **Operating leases** are **rental agreements** and all instalments are charged against profit.

- You must learn (through repeated practice) how to apply the actuarial method of **interest allocation**.

- You must also learn the **disclosure requirements of IAS 17** (revised) for lessees.

Quick Quiz

1 (a) ....leases transfer substantially all the risks and rewards of ownership.

   (b) ....leases are usually short-term rental agreements with the lessor being responsible for the repairs and maintenance of the asset.

2 A business acquires an asset under a finance lease. What is the double entry?

3 List the disclosures required under IAS 17 for lessees.

4 A lorry has an expected useful life of six years. It is acquired under a four year finance lease. Over which period should it be depreciated?

5 A company leases a photocopier under an operating lease which expires in June 20X2. Its office is leased under an operating lease due to expire in January 20X3. How should past and future operating leases be disclosed in its 31 December 20X1 accounts?

Answers to Quick Quiz

1 (a) Finance leases
   (b) Operating leases

2 DEBIT   Asset account
   CREDIT   Lessor account

3 See Para 2.4.

4 The four year term, being the shorter of the lease term and the useful life.

5 The total operating lease rentals charged though profit or loss should be disclosed. The payments committed to should be disclosed analysing them between those falling due in the next year and the second to fifth years.

Now try the questions below from the Exam Question Bank			
Number	Level	Marks	Time
20	Examination	10	18 mins
22	Examination	15	27 mins

17

Accounting for taxation

Topic list	Syllabus reference
1 Current tax	C9
2 Deferred tax	C9
3 Taxable temporary differences	C9
4 Deductible temporary differences	C9
5 Measurement and recognition of deferred tax	C9
6 Taxation in company accounts	C9

Introduction

In almost all countries entities are taxed on the basis of their trading income. In some countries this may be called corporation or corporate tax, but we will follow the terminology of IAS 12 *Income taxes* and call it income tax.

There are two aspects of income tax which must be accounted for: **current tax** and **deferred tax**. These will be discussed in Sections 1 and 2 respectively.

Note. Throughout this chapter we will assume a current corporate income tax rate of 30% and a current personal income tax rate of 20%, unless otherwise stated.

Study guide

		Intellectual level
9	**Taxation**	
(a)	account for current taxation in accordance with relevant accounting standards.	2
(b)	record entries relating to income tax in the accounting records.	2
(c)	explain the effect of taxable temporary differences on accounting and taxable profits.	2
(d)	compute and record deferred tax amounts in the financial statements.	2

1 Current tax

FAST FORWARD

Current tax is the amount payable to the tax authorities in relation to the trading activities of the period.

1.1 Introduction

You may have assumed until now that accounting for income tax was a very simple matter for companies. You would calculate the amount of tax due to be paid on the company's taxable profits and you would:

DEBIT   Tax charge (statement of comprehensive income)
CREDIT   Tax liability (statement of financial position)

with this amount.

Indeed, this aspect of corporate taxation – **current tax** – *is* ordinarily straightforward. Complexities arise, however, when we consider the future tax consequences of what is going on in the accounts now. This is an aspect of tax called **deferred tax**, which we will look at in the next section.

1.2 IAS 12 Income taxes

IAS 12 covers both current and deferred tax. The parts relating to current tax are fairly brief, because this is the simple and uncontroversial area of tax.

1.3 Definitions

These are some of the definitions given in IAS 12. We will look at the rest later.

Key terms

> - **Accounting profit**. Net profit or loss for a period before deducting tax expense.
> - **Taxable profit (tax loss)**. The profit (loss) for a period, determined in accordance with the rules established by the taxation authorities, upon which income taxes are payable (recoverable).
> - **Tax expense (tax income)**. The aggregate amount included in the determination of net profit or loss for the period in respect of current tax and deferred tax.
> - **Current tax**. The amount of income taxes payable (recoverable) in respect of the taxable profit (tax loss) for a period. *(IAS 12)*

Before we go any further, let us be clear about the difference between current and deferred tax.

(a) **Current tax** is the amount *actually payable* to the tax authorities in relation to the trading activities of the entity during the period.

(b) **Deferred tax** is an *accounting measure*, used to match the tax effects of transactions with their accounting impact and thereby produce less distorted results.

You should understand this a little better after working through Section 2.

1.4 Recognition of current tax liabilities and assets

IAS 12 requires any **unpaid tax** in respect of the current or prior periods to be recognised as a **liability**.

Conversely, any **excess tax** paid in respect of current or prior periods over what is due should be recognised as an **asset**.

Question	Current tax

In 20X8 Darton Co had taxable profits of $120,000. In the previous year (20X7) income tax on 20X7 profits had been estimated as $30,000.

Required

Calculate tax payable and the charge for 20X8 if the tax due on 20X7 profits was subsequently agreed with the tax authorities as:

(a) $35,000; or
(b) $25,000.

Any under or over payments are not settled until the following year's tax payment is due.

Answer

(a)

	$
Tax due on 20X8 profits ($120,000 × 30%)	36,000
Underpayment for 20X7	5,000
Tax charge and liability	41,000

(b)

	$
Tax due on 20X8 profits (as above)	36,000
Overpayment for 20X7	(5,000)
Tax charge and liability	31,000

Alternatively, the rebate due could be shown separately as income in the statement of comprehensive income and as an asset in the statement of financial position. An offset approach like this is, however, most likely.

Taking this a stage further, IAS 12 also requires recognition as an asset of the benefit relating to any tax loss that can be **carried back** to recover current tax of a previous period. This is acceptable because it is probable that the benefit will flow to the entity *and* it can be reliably measured.

1.5 Example: tax losses carried back

In 20X7 Eramu Co paid $50,000 in tax on its profits. In 20X8 the company made tax losses of $24,000. The local tax authority rules allow losses to be carried back to offset against current tax of prior years.

Required

Show the tax charge and tax liability for 20X8.

Solution

Tax repayment due on tax losses = 30% × $24,000 = $7,200.
The double entry will be:

DEBIT	Tax receivable (statement of financial position)	$7,200	
CREDIT	Tax repayment (statement of comprehensive income)		$7,200

The tax receivable will be shown as an asset until the repayment is received from the tax authorities.

1.6 Measurement

Measurement of current tax liabilities (assets) for the current and prior periods is very simple. They are measured at the **amount expected to be paid to (recovered from) the tax authorities**. The tax rates (and tax laws) used should be those enacted (or substantively enacted) by the end of the reporting period.

1.7 Recognition of current tax

Normally, current tax is recognised as income or expense and included in the net profit or loss for the period, except in two cases.

(a) Tax arising from a **business combination** is treated differently (Tax assets or liabilities of the acquired subsidiary will form part of the goodwill calculation).

(b) Tax arising from a transaction or event which is recognised **directly in equity** (in the same or a different period).

The rule in (b) is logical. If a transaction or event is charged or credited directly to equity, rather than to profit or loss, then the related tax should be also. An example of such a situation is where, under IAS 8, an adjustment is made to the **opening balance of retained earnings** due to either a change in accounting policy that is applied retrospectively, or to the correction of a material prior period error (see Chapter 7).

1.8 Presentation

In the statement of financial position, **tax assets and liabilities** should be shown separately from other assets and liabilities.

Current tax assets and liabilities can be **offset**, but this should happen only when certain conditions apply.

(a) The entity has a **legally enforceable right** to set off the recognised amounts.

(b) The entity intends to settle the amounts on a **net basis**, or to realise the asset and settle the liability at the same time.

The **tax expense (income)** related to the profit or loss from ordinary activities should be shown in the statement of comprehensive income.

The **disclosure requirements** of IAS 12 are extensive and we will look at these later in the chapter.

2 Deferred tax

FAST FORWARD

Deferred tax is an accounting measure used to match the tax effects of transactions with their accounting impact. It is quite complex.

Exam focus point

Students invariably find deferred tax very confusing. You are unlikely to be asked any very complicated questions on deferred tax in Paper 7, so concentrate on understanding and being able to explain the purpose of deferred tax and to carry out basic calculations.

2.1 What is deferred tax?

When a company recognises an asset or liability, it expects to **recover or settle the carrying amount** of that asset or liability. In other words, it expects to sell or use up assets, and to pay off liabilities. What happens if that recovery or settlement is likely to make future tax payments larger (or smaller) than they would otherwise have been if the recovery or settlement had no tax consequences? In these circumstances, IAS 12 requires companies to recognise a **deferred tax liability** (or **deferred tax asset**).

2.2 Definitions

Don't worry too much if you don't understand the concept of deferred tax yet; things should become clearer as you work through this section. First of all, here are the definitions relating to deferred tax given in IAS 12.

Key terms

> **Deferred tax liabilities** are the amounts of income taxes payable in future periods in respect of taxable temporary differences.
>
> **Deferred tax assets** are the amounts of income taxes recoverable in future periods in respect of:
>
> - Deductible temporary differences
> - The carry forward of unused tax losses
> - The carry forward of unused tax credits
>
> **Temporary differences** are differences between the carrying amount of an asset or liability in the statement of financial position and its tax base. Temporary differences may be either:
>
> - **Taxable temporary differences**, which are temporary differences that will result in taxable amounts in determining taxable profit (tax loss) of future periods when the carrying amount of the asset or liability is recovered or settled
>
> - **Deductible temporary differences**, which are temporary differences that will result in amounts that are deductible in determining taxable profit (tax loss) of future periods when the carrying amount of the asset or liability is recovered or settled
>
> The **tax base** of an asset or liability is the amount attributed to that asset or liability for tax purposes.
>
> *(IAS 12)*

We need to look at some of these definitions in more detail.

2.3 Tax base

We can expand on the definition given above by stating that the **tax base of an asset** is the amount that will be deductible for tax purposes against any taxable economic benefits that will flow to the enterprise when it recovers the carrying value of the asset. Where those economic benefits are not taxable, the tax base of the asset is the same as its carrying amount.

Question
Tax base (1)

State the tax base of each of the following assets.

(a)   A machine cost $10,000. For tax purposes, depreciation of $3,000 has already been deducted in the current and prior periods and the remaining cost will be deductible in future periods, either as depreciation or through a deduction on disposal. Revenue generated by using the machine is taxable, any gain on disposal of the machine will be taxable and any loss on disposal will be deductible for tax purposes.

(b)   Interest receivable has a carrying amount of $1,000. The related interest revenue will be taxed on a cash basis.

(c)   Trade receivables have a carrying amount of $10,000. The related revenue has already been included in taxable profit (tax loss).

(d)   A loan receivable has a carrying amount of $1m. The repayment of the loan will have no tax consequences.

Answer

(a)   The tax base of the machine is $7,000.
(b)   The tax base of the interest receivable is nil.

(c)   The tax base of the trade receivables is $10,000.
(d)   The tax base of the loan is $1m.

In the case of a **liability**, the tax base will be its carrying amount, less any amount that will be deducted for tax purposes in relation to the liability in future periods. For revenue received in advance, the tax base of the resulting liability is its carrying amount, less any amount of the revenue that will *not* be taxable in future periods.

| Question | Tax base (2) |

State the tax base of each of the following liabilities.

(a)   Current liabilities include accrued expenses with a carrying amount of $1,000. The related expense will be deducted for tax purposes on a cash basis.

(b)   Current liabilities include interest revenue received in advance, with a carrying amount of $10,000. The related interest revenue was taxed on a cash basis.

(c)   Current liabilities include accrued expenses with a carrying amount of $2,000. The related expense has already been deducted for tax purposes.

(d)   Current liabilities include accrued fines and penalties with a carrying amount of $100. Fines and penalties are not deductible for tax purposes.

(e)   A loan payable has a carrying amount of $1m. The repayment of the loan will have no tax consequences.

Answer

(a)   The tax base of the accrued expenses is nil.
(b)   The tax base of the interest received in advance is nil.
(c)   The tax base of the accrued expenses is $2,000.
(d)   The tax base of the accrued fines and penalties is $100.
(e)   The tax base of the loan is $1m.

IAS 12 gives the following examples of circumstances in which the carrying amount of an asset or liability will be **equal to its tax base**.

•   **Accrued expenses** which have already been deducted in determining an enterprise's current tax liability for the current or earlier periods.

•   A **loan payable** is measured at the amount originally received and this amount is the same as the amount repayable on final maturity of the loan.

•   **Accrued expenses** which will never be deductible for tax purposes.

•   **Accrued income** will never be taxable.

2.4 Temporary differences

You may have found the definition of temporary differences somewhat confusing. Remember that accounting profits form the basis for computing **taxable profits**, on which the tax liability for the year is calculated; however, accounting profits and taxable profits are different. There are two reasons for the differences.

(a)   **Permanent differences**. These occur when certain items of revenue or expense are excluded from the computation of taxable profits (for example, entertainment expenses may not be allowable for tax purposes).

(b)   **Temporary differences**. These occur when items of revenue or expense are included in both accounting profits and taxable profits, but not for the same accounting period. For example, an expense which is allowable as a deduction in arriving at taxable profits for 20X7 might not be included in the financial accounts until 20X8 or later. In the long run, the total taxable profits and total accounting profits will be the same (except for permanent differences) so that timing differences originate in one period and are capable of reversal in one or more subsequent periods. Deferred tax is the tax attributable to **temporary differences.**

The distinction made in the definition between **taxable temporary differences** and **deductible temporary differences** can be made clearer by looking at the explanations and examples given in the standard and its appendices.

2.5 Section summary

- Deferred tax is an **accounting device**. It does *not* represent tax payable to the tax authorities.
- The **tax base** of an asset or liability is the value of that asset or liability for tax purposes.
- You should understand the difference between **permanent and temporary differences**.
- Deferred tax is the tax attributable to **temporary differences**.

3 Taxable temporary differences

FAST FORWARD

Deferred tax assets and liabilities arise from taxable and deductible temporary differences.

Exam focus point

> The rule to remember here is that:
>
> 'All taxable temporary differences give rise to a deferred tax liability.'

3.1 Examples

The following are examples of circumstances that give rise to taxable temporary differences.

3.1.1 Transactions that affect the statement of comprehensive income

(a) **Interest revenue** received in arrears and included in accounting profit on the basis of time apportionment. It is included in taxable profit, however, on a cash basis.

(b) **Sale of goods revenue** is included in accounting profit when the goods are delivered, but only included in taxable profit when cash is received.

(c) **Depreciation** of an asset is accelerated for tax purposes. When new assets are purchased, allowances may be available against taxable profits which exceed the amount of depreciation chargeable on the assets in the financial accounts for the year of purchase.

(d) **Development costs** which have been capitalised will be amortised in the statement of comprehensive income, but they were deducted in full from taxable profit in the period in which they were incurred.

(e) **Prepaid expenses** have already been deducted on a cash basis in determining the taxable profit of the current or previous periods.

3.1.2 Transactions that affect the statement of financial position

(a) **Depreciation of an asset** is not deductible for tax purposes. No deduction will be available for tax purposes when the asset is sold/scrapped.

(b) A borrower records a **loan** at proceeds received (amount due at maturity) less transaction costs. The carrying amount of the loan is subsequently increased by amortisation of the transaction costs against accounting profit. The transaction costs were, however, deducted for tax purposes in the period when the loan was first recognised.

3.1.3 Fair value adjustments and revaluations

(a) **Current investments** or financial instruments are carried at fair value. This exceeds cost, but no equivalent adjustment is made for tax purposes.

(b) Property, plant and equipment is **revalued** by an entity (under IAS 16), but no equivalent adjustment is made for tax purposes. This also applies to long-term investments. As the tax base remains at the original value, there will be a difference between the carrying value and the tax base, leading to an increase in the deferred tax provision.

3.1.4 Differences that do not give rise to a deferred tax liability

Remember the rule we gave you above, that all taxable temporary differences give rise to a deferred tax liability? There are **two circumstances** given in the standard where this does *not* apply.

(a) The deferred tax liability arises from **goodwill** for which amortisation is not deductible for tax purposes.

(b) The deferred tax liability arises from the **initial recognition** of an asset or liability in a transaction which:

    (i) Is *not* a business combination, *and*
    (ii) At the time of the transaction affects neither accounting profit nor taxable profit

Try to **understand the reasoning** behind the recognition of deferred tax liabilities on taxable temporary differences.

(a) When an **asset is recognised**, it is expected that its carrying amount will be recovered in the form of economic benefits that flow to the entity in future periods.

(b) If the carrying amount of the asset is **greater than** its tax base, then taxable economic benefits will also be greater than the amount that will be allowed as a deduction for tax purposes.

(c) The difference is therefore a **taxable temporary difference** and the obligation to pay the resulting income taxes in future periods is a **deferred tax liability**.

(d) As the entity recovers the carrying amount of the asset, the taxable temporary difference will **reverse** and the enterprise will have taxable profit.

(e) It is then probable that economic benefits will flow from the entity in the form of **tax payments**, and so the recognition of all deferred tax liabilities (except those excluded above) is required by IAS 12.

3.2 Example: taxable temporary differences

A company purchased an asset costing $1,500. At the end of 20X8 the carrying amount is $1,000. The cumulative depreciation for tax purposes is $900 and the current tax rate is 25%.

Required

Calculate the deferred tax liability for the asset.

Solution

Firstly, what is the tax base of the asset? It is $1,500 – $900 = $600.

In order to recover the carrying value of $1,000, the enterprise must earn taxable income of $1,000, but it will only be able to deduct $600 as a taxable expense. The enterprise must therefore pay income tax of $400 × 25% = $100 when the carrying value of the asset is recovered.

The enterprise must therefore recognise a deferred tax liability of $400 × 25% = $100, recognising the difference between the carrying amount of $1,000 and the tax base of $600 as a taxable temporary difference.

3.3 Timing differences

Some temporary differences are often called **timing differences**, when income or expense is included in accounting profit in one period, but is included in taxable profit in a different period. The main types of taxable temporary differences which are timing differences and which result in deferred tax liabilities are included in the examples given above.

- **Interest received** which is accounted for on an accruals basis, but which for tax purposes is included on a cash basis.
- **Accelerated depreciation** for tax purposes.
- Capitalised and amortised **development costs**.

We will look briefly at other circumstances where temporary differences arise.

3.4 Revalued assets

Under IAS 16 assets may be revalued. If this affects the taxable profit for the current period, the tax base of the asset changes and **no temporary difference** arises.

If, however (as in some countries), the revaluation does *not* affect current taxable profits, the tax base of the asset is not adjusted. Consequently, the taxable flow of economic benefits to the entity as the carrying value of the asset is recovered will differ from the amount that will be deductible for tax purposes.

The difference between the carrying amount of a revalued asset and its tax base is a temporary difference and gives rise to a **deferred tax liability or asset**..

3.5 Initial recognition of an asset or liability

A temporary difference can arise on initial recognition of an asset or liability, eg if part or all of the cost of an asset will not be deductible for tax purposes. The **nature of the transaction** which led to the initial recognition of the asset is important in determining the method of accounting for such temporary differences.

If the transaction affects *either* accounting profit or taxable profit, an entity will **recognise any deferred tax liability** or asset. The resulting deferred tax expense or income will be recognised in profit or loss.

Where a transaction affects **neither accounting profit nor taxable profit** it would be normal for an entity to recognise a deferred tax liability or asset and adjust the carrying amount of the asset or liability by the same amount (unless exempted by IAS 12 as under Paragraph 3.1.4 above). However, IAS 12 does *not* permit this recognition of a deferred tax asset or liability as it would make the financial statements less transparent. This will be the case both on initial recognition and subsequently, nor should any subsequent changes in the unrecognised deferred tax liability or asset as the asset is depreciated be made.

3.6 Example: initial recognition

As an example of the last paragraph, suppose Petros Co intends to use an asset which cost $10,000 in 20X1 through its useful life of five years. Its residual value will then be nil. The tax rate is 40%. Any capital gain on disposal would not be taxable (and any capital loss not deductible). Depreciation of the asset is not deductible for tax purposes.

Required

State the deferred tax consequences in each of years 20X1 and 20X2.

Solution

As at 20X1, as it recovers the carrying amount of the asset, Petros Co will earn taxable income of $10,000 and pay tax of $4,000. The resulting deferred tax liability of $4,000 would not be recognised because it results from the initial recognition of the asset.

As at 20X2, the carrying value of the asset is now $8,000. In earning taxable income of $8,000, the enterprise will pay tax of $3,200. Again, the resulting deferred tax liability of $3,200 is not recognised, because it results from the initial recognition of the asset.

The following question on accelerated depreciation should clarify some of the issues and introduce you to the calculations which may be necessary in the exam.

Current and deferred tax

Question

Jonquil Co buys equipment for $50,000 and depreciates it on a straight line basis over its expected useful life of five years. For tax purposes, the equipment is depreciated at 25% per annum on a straight line basis. Tax losses may be carried back against taxable profit of the previous five years. In year 20X0, the entity's taxable profit was $25,000. The tax rate is 40%.

Required

Assuming nil profits/losses after depreciation in years 20X1 to 20X5 show the current and deferred tax impact in years 20X1 to 20X5 of the acquisition of the equipment.

Answer

Jonquil Co will recover the carrying amount of the equipment by using it to manufacture goods for resale. Therefore, the entity's current tax computation is as follows.

	Year				
	20X1	20X2	20X3	20X4	20X5
	$	$	$	$	$
Taxable income*	10,000	10,000	10,000	10,000	10,000
Depreciation for tax purposes	12,500	12,500	12,500	12,500	0
Taxable profit (tax loss)	(2,500)	(2,500)	(2,500)	(2,500)	10,000
Current tax expense (income) at 40%	(1,000)	(1,000)	(1,000)	(1,000)	4,000

* ie nil profit plus $50,000 ÷ 5 depreciation add-back.

The entity recognises a current tax asset at the end of years 20X1 to 20X4 because it recovers the benefit of the tax loss against the taxable profit of year 20X0.

The temporary differences associated with the equipment and the resulting deferred tax asset and liability and deferred tax expense and income are as follows.

	Year				
	20X1	20X2	20X3	20X4	20X5
	$	$	$	$	$
Carrying amount	40,000	30,000	20,000	10,000	0
Tax base	37,500	25,000	12,500	0	0
Taxable temporary difference	2,500	5,000	7,500	10,000	0
Opening deferred tax liability	0	1,000	2,000	3,000	4,000
Deferred tax expense (income): bal fig	1,000	1,000	1,000	1,000	(4,000)
Closing deferred tax liability @ 40%	1,000	2,000	3,000	4,000	0

The entity recognises the deferred tax liability in years 20X1 to 20X4 because the reversal of the taxable temporary difference will create taxable income in subsequent years. The entity's income statement is as follows.

	Year				
	20X1	20X2	20X3	20X4	20X5
	$	$	$	$	$
Income	10,000	10,000	10,000	10,000	10,000
Depreciation	10,000	10,000	10,000	10,000	10,000
Profit before tax	0	0	0	0	0
Current tax expense (income)	(1,000)	(1,000)	(1,000)	(1,000)	4,000
Deferred tax expense (income)	1,000	1,000	1,000	1,000	(4,000)
Total tax expense (income)	0	0	0	0	0
Net profit for the period	0	0	0	0	0

3.7 Section summary

- With one or two exceptions, all taxable temporary differences give rise to a **deferred tax liability**.
- Many taxable temporary differences are **timing differences**.
- Timing differences arise when income or an expense is included in accounting profit in one period, but in taxable profit in a **different period**.

4 Deductible temporary differences

4.1 Definition

Refer again to the definition given in Section 3 above.

Exam focus point

The rule to remember here is that:

'All deductible temporary differences give rise to a deferred tax asset.'

There is a proviso, however. The deferred tax asset must also satisfy the **recognition criteria** given in IAS 12. This is that a deferred tax asset should be recognised for all deductible temporary differences to the extent that it is **probable that taxable profit will be available** against which it can be utilised. This is an application of prudence. Before we look at this issue in more detail, let us consider the examples of deductible temporary differences given in the standard.

4.2 Transactions that affect the statement of comprehensive income

(a) **Retirement benefit costs** (pension costs) are deducted from accounting profit as service is provided by the employee. They are not deducted in determining taxable profit until the entity pays either retirement benefits or contributions to a fund. (This may also apply to similar expenses.)

(b) **Accumulated depreciation** of an asset in the financial statements is greater than the accumulated depreciation allowed for tax purposes up to the end of the reporting period.

(c) The **cost of inventories** sold before the end of the reporting period is deducted from accounting profit when goods/services are delivered, but is deducted from taxable profit when the cash is received. (*Note.* There is also a taxable temporary difference associated with the related trade receivable, as noted in Section 3 above.)

(d) The **NRV** of inventory, or the **recoverable amount** of an item of property, plant and equipment falls and the carrying value is therefore **reduced**, but that reduction is ignored for tax purposes until the asset is sold.

(e) **Research costs** (or organisation/other start-up costs) are recognised as an expense for accounting purposes but are not deductible against taxable profits until a later period.

(f) Income is **deferred** in the statement of financial position, but has already been included in taxable profit in current/prior periods.

(g) A **government grant** is included in the statement of financial position as deferred income, but it will not be taxable in future periods. (*Note.* A deferred tax asset may *not* be recognised here according to the standard.)

4.3 Fair value adjustments and revaluations

Current investments or **financial instruments** may be carried at fair value which is less than cost, but no equivalent adjustment is made for tax purposes.

4.4 Recognition of deductible temporary differences

We looked at the important recognition criteria in Section 4.1 above. As with temporary taxable differences, there are also circumstances where the overall rule for recognition of deferred tax asset is *not* allowed.

(a) Where the deferred tax asset arises from **negative goodwill** which is treated as deferred income in accordance with IAS 22.

(b) Where the deferred tax asset arises from **initial recognition** of an asset or liability in a transaction which:

    (i) Is not a business combination, *and*

    (ii) At the time of the transaction, affects neither accounting nor taxable profit/tax loss.

Let us lay out the reasoning behind the recognition of deferred tax assets arising from deductible temporary differences.

(a) When a **liability is recognised**, it is assumed that its carrying amount will be settled in the form of outflows of economic benefits from the entity in future periods.

(b) When these resources flow from the entity, part or all may be deductible in determining taxable profits of a **period later** than that in which the liability is recognised.

(c) A **temporary tax difference** then exists between the carrying amount of the liability and its tax base.

(d) A **deferred tax asset** therefore arises, representing the income taxes that will be recoverable in future periods when that part of the liability is allowed as a deduction from taxable profit.

(e) Similarly, when the carrying amount of an asset is **less than its tax base**, the difference gives rise to a deferred tax asset in respect of the income taxes that will be recoverable in future periods.

4.5 Example: deductible temporary differences

Pargatha Co recognises a liability of $10,000 for accrued product warranty costs on 31 December 20X7. These product warranty costs will not be deductible for tax purposes until the enterprise pays claims. The tax rate is 25%.

Required

State the deferred tax implications of this situation.

Solution

What is the tax base of the liability? It is nil (carrying amount of $10,000 less the amount that will be deductible for tax purposes in respect of the liability in future periods).

When the liability is settled for its carrying amount, the entity's future taxable profit will be reduced by $10,000 and so its future tax payments by $10,000 × 25% = $2,500.

The difference of $10,000 between the carrying amount ($10,000) and the tax base (nil) is a deductible temporary difference. The entity should therefore recognise a deferred tax asset of $10,000 × 25% = $2,500 **provided that** it is probable that the entity will earn sufficient taxable profits in future periods to benefit from a reduction in tax payments.

4.6 Taxable profits in future periods

When can we be sure that sufficient taxable profit will be available against which a deductible temporary difference can be utilised? IAS 12 states that this will be assumed when sufficient **taxable temporary differences** exist which relate to the same taxation authority and the same taxable entity. These should be expected to reverse:

(a) In the same period as the expected reversal of the deductible temporary difference, *or*

(b) In periods into which a tax loss arising from the deferred tax asset can be carried back or forward.

Only in these circumstances is the deferred tax asset **recognised**, in the period in which the deductible temporary differences arise.

4.7 Unused tax losses and unused tax credits

An entity may have unused tax losses or credits (ie which it can offset against taxable profits) at the end of a period. Should a deferred tax asset be recognised in relation to such amounts? IAS 12 states that a deferred tax asset may be recognised in such circumstances **to the extent that it is probable future taxable profit will be available against which the unused tax losses/credits can be utilised**.

4.8 Reassessment of unrecognised deferred tax assets

For *all* unrecognised deferred tax assets, at the end of each reporting period an entity should **reassess the availability of future taxable profits** and whether part or all of any unrecognised deferred tax assets should now be recognised. This may be due to an improvement in trading conditions which is expected to continue.

4.9 Section summary

- Deductible temporary differences give rise to a **deferred tax asset**.
- **Prudence** dictates that deferred tax assets can only be recognised when **sufficient future taxable profits** exist against which they can be utilised.

5 Measurement and recognition of deferred tax

5.1 Basis of provision of deferred tax

IAS 12 adopts the **full provision** method of accounting for deferred tax.

The **full provision method** has the **advantage** that it recognises that each timing difference at the end of the reporting period has an effect on future tax payments. If a company claims an accelerated tax allowance on an item of plant, future tax assessments will be bigger than they would have been otherwise. Future transactions may well affect those assessments still further, but that is not relevant in assessing the position at the end of the reporting period.

5.2 Example

Suppose that Girdo Co begins trading on 1 January 20X7. In its first year it makes profits of $5m, the depreciation charge is $1m and the tax allowances on those assets is $1.5m. The rate of income tax is 30%.

Solution: full provision

The tax liability is $1.35m (30% × $m(5.0 + 1.0 −1.5), but the debit to profit or loss is increased by the deferred tax liability of 30% × $0.5m = $150,000. The total charge to profit or loss is therefore $1.5m which is an effective tax rate of 30% on accounting profits (ie 30% × $5.0m).

5.3 Changes in tax rates

Where the corporate rate of income tax **fluctuates from one year to another**, a problem arises in respect of the amount of deferred tax to be credited (debited) to the statement of comprehensive income in later years.

IAS 12 requires deferred tax assets and liabilities to be measured at the tax rates expected to apply in the period **when the asset is realised or liability settled**, based on tax rates and laws enacted (or substantively enacted) at the end of the reporting period. In other words, IAS 12 requires the **liability method** to be used.

5.4 Discounting

Discounting is used to allow for the effect of the time value of money.

IAS 12 states that deferred tax assets and liabilities **should not be discounted** because of the complexities and difficulties involved. Discounting is applied to other non-current liabilities such as provisions and deferred payments.

5.5 Carrying amount of deferred tax assets

The carrying amount of deferred tax assets should be **reviewed at the end of each reporting period** and reduced where appropriate (insufficient future taxable profits). Such a reduction may be reversed in future years.

5.6 Recognition

As with current tax, deferred tax should normally be recognised as income or an expense and included in the net profit or loss for the period in the **statement of comprehensive income**. The exception is where the tax arises from a transaction or event which is recognised (in the same or a different period) **directly in equity**.

The figures shown for deferred tax in the statement of comprehensive income will consist of **two components**.

(a)   Deferred tax relating to **timing differences**.

(b)   Adjustments relating to **changes in the carrying amount of deferred tax assets/liabilities** (where there is no change in timing differences), eg changes in tax rates/laws, reassessment of the recoverability of deferred tax assets, or a change in the expected recovery of an asset.

Items in (b) will be recognised in profit or loss, *unless* they relate to items previously charged/credited to equity.

Deferred tax (and current tax) should be **charged/credited directly to equity** if the tax relates to items also charged/credited directly to equity (in the same or a different period).

Examples of IASs which allow certain items to be credited/charged directly to equity include:

(a)   **Revaluations** of property, plant and equipment (IAS 16), and

(b)   The effect of a **change in accounting policy** (applied retrospectively) or correction of a **material error** (IAS 8)

5.6.1 Example

Z Co owns a property which has a carrying value at the beginning of 20X9 of $1,500,000. At the year end it has entered into a contract to sell the property for $1,800,000. The tax rate is 30%. How will this be shown in the financial statements?

Solution

STATEMENT OF COMPREHENSIVE INCOME (EXTRACT)

	$'000
Profit for the year	X
Other comprehensive income:	
Gains on property revaluation	300
Income tax relating to components of other comprehensive income (300 × 30%)	(90)
Other comprehensive income for the year net of tax	210

The amounts will be posted as follows:

	Dr	Cr
	$'000	$'000
Property, plant and equipment	300	
Deferred tax		90
Revaluation surplus		210

5.7 Why do we recognise deferred tax?

(a) Adjustments for deferred tax are made in accordance with the **accruals concept** and in accordance with the definition of a **liability** in the Framework, ie a past event has given rise to an obligation in the form of increased taxation which will be payable in the future. The amount can be reliably estimated. A deferred tax asset similarly meets the definition of an **asset**.

(b) If the future tax consequences of transactions are not recognised, profit can be overstated, leading to overpayment of dividends and distortion of share price and EPS.

6 Taxation in company accounts

In the statement of financial position the liability for tax payable is the tax charge for the year. In the statement of comprehensive income the tax charge for the year is adjusted for transfers to or from deferred tax and for prior year under– or over-provisions.

We have now looked at the 'ingredients' of taxation in company accounts. There are two aspects to be learned:

(a) Taxation on profits in the statement of comprehensive income.
(b) Taxation payments due, shown as a liability in the statement of financial position.

6.1 Taxation in the statement of comprehensive income

The tax on profit on ordinary activities is calculated by **aggregating**:

(a) **Income tax** on taxable profits
(b) **Transfers to or from deferred taxation**
(c) Any **under provision or overprovision** of income tax on profits of previous years

When income tax on profits is calculated, **the calculation is only an estimate of what the company thinks its tax liability will be. In subsequent dealings with the tax authorities, a different income tax charge might eventually be agreed.**

The difference between the estimated tax on profits for one year and the actual tax charge finally agreed for the year is made as an adjustment to taxation on profits in the following year, **resulting in the disclosure of either an underprovision or an overprovision of tax.**

Question   Tax payable

In the accounting year to 31 December 20X3, Neil Down Co made an operating profit before taxation of $110,000.

Income tax on the operating profit has been estimated as $45,000. In the previous year (20X2) income tax on 20X2 profits had been estimated as $38,000 but it was subsequently agreed at $40,500.

A transfer to the credit of the deferred taxation account of $16,000 will be made in 20X3.

Required

(a) Calculate the tax on profits for 20X3 for disclosure in the accounts.
(b) Calculate the amount of tax payable.

(a)

	$
Income tax on profits (liability in the statement of FP)	45,000
Deferred taxation	16,000
Underprovision of tax in previous year $(40,500 – 38,000)	2,500
Tax on profits for 20X3 (income statement charge)	63,500

(b)

	$
Tax payable on 20X3 profits (liability)	45,000

6.2 Taxation in the statement of financial position

It should already be apparent from the previous examples that the income tax charge in the statement of comprehensive income will not be the same as income tax liabilities in the statement of financial position.

In the statement of financial position, there are several items which we might expect to find.

(a) **Income tax may be payable** in respect of (say) interest payments paid in the last accounting return period of the year, or accrued.

(b) If no tax is payable (or very little), then there might be an **income tax recoverable asset** disclosed in current assets (income tax is normally recovered by offset against the tax liability for the year).

(c) There will usually be a **liability for tax**, possibly including the amounts due in respect of previous years but not yet paid.

(d) We may also find a **liability on the deferred taxation account**. Deferred taxation is shown under 'non-current liabilities' in the statement of financial position.

Tax charge

For the year ended 31 July 20X4 Norman Kronkest Co made taxable trading profits of $1,200,000 on which income tax is payable at 30%.

(a) A transfer of $20,000 will be made to the deferred taxation account. The balance on this account was $100,000 before making any adjustments for items listed in this paragraph.

(b) The estimated tax on profits for the year ended 31 July 20X3 was $80,000, but tax has now been agreed at $84,000 and fully paid.

(c) Tax on profits for the year to 31 July 20X4 is payable on 1 May 20X5.

(d) In the year to 31 July 20X4 the company made a capital gain of $60,000 on the sale of some property. This gain is taxable at a rate of 30%.

Required

(a) Calculate the tax charge for the year to 31 July 20X4.

(b) Calculate the tax liabilities in the statement of financial position of Norman Kronkest as at 31 July 20X4.

(a) *Tax charge for the year*

		$
(i)	Tax on trading profits (30% of $1,200,000)	360,000
	Tax on capital gain	18,000
	Deferred taxation	20,000
		398,000
	Underprovision of taxation in previous years $(84,000 – 80,000)	4,000
	Tax charge on profit for the period	402,000

(ii) *Note.* The statement of comprehensive income will show the following.

	$
Profit before tax (1,200,000 + 60,000)	1,260,000
Income tax expense	(402,000)
Profit for the year	858,000

(b)

	$
Deferred taxation	
Balance brought forward	100,000
Transferred from profit or loss	20,000
Deferred taxation in the statement of financial position	120,000

The tax liability is as follows.

	$
Payable on 1 May 20X5	
Tax on profits (30% of $1,200,000)	360,000
Tax on capital gain (30% of $60,000)	18,000
Due on 1 May 20X5	378,000

Summary

	$
Current liabilities	
Tax, payable on 1 May 20X5	378,000
Non-current liabilities	
Deferred taxation	120,000

Note. It may be helpful to show the journal entries for these items.

		$	$
DEBIT	Tax charge (statement of comprehensive income)	402,000	
CREDIT	Tax payable		*382,000
	Deferred tax		20,000

* This account will show a debit balance of $4,000 until the underprovision is recorded, since payment has already been made: (360,000 + 18,000 + 4,000). The closing balance will therefore be $378.000.

6.3 Presentation of tax assets and liabilities

These should be **presented separately** from other assets and liabilities in the statement of financial position. Deferred tax assets and liabilities should be distinguished from current tax assets and liabilities.

In addition, deferred tax assets/liabilities should *not* be classified as current assets/liabilities, where an entity makes such a distinction.

There are only limited circumstances where **current tax** assets and liabilities may be **offset**. This should only occur if two things apply

(a) The entity has a legally enforceable right to set off the recognised amounts.

(b) The entity intends either to settle on a net basis, or to realise the asset and settle the liability simultaneously.

Similar criteria apply to the **offset of deferred tax assets and liabilities**.

6.4 Presentation of tax expense

The tax expense or income related to the profit or loss for the period should be presented in the statement of comprehensive income.

Chapter roundup

- Taxation consists of **two components**.

  - Current tax
  - Deferred tax

- **Current tax** is the amount payable to the tax authorities in relation to the trading activities during the period. It is generally straightforward.

- **Deferred tax** is an accounting measure, used to match the tax effects of transactions with their accounting impact. It is quite complex.

- **Deferred tax assets and liabilities** arise from deductible and taxable temporary differences.

- IAS 12 *Income taxes* covers both current and deferred tax.

Quick quiz

1   The tax expense related to the profit for the period should be shown in the statement of comprehensive income.

    True   ☐

    False   ☐

2   Deferred tax liabilities are the amounts of income taxes payable in future periods in respect of
    ....

3   Give three examples of temporary differences.

4   An entity has a tax overprovision relating to the prior year of $3,000. Taxable temporary differences have increased by $6,000 and profit for the year is $150,000. Tax is at 30%.
    What is the charge to profit or loss?

Answers to quick quiz

1   True

2   Taxable temporary differences

3   Any three of:
    - Interest revenue received in arrears
    - Depreciation accelerated for tax purposes
    - Development costs capitalised in the statement of financial position
    - Prepayments
    - Sale of goods revenue recognised before the cash is received

4   $43,800

	$
Tax on profit (150,000 × 30%)	45,000
Overprovision	(3,000)
Deferred tax increase (6,000 × 30%)	1,800
	43,800

Now try the question below from the Exam Question Bank

Number	Level	Marks	Time
23	Examination	15	27 mins

18

Earnings per share

Topic list	Syllabus reference
1 IAS 33 Earnings per share	C11
2 Basic EPS	C11
3 Effect on EPS of changes in capital structure	C11
4 Diluted EPS	C11
5 Presentation, disclosure and other matters	C11

Introduction

Earnings per share (EPS) is widely used by investors as a measure of a company's performance and is of particular importance in:

(a) **Comparing the results** of a company over a **period of time**

(b) **Comparing the performance** of one company's equity against the performance of **another company's equity**, and also against the returns obtainable from loan stock and other forms of investment.

The purpose of any earnings yardstick is to achieve as far as possible clarity of meaning, comparability between one company and another, one year and another, and attributability of profits to the equity shares. IAS 33 *Earnings per share* goes some way to ensuring that all these aims are achieved.

Study guide

		Intellectual level
C	**FINANCIAL STATEMENTS**	
11	**Reporting financial performance**	
(f)	earning per share (eps)	
(i)	calculate the eps in accordance with relevant accounting standards (dealing with bonus issues, full market value issues and rights issues)	2
(ii)	explain the relevance of the diluted eps and calculate the diluted eps involving convertible debt and share options (warrants)	2
(iii)	explain why the trend of eps may be a more accurate indicator of performance than a company's profit trend and the importance of eps as a stock market indicator.	2
(iv)	discuss the limitations of using eps as a performance measure.	2

1 IAS 33 Earnings per share

FAST FORWARD

> IAS 33 is a fairly straightforward standard. Make sure you follow all the calculations through and you should then be able to tackle questions easily.

1.1 Objective

The objective of IAS 33 is to improve the **comparison** of the performance of different entities in the same period and of the same entity in different accounting periods by prescribing methods for determining the number of shares to be included in the calculation of earnings per share and other amounts per share and by specifying their presentation.

1.2 Definitions

The following definitions are given in IAS 33 and IAS 32.

Key terms

- **Ordinary shares**: an equity instrument that is subordinate to all other classes of equity instruments.

- **Potential ordinary share:** a financial instrument or other contract that may entitle its holder to ordinary shares.

- **Options, warrants and their equivalents**: financial instruments that give the holder the right to purchase ordinary shares. *(IAS 33)*

- **Financial instrument**: any contract that gives rise to both a financial asset of one entity and a financial liability or equity instrument of another entity.

- **Equity instrument**: any contract that evidences a residual interest in the assets of an entity after deducting all of its liabilities. *(IAS 32)*

1.2.1 Ordinary shares

There may be more than one class of ordinary shares, but ordinary shares of the same class will have the same rights to receive dividends. Ordinary shares participate in the net profit for the period **only after other types of shares**, eg preference shares.

1.2.2 Potential ordinary shares

IAS 33 identifies the following examples of financial instruments and other contracts generating potential ordinary shares.

(a) **Debt or equity instruments**, including preference shares, that are convertible into ordinary shares

(b) **Share warrants and options**

(c) **Employee plans** that allow employees to receive ordinary shares as part of their remuneration and other share purchase plans

(d) Shares that would be issued upon the satisfaction of **certain conditions** resulting from contractual arrangements, such as the purchase of a business or other assets

1.3 Scope

IAS 33 has the following scope restrictions.

(a) Only companies with (potential) ordinary shares which are **publicly traded** need to present EPS (including companies in the process of being listed).

(b) EPS need only be presented on the basis of **consolidated results** where the parent's results are shown as well.

(c) Where companies **choose** to present EPS, even when they have no (potential) ordinary shares which are traded, they must do so in accordance with IAS 33.

2 Basic EPS

FAST FORWARD
You should know how to calculate basic EPS.

2.1 Measurement

Basic EPS should be calculated by dividing the **net profit** or loss for the period attributable to ordinary shareholders by the **weighted average number of ordinary shares** outstanding during the period.

$$\text{Basic EPS} = \frac{\text{Net profit/(loss) attributable to ordinary shareholders}}{\text{Weighted average number of ordinary shares outstanding during the period}}$$

2.2 Earnings

Earnings includes **all items of income and expense** (including tax and non-controlling interests) *less* net profit attributable to **preference shareholders**, including preference dividends.

Preference dividends deducted from net profit consist of:

(a) Preference dividends on non-cumulative preference shares declared in respect of the period

(b) The full amount of the required preference dividends for cumulative preference shares for the period, *whether or not* they have been declared (*excluding* those paid/declared during the period in respect of previous periods)

Note. In an exam question any preference shares will be redeemable and the dividend will already have been accounted for under finance costs.

2.3 Per share

The number of ordinary shares used should be the weighted average number of ordinary shares during the period. This figure (for all periods presented) should be **adjusted for events**, other than the conversion of potential ordinary shares, that have changed the number of shares outstanding without a corresponding change in resources.

The **time-weighting factor** is the number of days the shares were outstanding compared with the total number of days in the period; a reasonable approximation is usually adequate.

2.4 Example: weighted average number of shares

Justina Co, a listed company, has the following share transactions during 20X7.

Date	Details	Shares issued
1 January 20X7	Balance at beginning of year	170,000
31 May 20X7	Issue of new shares for cash	80,000
31 December 20X7	Balance at year end	250,000

Required

Calculate the weighted average number of shares outstanding for 20X7.

Solution

The weighted average number of shares can be calculated in two ways.

(a) (170,000 × 5/12) + (250,000 × 7/12) = 216,666 shares
(b) (170,000 × 12/12) + (80,000 × 7/12) = 216,666 shares

2.5 Consideration

Shares are usually included in the weighted average number of shares from the **date consideration is receivable** which is usually the date of issue; in other cases consider the specific terms attached to their issue (consider the substance of any contract). The treatment for the issue of ordinary shares in different circumstances is as follows.

Consideration	Start date for inclusion
In exchange for cash	When cash is receivable
As a result of the conversion of a debt instrument to ordinary shares	Date interest ceases accruing
In place of interest or principal on other financial instruments	Date interest ceases accruing
In exchange for the settlement of a liability of the entity	The settlement date
As consideration for the acquisition of an asset other than cash	The date on which the acquisition is recognised
For the rendering of services to the entity	As services are rendered

Ordinary shares issued as **purchase consideration** in an acquisition should be included as of the date of acquisition because the acquired entity's results will also be included from that date.

If ordinary shares are **partly paid**, they are treated as a fraction of an ordinary share to the extent they are entitled to dividends relative to fully paid ordinary shares.

Contingently issuable shares (including those subject to recall) are included in the computation when all necessary conditions for issue have been satisfied.

 Question | Basic EPS

Flame Co is a company with a called up and paid up capital of 100,000 ordinary shares of $1 each and 20,000 10% redeemable preference shares of $1 each. The company manufactures gas appliances. During its financial year to 31 December the company had to pay $50,000 compensation and costs arising from an uninsured claim for personal injuries suffered by a customer while on the company premises.

The gross profit was $200,000. Flame Co paid the required preference share dividend and declared an ordinary dividend of 42c per share. Assuming an income tax rate of 30% on the given figures show the trading results and EPS of the company.

Answer

FLAME CO
TRADING RESULTS FOR YEAR TO 31 DECEMBER

	$
Gross profit	200,000
Expense (50,000 + 2,000 preference dividend)	(52,000)
Profit before tax	148,000
Tax at 30%	(44,400)
Profit for the period	103,600

EARNINGS PER SHARE

$$\frac{103,600}{100,000} = 103.6c$$

3 Effect on EPS of changes in capital structure

 You also need to know how to deal with EPS following changes in capital structure.

3.1 Introduction

We looked at the effect of issues of new shares or buy-backs of shares on basic EPS above. In these situations, the corresponding figures for EPS for the previous year will be comparable with the current year because, as the weighted average number of shares has risen or fallen, there has been a **corresponding increase or decrease in resources**. Money has been received when shares were issued, and money has been paid out to repurchase shares. It is assumed that the sales or purchases have been made at full market price.

3.2 Example: earnings per share with a new issue

On 30 September 20X2, Boffin Co made an issue at full market price of 1,000,000 ordinary shares. The company's accounting year runs from 1 January to 31 December. Relevant information for 20X1 and 20X2 is as follows.

	20X2	20X1
Shares in issue as at 31 December	9,000,000	8,000,000
Profits after tax and preference dividend	$3,300,000	$3,280,000

Required

Calculate the EPS for 20X2 and the corresponding figure for 20X1.

Solution

	20X2	20X1
Weighted average number of shares		
8 million × 9/12	6,000,000	
9 million × 3/12	2,250,000	
	8,250,000	8,000,000
Earnings	$3,300,000	$3,280,000
EPS	40 cents	41 cents

In spite of the increase in total earnings by $20,000 in 20X2, the EPS is not as good as in 20X1, because there was extra capital employed for the final 3 months of 20X2.

There are other events, however, which change the number of shares outstanding, **without a corresponding change in resources**. In these circumstances it is necessary to make adjustments so that the current and prior period EPS figures are comparable.

Four such events are considered by IAS 33.

(a)   **Capitalisation or bonus issue** (sometimes called a stock dividend)
(b)   Bonus element in any other issue, eg a **rights issue** to existing shareholders
(c)   **Share split**
(d)   **Reverse share split** (consolidation of shares)

3.3 Capitalisation/bonus issue and share split/reverse share split

These two types of event can be considered together as they have a similar effect. In both cases, ordinary shares are issued to existing shareholders for **no additional consideration**. The number of ordinary shares has increased without an increase in resources.

This problem is solved by **adjusting the number of ordinary shares outstanding before the event** for the proportionate change in the number of shares outstanding as if the event had occurred at the beginning of the earliest period reported.

3.4 Example: earnings per share with a bonus issue

Greymatter Co had 400,000 shares in issue, until on 30 September 20X2 it made a bonus issue of 100,000 shares. Calculate the EPS for 20X2 and the corresponding figure for 20X1 if total earnings were $80,000 in 20X2 and $75,000 in 20X1. The company's accounting year runs from 1 January to 31 December.

Solution

	20X2	20X1
Earnings	$80,000	$75,000
Shares at 1 January	400,000	400,000
Bonus issue	100,000	100,000
	500,000 shares	500,000 shares
EPS	16c	15c

The number of shares for 20X1 must also be adjusted if the figures for EPS are to remain comparable.

3.5 Rights issue

A rights issue of shares is an issue of new shares to existing shareholders **at a price below the current market value**. The offer of new shares is made on the basis of x new shares for every y shares currently held; eg a 1 for 3 rights issue is an offer of 1 new share at the offer price for every 3 shares currently held. This means that there is a bonus element included.

To arrive at figures for EPS when a rights issue is made, we need to calculate first of all the **theoretical ex-rights price**. This is a weighted average value per share, and is perhaps explained most easily with a numerical example.

3.6 Example: theoretical ex-rights price

Suppose that Egghead Co has 10,000,000 shares in issue. It now proposes to make a 1 for 4 rights issue at a price of $3 per share. The market value of existing shares on the final day before the issue is made is $3.50 (this is the 'with rights' value). What is the theoretical ex-rights price per share?

Solution

	$
Before issue 4 shares, value $3.50 each	14.00
Rights issue 1 share, value $3	3.00
Theoretical value of 5 shares	17.00

$$\text{Theoretical ex-rights price} = \frac{\$17.00}{5} = \$3.40 \text{ per share}$$

Note that this calculation can alternatively be performed using the total value and number of outstanding shares.

3.7 Procedures

The procedures for calculating the EPS for the current year and a corresponding figure for the previous year are now as follows.

(a)   The **EPS for the corresponding previous period** should be multiplied by the following fraction. (*Note.* The market price on the last day of quotation is taken as the fair value immediately prior to exercise of the rights, as required by the standard.)

Formula to learn

$$\frac{\text{Theoretical ex - rights fair value per share}}{\text{Fair value per share immediately before the exercise of rights}}$$

(b)   To obtain the **EPS for the current year** you should:

(i)   Multiply the number of shares before the rights issue by the fraction of the year before the date of issue and by the following fraction

Formula to learn

$$\frac{\text{Fair value per share immediately before the exercise of rights}}{\text{Theoretical ex - rights fair value per share}}$$

(ii)   Multiply the number of shares after the rights issue by the fraction of the year after the date of issue and add to the figure arrived at in (i)

The total earnings should then be divided by the total number of shares so calculated.

3.8 Example: earnings per share with a rights issue

Brains Co had 100,000 shares in issue, but then makes a 1 for 5 rights issue on 1 October 20X2 at a price of $1. The market value on the last day of quotation with rights was $1.60.

Calculate the EPS for 20X2 and the corresponding figure for 20X1 given total earnings of $50,000 in 20X2 and $40,000 in 20X1.

Solution

Calculation of theoretical ex-rights price:

	$
Before issue 5 shares, value × $1.60	8.00
Rights issue 1 share, value × $1.00	1.00
Theoretical value of 6 shares	9.00

$$\text{Theoretical ex-rights price} = \frac{\$9}{6} = \$1.50$$

EPS for 20X1

EPS as calculated before taking into account the rights issue = 40c ($40,000 divided by 100,000 shares).

$$EPS = \frac{1.50}{1.60} \times 40c = 37\tfrac{1}{2}c$$

(Remember: this is the corresponding value for 20X1 which will be shown in the financial statements for Brains Co at the end of 20X2.)

EPS for 20X2

Number of shares before the rights issue was 100,000. 20,000 shares were issued.

Stage 1:	$100{,}000 \times \tfrac{9}{12} \times \dfrac{1.60}{1.50}$	80,000
Stage 2:	$120{,}000 \times \tfrac{3}{12}$	30,000
		110,000

$$EPS = \frac{\$50{,}000}{110{,}000} = 45\tfrac{1}{2}c$$

The figure for total earnings is the actual earnings for the year.

Marcoli Co has produced the following net profit figures for the years ending 31 December.

	$m
20X6	1.1
20X7	1.5
20X8	1.8

On 1 January 20X7 the number of shares outstanding was 500,000. During 20X7 the company announced a rights issue with the following details.

Rights:	1 new share for each 5 outstanding (100,000 new shares in total)
Exercise price:	$5.00
Last date to exercise rights:	1 March 20X7

The market (fair) value of one share in Marcoli immediately prior to exercise on 1 March 20X7 = $11.00.

Required

Calculate the EPS for 20X6, 20X7 and 20X8.

Answer

Computation of theoretical ex-rights price

This computation uses the total fair value and number of shares.

$$\frac{\text{Fair value of all outstanding shares + total received from exercise of rights}}{\text{No shares outstanding prior to exercise + no shares issued in exercise}}$$

$$= \frac{(\$11.00 \times 500{,}000) + (\$5.00 \times 100{,}000)}{500{,}000 + 100{,}000} = \$10.00$$

Computation of EPS

		20X6 $	20X7 $	20X8 $
20X6	EPS as originally reported $\dfrac{\$1{,}100{,}000}{500{,}000}$	2.20		
20X6	EPS restated for rights issue $\dfrac{\$1{,}100{,}000}{500{,}000} \times \dfrac{10}{11}$	2.00		

	20X6 $	20X7 $	20X8 $

20X7   EPS including effects of rights issue

$$\frac{\$1,500,000}{(500,000\times2/12\times11/10)+(600,000\times10/12)}$$

| | | 2.54 | |

20X8 $EPS = \dfrac{\$1,800,000}{600,000}$

| | | | 3.00 |

Exam focus point

You should know how to deal with the effect on EPS of bonus and rights issues and be able to calculate diluted EPS.

4 Diluted EPS

 FAST FORWARD

Diluted EPS is complicated, but you should be able to deal with a fairly straightforward situation.

4.1 Introduction

At the end of an accounting period, a company may have in issue some **securities** which do not (at present) have any 'claim' to a share of equity earnings, but **may give rise to such a claim in the future**. These securities include:

(a)   A **separate class of equity shares** which at present is not entitled to any dividend, but will be entitled after some future date

(b)   **Convertible loan stock** or **convertible preferred shares** which give their holders the right at some future date to exchange their securities for ordinary shares of the company, at a pre-determined conversion rate

(c)   **Options** or **warrants**

In such circumstances, the future number of ordinary shares in issue might increase, which in turn results in a fall in the EPS. In other words, a **future increase** in the **number of ordinary shares will cause a dilution or 'watering down' of equity**, and it is possible to calculate a **diluted earnings per share** (ie the EPS that would have been obtained during the financial period if the dilution had already taken place). This will indicate to investors the possible effects of a future dilution.

4.2 Earnings

The earnings calculated for basic EPS should be adjusted by the **post-tax** (including deferred tax) effect of:

(a)   Any **dividends** on dilutive potential ordinary shares that were deducted to arrive at earnings for basic EPS

(b)   **Interest recognised** in the period for the dilutive potential ordinary shares

(c)   Any **other changes in income or expenses** (fees or discount) that would result from the conversion of the dilutive potential ordinary shares

The conversion of some potential ordinary shares may lead to changes in **other income or expenses**. For example, the reduction of interest expense related to potential ordinary shares and the resulting increase in net profit for the period may lead to an increase in the expense relating to a non-discretionary employee profit-sharing plan. When calculating diluted EPS, the net profit or loss for the period is adjusted for any such consequential changes in income or expense.

4.3 Per share

The number of ordinary shares is the weighted average number of ordinary shares calculated for basic EPS plus the weighted average number of ordinary shares that would be issued on the conversion of all the **dilutive potential ordinary shares** into ordinary shares.

It should be assumed that dilutive ordinary shares were converted into ordinary shares at the **beginning of the period** or, if later, at the actual date of issue. There are two other points.

(a) The computation assumes the most **advantageous conversion rate** or exercise rate from the standpoint of the holder of the potential ordinary shares.

(b) **Contingently issuable** (potential) ordinary shares are treated as for basic EPS; if the conditions have not been met, the number of contingently issuable shares included in the computation is based on the number of shares that would be issuable if the end of the reporting period was the end of the contingency period. Restatement is not allowed if the conditions are not met when the contingency period expires.

4.4 Example: diluted EPS

In 20X7 Farrah Co had a basic EPS of 105c based on earnings of $105,000 and 100,000 ordinary $1 shares. It also had in issue $40,000 15% convertible loan stock which is convertible in two years' time at the rate of 4 ordinary shares for every $5 of stock. The rate of tax is 30%. In 20X7 gross profit of $200,000 and expenses of $50,000 were recorded, including interest payable of $6,000.

Required

Calculate the diluted EPS.

Solution

Diluted EPS is calculated as follows.

Step 1   **Number of shares**: the additional equity on conversion of the loan stock will be 40,000 × 4/5 = 32,000 shares

Step 2   **Earnings**: Farrah Co will save interest payments of $6,000 but this increase in profits will be taxed. Hence the earnings figure may be recalculated:

	$
Gross profit	200,000
Expenses (50,000 – 6,000)	(44,000)
Profit before tax	156,000
Tax expense (30%)	(46,800)
Earnings	109,200

Step 3   **Calculation**: Diluted EPS = $\dfrac{\$109,200}{132,000}$ = 82.7c

Step 4   **Dilution**: the dilution in earnings would be 105c – 82.7c = 22.3c per share.

Question   Diluted EPS

Ardent Co has 5,000,000 ordinary shares of 25 cents each in issue, and also had in issue in 20X4:

(a) $1,000,000 of 14% convertible loan stock, convertible in three years' time at the rate of 2 shares per $10 of stock;

(b) $2,000,000 of 10% convertible loan stock, convertible in one year's time at the rate of 3 shares per $5 of stock.

The total earnings in 20X4 were $1,750,000.

The rate of income tax is 35%.

Required

Calculate the basic EPS and diluted EPS.

Answer

(a) Basic EPS = $\dfrac{\$1,750,000}{5\ \text{million}}$ = 35 cents

(b) We must decide which of the potential ordinary shares (ie the loan stocks) are dilutive (ie would decrease the EPS if converted).

For the 14% loan stock, incremental EPS $= \dfrac{0.65 \times \$140,000}{200,000\ \text{shares}}$

$= 45.5c$

For the 10% loan stock, incremental EPS $= \dfrac{0.65 \times \$200,000}{1.2\text{m shares}}$

$= 10.8c$

The effect of converting the 14% loan stock is therefore to **increase** the EPS figure, since the incremental EPS of 45.5c is greater than the basic EPS of 35c. The 14% loan stock is not dilutive and is therefore excluded from the diluted EPS calculation.

The 10% loan stock is dilutive.

Diluted EPS $= \dfrac{\$1.75\text{m} + \$0.13\text{m}}{5\text{m} + 1.2\text{m}}$ = 30.3c

4.5 Treatment of options

It should be assumed that options are exercised and that the assumed proceeds would have been received from the issue of shares at **fair value**. Fair value for this purpose is calculated on the basis of the average price of the ordinary shares during the period.

Options and other share purchase arrangements are dilutive when they would result in the issue of ordinary shares for **less than fair value**. The amount of the dilution is fair value less the issue price. In order to calculate diluted EPS, each transaction of this type is treated as consisting of two parts.

(a) A contract to issue a certain number of ordinary shares at their **average market price** during the period. These shares are fairly priced and are assumed to be neither dilutive nor antidilutive. They are ignored in the computation of diluted earnings per share.

(b) A contract to issue the remaining ordinary shares for **no consideration**. Such ordinary shares generate no proceeds and have no effect on the net profit attributable to ordinary shares outstanding. Therefore such shares are dilutive and they are added to the number of ordinary shares outstanding in the computation of diluted EPS.

To the extent that **partly paid shares** are not entitled to participate in dividends during the period, they are considered the equivalent of **warrants** or **options**.

Question

Brand Co has the following results for the year ended 31 December 20X7.

Net profit for year	$1,200,000
Weighted average number of ordinary shares outstanding during year	500,000 shares
Average fair value of one ordinary share during year	$20.00

	Per share	Earnings $	Shares
Weighted average number of shares under option during year			100,000 shares
Exercise price for shares under option during year			$15.00

Required

Calculate both basic and diluted earnings per share.

Answer

	Per share	Earnings $	Shares
Net profit for year		1,200,000	
Weighted average shares outstanding during 20X7			500,000
Basic earnings per share	2.40		
Number of shares under option			100,000
Number of shares that would have been issued			
At fair value: (100,000 × $15.00/$20.00)			(75,000) *
Diluted earnings per share	2.29	1,200,000	525,000

* The earnings have not been increased as the total number of shares has been increased only by the number of shares (25,000) deemed for the purpose of the computation to have been issued for no consideration.

4.6 Dilutive potential ordinary shares

According to IAS 33, potential ordinary shares should be treated as dilutive when, and only when, their conversion to ordinary shares would **decrease net profit per share** from continuing operations. This point was illustrated in the question above.

5 Presentation, disclosure and other matters

> **FAST FORWARD**
>
> IAS 33 contains the following requirements on presentation and disclosure.

5.1 Presentation

Basic and diluted EPS should be presented by an entity in the statement of comprehensive income for each class of ordinary share that has a different right to share in the net profit for the period. The basic and diluted EPS should be presented with **equal prominence** for all periods presented.

Disclosure must still be made where the EPS figures (basic and/or diluted) are **negative** (ie a loss per share).

5.2 Disclosure

An entity should disclose the following.

(a) The amounts used as the **numerators** in calculating basic and diluted EPS, and a **reconciliation** of those amounts to the net profit or loss for the period

(b) The weighted average number of ordinary shares used as the **denominator** in calculating basic and diluted EPS, and a **reconciliation** of these denominators to each other.

5.3 Alternative EPS figures

An entity may present **alternative EPS figures if it wishes**. However, IAS 33 lays out certain rules where this takes place.

(a)   The weighted average number of shares as calculated under IAS 33 **must** be used.

(b)   A **reconciliation** must be given between the component of profit used in the alternative EPS (if it is not a line item in the statement of comprehensive income) and the line item for profit reported in the statement of comprehensive income.

(c)   Basic and diluted EPS must be shown with **equal prominence**.

5.4 Significance of earnings per share

Earnings per share (EPS) is one of the most frequently quoted statistics in financial analysis. Because of the widespread use of the price earnings **(P/E) ratio** as a yardstick for investment decisions, it became increasingly important.

Reported and forecast EPS can, through the P/E ratio, have a **significant effect on a company's share price**. Thus, a share price might fall if it looks as if EPS is going to be low.

There are a number of reasons why EPS should not be used to determine the value of a company's shares. IAS 32 concentrates on the **denominator** of EPS – ie. the number of shares. However, it is more difficult to regulate the **numerator** – earnings. Reported earnings can be affected by a number or factors – choice of accounting policy, asset valuation, taxation issues. Directors who want to present favourable EPS can find ways to boost reported earnings, as happened with Enron.

EPS has also served as a means of assessing the **stewardship and management** role performed by company directors and managers. Remuneration packages might be linked to EPS growth, thereby increasing the pressure on management to improve EPS. The danger of this, however, is that management effort may go into distorting results to produce a favourable EPS.

It should also be noted that EPS takes no account of other issues that affect whether a company is worth investing in, such as its risk profile and its investment requirements. Nevertheless, the market is sensitive to EPS.

Chapter roundup

- **Earnings per share** is a measure of the amount of profits earned by a company for each ordinary share. Earnings are profits after tax and preferred dividends.

- **Basic EPS** is calculated by dividing the net profit or loss for the period attributable to ordinary shareholders by the weighted average number of ordinary shares outstanding during the period.

- You should know how to calculate **basic EPS** and how to deal with related complications (issue of shares for cash, bonus issues, rights issues).

- **Diluted EPS** is calculated by adjusting the net profit attributable to ordinary shareholders and the weighted average number of shares outstanding for the effects of all dilutive potential ordinary shares.

- **Diluted EPS** is complicated, but you should be able to deal with a fairly straightforward situation, eg with convertible loan stock.

Quick quiz

1   How is basic EPS calculated?
2   Give the formula for the 'bonus element' of a rights issue.
3   Define 'dilutive potential ordinary share'.
4   Which numerator is used to decide whether potential ordinary shares are dilutive?
5   Why is the numerator adjusted for convertible bonds when calculating diluted EPS?

1   $$\frac{\text{Net profit/(loss) attributable to ordinary shareholders}}{\text{Weighted average number of ordinary shares outstanding during the period}}$$

2   $$\frac{\text{Actual cum} - \text{rights price}}{\text{Theoretical ex} - \text{rights price}}$$

3   See Para 4.1

4   Net profit from continuing operations only.

5   Because the issue of shares will affect earnings (the interest will no longer have to be paid).

Now try the question below from the Exam Question Bank

Number	Level	Marks	Time
24	–	15	27 mins

19

Analysing and interpreting financial statements

Topic list	Syllabus reference
1 The broad categories of ratio	E2
2 Profitability and return on capital	E2
3 Liquidity, gearing/leverage and working capital	E2
4 Shareholders' investment ratios	E2
5 Presentation of financial performance	E2

Introduction

This chapter looks at **interpretation of accounts**. We deal here with the calculation of ratios, how they can be analysed and interpreted, and how the results should be presented to management.

Study guide

		Intellectual level
E2	Calculation and interpretation of accounting ratios and trends to address users' and stakeholders' needs	
(a)	define and compute relevant financial ratios.	2
(b)	explain what aspects of performance specific ratios are intended to assess.	2
(c)	analyse and interpret ratios to given an assessment of an entity's performance and financial position in comparison with:	2
(i)	an entity's previous periods' financial statements	
(ii)	another similar entity for the same reporting period	
(iii)	industry average ratios.	
(d)	interpret an entity's financial statements to give advice from the perspectives of different stakeholders.	2
(e)	discuss how the interpretation of current value based financial statements would differ from those using historical cost based accounts.	1

1 The broad categories of ratio

FAST FORWARD Your syllabus requires you to **appraise and communicate** the position and prospects of a business based on given and prepared statements and ratios.

If you were to look at a statement of financial position or statement of comprehensive income, how would you decide whether the company was doing well or badly? Or whether it was financially strong or financially vulnerable? And what would you be looking at in the figures to help you to make your judgement?

Ratio analysis involves **comparing one figure against another** to produce a ratio, and assessing whether the ratio indicates a weakness or strength in the company's affairs.

1.1 The broad categories of ratios

Broadly speaking, basic ratios can be grouped into five categories.

- Profitability and return
- Long-term solvency and stability
- Short-term solvency and liquidity
- Efficiency (turnover ratios)
- Shareholders' investment ratios

Within each heading we will identify a number of standard measures or ratios that are normally calculated and generally accepted as meaningful indicators. One must stress however that each individual business must be considered separately, and a ratio that is meaningful for a manufacturing company may be completely meaningless for a financial institution. **Try not to be too mechanical** when working out ratios and constantly think about what you are trying to achieve.

The key to obtaining meaningful information from ratio analysis is **comparison**. This may involve comparing ratios over time within the same business to establish whether things are improving or declining, and comparing ratios between similar businesses to see whether the company you are analysing is better or worse than average within its specific business sector.

It must be stressed that ratio analysis on its own is not sufficient for interpreting company accounts, and that there are **other items of information** which should be looked at, for example:

(a) The content of any **accompanying commentary** on the accounts and other statements

(b) The age and nature of the **company's assets**

(c) **Current and future developments** in the company's markets, at home and overseas, recent acquisitions or disposals of a subsidiary by the company

(d) **Unusual** items separately disclosed in the statement of comprehensive income

(e) Any other **noticeable features** of the report and accounts, such as events after the end of the reporting period, contingent liabilities, a qualified auditors' report, the company's taxation position, and so on

1.2 Example: calculating ratios

To illustrate the calculation of ratios, the following **draft** statement of financial position and income statement figures will be used. We are using a separate income statement for this example as no items of other comprehensive income are involved.

FURLONG CO INCOME STATEMENT
FOR THE YEAR ENDED 31 DECEMBER 20X8

	Notes	20X8	20X7
		$	$
Revenue	1	3,095,576	1,909,051
Operating profit	1	359,501	244,229
Interest	2	17,371	19,127
Profit before taxation		342,130	225,102
Income tax expense		74,200	31,272
Profit for the yesr		267,930	193,830
Earnings per share		12.8c	9.3c

FURLONG CO STATEMENT OF FINANCIAL POSITION
AS AT 31 DECEMBER 20X8

	Notes	20X8	20X7
		$	$
Assets			
Non-current assets			
Property, plant and equipment		802,180	656,071
Current assets			
Inventory		64,422	86,550
Receivables	3	1,002,701	853,441
Cash at bank and in hand		1,327	68,363
		1,068,450	1,008,354
Total assets		1,870,630	1,664,425
Equity and liabilities			
Equity			
Ordinary shares 10c each	5	210,000	210,000
Share premium account		48,178	48,178
Retained earnings		651,721	410,591
		909,899	668,769
Non-current liabilities			
10% loan stock 20X4/20Y0		100,000	100,000
Current liabilities	4	860,731	895,656
Total equity and liabilities		1,870,630	1,664,425

		20X8	20X7
1	*Sales revenue and profit*	$	$
	Sales revenue	3,095,576	1,909,051
	Cost of sales	2,402,609	1,441,950
	Gross profit	692,967	467,101
	Administration expenses	333,466	222,872
	Operating profit	359,501	244,229
	Depreciation charged	151,107	120,147
2	*Interest*		
	Payable on bank overdrafts and other loans	8,115	11,909
	Payable on loan stock	10,000	10,000
		18,115	21,909
	Receivable on short-term deposits	744	2,782
	Net payable	17,371	19,127
3	*Receivables*		
	Amounts falling due within one year		
	Trade receivables	905,679	807,712
	Prepayments and accrued income	97,022	45,729
		1,002,701	853,441
4	*Current liabilities*		
	Trade payables	627,018	545,340
	Accruals and deferred income	81,279	280,464
	Corporate taxes	108,000	37,200
	Other taxes	44,434	32,652
		860,731	895,656
5	*Called-up share capital*		
	Authorised ordinary shares of 10c each	1,000,000	1,000,000
	Issued and fully paid ordinary shares of 10c each	210,000	210,000
6	Dividends paid	20,000	–

2 Profitability and return on capital

FAST FORWARD

Return on capital employed (ROCE) may be used by the shareholders or the Board to assess the performance of management.

In our example, the company made a profit in both 20X8 and 20X7, and there was an increase in profit between one year and the next:

(a)   Of 52% before taxation
(b)   Of 39% after taxation

Profit before taxation is generally thought to be a better figure to use than profit after taxation, because there might be unusual variations in the tax charge from year to year which would not affect the underlying profitability of the company's operations.

Another profit figure that should be calculated is PBIT, **profit before interest and tax**. This is the amount of profit which the company earned before having to pay interest to the providers of loan capital, such as loan notes and medium-term bank loans, which will be shown in the statement of financial position as non-current liabilities.

Formula to learn

Profit before interest and tax is therefore:

(a)   the profit on ordinary activities before taxation; **plus**
(b)   interest charges on loan capital.

Published accounts do not always give sufficient detail on interest payable to determine how much is interest on long-term finance. We will assume in our example that the whole of the interest payable ($18,115, note 2) relates to long-term finance.

PBIT in our example is therefore:

	20X8	20X7
	$	$
Profit on ordinary activities before tax	342,130	225,102
Interest payable	18,115	21,909
PBIT	360,245	247,011

This shows a 46% growth between 20X7 and 20X8.

2.1 Return on capital employed (ROCE)

It is impossible to assess profits or profit growth properly without relating them to the **amount of funds (capital) that were employed in making the profits**. The most important profitability ratio is therefore return on capital employed (ROCE), which states the profit as a percentage of the amount of capital employed.

Formula to learn

$$ROCE = \frac{Profit\ before\ interest\ and\ taxation}{Total\ assets\ less\ current\ liabilities} \times 100\%$$

Capital employed = Shareholders' equity plus non-current liabilities
(*or* total assets less current liabilities)

The underlying principle is that we must **compare like with like**, and so if capital means share capital and reserves plus non-current liabilities and debt capital, profit must mean the profit earned by all this capital together. This is PBIT, since interest is the return for loan capital.

In our example, capital employed = 20X8 $1,870,630 − $860,731 = $1,009,899
20X7 $1,664,425 − $895,656 = $768,769

These total figures are the total assets less current liabilities figures for 20X8 and 20X7 in the statement of financial position.

	20X8	20X7
ROCE	$\frac{\$360,245}{\$1,009,899} = 35.7\%$	$\frac{\$247,011}{\$768,769} = 32\%$

What does a company's ROCE tell us? What should we be looking for? There are three comparisons that can be made.

(a)   The **change in ROCE from one year to the next** can be examined. In this example, there has been an increase in ROCE by about 4 percentage points from its 20X7 level.

(b)   The **ROCE being earned by other companies**, if this information is available, can be compared with the ROCE of this company. Here the information is not available.

(c)   A comparison of the ROCE with **current market borrowing rates** may be made.

  (i)   What would be the cost of extra borrowing to the company if it needed more loans, and is it earning a ROCE that suggests it could make profits to make such borrowing worthwhile?

  (ii)   Is the company making a ROCE which suggests that it is getting value for money from its current borrowing?

  (iii)   Companies are in a risk business and commercial borrowing rates are a good independent yardstick against which company performance can be judged.

In this example, if we suppose that current market interest rates, say, for medium-term borrowing from banks, are around 10%, then the company's actual ROCE of 36% in 20X8 would not seem low. On the contrary, it might seem high.

However, it is easier to spot a low ROCE than a high one, because there is always a chance that the company's non-current assets, especially property, are **undervalued** in its statement of financial position, and so the capital employed figure might be unrealistically low. If the company had earned a ROCE, not of 36%, but of, say only 6%, then its return would have been below current borrowing rates and so disappointingly low.

2.2 Return on equity (ROE)

Return on equity gives a more restricted view of capital than ROCE, but it is based on the same principles.

Formula to learn

$$ROE = \frac{\text{Profit after tax and preference dividend}}{\text{Equity shareholders funds}} \times 100\%$$

In our example, ROE is calculated as follows.

	20X8	20X7
ROE	$\dfrac{\$267,930}{\$909,899} = 29.4\%$	$\dfrac{\$193,830}{\$668,769} = 29\%$

ROE is **not a widely-used ratio**, however, because there are more useful ratios that give an indication of the return to shareholders, such as earnings per share, dividend per share, dividend yield and earnings yield, which are described later.

2.3 Analysing profitability and return in more detail: the secondary ratios

We often sub-analyse ROCE, to find out more about why the ROCE is high or low, or better or worse than last year. There are two factors that contribute towards a return on capital employed, both related to sales revenue.

(a) **Profit margin**. A company might make a high or low profit margin on its sales. For example, a company that makes a profit of 25c per $1 of sales is making a bigger return on its revenue than another company making a profit of only 10c per $1 of sales.

(b) **Asset turnover**. Asset turnover is a measure of how well the assets of a business are being used to generate sales. For example, if two companies each have capital employed of $100,000 and Company A makes sales of $400,000 per annum whereas Company B makes sales of only $200,000 per annum, Company A is making a higher revenue from the same amount of assets (twice as much asset turnover as Company B) and this will help A to make a higher return on capital employed than B. Asset turnover is expressed as 'x times' so that assets generate x times their value in annual sales. Here, Company A's asset turnover is 4 times and B's is 2 times.

Profit margin and asset turnover together explain the ROCE and if the ROCE is the primary profitability ratio, these other two are the secondary ratios. The relationship between the three ratios can be shown mathematically.

Formula to learn

Profit margin × Asset turnover = ROCE

$$\therefore \quad \frac{\text{PBIT}}{\text{Sales}} \times \frac{\text{Sales}}{\text{Capital employed}} = \frac{\text{PBIT}}{\text{Capital employed}}$$

In our example:

		Profit margin		Asset turnover		ROCE
(a)	20X8	$\dfrac{\$360,245}{\$3,095,576}$	×	$\dfrac{\$3,095,576}{\$1,009,899}$	=	$\dfrac{\$360,245}{\$1,009,899}$
		11.64%	×	3.06 times	=	35.6%

		Profit margin		Asset turnover		ROCE
(b)	20X7	$\dfrac{\$247,011}{\$1,909,051}$	×	$\dfrac{\$1,909,051}{\$768,769}$	=	$\dfrac{\$247,011}{\$768,769}$
		12.94%	×	2.48 times	=	32.1%

In this example, the company's improvement in ROCE between 20X7 and 20X8 is attributable to a higher asset turnover. Indeed the profit margin has fallen a little, but the higher asset turnover has more than compensated for this.

It is also worth commenting on the change in sales revenue from one year to the next. You may already have noticed that Furlong achieved sales growth of over 60% from $1.9 million to $3.1 million between 20X7 and 20X8. This is very strong growth, and this is certainly one of the most significant items in the income statement and statement of financial position.

2.3.1 A warning about comments on profit margin and asset turnover

It might be tempting to think that a high profit margin is good, and a low asset turnover means sluggish trading. In broad terms, this is so. But there is a trade-off between profit margin and asset turnover, and you cannot look at one without allowing for the other.

(a)   A **high profit margin** means a high profit per $1 of sales, but if this also means that sales prices are high, there is a strong possibility that sales revenue will be depressed, and so asset turnover lower.

(b)   A **high asset turnover** means that the company is generating a lot of sales, but to do this it might have to keep its prices down and so accept a low profit margin per $1 of sales.

Consider the following.

Company A		Company B	
Sales revenue	$1,000,000	Sales revenue	$4,000,000
Capital employed	$1,000,000	Capital employed	$1,000,000
PBIT	$200,000	PBIT	$200,000

These figures would give the following ratios.

ROCE	=	$\dfrac{\$200,000}{\$1,000,000}$	= 20%	ROCE	=	$\dfrac{\$200,000}{\$1,000,000}$	= 20%
Profit margin	=	$\dfrac{\$200,000}{\$1,000,000}$	= 20%	Profit margin	=	$\dfrac{\$200,000}{\$4,000,000}$	= 5%
Asset turnover	=	$\dfrac{\$1,000,000}{\$1,000,000}$	= 1	Asset turnover	=	$\dfrac{\$4,000,000}{\$1,000,000}$	= 4

The companies have the same ROCE, but it is arrived at in a very different fashion. Company A operates with a low asset turnover and a comparatively high profit margin whereas company B carries out much more business, but on a lower profit margin. Company A could be operating at the luxury end of the market, whilst company B is operating at the popular end of the market.

2.4 Gross profit margin, net profit margin and profit analysis

Depending on the format of the income statement, you may be able to calculate the gross profit margin as well as the net profit margin. **Looking at the two together** can be quite informative.

For example, suppose that a company has the following summarised income statement for two consecutive years.

	Year 1	Year 2
	$	$
Revenue	70,000	100,000
Cost of sales	42,000	55,000
Gross profit	28,000	45,000
Expenses	21,000	35,000
Net profit	7,000	10,000

Although the net profit margin is the same for both years at 10%, the gross profit margin is not.

In year 1 it is: $\dfrac{\$28,000}{\$70,000}$ = 40%

and in year 2 it is: $\dfrac{\$45,000}{\$100,000}$ = 45%

The improved gross profit margin has not led to an improvement in the net profit margin. This is because expenses as a percentage of sales have risen from 30% in year 1 to 35% in year 2.

2.5 Historical vs current cost

In this chapter we are dealing with interpretation of financial statements based on historical cost accounts.

It is worth considering how the analysis would change if we were dealing with financial statements based on some form of current value accounting (which we will go on to look at in Chapter 21).

These are some of the issues that would arise:

- Non-current asset values would probably be stated at fair value. This may be higher than depreciated historical cost. Therefore capital employed would be higher. This would lead to a reduction in ROCE.
- Higher asset values would lead to a higher depreciation charge, which would reduce net profit.
- If opening inventory were shown at current value, this would increase cost of sales and reduce net profit.

So you can see that ROCE based on historical cost accounts is probably overstated in real terms.

3 Liquidity, gearing/leverage and working capital

FAST FORWARD

Banks and other lenders will be interested in a company's gearing level.

3.1 Long-term solvency: debt and gearing ratios

Debt ratios are concerned with **how much the company owes in relation to its size**, whether it is getting into heavier debt or improving its situation, and whether its debt burden seems heavy or light.

(a)   When a company is heavily in debt banks and other potential lenders may be unwilling to advance further funds.

(b)   When a company is earning only a modest profit before interest and tax, and has a heavy debt burden, there will be very little profit left over for shareholders after the interest charges have been paid. And so if interest rates were to go up (on bank overdrafts and so on) or the company were to borrow even more, it might soon be incurring interest charges in excess of PBIT. This might eventually lead to the liquidation of the company.

These are two big reasons why companies should keep their debt burden under control. There are four ratios that are particularly worth looking at, the debt ratio, gearing ratio, interest cover and cash flow ratio.

3.2 Debt ratio

Formula to learn

> The **debt ratio** is the ratio of a company's total debts to its total assets.

(a)   Assets consist of non-current assets at their carrying value, plus current assets.
(b)   Debts consist of all payables, whether they are due within one year or after more than one year.

You can ignore other non-current liabilities, such as deferred taxation.

There is no absolute guide to the maximum safe debt ratio, but as a very general guide, you might regard 50% as a safe limit to debt. In practice, many companies operate successfully with a higher debt ratio than this, but 50% is nonetheless a helpful benchmark. In addition, if the debt ratio is over 50% and getting worse, the company's debt position will be worth looking at more carefully.

In the case of Furlong the debt ratio is as follows.

	20X8	20X7
Total debts	$ (860,731 + 100,000)	$ (895,656 + 100,000)
Total assets	$1,870,630	$1,664,425
	= 51%	= 60%

In this case, the debt ratio is quite high, mainly because of the large amount of current liabilities. However, the debt ratio has fallen from 60% to 51% between 20X7 and 20X8, and so the company appears to be improving its debt position.

3.3 Gearing/leverage

Gearing or leverage is concerned with a company's **long-term capital structure**. We can think of a company as consisting of non-current assets and net current assets (ie working capital, which is current assets minus current liabilities). These assets must be financed by long-term capital of the company, which is one of two things.

(a) Issued share capital which can be divided into:

    (i) Ordinary shares plus other equity (eg reserves)
    (ii) Non-redeemable preference shares (unusual)

(b) Long-term debt including redeemable preference shares.

Preference share capital is normally classified as a non-current liability in accordance with IAS 32, and preference dividends (paid or accrued) are included in finance costs in the income statement.

The **capital gearing ratio** is a measure of the proportion of a company's capital that is debt. It is measured as follows.

Formula to learn

$$\text{Gearing} = \frac{\text{Interest bearing debt}}{\text{Shareholders' equity} + \text{interest bearing debt}} \times 100\%$$

As with the debt ratio, there is **no absolute limit** to what a gearing ratio ought to be. A company with a gearing ratio of more than 50% is said to be high-geared (whereas low gearing means a gearing ratio of less than 50%). Many companies are high geared, but if a high geared company is becoming increasingly high geared, it is likely to have difficulty in the future when it wants to borrow even more, unless it can also boost its shareholders' capital, either with retained profits or by a new share issue.

Leverage is an alternative term for gearing; the words have the same meaning. Note that leverage (or gearing) can be looked at conversely, by calculating the proportion of total assets financed by equity, and which may be called the equity to assets ratio. It is calculated as follows.

Formula to learn

$$\text{Equity to assets ratio} = \frac{\text{Shareholders' equity}}{\text{Shareholders' equity} + \text{interest bearing debt}} \times 100\%$$

$$\text{or} \quad \frac{\text{Shareholders' equity}}{\text{Total assets less current liabilities}}$$

In the example of Furlong, we find that the company, although having a high debt ratio because of its current liabilities, has a low gearing ratio. It has no preference share capital and its only long-term debt is the 10% loan stock. The equity to assets ratio is therefore high.

		20X8	20X7
Gearing ratio	=	$\dfrac{\$100,000}{\$1,009,899}$	$\dfrac{\$100,000}{\$768,769}$
		= 10%	= 13%
Equity to assets ratio	=	$\dfrac{\$909,899}{\$1,009,899}$	$\dfrac{\$668,769}{\$768,769}$
		= 90%	= 87%

As you can see, the equity to assets ratio is the mirror image of gearing.

3.4 The implications of high or low gearing/leverage

We mentioned earlier that **gearing or leverage** is, amongst other things, an attempt to **quantify the degree of risk involved in holding equity shares in a company**, risk both in terms of the company's ability to remain in business and in terms of expected ordinary dividends from the company. The problem with a highly geared company is that by definition there is a lot of debt. Debt generally carries a fixed rate of interest (or fixed rate of dividend if in the form of preference shares), hence there is a given (and large) amount to be paid out from profits to holders of debt before arriving at a residue available for distribution to the holders of equity. The riskiness will perhaps become clearer with the aid of an example.

	Company A $'000	Company B $'000	Company C $'000
Ordinary shares	600	400	300
Retained earnings	200	200	200
Revaluation reserve	100	100	100
	900	700	600
6% preference shares (redeemable)	–	–	100
10% loan stock	100	300	300
Capital employed	1,000	1,000	1,000
Gearing ratio	10%	30%	40%
Equity to assets ratio	90%	70%	60%

Now suppose that each company makes a profit before interest and tax of $50,000, and the rate of tax on company profits is 30%. Amounts available for distribution to equity shareholders will be as follows.

	Company A $'000	Company B $'000	Company C $'000
Profit before interest and tax	50	50	50
Interest/preference dividend	10	30	36
Taxable profit	40	20	14
Taxation at 30%	12	6	6
Profit for the period	28	14	8

If in the subsequent year profit before interest and tax falls to $40,000, the amounts available to ordinary shareholders will become as follows.

	Company A $'000	Company B $'000	Company C $'000
Profit before interest and tax	40	40	40
Interest/preference dividend	10	30	36
Taxable profit	30	10	4
Taxation at 30%	9	3	3
Profit for the period	21	7	1

Note the following.

Gearing ratio	10%	30%	40%
Equity to assets ratio	90%	70%	60%
Change in PBIT	–20%	–20%	–20%
Change in profit available for ordinary shareholders	–25%	–50%	–87.5%

The more highly geared the company, the greater the risk that little (if anything) will be available to distribute by way of dividend to the ordinary shareholders. The example clearly displays this fact in so far as the more highly geared the company, the greater the percentage change in profit available for ordinary shareholders for any given percentage change in profit before interest and tax. The relationship similarly holds when profits increase, and if PBIT had risen by 20% rather than fallen, you would find that once again the largest percentage change in profit available for ordinary shareholders (this means an increase) will be for the highly geared company. This means that there will be greater *volatility* of amounts available for ordinary shareholders, and presumably therefore greater volatility in dividends paid to those shareholders, where a company is highly geared. That is the risk: you may do extremely well or extremely badly without a particularly large movement in the PBIT of the company.

The risk of a company's ability to remain in business was referred to earlier. Gearing or leverage is relevant to this. A highly geared company has a large amount of interest to pay annually (assuming that the debt is external borrowing rather than preference shares). If those borrowings are **'secured'** in any way (and loan notes in particular are secured), then the **holders of the debt are perfectly entitled to force the company** to **realise assets to pay their interest** if funds are not available from other sources. Clearly the more highly geared a company the more likely this is to occur when and if profits fall.

3.5 Interest cover

The interest cover ratio shows whether a company is earning enough profits before interest and tax to pay its interest costs comfortably, or whether its interest costs are high in relation to the size of its profits, so that a fall in PBIT would then have a significant effect on profits available for ordinary shareholders.

Formula to learn

$$\text{Interest cover} = \frac{\text{Profit before interest and tax}}{\text{Interest charges}}$$

An interest cover of 2 times or less would be low, and should really exceed 3 times before the company's interest costs are to be considered within acceptable limits.

Returning first to the example of Companies A, B and C, the interest cover was as follows.

		Company A	*Company B*	*Company C*
(a)	When PBIT was $50,000 =	$\frac{\$50,000}{\$10,000}$	$\frac{\$50,000}{\$30,000}$	$\frac{\$50,000}{\$30,000}$
		5 times	1.67 times	1.67 times
(b)	When PBIT was $40,000 =	$\frac{\$40,000}{\$10,000}$	$\frac{\$40,000}{\$30,000}$	$\frac{\$40,000}{\$30,000}$
		4 times	1.33 times	1.33 times

Both B and C have a low interest cover, which is a warning to ordinary shareholders that their profits are highly vulnerable, in percentage terms, to even small changes in PBIT.

Question

Interest cover

Returning to the example of Furlong in Paragraph 1.2, what is the company's interest cover?

Interest payments should be taken gross, from the note to the accounts, and not net of interest receipts as shown in the income statement.

	20X8	20X7
PBIT	360,245	247,011
Interest payable	18,115	21,909
	= 20 times	= 11 times

Furlong has more than sufficient interest cover. In view of the company's low gearing, this is not too surprising and so we finally obtain a picture of Furlong as a company that does not seem to have a debt problem, in spite of its high (although declining) debt ratio.

3.6 Cash flow ratio

The cash flow ratio is the ratio of a company's **net cash inflow to its total debts**.

(a) **Net cash inflow** is the amount of cash which the company has coming into the business from its operations. A suitable figure for net cash inflow can be obtained from the cash flow statement of cash flows.

(b) **Total debts** are short-term and long-term payables, including provisions. A distinction can be made between debts payable within one year and other debts and provisions.

Obviously, a company needs to be earning enough cash from operations to be able to meet its foreseeable debts and future commitments, and the cash flow ratio, and changes in the cash flow ratio from one year to the next, provide a **useful indicator of a company's cash position**.

3.7 Short-term solvency and liquidity

Profitability is of course an important aspect of a company's performance and gearing or leverage is another. Neither, however, addresses directly the key issue of *liquidity*.

Key term

> **Liquidity** is the amount of cash a company can put its hands on quickly to settle its debts (and possibly to meet other unforeseen demands for cash payments too).

Liquid funds consist of:

(a) Cash

(b) Short-term investments for which there is a ready market

(c) Fixed-term deposits with a bank or other financial institution, for example, a six month high-interest deposit with a bank

(d) Trade receivables (because they will pay what they owe within a reasonably short period of time)

(e) Bills of exchange receivable (because like ordinary trade receivables, these represent amounts of cash due to be received within a relatively short period of time)

In summary, **liquid assets are current asset items that will or could soon be converted into cash, and cash itself.** Two common definitions of liquid assets are:

• All current assets without exception
• All current assets with the exception of inventories

A company can obtain liquid assets from sources other than sales of goods and services, such as the issue of shares for cash, a new loan or the sale of non-current assets. But a company cannot rely on these at all times, and in general, obtaining liquid funds depends on making sales revenue and profits. Even so, profits do not always lead to increases in liquidity. This is mainly because funds generated from trading may be immediately invested in non-current assets or paid out as dividends.

The reason why a company needs liquid assets is so that it can meet its debts when they fall due. Payments are continually made for operating expenses and other costs, and so there is a **cash cycle** from trading activities of cash coming in from sales and cash going out for expenses.

3.8 The cash cycle

To help you to understand liquidity ratios, it is useful to begin with a brief explanation of the cash cycle. The cash cycle describes **the flow of cash out of a business and back into it again as a result of normal trading operations.**

Cash goes out to pay for supplies, wages and salaries and other expenses, although payments can be delayed by taking some credit. A business might hold inventory for a while and then sell it. Cash will come back into the business from the sales, although customers might delay payment by themselves taking some credit.

The main points about the cash cycle are as follows.

(a)   The timing of cash flows in and out of a business does not coincide with the time when sales and costs of sales occur. **Cash flows out can be postponed by taking credit. Cash flows in can be delayed by having receivables.**

(b)   **The time between making a purchase and making a sale also affects cash flows.** If inventories are held for a long time, the delay between the cash payment for inventory and cash receipts from selling it will also be a long one.

(c)   **Holding inventories and having receivables can therefore be seen as two reasons why cash receipts are delayed.** Another way of saying this is that if a company invests in working capital, its cash position will show a corresponding decrease.

(d)   Similarly, **taking credit from creditors can be seen as a reason why cash payments are delayed.** The company's liquidity position will worsen when it has to pay the suppliers, unless it can get more cash in from sales and receivables in the meantime.

The liquidity ratios and working capital turnover ratios are used to test a company's liquidity, length of cash cycle, and investment in working capital.

3.9 Liquidity ratios: current ratio and quick ratio

The 'standard' test of liquidity is the **current ratio**. It can be obtained from the statement of financial position.

Formula to learn

$$\text{Current ratio} = \frac{\text{Current assets}}{\text{Current liabilities}}$$

The idea behind this is that a company should have enough current assets that give a promise of 'cash to come' to meet its future commitments to pay off its current liabilities. Obviously, a **ratio in excess of 1 should be expected**. Otherwise, there would be the prospect that the company might be unable to pay its debts on time. In practice, a ratio comfortably in excess of 1 should be expected, but what is 'comfortable' varies between different types of businesses.

Companies are not able to convert all their current assets into cash very quickly. In particular, some manufacturing companies might hold large quantities of raw material inventories, which must be used in production to create finished goods inventory. These might be warehoused for a long time, or sold on lengthy credit. In such businesses, where inventory turnover is slow, most inventories are not very 'liquid' assets, because the cash cycle is so long. For these reasons, we calculate an additional liquidity ratio, known as the quick ratio or acid test ratio.

The **quick ratio**, or **acid test ratio**, is calculated as follows.

$$\text{Quick ratio} = \frac{\text{Current assets less inventory}}{\text{Current liabilities}}$$

This ratio should ideally be **at least 1** for companies with a slow inventory turnover. For companies with a fast inventory turnover, a quick ratio can be comfortably less than 1 without suggesting that the company could be in cash flow trouble.

Both the current ratio and the quick ratio offer an indication of the company's liquidity position, but the absolute figures **should not be interpreted too literally**. It is often theorised that an acceptable current ratio is 1.5 and an acceptable quick ratio is 0.8, but these should only be used as a guide. Different businesses operate in very different ways. A supermarket group for example might have a current ratio of 0.52 and a quick ratio of 0.17. Supermarkets have low receivables (people do not buy groceries on credit), low cash (good cash management), medium inventories (high inventories but quick turnover, particularly in view of perishability) and very high payables.

Compare this with a manufacturing and retail organisation, with a current ratio of 1.44 and a quick ratio of 1.03. Such businesses operate with liquidity ratios closer to the standard.

What is important is the **trend** of these ratios. From this, one can easily ascertain whether liquidity is improving or deteriorating. If a supermarket has traded for the last 10 years (very successfully) with current ratios of 0.52 and quick ratios of 0.17 then it should be supposed that the company can continue in business with those levels of liquidity. If in the following year the current ratio were to fall to 0.38 and the quick ratio to 0.09, then further investigation into the liquidity situation would be appropriate. It is the relative position that is far more important than the absolute figures.

Don't forget the other side of the coin either. A current ratio and a quick ratio can get **bigger than they need to be**. A company that has large volumes of inventories and receivables might be over-investing in working capital, and so tying up more funds in the business than it needs to. This would suggest poor management of receivables (credit) or inventories by the company.

3.10 Efficiency ratios: control of receivables and inventories

A rough measure of the average length of time it takes for a company's customers to pay what they owe is the accounts receivable collection period.

The estimated average accounts receivable collection period is calculated as:

$$\frac{\text{Trade receivables}}{\text{Sales}} \times 365 \text{ days}$$

The figure for sales should be taken as the sales revenue figure in the income statement. Note that any **cash sales should be excluded** – this ratio only uses credit sales. The trade receivables are not the total figure for receivables in the statement of financial position, which includes prepayments and non-trade receivables. The trade receivables figure will be itemised in an analysis of the receivable total, in a note to the accounts.

The estimate of the accounts receivable collection period is **only approximate**.

(a)   The value of receivables in the statement of financial position might be abnormally high or low compared with the 'normal' level the company usually has.

(b)   Sales revenue in the income statement is exclusive of sales taxes, but receivables in the statement of financial position are inclusive of sales tax. We are not strictly comparing like with like.

Sales are usually made on 'normal credit terms' of payment within 30 days. A collection period significantly in excess of this might be representative of poor management of funds of a business. However, some companies must allow generous credit terms to win customers. Exporting companies in particular may have to carry large amounts of receivables, and so their average collection period might be well in excess of 30 days.

The **trend of the collection period over time** is probably the best guide. If the collection period is increasing year on year, this is indicative of a poorly managed credit control function (and potentially therefore a poorly managed company).

3.11 Accounts receivable collection period: examples

Using the same types of company as examples, the collection period for each of the companies was as follows.

Company	Trade receivables / Sales	Collection period (× 365)	Previous year	Collection period (× 365)
Supermarket	$\dfrac{\$5,016K}{\$284,986K}=$	6.4 days	$\dfrac{\$3,977K}{\$290,668K}=$	5.0 days
Manufacturer	$\dfrac{\$458.3m}{\$2,059.5m}=$	81.2 days	$\dfrac{\$272.4m}{\$1,274.2m}=$	78.0 days
Sugar refiner and seller	$\dfrac{\$304.4m}{\$3,817.3m}=$	29.3 days	$\dfrac{\$287.0m}{\$3,366.3m}=$	31.1 days

The differences in collection period reflect the differences between the types of business. Supermarkets have hardly any trade receivables at all, whereas the manufacturing companies have far more. The collection periods are fairly constant from the previous year for all three companies.

3.12 Inventory turnover period

Another ratio worth calculating is the inventory turnover period. This is another estimated figure, obtainable from published accounts, which indicates the average number of days that items of inventory are held for. As with the average receivable collection period, however, it is only an approximate estimated figure, but one which should be reliable enough for comparing changes year on year.

Formula to learn

The inventory turnover period is calculated as:

$$\frac{\text{Inventory}}{\text{Cost of sales}} \times 365 \text{ days}$$

This is another measure of how vigorously a business is trading. A lengthening inventory turnover period from one year to the next indicates:

(a) a slowdown in trading; or
(b) a build-up in inventory levels, perhaps suggesting that the investment in inventories is becoming excessive.

Generally the **higher the inventory turnover the better**, ie the lower the turnover period the better, but several aspects of inventory holding policy have to be balanced.

(a) Lead times
(b) Seasonal fluctuations in orders
(c) Alternative uses of warehouse space
(d) Bulk buying discounts
(e) Likelihood of inventory perishing or becoming obsolete

Presumably if we add together the inventory turnover period and receivables collection period, this should give us an indication of how soon inventory is converted into cash. Both receivables collection period and inventory turnover period therefore give us a further indication of the company's liquidity.

3.13 Inventory turnover period: example

The estimated inventory turnover periods for a supermarket are as follows.

Company	Inventory / Cost of sales	Inventory turnover period (days× 365)	Previous year		
Supermarket	$\dfrac{\$15,554K}{\$254,571K}$	22.3 days	$\dfrac{\$14,094K}{\$261,368K}$	× 365	= 19.7 days

3.14 Accounts payable payment period

Formula to learn

> **Accounts payable payment period** is ideally calculated by the formula:
>
> $$\frac{\text{Trade accounts payable}}{\text{Purchases}} \times 365 \ \text{days}$$

It is rare to find purchases disclosed in published accounts and so **cost of sales serves as an approximation**. The payment period often helps to assess a company's liquidity; an increase is often a sign of lack of long-term finance or poor management of current assets, resulting in the use of extended credit from suppliers, increased bank overdraft and so on.

Question

Liquidity and working capital

Calculate liquidity and working capital ratios from the accounts of TEB Co, a business which provides service support (cleaning etc) to customers worldwide. Comment on the results of your calculations.

	20X7 $m	20X6 $m
Sales revenue	2,176.2	2,344.8
Cost of sales	1,659.0	1,731.5
Gross profit	517.2	613.3
Current assets		
Inventories	42.7	78.0
Receivables (note 1)	378.9	431.4
Short-term deposits and cash	205.2	145.0
	626.8	654.4
Current liabilities		
Loans and overdrafts	32.4	81.1
Tax on profits	67.8	76.7
Accruals	11.7	17.2
Payables (note 2)	487.2	467.2
	599.1	642.2
Net current assets	27.7	12.2
Notes		
1 Trade receivables	295.2	335.5
2 Trade payables	190.8	188.1

Answer

	20X7	20X6
Current ratio	$\dfrac{626.8}{599.1} = 1.05$	$\dfrac{654.4}{642.2} = 1.02$
Quick ratio	$\dfrac{584.1}{599.1} = 0.97$	$\dfrac{576.4}{642.2} = 0.90$

	20X7	20X6

Accounts receivable collection period: $\dfrac{295.2}{2,176.2} \times 365 = 49.5$ days $\dfrac{335.5}{2,344.8} \times 365 = 52.2$ days

Inventory turnover period: $\dfrac{42.7}{1,659.0} \times 365 = 9.4$ days $\dfrac{78.0}{1,731.5} \times 365 = 16.4$ days

Accounts payable payment period: $\dfrac{190.8}{1,659.0} \times 365 = 42.0$ days $\dfrac{188.1}{1,731.5} \times 365 = 40.0$ days

The company's current ratio is a little lower than average but its quick ratio is better than average and very little less than the current ratio. This suggests that inventory levels are strictly controlled, which is reinforced by the low inventory turnover period. It would seem that working capital is tightly managed, to avoid the poor liquidity which could be caused by a long receivables collection period and comparatively high payables.

The company in the exercise is a service company and hence it would be expected to have very low inventory and a very short inventory turnover period. The similarity of receivables collection period and payables payment period means that the company is passing on most of the delay in receiving payment to its suppliers.

Question   Operating cycle

(a)   Calculate the operating cycle for Moribund plc for 20X2 on the basis of the following information.

		$
Inventory:	raw materials	150,000
	work in progress	60,000
	finished goods	200,000
Purchases		500,000
Trade accounts receivable		230,000
Trade accounts payable		120,000
Sales		900,000
Cost of goods sold		750,000

Tutorial note. You will need to calculate inventory turnover periods (total year end inventory over cost of goods sold), receivables as daily sales, and payables in relation to purchases, all converted into 'days'.

(b)   List the steps which might be taken in order to improve the operating cycle.

Answer

(a)   The operating cycle can be found as follows.

Inventory turnover period: $\dfrac{\text{Total closing inventory} \times 365}{\text{Cost of goods sold}}$

plus

Accounts receivable collection period: $\dfrac{\text{Closing trade receivables} \times 365}{\text{Sales}}$

less

Accounts payable payment period: $\dfrac{\text{Closing trade payables} \times 365}{\text{Purchases}}$

	20X2
Total closing inventory ($)	410,000
Cost of goods sold ($)	750,000
Inventory turnover period	199.5 days
Closing receivables ($)	230,000

	20X2
Sales ($)	900,000
Receivables collection period	93.3 days
Closing payables ($)	120,000
Purchases ($)	500,000
Payables payment period	(87.6 days)
Length of operating cycle (199.5 + 93.3 – 87.6)	205.2 days

(b)   The steps that could be taken to reduce the operating cycle include the following.

(i)   Reducing the raw material inventory turnover period.

(ii)   Reducing the time taken to produce goods. However, the company must ensure that quality is not sacrificed as a result of speeding up the production process.

(iii)   Increasing the period of credit taken from suppliers. The credit period already seems very long – the company is allowed three months credit by its suppliers, and probably could not be increased. If the credit period is extended then the company may lose discounts for prompt payment.

(iv)   Reducing the finished goods inventory turnover period.

(v)   Reducing the receivables collection period. The administrative costs of speeding up debt collection and the effect on sales of reducing the credit period allowed must be evaluated. However, the credit period does already seem very long by the standards of most industries. It may be that generous terms have been allowed to secure large contracts and little will be able to be done about this in the short term.

4 Shareholders' investment ratios

FAST FORWARD

These are the ratios which help equity shareholders and other investors to **assess the value and quality of an investment in the ordinary shares of a company.**

They are:

(a)   Earnings per share
(b)   Dividend per share
(c)   Dividend cover
(d)   P/E ratio
(e)   Dividend yield

The value of an investment in ordinary shares in a company **listed on a stock exchange** is its market value, and so investment ratios must have regard not only to information in the company's published accounts, but also to the current price, and the fourth and fifth ratios involve using the share price.

4.1 Earnings per share

It is possible to calculate the return on each ordinary share in the year. This is the earnings per share (EPS). Earnings per share is the amount of net profit for the period that is attributable to each ordinary share which is outstanding during all or part of the period (see Chapter 17).

4.2 Dividend per share and dividend cover

The **dividend per share** in cents is self-explanatory, and clearly an item of some interest to shareholders.

Formula to learn

Dividend cover is a ratio of: $\dfrac{\text{Earnings per share}}{\text{Dividend per (ordinary) share}}$

It shows the **proportion of profit for the year that is available for distribution to shareholders that has been paid (or proposed) and what proportion will be retained in the business to finance future growth.** A dividend cover of 2 times would indicate that the company had paid 50% of its distributable profits as dividends, and retained 50% in the business to help to finance future operations. Retained profits are an important source of funds for most companies, and so the dividend cover can in some cases be quite high.

A **significant change** in the dividend cover from one year to the next would be worth looking at closely. For example, if a company's dividend cover were to fall sharply between one year and the next, it could be that its profits had fallen, but the directors wished to pay at least the same amount of dividends as in the previous year, so as to keep shareholder expectations satisfied.

4.3 P/E ratio

Formula to learn

> The **Price/Earnings (P/E) ratio** is the ratio of a company's current share price to the earnings per share.

A high P/E ratio indicates strong shareholder **confidence** in the company and its future, eg in profit growth, and a lower P/E ratio indicates lower confidence.

The P/E ratio of one company can be compared with the P/E ratios of:

- Other companies in the same business sector
- Other companies generally

It is often used in **stock exchange reporting** where prices are readily available.

4.4 Dividend yield

Dividend yield is the return a shareholder is currently expecting on the shares of a company.

Formula to learn

> $$\text{Dividend yield} = \frac{\text{Dividend on the share for the year}}{\text{Current market value of the share (ex div)}} \times 100\%$$

(a) The dividend per share is taken as the dividend for the previous year.
(b) Ex-div means that the share price does *not* include the right to the most recent dividend.

Shareholders look for **both dividend yield and capital growth**. Obviously, dividend yield is therefore an important aspect of a share's performance.

Question | Dividend yield

In the year to 30 September 20X8, an advertising agency declares an interim ordinary dividend of 7.4c per share and a final ordinary dividend of 8.6c per share. Assuming an ex div share price of 315 cents, what is the dividend yield?

Answer

The total dividend per share is (7.4 + 8.6) = 16 cents

$$\frac{16}{315} \times 100 = 5.1\%$$

5 Presentation of financial performance

You should begin your report with a heading showing who it is from, the name of the addressee, the subject of the report and a suitable date.

A good approach is often to head up a **'schedule of ratios and statistics'** which will form an appendix to the main report. Calculate the ratios in a logical sequence, dealing in turn with operating and profitability ratios, use of assets (eg turnover period for inventories, collection period for receivables), liquidity and gearing/leverage.

As you calculate the ratios you are likely to be struck by **significant fluctuations and trends**. These will form the basis of your comments in the body of the report. The report should begin with some introductory comments, setting out the scope of your analysis and mentioning that detailed figures have been included in an appendix. You should then go on to present your analysis under any categories called for by the question (eg separate sections for management, shareholders and creditors, or separate sections for profitability and liquidity).

Finally, look out for opportunities to **suggest remedial action** where trends appear to be unfavourable. Questions sometimes require you specifically to set out your advice and recommendations.

5.1 Planning your answers

This is as good a place as any to stress the importance of planning your answers. This is particularly important for 'wordy' questions. While you may feel like breathing a sigh of relief after all that number crunching, you should not be tempted to 'waffle'. The best way to avoid going off the point is to **prepare an answer plan**. This has the advantage of making you think before you write and structure your answer logically.

The following approach may be adopted when preparing an answer plan.

(a) Read the question **requirements**.

(b) **Skim through the question** to see roughly what it is about.

(c) Read through the question carefully, **underlining any key words**.

(d) Set out the **headings** for the main parts of your answer. Leave space to insert points within the headings.

(e) **Jot down points** to make within the main sections, underlining points on which you wish to expand.

(f) Write your **full answer**.

You should allow yourself the full time allocation for written answers, that is 1.8 minutes per mark. If, however, you run out of time, a clear answer plan with points in note form will earn you more marks than an introductory paragraph written out in full.

Question		Ratios

The following information has been extracted from the recently published accounts of DG.

EXTRACTS FROM THE INCOME STATEMENTS TO 30 APRIL

	20X9	20X8
	$'000	$'000
Sales	11,200	9,750
Cost of sales	8,460	6,825
Net profit before tax	465	320

	20X9	20X8
	$'000	$'000
This is after charging:		
Depreciation	360	280
Loan note interest	80	60
Interest on bank overdraft	15	9
Audit fees	12	10

STATEMENTS OF FINANCIAL POSITION AS AT 30 APRIL

	20X9		20X8	
	$'000	$'000	$'000	$'000
Assets				
Non-current assets		1,850		1,430
Current assets				
Inventory	640		490	
Receivables	1,230		1,080	
Cash	80		120	
		1,950		1,690
Total assets		3,800		3,120
Equity and liabilities				
Equity				
Ordinary share capital	800		800	
Retained earnings	1,310		930	
		2,110		1,730
Non-current liabilities				
10% loan stock		800		600
Current liabilities				
Bank overdraft	110		80	
Payables	750		690	
Taxation	30		20	
		890		790
Total equity and liabilities		3,800		3,120

The following ratios are those calculated for DG, based on its published accounts for the previous year, and also the latest industry average ratios:

	DG 30 April 20X8	Industry average
ROCE (capital employed = equity and debentures)	16.70%	18.50%
Profit/sales	3.90%	4.73%
Asset turnover	4.29	3.91
Current ratio	2.00	1.90
Quick ratio	1.42	1.27
Gross profit margin	30.00%	35.23%
Accounts receivable collection period	40 days	52 days
Accounts payable payment period	37 days	49 days
Inventory turnover (times)	13.90	18.30
Gearing	26.37%	32.71%

Required

(a) Calculate comparable ratios (to two decimal places where appropriate) for DG for the year ended 30 April 20X9. All calculations must be clearly shown.

(b) Write a report to your board of directors analysing the performance of DG, comparing the results against the previous year and against the industry average.

(a)

	20X8	20X9	Industry average
ROCE	$\frac{320+60}{2,330}=16.30\%$	$\frac{465+80}{2,910}=18.72\%$	18.50%
Profit/sales	$\frac{320+60}{9,750}=3.90\%$	$\frac{465+80}{11,200}=4.87\%$	4.73%
Asset turnover	$\frac{9,750}{2,330}=4.18x$	$\frac{11,200}{2,910}=3.85x$	3.91x
Current ratio	$\frac{1,690}{790}=2.10$	$\frac{1,950}{890}=2.20$	1.90
Quick ratio	$\frac{1,080+120}{790}=1.52$	$\frac{1,230+80}{890}=1.47$	1.27
Gross profit margin	$\frac{9,750-6,825}{9,750}=30.00\%$	$\frac{11,200-8,460}{11,200}=24.46\%$	35.23%
Accounts receivable collection period	$\frac{1,080}{9,750}\times365=40\text{days}$	$\frac{1,230}{11,200}\times365=40\text{days}$	52 days
Accounts payable payment period	$\frac{690}{6,825}\times365=37\text{days}$	$\frac{750}{8,460}\times365=32\text{days}$	49 days
Inventory turnover (times)	$\frac{6,825}{490}=13.9x$	$\frac{8,460}{640}=13.2x$	18.30x
Gearing	$\frac{600}{2,330}=25.75\%$	$\frac{800}{2,910}=27.5\%$	32.71%

(b) (i) REPORT

To: Board of Directors
From: Accountant   Date: xx/xx/xx
Subject: Analysis of performance of DG

This report should be read in conjunction with the appendix attached which shows the relevant ratios (from part (a)).

Trading and profitability

Return on capital employed has improved considerably between 20X8 and 20X9 and is now higher than the industry average.

Net income as a proportion of sales has also improved noticeably between the years and is also now marginally ahead of the industry average. Gross margin, however, is considerably lower than in the previous year and is only some 70% of the industry average. This suggests either that there has been a change in the cost structure of DG or that there has been a change in the method of cost allocation between the periods. Either way, this is a marked change that requires investigation. The company may be in a period of transition as sales have increased by nearly 15% over the year and it would appear that new non-current assets have been purchased.

Asset turnover has declined between the periods although the 20X9 figure is in line with the industry average. This reduction might indicate that the efficiency with which assets are used has deteriorated or it might indicate that the assets acquired in 20X9 have not yet fully contributed to the business. A longer term trend would clarify the picture.

(ii) Liquidity and working capital management

The current ratio has improved slightly over the year and is marginally higher than the industry average. It is also in line with what is generally regarded as satisfactory (2:1).

The quick ratio has declined marginally but is still better than the industry average. This suggests that DG has no short term liquidity problems and should have no difficulty in paying its debts as they become due.

Receivables as a proportion of sales is unchanged from 20X8 and are considerably lower than the industry average. Consequently, there is probably little opportunity to reduce this further and there may be pressure in the future from customers to increase the period of credit given. The period of credit taken from suppliers has fallen from 37 days' purchases to 32 days' and is much lower than the industry average; thus, it may be possible to finance any additional receivables by negotiating better credit terms from suppliers.

Inventory turnover has fallen slightly and is much slower than the industry average and this may partly reflect stocking up ahead of a significant increase in sales. Alternatively, there is some danger that the inventory could contain certain obsolete items that may require writing off. The relative increase in the level of inventory has been financed by an increased overdraft which may reduce if the inventory levels can be brought down.

The high levels of inventory, overdraft and receivables compared to that of payables suggests a labour intensive company or one where considerable value is added to bought-in products.

(iii)   Gearing

The level of gearing has increased only slightly over the year and is below the industry average. Since the return on capital employed is nearly twice the rate of interest on the loan stock, profitability is likely to be increased by a modest increase in the level of gearing.

Signed: Accountant

- This lengthy chapter has gone into quite a lot of detail about basic ratio analysis. The ratios you should be able to calculate and/or comment on are as follows.

  - **Profitability ratios**

    - Return on capital employed
    - Net profit as a percentage of sales
    - Asset turnover ratio
    - Gross profit as a percentage of sales

  - **Debt and gearing/leverage ratios**

    - Debt ratio
    - Gearing ratio/leverage
    - Interest cover
    - Cash flow ratio

  - **Liquidity and working capital ratios**

    - Current ratio
    - Quick ratio (acid test ratio)
    - Accounts receivable collection period
    - Accounts payable payment period
    - Inventory turnover period

  - **Ordinary shareholders' investment ratios**

    - Earnings per share
    - Dividend cover
    - P/E ratio
    - Dividend yield

- With the exception of the last two ratios, where the share's market price is required, all of these ratios **can be calculated from information in a company's published accounts.**

- Ratios provide information through **comparison**.

  - **Trends** in a company's ratios from **one year to the next**, indicating an improving or worsening position.

  - In some cases, **against a 'norm' or 'standard'**.

  - In some cases, **against the ratios of other companies**, although differences between one company and another should often be expected.

- You must realise that, however many ratios you can find to calculate, **numbers alone will not answer a question**. You *must* interpret all the information available to you and support your interpretation with ratio calculations.

Quick quiz

1   List the main categories of ratio.

2   ROCE is $\dfrac{\text{Profit before interest and tax}}{\text{Capital employed}} \times 100\%$

    True   ☐
    False ☐

3   Company Q has a profit margin of 7%. Briefly comment on this.

4   The debt ratio is a company's long-term debt divided by its net assets.

    True   ☐
    False ☐

5   The cash flow ratio is the ratio of:

    A   Gross cash inflow to total debt
    B   Gross cash inflow to net debt
    C   Net cash inflow to total debt
    D   Net cash inflow to net debt

6   List the formulae for:

    (a)   Current ratio   (c)   Accounts receivable collection period
    (b)   Quick ratio   (d)   Inventory turnover period

Answers to quick quiz

1   See Section 1.1.

2   True

3   You should be careful here. You have very little information. This is a low margin but you need to know what industry the company operates in. 7% may be good for a major retailer.

4   False (see Section 3.2)

5   C (see Section 3.6)

6   See Sections 3.9, 3.10 and 3.12.

Now try the questions below from the Exam Question Bank			
Number	**Level**	**Marks**	**Time**
25	Examination	25	45 mins

19: Analysing and interpreting financial statements | F7 Financial reporting

Limitations of financial statements and interpretation techniques

20

Topic list	Syllabus reference
1 Limitations of financial statements	E1
2 Accounting polices and the limitations of ratio analysis	E3

Introduction

In the least chapter we looked at how we interpret financial statements. In this chapter we take a look at how far we can rely on such interpretation.

Study guide

		Intellectual level
E	**ANALYSING AND INTERPRETING FINANCIAL STATEMENTS**	
1	**Limitations of financial statements**	
	(a) indicate the problems of using historic information to predict future performance and trends.	2
	(b) discuss how financial statements may be manipulated to produce a desired effect (creative accounting, window dressing)	2
	(c) recognise how related party relationships have the potential to mislead users.	2
	(d) explain why figures in the statement of financial position may not be representative of average values throughout the period for example, due to:	2
	(i) seasonal trading	
	(ii) major asset acquisitions near the end of the accounting period.	
3	**Limitations of interpretation techniques**	
	(a) discuss the limitations in the use of ratio analysis for assessing corporate performance.	2
	(b) discuss the effect that changes in accounting policies or the use of different accounting policies between entities can have on the ability to interpret performance.	2
	(c) indicate other information, including non-financial information, that may be of relevance to the assessment of an entity's performance.	1

Exam guide

These issues are unlikely to form a whole question but could well appear in a question on interpretation of accounts.

1 Limitations of financial statements

FAST FORWARD

Financial statements are affected by the obvious shortcomings of historic cost information and are also subject to manipulation.

Financial statements are intended to give a fair presentation of the financial performance of an entity over a period and its financial position at the end of that period. The IASB *Framework* and the IASs/IFRSs are there to ensure as far as possible that they do. However, there are a number of reasons why the information in financial statements should not just be taken at its face value.

1.1 Problems of historic cost information

Historic cost information is reliable and can be verified, but it becomes less relevant as time goes by. The value shown for assets carried in the statement of financial position at historic cost may bear no relation whatever to what their current value is and what it may cost to replace them. The corresponding depreciation charge will also be low, leading to the overstatement of profits in real terms. The financial statements do not show the real cost of using such assets.

This is particularly misleading when attempting to predict future performance. It could be that a major asset will need to be replaced in two years time, at vastly more than the original cost of the asset currently shown in the statement of financial position. This will then entail much higher depreciation and interest payments (if a loan or finance lease is used). In addition, overstatement of profit due to the low depreciation charge can have led to too much profit having been distributed, increasing the likelihood of new asset purchases having to be financed by loans. This information could not have been obtained just from looking at the financial statements.

In a period of inflation, financial statements based on historic cost are subject to an additional distortion. Sales revenue will be keeping pace with inflation and so will the cost of purchases. However, using FIFO (and to some degree the weighted average method) inventory being used will be valued as the earliest (and therefore cheapest) purchases. This leads to understatement of cost of sales and overstatement of profits. This is the result of inventory carried at historic cost.

1.2 Creative accounting

Listed companies produce their financial statements with one eye on the stock market and, where possible, they like to produce financial statements which show analysts what they are expecting to see. For instance, a steady rise in profits, with no peaks or troughs, is reassuring to potential investors. Companies could sometimes achieve this by using provisions to smooth out the peaks and troughs. This has been largely outlawed by IAS 37 (see Chapter 12), but companies can still achieve similar effects by delaying or advancing invoicing or manipulating cut-offs or accruals. Directors who are paid performance bonuses will favour the steady rise (enough to secure the bonus each year, rather than up one year, down the next) while those who hold share options may be aiming for one spectacular set of results just before they sell.

An important aspect of improving the appearance of the statement of financial position is keeping gearing as low as possible. Investors know that interest payments reduce the amount available for distribution and potential lenders will be less willing to lend to a company which is already highly geared.

A number of creative accounting measures are aimed at reducing gearing. In the past parent companies could find reasons to exclude highly-geared subsidiaries from the consolidation and could obtain loans in the first place via such 'quasi subsidiaries', so that the loan never appeared in the consolidated statement of financial position. This loophole has been effectively closed by IAS 27, but other means of keeping debt out of the statement of financial position exist. Finance leases can be treated as operating leases, so that the asset and the loan are kept off-balance sheet. Assets can be 'sold' under a sale and leaseback agreement, which is in effect a disguised loan. And if all else fails, a last minute piece of 'window dressing' can be undertaken. For instance, a loan can be repaid just before the year end and taken out again at the beginning of the next year.

1.3 The effect of related parties

The objective of IAS 24 is to "ensure that an entity's financial statements contain the disclosures necessary to draw attention to the possibility that its financial position and profit or loss may have been affected by the existence of related parties and by transactions and outstanding balances with such parties".

Related parties are a normal feature of business. It is common for entities to carry on activities with or through subsidiaries and associates, or occasionally to engage in transactions with directors or their families. The point is that such transactions cannot be assumed to have been engaged in 'at arm's length' or in the best interests of the entity itself, which is why investors and potential investors need to be made aware of them. Transfer pricing can be used to transfer profit from one company to another and inter-company loans and transfers of non-current assets can also be used in the same way.

Despite IAS 24, companies which wish to disguise a related party relationship can probably still find complex ways to do it (the Enron scandal revealed the existence of numerous related party transactions) and financial statements do not show the unseen effects of such a relationship. For instance, a subsidiary may not have been allowed to tender for a contract in competition with another group company. Its shareholders will never know about such missed opportunities.

1.4 Seasonal trading

This is another issue that can distort reported results. Many companies whose trade is seasonal position their year end after their busy period, to minimise time spent on the inventory count. At this point in time, the statement of financial position will show a healthy level of cash and/or receivables and a low level of trade payables, assuming most of them have been paid. Thus the position is reported at the moment when the company is at its most solvent. A statement of financial position drawn up a few months earlier, or even perhaps a few months later, when trade is still slack but fixed costs still have to be paid, may give a very different picture.

1.5 Asset acquisitions

Major asset acquisitions just before the end of an accounting period can also distort results. The statement of financial position will show an increased level of assets and corresponding liabilities (probably a loan or lease payable), but the income which will be earned from utilisation of the asset will not yet have materialised. This will adversely affect the company's return on capital employed.

1.6 IAS 10: *Events after the reporting period*

The standard gives the following definition.

Key term

> **Events occurring after the reporting period** are those events, both favourable and unfavourable, that occur between the end of the reporting period and the date on which the financial statements are authorised for issue. Two types of events can be identified.
>
> - Those that provide evidence of conditions that existed at the end of the reporting period – *adjusting*
> - Those that are indicative of conditions that arose after the reporting period – *non-adjusting*
>
> *(IAS 10)*

Between the end of the reporting period and the date the financial statements are authorised (ie for issue outside the organisation), events may occur which show that assets and liabilities at the end of the reporting period should be adjusted, or that disclosure of such events should be given.

1.6.1 Events requiring adjustment

The standard requires adjustment of assets and liabilities in certain circumstances.

> An entity shall adjust the amounts recognised in its financial statements to reflect adjusting events after the reporting period. An entity shall not adjust the amounts recognised in its financial statements to reflect non-adjusting events after the reporting period. *(IAS 10)*

An **example** of additional evidence which becomes available after the reporting period is where a **customer goes bankrupt, thus confirming that the trade account receivable balance at the year end is uncollectable.**

In relation to **going concern**, the standard states that, where operating results and the financial position have deteriorated after the reporting period, it may be necessary to reconsider whether the going concern assumption is appropriate in the preparation of the financial statements.

Examples of **adjusting events** would be:

- evidence of a permanent diminution in property value prior to the year end
- sale of inventory after the reporting period for less than its carrying value at the year end
- insolvency of a customer with a balance owing at the year end
- amounts received or paid in respect of legal or insurance claims which were in negotiation at the year end
- determination after the year end of the sale or purchase price of assets sold or purchased before the year end

- evidence of a permanent diminution in the value of a long-term investment prior to the year end
- discovery of error or fraud which shows that the financial statements were incorrect

1.6.2 Events not requiring adjustment

The standard then looks at events which do **not** require adjustment.

The standard gives the following examples of events which do **not** require adjustments:

- acquisition of, or disposal of, a subsidiary after the year end
- announcement of a plan to discontinue an operation
- major purchases and disposals of assets
- destruction of a production plant by fire after the reporting period
- announcement or commencing implementation of a major restructuring
- share transactions after the reporting period
- litigation commenced after the reporting period

But note that, while they may be non-adjusting, some events after the reporting period will require disclosure.

> If non-adjusting events after the reporting period are material, non-disclosure could influence the economic decisions of users taken on the basis of the financial statements. Accordingly, an entity shall disclose the following for each material category of non-adjusting event after the reporting period:
>
> (a)   the nature of the event; and
> (b)   an estimate of its financial effect, or a statement that such an estimate cannot be made.
>
> *(IAS 10)*

The **example** given by the standard of such an event is where the **value of an investment falls between the end of the reporting period and the date the financial statements are authorised** for issue. The fall in value represents circumstances during the current period, not conditions existing at the end of the previous reporting period, so it is not appropriate to adjust the value of the investment in the financial statements. Disclosure is an aid to users, however, indicating 'unusual changes' in the state of assets and liabilities after the reporting period.

The rule for **disclosure** of events occurring after the reporting period which relate to conditions that arose after that date, is that disclosure should be made if non-disclosure would hinder the user's ability to make **proper evaluations** and decisions based on the financial statements. An example might be the acquisition of another business.

2 Accounting policies and the limitations of ratio analysis

FAST FORWARD

> We discussed the disclosure of accounting policies in our examination of IAS 1. The choice of accounting policy and the effect of its implementation are almost as important as its disclosure in that the results of a company can be altered significantly by the choice of accounting policy.

2.1 The effect of choice of accounting policies

Where accounting standards allow alternative treatment of items in the accounts, then the accounting policy note should declare which policy has been chosen. It should then be applied consistently.

You should be able to think of examples of how the choice of accounting policy can affect the financial statements eg whether to revalue property in IAS 16, or whether to capitalise the cost of interest in self-constructed assets in IAS 23.

2.2 Changes in accounting policy

The effect of a change of accounting policy is treated as a prior year adjustment according to IAS 8 (see Chapter 4). This just means that the comparative figures are adjusted for the change in accounting policy for comparative purposes and an adjustment is put through retained earnings.

Under **consistency of presentation** in IAS 1, any change in policy may only be made if it can be justified on the grounds that the new policy is preferable to the one it replaces because it will give a fairer presentation of the result and of the financial position of a reporting entity.

The problem with this situation is that the directors may be able to **manipulate the results** through change(s) of accounting policies. This would be done to avoid the effect of an old accounting policy or gain the effect of a new one. It is likely to be done in a sensitive period, perhaps when the company's profits are low or the company is about to announce a rights issue. The management would have to convince the auditors that the new policy was much better, but it is not difficult to produce reasons in such cases.

The effect of such a change is very **short-term**. Most analysts and sophisticated users will discount its effect immediately, except to the extent that it will affect any dividend (because of the effect on distributable profits). It may help to avoid breaches of banking covenants because of the effect on certain ratios.

Obviously, the accounting policy for any item in the accounts could only be changed once in quite a long period of time. Auditors would not allow another change, even back to the old policy, unless there was a wholly exceptional reason.

The managers of a company can choose accounting policies **initially** to suit the company or the type of results they want to get. Any changes in accounting policy must be justified, but some managers might try to change accounting policies just to manipulate the results.

2.3 Limitations of ratio analysis

The consideration of how accounting policies may be used to manipulate company results leads us to some of the other limitations of ratio analysis.

The most important ones are:

- In a company's first year of trading there will be no comparative figures. So there will be no indication of whether or not a ratio is improving.
- Comparison against industry averages may not be that revealing. A business may be subject to factors which hare not common in the industry.
- Ratios based on historic cost accounts are subject to the distortions described in 1.1 above. In particular, undervalued assets will distort ROCE and exaggerate gearing.
- Ratios are influenced by the choice of accounting policy. For instance, a company seeking to maintain or increase its ROCE may choose not to revalue its assets.
- Financial statements are subject to manipulation and so are the ratios based on them. Creative accounting is undertaken with key ratios in mind.
- Inflation over a period will distort results and ratios. Net profit, and therefore ROCE, can be inflated where FIFO is applied during an inflationary period.
- No two companies, even operating in the same industry, will have the same financial and business risk profile. For instance, one may have better access to cheap borrowing than the other and so may be able to sustain a higher level of gearing.

2.4 Other issues

Are there other issues which should be looked at when assessing an entity's performance? Factors to consider are:

- How technologically advanced is it? If it is not using the latest equipment and processes it risks being pushed out of the market at some point or having to undertake a high level of capital expenditure.
- What are its environmental policies? Is it in danger of having to pay for cleanup if the law is tightened? Does it appeal to those seeking 'ethical investment'?
- What is the reputation of its management? If it has attracted good people and kept them, that is a positive indicator.
- What is its mission statement? To what degree does it appear to be fulfilling it?
- What is its reputation as an employer? Do people want to work for this company? What are its labour relations like?
- What is the size of its market? Does it trade in just one or two countries or worldwide?
- How strong is its competition? Is it in danger of takeover?

You can probably think of other factors that you would consider important. In some cases you can also look at the quality of the product that a company produces.

Question	Company analysis

Analyse a company that you know something about against these criteria.

Exam focus point

In any interpretation of accounts question, bear the issues in this chapter in mind. The examiner expects you to be able to look critically at financial information.

Chapter Roundup

- Financial statements are affected by the obvious shortcoming of historic cost information and are also subject to manipulation.
- The choice of accounting policy and the effect of its implementation are almost as important as its disclosure, in that the results of a company can be altered significantly by the choice of accounting policy.

Quick Quiz

1   What is the effect of inventory carried at historical cost in a period of inflation?
2   What is 'window dressing'?
3   How can companies attempt to transfer profits from one group company to another?
4   Will two companies in the same industry have the same ROCE?

Answers to Quick Quiz

1   Overstatement of profits (see 1.1).
2   An accounting adjustment made just before the year end to improve the appearance of the financial statements (1.2).
3   Transfer pricing, intercompany loans, transfers of fixed assets (1.3).
4   Probably not, there may be many other differences between them.

Now try the questions below from the Exam Question Bank

Number	Level	Marks	Time
26	Examination	25	45 mins

Statements of cash flows

Topic list	Syllabus reference
1 IAS 7 Statement of cash flows	C1
2 Preparing a statement of cash flows	C1
3 Interpretation of statements of cash flows	C1

Introduction

You have already covered much of the material on statements of cash flows in your earlier studies. Much of this is repeated here for revision.

The importance of the distinction between cash and profit and the scant attention paid to this by the income statement has resulted in the development of statements of cash flows.

This chapter adopts a systematic approach to the preparation of statements of cash flows in examinations; you should learn this method and you will then be equipped for any problems in the exam.

The third section of the chapter looks at the information which is provided by statements of cash flows and how it should be analysed.

Study guide

		Intellectual level
C1	FINANCIAL STATEMENTS	
	Statements of cash flows	
(a)	prepare a statement of cash flows for a single entity (not a group) in accordance with relevant accounting standards using the direct and the indirect method.	2
(b)	compare the usefulness of cash flow information with that of an income statement or statement of comprehensive income.	2
(c)	interpret a statement of cash flows (together with other financial information) to assess the performance and financial position of an entity.	2

Exam guide

Statements of cash flows were tested regularly under the old syllabus, and as this syllabus has the same examiner, we may assume that he will also test them regularly.

1 IAS 7 Statement of cash flows

FAST FORWARD

A statement of cash flows is a useful addition to a company's financial statements as a measure of performance.

1.1 Introduction

It has been argued that 'profit' does not always give a useful or meaningful picture of a company's operations. Readers of a company's financial statements might even be **misled by a reported profit figure**.

(a) Shareholders might believe that if a company makes a profit after tax, of say, $100,000 then this is the amount which it could afford to **pay as a dividend**. Unless the company has **sufficient cash** available to stay in business and also to pay a dividend, the shareholders' expectations would be wrong.

(b) Employees might believe that if a company makes profits, it can afford to **pay higher wages** next year. This opinion may not be correct: the ability to pay wages depends on the **availability of cash**.

(c) Survival of a business entity depends not so much on profits as on its **ability to pay its debts when they fall due**. Such payments might include 'revenue' items such as material purchases, wages, interest and taxation etc, but also capital payments for new non-current assets and the repayment of loan capital when this falls due (for example on the redemption of debentures).

From these examples, it may be apparent that a company's performance and prospects depend not so much on the 'profits' earned in a period, but more realistically on liquidity or **cash flows**.

1.2 Funds flow and cash flow

Some countries, either currently or in the past, have required the disclosure of additional statements based on **funds flow** rather than cash flow. However, the definition of 'funds' can be very vague and such statements often simply require a rearrangement of figures already provided in the statement of financial position and income statement. By contrast, a statement of cash flows is unambiguous and provides information which is additional to that provided in the rest of the accounts. It also lends itself to organisation by activity and not by classification in the statement of financial position.

Statements of cash flows are frequently given as an **additional statement**, supplementing the statement of financial position, statement of comprehensive income and related notes. The group aspects of statements of cash flows (and certain complex matters) have been excluded as they are beyond the scope of your syllabus.

1.3 Objective of IAS 7

The aim of IAS 7 is to provide information to users of financial statements about the entity's **ability to generate cash and cash equivalents**, as well as indicating the cash needs of the entity. The statement of cash flows provides *historical* information about cash and cash equivalents, classifying cash flows between operating, investing and financing activities.

1.4 Scope

A statement of cash flows should be presented as an **integral part** of an entity's financial statements. All types of entity can provide useful information about cash flows as the need for cash is universal, whatever the nature of their revenue-producing activities. Therefore **all entities are required by the standard to produce a statement of cash flows**.

1.5 Benefits of cash flow information

The use of statements of cash flows is very much **in conjunction** with the rest of the financial statements. Users can gain further appreciation of the change in net assets, of the entity's financial position (liquidity and solvency) and the entity's ability to adapt to changing circumstances by affecting the amount and timing of cash flows. Statements of cash flows **enhance comparability** as they are not affected by differing accounting policies used for the same type of transactions or events.

Cash flow information of a historical nature can be used as an indicator of the amount, timing and certainty of future cash flows. Past forecast cash flow information can be **checked for accuracy** as actual figures emerge. The relationship between profit and cash flows can be analysed as can changes in prices over time.

1.6 Definitions

The standard gives the following definitions, the most important of which are **cash** and **cash equivalents**.

Key terms

- **Cash** comprises cash on hand and demand deposits.
- **Cash equivalents** are short-term, highly liquid investments that are readily convertible to known amounts of cash and which are subject to an insignificant risk of changes in value.
- **Cash flows** are inflows and outflows of cash and cash equivalents.
- **Operating activities** are the principal revenue-producing activities of the entity and other activities that are not investing or financing activities.
- **Investing activities** are the acquisition and disposal of non-current assets and other investments not included in cash equivalents.
- **Financing activities** are activities that result in changes in the size and composition of the equity capital and borrowings of the entity.

(IAS 7)

1.7 Cash and cash equivalents

The standard expands on the definition of cash equivalents: they are not held for investment or other long-term purposes, but rather to meet short-term cash commitments. To fulfil the above definition, an investment's **maturity date should normally be within three months from its acquisition date**. It would usually be the case then that equity investments (ie shares in other companies) are *not* cash equivalents. An exception would be where preferred shares were acquired with a very close maturity date.

Loans and other borrowings from banks are classified as investing activities. In some countries, however, **bank overdrafts** are repayable on demand and are treated as part of an entity's total cash management system. In these circumstances an overdrawn balance will be included in cash and cash equivalents. Such banking arrangements are characterised by a balance which fluctuates between overdrawn and credit.

Movements between different types of cash and cash equivalent are not included in cash flows. The investment of surplus cash in cash equivalents is part of cash management, not part of operating, investing or financing activities.

1.8 Presentation of a statement of cash flows

IAS 7 requires statements of cash flows to report cash flows during the period classified by **operating, investing and financing activities**.

1.9 Example: simple statement of cash flows

Flail Co commenced trading on 1 January 20X1 with a medium-term loan of $21,000 and a share issue which raised $35,000. The company purchased non-current assets for $21,000 cash, and during the year to 31 December 20X1 entered into the following transactions.

(a)   Purchases from suppliers were $19,500, of which $2,550 was unpaid at the year end.
(b)   Wages and salaries amounted to $10,500, of which $750 was unpaid at the year end.
(c)   Interest on the loan of $2,100 was fully paid in the year and a repayment of $5,250 was made.
(d)   Sales revenue was $29,400, including $900 receivables at the year end.
(e)   Interest on cash deposits at the bank amounted to $75.
(f)   A dividend of $4,000 was proposed as at 31 December 20X1.

You are required to prepare a historical statement of cash flows for the year ended 31 December 20X1.

Solution

FLAIL CO
STATEMENT OF CASH FLOWS
THE YEAR ENDED 31 DECEMBER 20X1

	$	$
Cash flows from operating activities		
Cash received from customers ($29,400 – $900)	28,500	
Cash paid to suppliers ($19,500 – $2,550)	(16,950)	
Cash paid to and on behalf of employees ($10,500 – $750)	(9,750)	
Interest paid	(2,100)	
Net cash used in operating activities		(300)
Cash flows from investing activities		
Purchase of non-current assets	(21,000)	
Interest received	75	
Net cash used in investing activities		
		(20,925)
Cash flows from financing activities		
Issue of shares	35,000	
Proceeds from medium-term loan	21,000	
Repayment of medium-term loan	(5,250)	
Net cash from financing activities		50,750
Net increase in cash and cash equivalents		29,525
Cash and cash equivalents at 1 January 20X1		–
Cash and cash equivalents at 31 December 20X1		29,525

Note that the dividend is only proposed and so there is no related cash flow in 20X1.

The managers of Flail Co have the following information in respect of projected cash flows for the year to 31 December 20X2.

(a) Non-current asset purchases for cash will be $3,000.

(b) Further expenses will be:

   (i)   purchases from suppliers – $18,750 ($4,125 owed at the year end);
   (ii)   wages and salaries – $11,250 ($600 owed at the year end);
   (iii) loan interest – $1,575.

(c) Sales revenue will be $36,000 ($450 receivables at the year end).

(d) Interest on bank deposits will be $150.

(e) A further capital repayment of $5,250 will be made on the loan.

(f) A dividend of $5,000 will be proposed and last year's final dividend paid.

(g) Income taxes of $2,300 will be paid in respect of 20X1.

Prepare the cash flow forecast for the year to 31 December 20X2.

Answer

FLAIL CO
STATEMENT OF FORECAST CASH FLOWS FOR
THE YEAR ENDING 31 DECEMBER 20X2

	$	$
Cash flows from operating activities		
Cash received from customers	36,450	
($36,000 + $900 – $450)		
Cash paid to suppliers ($18,750 + $2,550 – $4,125)	(17,175)	
Cash paid to and on behalf of employees		
($11,250 + $750 – $600)	(11,400)	
Interest paid	(1,575)	
Taxation	(2,300)	
Net cash paid from operating activities		4,000
Cash flow from investing activities		
Purchase of non-current assets	(3,000)	
Interest received	150	
Net cash used in investing activities		(2,850)
Cash flows from financing activities		
Repayment of medium-term loan	(5,250)	
Dividend payment	(4,000)	
Net cash used in financing activities		(9,250)
Forecast net decrease in cash and cash equivalents		(8,100)
Cash and cash equivalents as at 31 December 20X1		29,525
Forecast cash and cash equivalents as at 31 December 20X2		21,425

1.10 Activities

The manner of presentation of cash flows between operating, investing and financing activities **depends on the nature of the entity**. By classifying cash flows between different activities in this way users can see the impact on cash and cash equivalents of each one, and their relationships with each other. We can look at each in more detail.

1.10.1 Operating activities

This is perhaps the key part of the statement of cash flows because it shows whether, and to what extent, companies can **generate cash from their operations**. It is these operating cash flows which must, in the end pay for all cash outflows relating to other activities, ie paying loan interest, dividends and so on.

Most of the components of cash flows from operating activities will be those items which **determine the net profit or loss of the entity**, ie they relate to the main revenue-producing activities of the entity. The standard gives the following as examples of cash flows from operating activities.

(a) Cash receipts from the sale of goods and the rendering of services
(b) Cash receipts from royalties, fees, commissions and other revenue
(c) Cash payments to suppliers for goods and services
(d) Cash payments to and on behalf of employees

Certain items may be included in the net profit or loss for the period which do *not* relate to operational cash flows, for example the profit or loss on the sale of a piece of plant will be included in net profit or loss, but the cash flows will be classed as **investing**.

1.10.2 Investing activities

The cash flows classified under this heading show the extent of new investment in **assets which will generate future profit and cash flows**. The standard gives the following examples of cash flows arising from investing activities.

(a) Cash payments to acquire property, plant and equipment, intangibles and other non-current assets, including those relating to capitalised development costs and self-constructed property, plant and equipment
(b) Cash receipts from sales of property, plant and equipment, intangibles and other non-current assets
(c) Cash payments to acquire shares or debentures of other entities
(d) Cash receipts from sales of shares or debentures of other entities
(e) Cash advances and loans made to other parties
(f) Cash receipts from the repayment of advances and loans made to other parties

1.10.3 Financing activities

This section of the statement of cash flows shows the share of cash which the entity's capital providers have claimed during the period. This is an indicator of **likely future interest and dividend payments**. The standard gives the following examples of cash flows which might arise under this heading.

(a) Cash proceeds from issuing shares
(b) Cash payments to owners to acquire or redeem the entity's shares
(c) Cash proceeds from issuing debentures, loans, notes, bonds, mortgages and other short or long-term borrowings
(d) Principal repayments of amounts borrowed under finance leases

Item (d) needs more explanation. Where the reporting entity uses an asset held under a finance lease, the amounts to go in the statement of cash flows as financing activities are repayments of the **principal (capital)** rather than the **interest**. The interest paid will be shown under operating activities.

1.11 Example: finance lease rental

The notes to the financial statements of Hayley Co show the following in respect of obligations under finance leases.

Year ended 30 June	20X5	20X4
	$'000	$'000
Amounts payable within one year	12	8
Within two to five years	110	66
	122	74
Less finance charges allocated to future periods	(14)	(8)
	108	66

Interest paid on finance leases in the year to 30 June 20X5 amounted to $6m. Additions to tangible non-current assets acquired under finance leases were shown in the non-current asset note at $56,000.

Required

Calculate the capital repayment to be shown in the statement of cash flows of Hayley Co for the year to 30 June 20X5.

Solution

OBLIGATIONS UNDER FINANCE LEASES

	$'000		$'000
Capital repayment (bal fig)	14	Bal 1.7.X4	66
Bal 30.6.X5	108	Additions	56
	122		122

1.12 Reporting cash flows from operating activities

The standard offers a choice of method for this part of the statement of cash flows.

(a) **Direct method:** disclose major classes of gross cash receipts and gross cash payments

(b) **Indirect method**: net profit or loss is adjusted for the effects of transactions of a non-cash nature, any deferrals or accruals of past or future operating cash receipts or payments, and items of income or expense associated with investing or financing cash flows

The **direct method is the preferred method** because it discloses information, not available elsewhere in the financial statements, which could be of use in estimating future cash flows. The example below shows both methods.

1.12.1 Using the direct method

There are different ways in which the **information about gross cash receipts and payments** can be obtained. The most obvious way is simply to extract the information from the accounting records. This may be a laborious task, however, and the indirect method below may be easier. The example and question above used the direct method.

1.12.2 Using the indirect method

This method is undoubtedly **easier** from the point of view of the preparer of the statement of cash flows. The net profit or loss for the period is adjusted for the following.

(a) Changes during the period in inventories, operating receivables and payables
(b) Non-cash items, eg depreciation, provisions, profits/losses on the sales of assets
(c) Other items, the cash flows from which should be classified under investing or financing activities.

A **proforma** of such a calculation, taken from the IAS, is as follows and this method may be more common in the exam. (The proforma has been amended to reflect changes to IFRS.)

	$
Cash flows from operating activities	
Profit before taxation	X
Adjustments for:	
Depreciation	X
Foreign exchange loss	X
Investment income	(X)
Interest expense	X
	X
Increase in trade and other receivables	(X)
Decrease in inventories	X
Decrease in trade payables	(X)
Cash generated from operations	X
Interest paid	(X)
Income taxes paid	(X)
Net cash from operating activities	X

It is important to understand why **certain items are added and others subtracted**. Note the following points.

(a) Depreciation is not a cash expense, but is deducted in arriving at profit. It makes sense, therefore, to eliminate it by adding it back.

(b) By the same logic, a loss on a disposal of a non-current asset (arising through underprovision of depreciation) needs to be added back and a profit deducted.

(c) An increase in inventories means less cash – you have spent cash on buying inventory.

(d) An increase in receivables means the company's debtors have not paid as much, and therefore there is less cash.

(e) If we pay off payables, causing the figure to decrease, again we have less cash.

1.12.3 Indirect versus direct

The direct method is encouraged where the necessary information is not too costly to obtain, but IAS 7 does not require it. In practice the indirect method is more commonly used, since it is quicker and easier.

1.13 Interest and dividends

Cash flows from interest and dividends received and paid should each be **disclosed separately**. Each should be classified in a consistent manner from period to period as either operating, investing or financing activities.

Dividends paid by the entity can be classified in **one of two ways**.

(a) As a **financing cash flow**, showing the cost of obtaining financial resources.

(b) As a component of **cash flows from operating activities** so that users can assess the entity's ability to pay dividends out of operating cash flows.

1.14 Taxes on income

Cash flows arising from taxes on income should be **separately disclosed** and should be classified as cash flows from operating activities *unless* they can be specifically identified with financing and investing activities.

Taxation cash flows are often **difficult to match** to the originating underlying transaction, so most of the time all tax cash flows are classified as arising from operating activities.

1.15 Components of cash and cash equivalents

The components of cash and cash equivalents should be disclosed and a **reconciliation** should be presented, showing the amounts in the statement of cash flows reconciled with the equivalent items reported in the statement of financial position.

It is also necessary to disclose the **accounting policy** used in deciding the items included in cash and cash equivalents, in accordance with IAS 1 *Presentation of Financial Statements*, but also because of the wide range of cash management practices worldwide.

1.16 Other disclosures

All entities should disclose, together with a **commentary by management**, any other information likely to be of importance, for example:

(a)   Restrictions on the use of or access to any part of cash equivalents

(b)   The amount of undrawn borrowing facilities which are available

(c)   Cash flows which increased operating capacity compared to cash flows which merely maintained operating capacity

(d)   Cash flows arising from each reported industry and geographical segment

1.17 Example of a statement of cash flows

In the next section we will look at the procedures for preparing a statement of cash flows. First, look at this **example**, adapted from the example given in the standard (which is based on a group and therefore beyond the scope of your syllabus).

1.17.1 Direct method

STATEMENT OF CASH FLOWS (DIRECT METHOD)
YEAR ENDED 31 DECEMBER 20X7

	$m	$m
Cash flows from operating activities		
Cash receipts from customers	30,330	
Cash paid to suppliers and employees	(27,600)	
Cash generated from operations	2,730	
Interest paid	(270)	
Income taxes paid	(900)	
Net cash from operating activities		1,560
Cash flows from investing activities		
Purchase of property, plant and equipment	(900)	
Proceeds from sale of equipment	20	
Interest received	200	
Dividends received	200	
Net cash used in investing activities		(480)
Cash flows from financing activities		
Proceeds from issue of share capital	250	
Proceeds from long-term borrowings	250	
Dividends paid*	(1,290)	
Net cash used in financing activities		(790)
Net increase in cash and cash equivalents		290
Cash and cash equivalents at beginning of period (Note)		120
Cash and cash equivalents at end of period (Note)		410

* This could also be shown as an operating cash flow

1.17.2 Indirect method

STATEMENT OF CASH FLOWS (INDIRECT METHOD)
YEAR ENDED 31 DECEMBER 20X7

	$m	$m
Cash flows from operating activities		
Profit before taxation	3,570	
Adjustments for:		
Depreciation	450	
Investment income	(500)	
Interest expense	400	
	3,920	
Increase in trade and other receivables	(500)	
Decrease in inventories	1,050	
Decrease in trade payables	(1,740)	
Cash generated from operations	2,730	
Interest paid	(270)	
Income taxes paid	(900)	
Net cash from operating activities		1,560
Cash flows from investing activities		
Purchase of property, plant and equipment	(900)	
Proceeds from sale of equipment	20	
Interest received	200	
Dividends received	200	
Net cash used in investing activities		(480)
Cash flows from financing activities		
Proceeds from issue of share capital	250	
Proceeds from long-term borrowings	250	
Dividends paid*	(1,290)	
Net cash used in financing activities		(790)
Net increase in cash and cash equivalents		290
Cash and cash equivalents at beginning of period		120
Cash and cash equivalents at end of period		410

* This could also be shown as an operating cash flow

2 Preparing a statement of cash flows

2.1 Introduction

In essence, preparing a statement of cash flows is very straightforward. You should therefore simply learn the format and apply the steps noted in the example below. Note that the following items are treated in a way that might seem confusing, but the treatment is logical if you **think in terms of cash**.

(a)   **Increase in inventory** is treated as **negative** (in brackets). This is because it represents a cash **outflow**; cash is being spent on inventory.

(b)   An **increase in receivables** would be treated as **negative** for the same reasons; more receivables means less cash.

(c)   By contrast an **increase in payables is positive** because cash is being retained and not used to settle accounts payable. There is therefore more of it.

2.2 Example: preparation of a statement of cash flows

Kane Co's income statement for the year ended 31 December 20X2 and statements of financial position at 31 December 20X1 and 31 December 20X2 were as follows.

KANE CO
INCOME STATEMENT FOR THE YEAR ENDED 31 DECEMBER 20X2

	$'000	$'000
Sales		720
Raw materials consumed	70	
Staff costs	94	
Depreciation	118	
Loss on disposal of non-current asset	18	
		300
Operating profit		420
Interest payable		28
Profit before tax		392
Taxation		124
Profit for the year		268

KANE CO
STATEMENTS OF FINANCIAL POSITION AS AT 31 DECEMBER

	20X2	20X1
	$'000	$'000
Non-current assets		
Cost	1,596	1,560
Depreciation	(318)	(224)
	1,278	1,336
Current assets		
Inventory	24	20
Trade receivables	76	58
Bank	48	56
	148	134
Total assets	1,426	1,470
Equity and liabilities		
Equity		
Share capital	360	340
Share premium	36	24
Retained earnings	716	514
	1,112	878
Non-current liabilities		
Long-term loans	200	500
Current liabilities		
Trade payables	12	6
Taxation	102	86
	114	92
Total equity and liabilities	1,426	1,470

Dividends paid were $66,000

During the year, the company paid $90,000 for a new piece of machinery.

Required

Prepare a statement of cash flows for Kane Co for the year ended 31 December 20X2 in accordance with the requirements of IAS 7, using the indirect method.

Solution

Step 1   **Set out the proforma statement of cash flows** with the headings required by IAS 7. You should leave plenty of space. Ideally, use three or more sheets of paper, one for the main statement, one for the notes and one for your workings. It is obviously essential to know the formats very well.

Step 2   Begin with the **cash flows from operating activities** as far as possible. When preparing the statement from statements of financial position, you will usually have to calculate such items as depreciation, loss on sale of non-current assets, profit for the year and tax paid (see Step 4). Note that you may not be given the tax charge in the income statement. You will then have to assume that the tax paid in the year is last year's year-end provision and calculate the charge as the balancing figure.

Step 3   Calculate the cash flow figures for **purchase or sale of non-current assets, issue of shares and repayment of loans** if these are not already given to you (as they may be).

Step 4   If you are not given the profit figure, open up a **working for profit or loss**. Using the opening and closing balances of retained earnings, the taxation charge and dividends paid and proposed, you will be able to calculate profit for the year as the balancing figure to put in the cash flows from operating activities section.

Step 5   You will now be able to **complete the statement** by slotting in the figures given or calculated.

KANE CO
STATEMENT OF CASH FLOWS FOR THE YEAR ENDED 31 DECEMBER 20X2

	$'000	$'000
Cash flows from operating activities		
Profit before tax	392	
Depreciation charges	118	
Loss on sale of tangible non-current assets	18	
Interest expense	28	
Increase in inventories	(4)	
Increase in receivables	(18)	
Increase in payables	6	
Cash generated from operations	540	
Interest paid	(28)	
Dividends paid	(66)	
Tax paid (86 + 124 − 102)	(108)	
Net cash from operating activities		338
Cash flows from investing activities		
Payments to acquire tangible non-current assets	(90)	
Receipts from sales of tangible non-current assets (W)	12	
Net cash used in investing activities		(78)
Cash flows from financing activities		
Issues of share capital (360 + 36 − 340 − 24)	32	
Long-term loans repaid (500 − 200)	(300)	
Net cash used in financing activities		(268)
Decrease in cash and cash equivalents		(8)
Cash and cash equivalents at 1.1.X2		56
Cash and cash equivalents at 31.12.X2		48

Working: non-current asset disposals

COST

	$'000		$'000
At 1.1.X2	1,560	At 31.12.X2	1,596
Purchases	90	Disposals (balance)	54
	1,650		1,650

ACCUMULATED DEPRECIATION

	$'000		$'000
At 31.12.X2	318	At 1.1.X2	224
Depreciation on disposals		Charge for year	118
(balance)	24		
	342		342

NBV of disposals	30
Net loss reported	(18)
Proceeds of disposals	12

Question   **Prepare a statement of cash flows**

Set out below are the financial statements of Emma Co. You are the financial controller, faced with the task of implementing IAS 7 *Statement of cash flows*.

EMMA CO
INCOME STATEMENT FOR THE YEAR ENDED 31 DECEMBER 20X2

	$'000
Revenue	2,553
Cost of sales	(1,814)
Gross profit	739
Other income: interest received	25
Distribution costs	(125)
Administrative expenses	(264)
Finance costs	(75)
Profit before tax	300
Income tax expense	(140)
Profit for the year	160

EMMA CO
STATEMENTS OF FINANCIAL POSITION AS AT 31 DECEMBER

	20X2	20X1
Assets	$'000	$'000
Non-current assets		
Property, plant and equipment	380	305
Intangible assets	250	200
Investments	–	25
Current assets		
Inventories	150	102
Receivables	390	315
Short-term investments	50	–
Cash in hand	2	1
Total assets	1,222	948
Equity and liabilities		
Equity		
Share capital ($1 ordinary shares)	200	150
Share premium account	160	150
Revaluation reserve	100	91
Retained earnings	260	180
Non-current liabilities		
Long-term loan	170	50
Current liabilities		
Trade payables	127	119
Bank overdraft	85	98
Taxation	120	110
Total equity and liabilities	1,222	948

The following information is available.

(a) The proceeds of the sale of non-current asset investments amounted to $30,000.

(b) Fixtures and fittings, with an original cost of $85,000 and a net book value of $45,000, were sold for $32,000 during the year.

(c) The following information relates to property, plant and equipment.

	31.12.20X2	31.12.20X1
	$'000	$'000
Cost	720	595
Accumulated depreciation	340	290
Net book value	380	305

(d) 50,000 $1 ordinary shares were issued during the year at a premium of 20c per share.

(e) The short-term investments are highly liquid and are close to maturity.

(f) Dividends of $80,000 were paid during the year.

Required

Prepare a statement of cash flows for the year to 31 December 20X2 using the format laid out in IAS 7.

Answer

EMMA CO
STATEMENT OF CASH FLOWS FOR THE YEAR ENDED 31 DECEMBER 20X2

	$'000	$'000
Cash flows from operating activities		
Profit before tax	300	
Depreciation charge (W1)	90	
Loss on sale of property, plant and equipment (45 – 32)	13	
Profit on sale of non-current asset investments	(5)	
Interest expense (net)	50	
(Increase)/decrease in inventories	(48)	
(Increase)/decrease in receivables	(75)	
Increase/(decrease) in payables	8	
	333	
Interest paid	(75)	
Dividends paid	(80)	
Tax paid (110 + 140 – 120)	(130)	
Net cash from operating activities		48
Cash flows from investing activities		
Payments to acquire property, plant and equipment (W2)	(201)	
Payments to acquire intangible non-current assets	(50)	
Receipts from sales of property, plant and equipment	32	
Receipts from sale of non-current asset investments	30	
Interest received	25	
Net cash flows from investing activities		(164)
Cash flows from financing activities		
Issue of share capital	60	
Long-term loan	120	
Net cash flows from financing		180
Increase in cash and cash equivalents		64
Cash and cash equivalents at 1.1.X2		(97)
Cash and cash equivalents at 31.12.X2		(33)

Workings

1   *Depreciation charge*

	$'000	$'000
Depreciation at 31 December 20X2		340
Depreciation 31 December 20X1	290	
Depreciation on assets sold (85 − 45)	40	
		250
Charge for the year		90

2   *Purchase of property, plant and equipment*

PROPERTY, PLANT AND EQUIPMENT (COST)

	$'000		$'000
1.1.X2 Balance b/d	595	Disposals	85
Revaluation (100 − 91)	9		
Purchases (bal fig)	201	31.12.X2 Balance c/d	720
	805		805

Note. In the exam you may have a number of issues to deal with in the statement of cash flows. Examples are:

- Share capital issues. The proceeds will be split between share capital and share premium.
- Bonus issues. These do *not* involve cash.
- Revaluation of non-current assets. This must be taken into account in calculating acquisitions and disposals.
- Movement on deferred tax. This must be taken into account in calculating tax paid.
- Finance leases. Assets acquired under finance leases must be adjusted for in non-current asset calculations and the amount paid under the finance lease must appear as a cash flow.

Make sure you attempt Question 27 in the question bank which includes a finance lease.

3 Interpretation of statements of cash flows

IAS 7 *Statement of cash flows* was introduced on the basis that it would provide better, more comprehensive and more useful information than what was already shown in the financial statements.

3.1 Introduction

So what kind of information does the statement of cash flows, along with its notes, provide?

Some of the main areas where IAS 7 should provide information not found elsewhere in the financial statements are as follows.

(a)   The **relationships between profit and cash** can be seen clearly and analysed accordingly.
(b)   **Cash equivalents** are highlighted, giving a better picture of the liquidity of the company.
(c)   **Financing inflows and outflows must be shown, rather than simply passed through reserves**.

One of the most important things to realise at this point is that it is wrong to try to assess the health or predict the death of a reporting entity solely on the basis of a single indicator. When analysing cash flow data, the **comparison should not just be between cash flows and profit, but also between cash flows over a period of time** (say three to five years).

Cash is not synonymous with profit on an annual basis, but you should also remember that the 'behaviour' of profit and cash flows will be very different. **Profit is smoothed out** through accruals, prepayments, provisions and other accounting conventions. This does not apply to cash, so the **cash flow figures** are likely to be **'lumpy'** in comparison. You must distinguish between this 'lumpiness' and the trends which will appear over time.

The **relationship between profit and cash flows will vary constantly**. Note that healthy companies do not always have reported profits exceeding operating cash flows. Similarly, unhealthy companies can have operating cash flows well in excess of reported profit. The value of comparing them is in determining the extent to which earned profits are being converted into the necessary cash flows.

Profit is not as important as the extent to which a company can **convert its profits into cash on a continuing basis.** This process should be judged over a period longer than one year. The cash flows should be compared with profits over the same periods to decide how successfully the reporting entity has converted earnings into cash.

Cash flow figures should also be considered in terms of their specific relationships with each other over time. A form of **'cash flow gearing'** can be determined by comparing operating cash flows and financing flows, particularly borrowing, to establish the extent of dependence of the reporting entity on external funding.

Other relationships can be examined.

(a)   Operating cash flows and investment flows can be related to match cash recovery from investment to investment.

(b)   Investment can be compared to distribution to indicate the proportion of total cash outflow designated specifically to investor return and reinvestment.

(c)   A comparison of tax outflow to operating cash flow minus investment flow will establish a 'cash basis tax rate'.

The 'ratios' mentioned above can be monitored **inter– and intra-firm** and the analyses can be undertaken in monetary, general price-level adjusted, or percentage terms.

3.2 The advantages of cash flow accounting

The advantages of cash flow accounting are as follows.

(a)   Survival in business depends on the **ability to generate** cash. Cash flow accounting directs attention towards this critical issue.

(b)   Cash flow is **more comprehensive** than 'profit' which is dependent on accounting conventions and concepts.

(c)   **Creditors** (long and short-term) are more interested in an entity's ability to repay them than in its profitability. Whereas 'profits' might indicate that cash is likely to be available, cash flow accounting is more direct with its message.

(d)   Cash flow reporting provides a better means of **comparing the results** of different companies than traditional profit reporting.

(e)   Cash flow reporting **satisfies the needs of all users** better.

    (i)   For **management**, it provides the sort of information on which decisions should be taken (in management accounting, 'relevant costs' to a decision are future cash flows); traditional profit accounting does not help with decision-making.

    (ii)   For **shareholders and auditors**, cash flow accounting can provide a satisfactory basis for stewardship accounting.

    (iii)   As described previously, the information needs of **creditors and employees** will be better served by cash flow accounting.

(f)   Cash flow forecasts are **easier to prepare**, as well as more useful, than profit forecasts.

(g)   They can in some respects be **audited more easily** than accounts based on the accruals concept.

(h)   The accruals concept is confusing, and cash flows are **more easily understood**.

(i)   Cash flow accounting should be both retrospective, and also include a forecast for the future. This is of **great information value** to all users of accounting information.

(j)   **Forecasts** can subsequently be **monitored** by the publication of variance statements which compare actual cash flows against the forecast.

Question Disadvantages

Can you think of some possible disadvantages of cash flow accounting?

Answer

The main disadvantages of cash accounting are essentially the advantages of accruals accounting (proper matching of related items). There is also the practical problem that few businesses keep historical cash flow information in the form needed to prepare a historical statement of cash flows and so extra record keeping is likely to be necessary.

Exam focus point

A statement of cash flows is very likely to come up as Question 3 in your exam. In this chapter we give you the basics, but you should also do as many as possible of the statement of cash flows questions in the Practice and Revision Kit. These will give you practice at the various items that you may have to deal with in a cash flow question.

3.3 Criticisms of IAS 7

The inclusion of **cash equivalents** has been criticised because it does not reflect the way in which businesses are managed: in particular, the requirement that to be a cash equivalent an investment has to be within three months of maturity is considered **unrealistic**.

The management of assets similar to cash (ie 'cash equivalents') is not distinguished from other investment decisions.

Chapter roundup

- **Statements of cash flows** are a useful addition to the financial statements of companies because it is recognised that accounting profit is not the only indicator of a company's performance.

- Statements of cash flows concentrate on the sources and uses of cash and are a useful indicator of a company's **liquidity and solvency**.

- You need to be aware of the **format** of the statement as laid out in **IAS 7**; setting out the format is an essential first stage in preparing the statement, so this format must be learnt.

- Remember the **step-by-step preparation procedure** and use it for all the questions you practise.

- Note that you may be expected to **analyse** or **interpret** a statement of cash flows.

1   What is the aim of a statement of cash flows?

2   The standard headings in IAS 7 *Statement of cash flows* are:

- O................. a...............
- I.................. a...................
- F..................... a.....................
- Net................... in C..................... and ....

3   Cash equivalents are current asset investments which will mature or can be redeemed within three months of the year end.

True   ☐

False   ☐

4   Why are you more likely to encounter the indirect method as opposed to the direct method?

5   List five advantages of cash flow accounting.

Answers to quick quiz

1   To indicate an entity's ability to generate cash and cash equivalents.

2
- Operating activities
- Investing activities
- Financing activities
- Net increase (decrease) in cash and cash equivalents

3   False. See the definition in paragraph 1.6 if you are not sure about this.

4   The indirect method utilises figures which appear in the financial statements. The figures required for the direct method may not be readily available.

5   See paragraph 3.2

Now try the question below from the Exam Question Bank

Number	Level	Marks	Time
27	–	20	36 mins
28	Examination	25	45 mins

Alternative models and practices

Topic list	Syllabus reference
1 Historical cost versus current value	A5
2 Concepts of capital and capital maintenance	A5
3 Current purchasing power (CPP)	A5
4 Current cost accounting (CCA)	A5

Introduction

In this chapter we look at the alternatives to historical cost accounting.

Study guide

		Intellectual level
5	**Alternative models and practices**	
	(a) describe the advantages and disadvantages of the use of historical cost accounting.	2
	(b) discuss whether the use of current value accounting overcomes the problems of historical cost accounting.	2
	(c) describe the concept of financial and physical capital maintenance and how this affects the determination of profits.	1

Exam guide

This is a topical issue which could come up as part of a discussion question.

1 Historical cost versus current value

FAST FORWARD A number of alternatives to historical cost accounting are presently under discussion, some progress have been made and more can be expected in the future.

1.1 Advantages of historical cost accounting

As we are still using historical cost accounting, it may be supposed to have a number of advantages. The most important ones are:

- Amounts used are objective and free from bias.
- Amounts are reliable, they can always be verified, they exist on invoices and documents.
- Amounts in the statement of financial position can be matched perfectly with amounts in the statement of cash flows.
- Opportunities for creative accounting are less than under systems which allow management to apply their judgement to the valuation of assets.
- It has been used for centuries and is easily understood.

1.2 Disadvantages of historical cost accounting

Historical cost accounting has a number of distinct advantages. They arise as particular problems in periods of inflation. The mains ones are:

- It can lead to understatement of assets in the statement of financial position. A building purchased 50 years ago will appear at the price that was paid for it 50 years ago.
- Because assets are understated, depreciation will also be understated. While the purpose of depreciation is not to set aside funds for replacement of assets, if an asset has to be replaced at twice the price that was paid for its predecessor, the company may decide that it may have been prudent to make some provision for this in earlier years.
- When inventory prices are rising, and when the company is operating a FIFO system, the cheapest inventories are being charged to cost of sales and the most expensive are being designated as closing inventory in the statement of financial position. This leads to understatement of cost of sales.
- An organisation selling in an inflationary market will see its revenue and profits rise, but this is 'paper profit', distorted by the understated depreciation and cost of sales.

From these disadvantages various issues arise:

- Understatement of assets will depress a company's share price and make it vulnerable to takeover. In practice, listed companies avoid this by revaluing land and buildings in line with market values.

- Understated depreciation and understated cost of sales lead to overstatement of profits, compounded by price inflation.
- Overstated profits can lead to too much being distributed to shareholders, leaving insufficient amounts for investment.
- Overstated profits will lead shareholders to expect higher dividends and employees to demand higher wages.
- Overstated profits lead to overstated tax bills.

During periods where price inflation is low, profit overstatement will be marginal. The disadvantages of historical cost accounting become most apparent in periods of inflation. It was during the inflationary period of the 70s that alternatives were sought and that an attempt was made to introduce Current Cost Accounting (CCA). As inflation came back under control, the debate died down, but it is becoming increasingly recognised that historical cost accounting has shortcomings which need to be addressed.

1.3 Current value accounting

The move towards current value accounting has already taken a number of steps. Entities are now permitted to revalue non-current assets such as land and buildings in line with market value and financial assets and liabilities such as securities and investments can be carried at **fair value**, defined in IAS 39 as: 'the amount for which an asset could be exchanged, or a liability settled, between knowledgeable, willing parties in an arm's length transaction'.

These developments, and the use of fair values in acquisition accounting (to measure the assets of the subsidiary and thus arrive at a realistic goodwill valuation) are relatively uncontroversial. However, there are those who would like fair value to be used more widely as a system of current value. The European Central Bank recently produced a paper on the possible use of Full Fair Value Accounting (FFVA) in the banking industry.

In the US a similar move is being advocated towards Current Value Accounting (CVA). Under CVA the original cost of an asset would be replaced with its discounted present value ie. the present value of its future cash flows. This is obviously suitable for monetary items such as receivables and payables. The expected inflows and outflows would be discounted to present value using an interest rate which reflects the current time value of money. For assets such as vehicles, which do not yield a pre-determined future cash flow, current cost would be a more applicable measure – based either on the current cost of the original asset or on its replacement by a more up-to-date version. For inventories, current replacement cost or NRV would be indicated. Under this measurement basis, the LIFO/FIFO distinction would no longer apply.

1.4 Historical cost accounting; does it have a future?

Investment analysts have argued that historical cost information is out of date and not relevant and that fair value information, where based on active market prices, is the best available measure of future cash flows which an asset can be expected to generate.

This is heard increasingly in the US, where investors are the most highly-regarded user group for financial information, and the issue is likely to arise in the context of the IASB/FASB discussion on a joint conceptual framework.

We will now go on to look at two alternative systems which have sought in the past to address the shortcomings of historical cost accounting - **current purchasing power (CPP)** and **Current cost accounting (CCA)**. We begin by looking at the fundamental difference between these two systems - a different concept of capital maintenance and therefore of profit.

2 Concepts of capital and capital maintenance

 The concept of capital selected should be appropriate to the needs of the users of an entity's financial statements.

Most entities use a **financial concept of capital** when preparing their financial statements.

2.1 Concepts of capital maintenance and the determination of profit

First of all, we need to define the different concepts of capital.

Key term

> **Capital**. Under a **financial concept of capital**, such as invested money or invested purchasing power, capital is the net assets or equity of the entity. The financial concept of capital is adopted by most entities.
>
> Under a **physical concept of capital**, such as operating capability, capital is the productive capacity of the entity based on, for example, units of output per day. *(Framework)*

The definition of profit is also important.

Key term

> **Profit**. The residual amount that remains after expenses (including capital maintenance adjustments, where appropriate) have been deducted from income. Any amount over and above that required to maintain the capital at the beginning of the period is profit.
>
> *(Framework)*

The main difference between the two concepts of capital maintenance is the treatment of the **effects of changes in the prices of assets and liabilities** of the entity. In general terms, an entity has maintained its capital if it has as much capital at the end of the period as it had at the beginning of the period. Any amount over and above that required to maintain the capital at the beginning of the period is profit.

(a) **Financial capital maintenance**: profit is the increase in nominal money capital over the period. This is the concept used in CPP, and used under historical cost accounting.

(b) **Physical capital maintenance**: profit is the increase in the physical productive capacity over the period. This is the concept used in CCA.

2.2 Capital maintenance in times of inflation

Profit can be measured as the **difference between how wealthy a company is at the beginning and at the end of an accounting period.**

(a) This wealth can be expressed in terms of the capital of a company as shown in its opening and closing statements of financial position.

(b) A business which maintains its capital unchanged during an accounting period can be said to have broken even.

(c) Once **capital has been maintained**, **anything** achieved **in excess represents profit.**

For this analysis to be of any use, we must be able to draw up a company's statement of financial position at the beginning and at the end of a period, so as to place a value on the opening and closing capital. There are particular difficulties in doing this during a **period of rising prices**.

In conventional historical cost accounts, assets are stated in the statement of financial position at the amount it cost to acquire them (less any amounts written off in respect of depreciation or impairment in value). Capital is simply the **difference between assets and liabilities**.

Exam focus point

> If prices are rising, it is possible for a company to show a profit in its historical cost accounts despite having identical physical assets and owing identical liabilities at the beginning and end of its accounting period.

For example, consider the following opening and closing statements of financial position of a company.

	Opening $	Closing $
Inventory (100 items at cost)	500	600
Other net assets	1,000	1,000
Capital	1,500	1,600

Assuming that no new capital has been introduced during the year, and no capital has been distributed as dividends, the profit shown in historical cost accounts would be $100, being the excess of closing capital over opening capital. And yet in physical terms the company is no better off: it still has 100 units of inventory (which cost $5 each at the beginning of the period, but $6 each at the end) and its other net assets are identical. The 'profit' earned has merely enabled the company to keep pace with inflation.

An alternative to the concept of capital maintenance based on historical costs is to express capital in **physical** terms. On this basis, no profit would be recognised in the example above because the physical substance of the company is unchanged over the accounting period. Capital is maintained if at the end of the period the company is in a position to achieve the same physical output as it was at the beginning of the period. You should bear in mind that financial definitions of capital maintenance are not the only ones possible; in theory at least, there is no reason why profit should not be measured as the increase in a company's *physical* capital over an accounting period.

3 Current purchasing power (CPP)

3.1 The unit of measurement

Another way to tackle the problems of capital maintenance in times of rising prices is to look at the **unit of measurement** in which accounting values are expressed.

It is an axiom of conventional accounting, as it has developed over the years, that value should be measured in terms of money. It is also **implicitly assumed** that **money values are stable**, so that $1 at the start of the financial year has the same value as $1 at the end of that year. But when **prices are rising**, this assumption is invalid: **$1 at the end of the year has less value (less purchasing power) than it had one year previously**.

This leads to problems when aggregating amounts which have arisen at different times. For example, a company's non-current assets may include items bought at different times over a period of many years. They will each have been recorded in $s, but the value of $1 will have varied over the period. In effect the **non-current asset figure in a historical cost statement of financial position is an aggregate of a number of items expressed in different units**. It could be argued that such a figure is **meaningless**.

Faced with this argument, one possibility would be to re-state all accounts items in terms of a stable monetary unit. There would be difficulties in practice, but in theory there is no reason why a stable unit ($ CPP = $s of current purchasing power) should not be devised. In this section we will look at a system of accounting (current purchasing power accounting, or CPP) based on precisely this idea.

3.2 Specific and general price changes

We can identify two different types of price inflation.

When prices are rising, it is likely that the **current value of assets will also rise**, but not necessarily by the general rate of inflation. For example, if the replacement cost of a machine on 1 January 20X2 was $5,000, and the general rate of inflation in 20X2 was 8%, we would not necessarily expect the replacement cost of the machine at 31 December 20X2 to be $5,000 plus 8% = $5,400. The rate of price increase on the machinery might have been less than 8% or more than 8%. (Conceivably, in spite of general inflation, the replacement cost of the machinery might have gone down.)

(a)   There is **specific price inflation**, which measures price changes over time for a specific asset or group of assets.
(b)   There is **general price inflation**, which is the average rate of inflation, which reduces the general purchasing power of money.

To counter the problems of specific price inflation some system of current value accounting may be used (such as current cost accounting). The capital maintenance concepts underlying current value systems do not attempt to allow for the maintenance of real value in money terms.

Current purchasing power (CPP) accounting is based on a different concept of capital maintenance.

> **CPP** measures profits as the increase in the current purchasing power of equity. Profits are therefore stated after allowing for the declining purchasing power of money due to price inflation.

When applied to historical cost accounting, CPP is a system of accounting which makes adjustments to income and capital values to allow for the general rate of price inflation.

3.3 Monetary and non-monetary items

It is obvious that during a period of inflation borrowers benefit at the expense of lenders. A sum borrowed at the beginning of the year will cost less to repay at the end of the year (although lenders will seek to allow for this in higher interest charges). Similarly, customers with balances owing benefit at the expense of suppliers. CPP accounting seeks to remove this element of 'holding gain'.

Monetary items (cash, receivables, payables) cannot be restated as their amount is fixed. Non-monetary items (not-current assets and inventories) are restated in line with the general price index (at $c) and the balancing figure is equity.

Question

CPP profits

Rice and Price set up in business on 1 January 20X5 with no non-current assets, and cash of $5,000. On 1 January they acquired inventories for the full $5,000, which they sold on 30 June 20X5 for $6,000. On 30 November they obtained a further $2,100 of inventory on credit. The index of the general price level gives the following index figures.

Date	Index
1 January 20X5	300
30 June 20X5	330
30 November 20X5	350
31 December 20X5	360

Calculate the CPP profits (or losses) of Rice and Price for the year to 31 December 20X5.

Answer

The approach is to prepare a CPP income statement.

	$c	$c
Sales (6,000 × 360/330)		6,545
Less cost of goods sold (5,000 × 360/300)		6,000
		545
Loss on holding cash for 6 months*	(545)	
Gain by owing payables for 1 month**	60	
		485
CPP profit		60

* ($6,000 × 360/330) – $6,000 = $c 545
**($2,100 × 360/350) – $2,100 = $c 60
Note that under historic cost accounting the gross profit would be $1,000 ($6,000 – $5,000).

3.4 The advantages and disadvantages of CPP accounting

3.4.1 Advantages

(a)   The restatement of asset values in terms of a **stable money value** provides **a more meaningful basis of comparison** with other companies. Similarly, provided that previous years' profits are re-valued into CPP terms, it is also possible to compare the current year's results with past performance.

(b) **Profit** is measured in **'real' terms** and excludes 'inflationary value increments'. This enables better forecasts of future prospects to be made.

(c) CPP **avoids the subjective valuations** of current value accounting, because a single price index is applied to all non-monetary assets.

(d) CPP **provides a stable monetary** unit with which to value profit and capital; ie $c.

(e) Since it is based on historical cost accounting, **raw data is easily verified**, and measurements of value can be readily audited.

3.4.2 Disadvantages

(a) It is not **clear what $c means**. 'Generalised purchasing power' as measured by a retail price index, or indeed any other general price index, has no obvious practical significance.

'Generalised purchasing power has no relevance to any person or entity because no such thing exists in reality, except as a statistician's computation.'   (T A Lee)

(b) The use of indices inevitably involves **approximations** in the measurements of value.

(c) The value **of assets in a CPP statement of financial position has less meaning than a current value statement of financial position**. It cannot be supposed that the CPP value of net assets reflects:

   (i) The general goods and services that could be bought if the assets were released
   (ii) The consumption of general goods and services that would have to be forgone to replace those assets

In this respect, a CPP statement of financial position has similar drawbacks to an historical cost statement of financial position.

4 Current cost accounting (CCA)

4.1 Value to the business (deprival value)

Current cost accounting (CCA) reflects an approach to capital maintenance based on maintaining the **operating capability** of a business. The conceptual basis of CCA is that the value of assets consumed or sold, and the value of assets in the statement of financial position, should be stated at their **value to the business** (also known as 'deprival value').

Key term

> The **deprival value** of an asset is the loss which a business entity would suffer if it were deprived of the use of the asset.

(a) A basic assumption in CCA is that 'capital maintenance' should mean maintenance of the 'business substance' or 'operating capability' of the business entity. As we have seen already, it is generally accepted that profit is earned only after a sufficient amount has been charged against sales to ensure that the capital of the business is maintained. In CCA, a **physical** rather than financial definition of capital is used: capital maintenance is measured by the ability of the business entity to keep up the same level of operating capability.

(b) 'Value to the business' is the required method of valuation in current cost accounting, because it reflects the extra funds which would be required to maintain the operating capability of the business entity if it suddenly lost the use of an asset.

Value to the business, or deprival value, can be any of the following values.

(a) **Replacement cost**: in the case of non-current assets, it is assumed that the replacement cost of an asset would be its net replacement cost (NRC), its gross replacement cost minus an appropriate provision for depreciation to reflect the amount of its life already 'used up'.

(b)　**Net realisable value** (NRV): what the asset could be sold for, net of any disposal costs.

(c)　**Economic value** (EV), or value in use: what the existing asset will be worth to the company over the rest of its useful life.

The choice of deprival value from one of the three values listed will depend on circumstances. In simple terms you should remember that in **CCA deprival value is nearly always replacement cost**.

If the asset is worth replacing, its deprival value will always be net replacement cost. If the asset is not worth replacing, it might have been disposed of straight away, or else it might have been kept in operation until the end of its useful life.

You may therefore come across a statement that deprival value is the **lower of**:

* **Net replacement cost (NRC)**
* The **higher of net realisable value and economic value**

We have already seen that if an asset is not worth replacing, the deprival value will be NRV or EV. However, there are many assets which will not be replaced either:

(a)　Because the asset is **technologically obsolete**, and has been (or will be) superseded by more modern equipment

(b)　Because the business is **changing the nature of its operations** and will not want to continue in the same line of business once the asset has been used up

Such assets, even though there are reasons not to replace them, would still be valued (usually) at net replacement cost, because this 'deprival value' still provides an estimate of the **operating capability** of the company.

4.2 CCA profits and deprival value

The deprival value of assets is reflected in the CCA income statement by the following means.

(a)　**Depreciation** is charged on non-current assets on the basis of **gross replacement cost** of the asset (where NRC is the deprival value).

(b)　Where **NRV or EV** is the deprival value, the charge against CCA profits will be the **loss in value of the asset** during the accounting period; ie from its previous carrying value to its current NRV or EV.

(c)　**Goods sold** are charged at their **replacement cost**. Thus if an item of inventory cost $15 to produce, and sells for $20, by which time its replacement cost has risen to $17, the CCA profit would be $3.

	$
Sales	20
Less replacement cost of goods sold	17
Current cost profit	3

4.3 Example: CCA v accounting for inflation

Suppose that Arthur Smith Co buys an asset on 1 January for $10,000. The estimated life of the asset is 5 years, and straight line depreciation is charged. At 31 December the gross replacement cost of the asset is $10,500 (5% higher than on 1 January) but general inflation during the year, as measured by the retail price index, has risen 20%.

(a)　To maintain the value of the business against inflation, the asset should be revalued as follows.

	$
Gross ($10,000 × 120%)	12,000
Depreciation charge for the year (@ 20%)	2,400
Net value in the statement of financial position	9,600

(b)　In CCA, the business maintains its operating capability if we revalue the asset as follows.

	$
Gross replacement cost	10,500
Depreciation charge for the year (note)	2,100
NRC; value in the statement of financial position	8,400

Note	$
Historical cost depreciation	2,000
CCA depreciation adjustment (5%)	100
Total CCA depreciation cost	2,100

CCA preserves the operating capability of the company but does not necessarily preserve it against the declining value in the purchasing power of money (against inflation). As mentioned previously, CCA is a system which takes account of specific price inflation (changes in the prices of specific assets or groups of assets) but **not of general price inflation.**

A strict view of current cost accounting might suggest that a set of CCA accounts should be prepared from the outset on the basis of deprival values. In practice, current cost accounts are usually prepared by **starting from historical cost accounts and making appropriate adjustments.**

4.4 CCA accounts

CAC accounts will include the following adjustments:

(1)   Depreciation adjustment – to amend depreciation in line with the gross replacement cost of the asset.

(2)   Cost of sales adjustment – to take account of increases in inventory prices and remove any element of profit based on this.

(3)   Working capital adjustment – to remove any element of profit or loss based on holding payables or receivables in a period of inflation.

You do not need to know how to do these adjustment, but you can see that they attempt to deal with the areas where inflation can lead to 'holding gains'.

4.5 The advantages and disadvantages of current cost accounting

4.5.1 Advantages

(a)   By excluding holding gains from profit, CCA can be used to indicate whether the dividends paid to shareholders will **reduce the operating capability** of the business.

(b)   Assets are valued after management has considered the **opportunity cost** of holding them, and the expected benefits from their future use. CCA is therefore a useful guide for management in deciding whether to hold or sell assets.

(c)   It is **relevant** to the needs of information users in:

(i)   Assessing the stability of the business entity

(ii)   Assessing the vulnerability of the business (eg to a takeover), or the liquidity of the business

(iii)   Evaluating the performance of management in maintaining and increasing the business substance

(iv)   Judging future prospects

(d)   It can be **implemented fairly easily** in practice, by making simple adjustments to the historical cost accounting profits. A current cost statement of financial position can also be prepared with reasonable simplicity.

4.5.2 Disadvantages

(a)   It is impossible to make valuations of EV or NRV without **subjective judgements**. The measurements used are therefore not objective.

(b)   There are several problems to be overcome in deciding how to provide an **estimate of replacement** costs for non-current assets.

(c)   The mixed value approach to valuation means that some assets will be valued at replacement cost, but others will be valued at net realisable value or economic value. It is arguable that the **total**

assets will, therefore, have an **aggregate value** which is **not particularly meaningful** because of this mixture of different concepts.

(d) It can be argued that **'deprival value'** is an **unrealistic concept**, because the business entity has not been deprived of the use of the asset. This argument is one which would seem to reject the fundamental approach to 'capital maintenance' on which CCA is based.

Chapter Roundup

- **Profit** is an important measure in accounting statements.
  - It measures the efficiency of the company's **management** and helps in decision making.
  - It helps **creditors and investors** to decide whether they can safely lend money.
  - The **government** may use profit as a means of imposing direct taxation.

- **Profit** therefore has a variety of uses and users, but its **measurement depends** on the **methods used to value capital** (assets and liabilities) and on the method, if any, of accounting for price level changes.

- Alternative methods of accounting based on **current value concepts** use methods such as **deprival value** to value assets.

- **CPP accounting** is a method of accounting for general (not specific) inflation. It does so by expressing asset values in a stable monetary unit, the $c or $ of current purchasing power.

- In the **CPP statement of financial position**, **monetary items** are stated at their **face value**. **Non-monetary items** are stated at their **current purchasing power** as at the end of the reporting period.

- **CCA** is an alternative to the historical cost convention which attempts to overcome the problems of accounting for **specific price inflation**. Unlike CPP accounting, it does not attempt to cope with general inflation.

- CCA is based on a **physical concept of capital maintenance**. Profit is recognised after the operating capability of the business has been maintained.

- To recognise **holding gains** as part of current cost profit would conflict with the principle of maintaining operating capability.

- The current cost income statement is constructed by taking **historical cost** profit before interest and taxation as a starting point.
  - Current cost **operating adjustments** in respect of **cost of sales**, **monetary working capital** and **depreciation** are made so as to arrive at **current cost operating profit**.

Quick Quiz

1 Can methods of current value accounting be described as systems for accounting for inflation?
2 Distinguish between specific price inflation and general price inflation.
3 What is an asset's deprival value if it is not worth replacing?

Answers to Quick Quiz

1 No
2 • Specific price inflation measures price changes over time for a specific asset or group of assets
  • General price inflation measures the continual reduction in the general purchasing power of money
3 The higher of net realisable value and economic value

Now try the questions below from the Exam Question Bank

Number	Level	Marks	Time
29	Examination	15	27 mins

Specialised, not-for-profit and public sector entities

Topic list	Syllabus reference
1 Primary aims	
2 Regulatory framework	
3 Performance measurement	

Introduction

In this chapter we look at the application of financial reporting requirements to not-for-profit and public sector entities.

Study guide

			Intellectual level
3	**Specialised, not-for-profit and public sector entities**		
	(a)	distinguish between the primary aims of not-for-profit and public sector entities and those of profit oriented entities.	1
	(b)	discuss the extent to which International Financial Reporting Standards (IFRSs) are relevant to specialised, not-for-profit and public sector entities.	1
4	**Specialised, not-for-profit and public sector entities**		
	(a)	discuss the different approaches that may be required when assessing the performance of specialised, not-for-profit and public sector organisations.	1

Exam guide

In the pilot paper, there was a 5-mark part of a question on this topic.

1 Primary aims

FAST FORWARD

The accounting requirements for not-for-profit and public sector entities are moving closer to those required for profit-making entities. However, they do have different goals and purposes.

What organisations do we have in mind when we refer to **Not-for-profit and public sector entities**? These are the most obvious examples:

(a) Central government departments and agencies
(b) Local or federal government departments
(c) Publicly-funded bodies providing healthcare (in the UK this would be the NHS) and social housing
(d) Further and higher education institutions
(e) Charitable bodies

The first four are **public sector entities**. Charities are **private** not-for-profit entities.

Not-for-profit entities have different goals and purposes to profit-making entities and are responsible to different stakeholders. However, they are dealing in very large sums of money and it is important that they are properly managed and that their accounts present fairly the results of their operations.

Until recently, **public sector** accounts were prepared on a **cash basis**. A transition is still in progress which will get them operating on an **accruals basis**, in line with normal practice in the private sector.

1.1 Conceptual framework for not-for profit entities

The IASB and the FASB are currently in a project to produce a new, improved conceptual framework for financial reporting, entitled: *The Objective of Financial Reporting and Qualitative Characteristics of Decision-Useful Financial Reporting Information*. This project is being undertaken in phases. Phase G is entitled *Application to not-for-profit entities in the private and public sector*. A monitoring group, including ASB members, set up to advise on this has made the following points:

(a) Not-for profit entities have different objectives, different operating environments and other different characteristics to private sector businesses.

(b) The following issues exist regarding application of the proposals to not-for-profit entities:

- Insufficient emphasis on accountability/stewardship
- A need to broaden the definition of users and user groups

- The emphasis on future cash flows is inappropriate to not-for-profit entities
- Insufficient emphasis on budgeting

1.2 Accountability/stewardship

Not-for-profit entities are not reporting to shareholders, but it is very important that they can account for funds received and show how they have been spent. In some cases, resources may be contributed for specific purposes and management is required to show that they have been utilised for that purpose. Perhaps most importantly, taxpayers are entitled to see how the government is spending their money.

1.3 Users and user groups

The primary user group for not-for-profit entities is providers of funds. In the case of public bodies, such as government departments, this primary group will consist of taxpayers. In the case of private bodies such as charities it will be financial supporters, and also potential future financial supporters. There is also a case for saying that a second primary user group should be recognised, being the recipients of the goods and services provided by the not-for-profit entity.

1.4 Cash flow focus

The new framework, like the existing framework, emphasises the need to provide information which will enable users to assess an entity's ability to generate net cash inflows. Not-for-profit entities also need to generate cash flows, but other aspects are generally more significant – for instance, the resources the entity has available to deliver future goods and services, the cost and effectiveness of those it has delivered in the past and the degree to which it is meeting its objectives.

1.5 Budgeting

The IASB has decided to leave consideration of whether financial reporting should include forecast information until later in the project. However, for not-for-profit entities, budgets and variance analyses are more important. In some cases, funding is supplied on the basis of a formal, published budget.

2 Regulatory framework

FAST FORWARD

There is a general move to get public bodies reporting under the accruals system. Many private not-for-profit organisations still use cash accounting.

Regulation of public not-for-profit entities, principally local and national governments and governmental agencies, is by the International Public Sector Accounting Standards Board (IPSAB), which comes under the International Federation of Accountants (IFAC).

2.1 International public sector accounting standards

The IPSASB is developing a set of International Public Sector Accounting Standards (IPSASs), based on IFRSs. To date the following IPSASs have been issued:

1 Presentation of Financial Statements
2 Cash Flow Statements
3 Net Surplus or Deficit for the Period, Fundamental Errors and Changes in Accounting Policies
4 The Effect of Changes in Foreign Exchange Rates
5 Borrowing Costs
6 Consolidated Financial Statements and Accounting for Controlled Entities
7 Accounting for investments in Associates
8 Financial Reporting of Interests in Joint Ventures
9 Revenue from Exchange Transactions
10 Financial Reporting in Hyperinflationary Economies

11	Construction Contracts
12	Inventories
13	Leases
14	Events After the Reporting Date
15	Financial Instruments: Disclosure and Presentation
16	Investment Property
17	Property, Plant and Equipment
18	Segment Reporting
19	Provisions, Contingent Liabilities and Contingent Assets
10	Related Party Disclosures
21	Impairment of Non-Cash-Generating Assets

You are not required to remember this list of IPSAs, or know any of their detailed provisions, but you can see that they closely mirror the IAS/IFRSes and each one is based on the relevant International Accounting Standard.

The IPSAs are all based on the **accrual method** of accounting and one of the aims of the IPSAB is to move public sector organisations from the cash to the accruals basis of accounting.

2.2 Characteristics of Not-for-profit Entities

As part of its preliminary report on the new *Framework*, the IASB sets out some of the characteristics of not-for-profit entities as follows:

2.2.1 Private Sector

Not-for-profit entities in the private sector have the following characteristics:

- Their objective is to provide goods and services to various recipients and not to make a profit
- They are generally characterised by the absence of defined ownership interests (shares) that can be sold, transferred or redeemed
- They may have a wide group of stakeholders to consider (including the public at large in some cases)
- Their revenues generally arise from contributions (donations or membership dues) rather than sales
- Their capital assets are typically acquired and held to deliver services without the intention of earning a return on them

2.2.2 Public Sector

Nor-for-profit entities in the public sector have similar key characteristics to those in the private sector. They are typically established by legislation and:

- Their objective is to provide goods and services to various recipients or to develop or implement policy on behalf of governments and not to make a profit
- They are characterised by the absence of defined ownership interests that can be sold, transferred or redeemed
- They typically have a wide group of stakeholders to consider (including the public at large)
- Their revenues are generally derived from taxes or other similar contributions obtained through the exercise of coercive powers
- Their capital assets are typically acquired and held to deliver services without the intention of earning a return on them

2.3 Not-for-profit entities – specific issues

While the general trend is to get not-for-profit entities producing accounts which are based as far as possible on the provisions of IFRS and which are generally comparable to those produced for profit-making entities, there are two issues which have yet to be resolved.

2.3.1 Cost of transition

While there has been a general assumption that for public sector entities the move to the accruals basis will result in more relevant and better quality financial reporting, no actual cost-benefit analysis has been undertaken on this.

One of the arguments in favour of the adoption of the accruals basis is that it will be possible to compare the cost of providing a service against the same cost in the private sector. It will then be possible to see how goods and services can be most cheaply sourced.

However, it is questionable whether governments get a good deal anyway when they involve themselves with the private sector and the move to accruals accounting has not gained universal acceptance. The governments of Germany, Italy and Holland have so far made no plans for the transition and the governments of China, Japan, Malaysia and Singapore have decided against it. The main issue is the huge cost involved in terms of the number of qualified accountants required. For developing countries this cost is considered to be prohibitive.

2.3.2 Definition of a liability

The *Framework* defines a liability as 'a present obligation of the entity arising from past events, the settlement of which is expected to result in an outflow from the entity of resources embodying economic benefits'. A liability is recognised when the amount of the outflow can be reliably measured.

Public benefit entities are subject to a commitment to provide public benefits, but there is an issue to be resolved over whether this commitment meets the definition of a liability. In this situation there has been no 'exchange'. The entity has not received any goods or services for which it is required to make 'settlement'. A distinction can be drawn between 'general commitments to provide public benefits' and 'specific commitments to provide public benefits'. The specific commitment can be regarded as a 'present obligation', but it can be argued that the obligation only arises when the entity formally undertakes to provide something such as a non-performance-related grant. (If the grant were performance-related, the entity would be able to withdraw from the agreement if the performance targets were not reached.)

There is also the issue of 'reliable measurement'. Governments in particular often find themselves funding projects which go a long way over budget, suggesting that reliable measurement was not obtained at the outset.

This issue is still being debated by the IPSAB. It is of major importance in the financial reporting of the social policies of governments.

2.4 Charities

Charities are regulated by accounting standards, charity law, relevant company law and best practice. This will vary from country to country. Here we are taking the UK as a typical example.

2.4.1 Statement of financial activities

In addition to a statement of financial position, charities also produce a Statement of Financial Activities (SOFA), an Annual Report to the Charity Commission and sometimes an income and expenditure account. The Statement of Financial Activities is the primary statement showing the results of the charity's activities for the period.

The SoFA shows Incoming resources, Resources expended, and the resultant Net movement in funds. Under incoming resources, income from all sources of funds are listed. These can include:

- Subscriptions or membership fees
- Public donations
- Donations from patrons
- Government grants
- Income from sale of goods
- Investment income

- Publication sales
- Royalties

The resources expended will show the amount spent directly in furtherance of the Charity's objects. It will also show items which form part of any income statement, such as salaries, depreciation, travelling and entertaining, audit and other professional fees. These items can be very substantial.

Charities, especially the larger charities, now operate very much in the way that profit-making entities do. They run high-profile campaigns which cost money and they employ professional people who have to be paid. At the same time, their stakeholders will want to see that most of their donation is not going on running the business, rather than achieving the aims for which funds were donated.

One of the problems charities experience is that, even although the accruals basis is being applied, they will still have income and expenditure recognised in different periods, due to the difficulty of correlating them. The extreme example is a campaign to persuade people to leave money to the charity in their will. The costs will have to be recognised, but there is no way to predict when the income will arise.

3 Performance measurement

FAST FORWARD

Not-for-profit and public sector entities are required to manage their funds efficiently but are not expected to show a profit. Their performance is measured in terms of achievement of their stated purpose.

Not-for-profit and public sector entities produce financial statements in the same way as profit-making entities do but, while they are expected to remain solvent, their performance cannot be measured simply by the bottom line.

A public sector entity is not expected to show a profit or to underspend its budget. In practice, central government and local government departments know that if they underspend the budget, next year's allocation will be correspondingly reduced. This leads to a rash of digging up the roads and other expenditure just before the end of the financial year as councils strive to spend any remaining funds.

Private and public sector entities are judged principally on the basis of what they have achieved, not how much or how little they have spent in achieving it. So how is performance measured?

3.1 Public sector entities

These will have performance measures laid down by government. The emphasis is on economy, efficiency and effectiveness. Departments and local councils have to show how they have spent public money and what level of service they have achieved. Performance measurement will be based on Key Performance Indicators (KPIs). Examples of these for a local council could be:

- Number of homeless people rehoused
- % of rubbish collections made on time
- Number of children in care adopted

Public sector entities use the services of outside contractors for a variety of functions. They then have to be able to show that they have obtained the best possible value for what they have spent on outside services. This principle is usually referred to as Value For Money (VFM). In the UK, local authorities are required to report under a system known as Best Value. They have to show that they applied 'fair competition' in awarding contracts.

Best Value is based on the principle of the 'four Cs':

1   **Challenging** why, how and by whom a service is provided
2   **Comparing** performance against other local authorities
3   **Consulting** service users, the local community etc.
4   Using fair **Competition** to secure efficient and effective services

3.2 Charities

While charities must demonstrate that they have made proper use of whatever funds they have received, their stakeholders will be more interested in what they have achieved in terms of their stated mission. People who donate money to a relief fund for earthquake victims will want to know what help has been given to survivors, before enquiring how well the organisation has managed its funds. Although it must be said that any mismanagement of funds by a charity is taken very seriously by the donating public.

Some charities produce 'impact reports' which highlight what the charity set out to achieve, what it has achieved and what it has yet to do. Stakeholders should know what the organisation is aiming to achieve and how it is succeeding. Each charity will have its own performance indicators which enable it to measure this.

Question	Performance measurement

Choose a charity with which you are familiar and produce a possible set of performance indicators for it.

Exam focus point

> You will not be asked anything detailed or specific on this topic. The examiner has said that the question in the pilot paper (3(c)) is typical of what he will ask.

Chapter Roundup

- The accounting requirements for not-for-profit and public sector entities are moving closer to those required for profit-making entities. However, they do have different goals and purposes.

- There is a general move to get public bodies reporting under the accruals system. Many private not-for-profit organisations still use cash accounting.

- Not-for-profit and public sector entities are required to manage their funds efficiently but are not expected to show a profit. Their performance is measured in terms of achievement of their stated purpose.

Quick Quiz

1 Give some examples of not-for-profit and public sector entities.
2 What are some of the characteristics of **private sector** not-for-profit entities?
3 What are the 'four Cs'?

Answers to Quick Quiz

1 Central and local government departments, schools, hospitals, charities.
2 See paragraph 2.2.1.
3 See paragraph 3.1

Now try the questions below from the Exam Question Bank

Number	Level	Marks	Time
3(b)	–	5	9 mins

Exam question and answer bank

1 Conceptual framework

18 mins

(a)   Explain and give an example of the effect on a set of published financial statements if the going concern convention is held not to apply.

(b)   Explain in general terms what the IASB *Framework* is trying to achieve.

(10 marks)

2 Regulators

18 mins

State three different regulatory influences on the preparation of the published accounts of quoted companies and briefly explain the role of each one. Comment briefly on the effectiveness of this regulatory system.

(10 marks)

3 Standard setters

18 mins

There are those who suggest that any standard setting body is redundant because accounting standards are unnecessary. Other people feel that such standards should be produced, but by the government, so that they are a legal requirement.

Required

(a)   Discuss the statement that accounting standards are unnecessary for the purpose of regulating financial statements.

(b)   Discuss whether or not the financial statements of not-for-profit entities should be subject to regulation.

(10 marks)

4 Polymer

The following list of account balances has been prepared by Polymer Co, plastics manufacturers, on 31 May 20X8, which is the end of the company's accounting period:

	$	$
Authorised and issued 300,000 ordinary shares of $1 each, fully paid		300,000
100,000 8.4% cumulative preference shares of $1 each, fully paid		100,000
Revaluation surplus		50,000
Share premium reserve		100,000
General reserve		50,000
Retained earnings – 31 May 20X7		283,500
Patents and trademarks	215,500	
Freehold land at cost	250,000	
Leasehold property at cost	75,000	
Amortisation of leasehold property – 31 May 20X7		15,000
Factory plant and equipment at cost	150,000	
Accumulated depreciation – plant and equipment – 31 May 20X7		68,500
Furniture and fixtures at cost	50,000	
Accumulated depreciation – furniture and fixtures – 31 May 20X7		15,750
Motor vehicles at cost	75,000	
Accumulated depreciation – motor vehicles – 31 May 20X7		25,000
10% loan notes (20Y0 – 20Y5)		100,000
Trade receivables/ trade payables	177,630	97,500
Bank overdraft		51,250
Inventories – raw materials at cost – 31 May 20X7	108,400	
Purchases – raw materials	750,600	
Carriage inwards – raw materials	10,500	
Manufacturing wages	250,000	
Manufacturing overheads	125,000	
Cash	5,120	
Work in progress – 31 May 20X7	32,750	
Sales		1,526,750
Administrative expenses	158,100	
Selling and distribution expenses	116,800	
Legal and professional expenses	54,100	
Allowance for receivables – 31 May 20X8		5,750
Inventories – finished goods – 31 May 20X7	184,500	
	2,789,000	2,789,000

Additional information:

(1) Inventories at 31 May 20X8 were:

	$
Raw materials	112,600
Finished goods	275,350
Work in progress	37,800

(2) Depreciation for the year is to be charged as follows:
Plant and equipment 8% on cost – charged to production
Furniture and fixtures 10% on cost – charged to admin
Motor vehicles   20% on reducing value   – 25% admin
                                                – 75% selling and distribution

(3) Financial, legal and professional expenses include:

	$
Solicitors' fees for purchase of freehold land during year	5,000

(4) Provision is to be made for a full year's interest on the loan notes.

(5) Income tax on the profits for the year is estimated at $40,000 and is due for payment on 28 February 20X9.

(6) The directors recommended on 30 June that a dividend of 3.5c per share be paid on the ordinary share capital. No ordinary dividend was paid during the year ended 31 May 20X7.

(7) The leasehold land and buildings are held on a 50 year lease, acquired ten years ago.

Required

From the information given above, prepare the income statement of Polymer Co for the year to 31 May 20X8 and a statement of financial position at that date for publication in accordance with International Financial Reporting Standards.

Notes to the financial statements are not required. **(25 marks)**

5 Winger **45 mins**

(Adapted from past ACCA exam paper 2.5 Pilot paper)

The following list of account balances relates to Winger at 31 March 20X1.

	$'000	$'000
Sales revenue (note a)		358,450
Cost of sales	185,050	
Distribution costs	28,700	
Administration expenses	15,000	
Lease rentals (note b)	20,000	
Loan note interest paid	2,000	
Dividend paid	12,000	
Property at cost (note c)	200,000	
Plant and equipment cost	154,800	
Depreciation 1 April 20X0 – plant and equipment		34,800
Development expenditure (note d)	30,000	
Profit on disposal of non-current assets (note c)		45,000
Trade accounts receivable	55,000	
Inventories: 31 March 20X1	28,240	
Cash and bank	10,660	
Trade accounts payable		29,400
Taxation: over provision in year to 31 March 20X0		2,200
Equity shares of 25c each		150,000
8% loan note (issued in 20W9)		50,000
Retained earnings 1 April 20X0		71,600
	741,450	741,450

The following notes are relevant.

(a) Included in sales revenue is $27 million, which relates to sales made to customers under sale or return agreements. The expiry date for the return of these goods is 30 April 20X1. Winger has charged a mark-up of 20% on cost for these sales.

(b) A lease rental of $20 million was paid on 1 April 20X0. It is the first of five annual payments in advance for the rental of an item of equipment that has a cash purchase price of $80 million. The auditors have advised that this is a finance lease and have calculated the implicit interest rate in the lease as 12% per annum. Leased assets should be depreciated on a straight-line basis over the life of the lease.

(c) On 1 April 20X0 Winger acquired a new property at a cost of $200 million. For the purpose of calculating depreciation only, the asset has been separated into the following elements.

Separate asset	Cost	Life
	$'000	
Land	50,000	freehold
Heating system	20,000	10 years
Lifts	30,000	15 years
Building	100,000	50 years

The depreciation of the elements of the property should be calculated on a straight-line basis. The new property replaced an existing one that was sold on the same date for $95 million. It had cost $50 million and had a carrying value of $80 million at the date of sale. The profit on this property has been calculated on the original cost. It had not been depreciated on the basis that the depreciation charge would not be material.

Plant and machinery is depreciated at 20% on the reducing balance basis.

(d) The figure for development expenditure in the list of account balances represents the amounts deferred in previous years in respect of the development of a new product. Unfortunately, during the current year, the government has introduced legislation which effectively bans this type of product. As a consequence of this the project has been abandoned. The directors of Winger are of the opinion that writing off the development expenditure, as opposed to its previous deferment, represents a change of accounting policy and therefore wish to treat the write off as a prior period adjustment.

(e) A provision for income tax for the year to 31 March 20X1 of $15 million is required.

Required

(a) Prepare the income statement of Winger for the year to 31 March 20X1. **(9 marks)**

(b) Prepare a statement of financial position as at 31 March 20X1 in accordance with International Accounting Standards as far as the information permits. **(11 marks)**

(c) Discuss the acceptability of the company's previous policy in respect of non-depreciation of property and the proposed treatment of the deferred development expenditure. **(5 marks)**

(Total = 25 marks)

6 Hewlett

Hewlett is a quoted company reporting under IFRS. During the year end 31 December 20X2, the company changed its accounting policy with respect to property valuation. There are also a number of other issues that need to be finalised before the financial statements can be published.

Hewlett's trial balance from the general ledger at 31 December 20X2 showed the following balances:

	$'m	$'m
Revenue		2,648
Loan note interest paid	3	
Purchases	1,669	
Distribution costs	514	
Administrative expenses	345	
Interim dividend paid	6	
Inventories at 1 January 20X2	444	
Trade receivables	545	
Trade payables		434
Cash and cash equivalents	28	
50c ordinary shares		100
Share premium		244
General reserve		570
Retained earnings at 1 January 20X2		349
4% loan note repayable 20X8 (issued 20X0)		150
Land and buildings: cost (including $60m land)	380	
accumulated depreciation at 1 January 20X2		64
Plant and equipment: cost	258	
accumulated depreciation at 1 January 20X2		126
Investment property at 1 January 20X2	548	
Rental income		48
Proceeds from sale of equipment		7
	4,740	4,740

Further information to be taken into account:

(i)   Closing inventories were counted and amounted to $388m at cost. However, shortly after the year end out-of-date inventories with a cost of $15m were sold for $8m.

(ii) The company decided to change its accounting policy with respect to its 10 year old land and buildings from the cost model to the revaluation model. The revalued amounts at 1 January 20X2 were $800m (including $100m for the land). No further revaluation was necessary at 31 December 20X2. The company wishes to treat the revaluation surplus as being realised over the life of the asset.

(iii) Due to a change in the company's product portfolio plans, an item of plant with a carrying value $22m at 31 December 20X1 (after adjusting for depreciation for the year) may be impaired due to a change in use. An impairment test conducted at 31 December, revealed its fair value less costs to sell to be $16m. The asset is now expected to generate an annual net income stream of $3.8m for the next 5 years at which point the asset would be disposed for $4.2m. An appropriate discount rate is 8%. 5 year discount factors at 8% are:

	Simple	Cumulative
	0.677	3.993

(iv) The income tax liability for the year is estimated at $27m. Ignore deferred tax.

(v)   An interim dividend of 3c per share was paid on 30 June 20X2. A final dividend of 1.5c per share was declared by the directors on 28 January 20X3. No dividends were paid or declared in 20X1.

(vi) During the year, Hewlett Co disposed of some malfunctioning equipment for $7m. The equipment had cost $15m and had accumulated depreciation brought forward at 1 January 20X2 of $3m.

There were no other additions or disposal to property, plant and equipment in the year.

(vii) The company treats depreciation on plant and equipment as a cost of sale and on land and buildings as an administration cost. Depreciation rates as per the company's accounting policy note are as follows:

Buildings	Straight line over 50 years
Plant and equipment	20% reducing balance

Hewlett's accounting policy is to charge a full year's depreciation in the year of an asset's purchase and none in the year of disposal.

(viii) During the year on 1 July 20X2, Hewlett made a 1 for 4 bonus issue, capitalising its general reserve. This transaction had not yet been accounted for. The fair value of the company's shares on the date of the bonus issue was $7.50 each.

(ix) Hewlett uses the fair value model of IAS 40. The fair value of the investment property at 31 December 20X2 was $586m.

Required

Prepare the statement of comprehensive income and statement of changes in equity for Hewlett Co for the year to 31 December 20X2 and a statement of financial position at that date in accordance with IFRS insofar as the information permits.

Notes to the financial statements are not required, but all workings should be clearly shown.

Work to the nearest $1m. Comparative information is not required. **(25 marks)**

7 Gains

Required

Using the information below prepare the Statement of changes in equity for Gains Co for the year ended 31 December 20X9. **(10 marks)**

(a) **Gains Co**
Statement of comprehensive income (extract)

	$'000
Profit before interest and tax	792
Finance income	24
Finance cost	(10)
Profit before tax	806
Income tax expense	(240)
PROFIT FOR THE YEAR	566
Other comprehensive income:	
Gain on property revaluation	120
TOTAL COMPREHENSIVE INCOME FOR THE YEAR	686

(b) *Non-current assets*

(i) Assets held at cost were impaired by $25,000.
(ii) Freehold land and buildings were revalued to $500,000 (Book value $380,000).

(iii) A previously revalued asset was sold for $60,000.

Details of the revaluation are as follows:

	$
Book value at revaluation	30,000
Revaluation	50,000
	80,000
Depreciation (80,000/10) × 3	24,000
	56,000

Gains Co has been following paragraph 41 of IAS 16 which allows a reserve transfer of the realised revaluation surplus (the difference between depreciation based on revalued amount and depreciation based on cost) as the asset is used to retained earnings.

(iv) Details of investment properties are as follows:

	$
Original cost	120,000
Revaluation surplus	40,000
Value at 1.1.20X9	160,000

The properties had a valuation on 31 December 20X9 of $110,000. Gains Co previously accounted for its investment properties by crediting gains to a revaluation surplus as allowed by local GAAP. Gains Co now wishes to apply the fair value model of IAS 40 which states that gains and losses should be accounted for in profit or loss. The elimination of the previous revaluation surplus is to be treated as a change in accounting policy in accordance with IAS 8. No adjustment has yet been made for the change in accounting policy or subsequent fall in value.

(c) Share capital

During the year the company had the following changes to its capital structure:

(i) An issue of $200,000 $1 ordinary bonus shares capitalising its share premium reserve
(ii) An issue of 400,000 $1 ordinary shares (issue price $1.40 per share).

(d) Equity

The book value of equity at the start of the year was as follows:

	$
Share capital	2,800,000
Share premium	1,150,000
Retained earnings	2,120,000
Revaluation surplus	750,000
	6,820,000

(e) Dividends

Dividends paid during the year amounted to $200,000.

8 Multiplex

(Adapted from past ACCA exam paper 2.5 Pilot paper)

On 1 January 20X0 Multiplex acquired Steamdays, a company that operates a scenic railway along the coast of a popular tourist area. The summarised statement of financial position at fair values of Steamdays on 1 January 20X0, reflecting the terms of the acquisition was:

	$'000
Goodwill	200
Operating licence	1,200
Property – train stations and land	300
Rail track and coaches	300
Two steam engines	1,000
Purchase consideration	3,000

The operating licence is for ten years. It was renewed on 1 January 20X0 by the transport authority and is stated at the cost of its renewal. The carrying values of the property and rail track and coaches are based on their value in use. The engines are valued at their net selling prices.

On 1 February 20X0 the boiler of one of the steam engines exploded, completely destroying the whole engine. Fortunately no one was injured, but the engine was beyond repair. Due to its age a replacement could not be obtained. Because of the reduced passenger capacity the estimated value in use of the whole of the business after the accident was assessed at $2 million.

Passenger numbers after the accident were below expectations even allowing for the reduced capacity. A market research report concluded that tourists were not using the railway because of their fear of a similar accident occurring to the remaining engine. In the light of this the value in use of the business was re-assessed on 31 March 20X0 at $1.8 million. On this date Multiplex received an offer of $900,000 in respect of the operating licence (it is transferable). The realisable value of the other net assets has not changed significantly.

Required

Calculate the carrying value of the assets of Steamdays (in Multiplex's consolidated statement of financial position) at 1 February 20X0 and 31 March 20X0 after recognising the impairment losses. **(15 marks)**

9 Barcelona and Madrid

Barcelona acquired 60% of Madrid's ordinary share capital on 30 June 20X2 at a price $1.06 per share. The balance on Madrid's retained earnings at that date was $104m and the general reserve stood at $11m.

Their respective statements of financial position as at 30 September 20X6 are as follows:

	Barcelona $m	Madrid $m
Non-current assets:		
Property, plant & equipment	2,848	354
Patents	45	–
Investment in Madrid	159	–
	3,052	354
Current assets		
Inventories	895	225
Trade and other receivables	1,348	251
Cash and cash equivalents	212	34
	2,455	510
	5,507	864

Equity		
Share capital (20c ordinary shares)	920	50
General reserve	775	46
Retained earnings	2,086	394
	3,781	490
Non-current liabilities		
Long-term borrowings	558	168
Current liabilities		
Trade and other payables	1,168	183
Current portion of long-term borrowings	–	23
	1,168	206
	5,507	864

Annual impairment tests have revealed cumulative impairment losses relating to recognised goodwill of $17m to date.

Required

Produce the consolidated statement of financial position for the Barcelona Group as at 30 September 20X6. It is the group policy to value the non-controlling interest at its proportionate share of the fair value of the subsidiary's identifiable net assets. **(10 marks)**

10 Reprise
36 mins

Reprise purchased 75% of Encore for $2,000,000 10 years ago when the balance on its retained earnings was $1,044,000. The statements of financial position of the two companies as at 31 March 20X4 are as follows:

	Reprise	Encore
	$'000	$'000
NON-CURRENT ASSETS		
Investment in Encore	2,000	–
Land and buildings	3,350	–
Plant and equipment	1,010	2,210
Motor vehicles	510	345
	6,870	2,555
CURRENT ASSETS		
Inventories	890	352
Trade receivables	1,372	514
Cash and cash equivalents	89	51
	2,351	917
	9,221	3,472
EQUITY		
Share capital – $1 ordinary shares	1,000	500
Revaluation surplus	2,500	–
Retained earnings	4,225	2,610
	7,725	3,110
NON-CURRENT LIABILITIES		
10% debentures	500	–
CURRENT LIABILITIES		
Trade payables	996	362
	9,221	3,472

The following additional information is available:

(1) Included in trade receivables of Reprise are amounts owed by Encore of $75,000. The current accounts do not at present balance due to a payment for $39,000 being in transit at the year end from Encore.

(2) Included in the inventories of Encore are items purchased from Reprise during the year for $31,200. Reprise marks up its goods by 30% to achieve its selling price.

(3) $180,000 of the recognised goodwill arising is to be written off due to impairment losses.

(4) Encore shares were trading at $4.40 just prior to acquisition by Reprise.

Required

Prepare the consolidated statement of financial position for the Reprise group of companies as at 31 March 20X4. It is the group policy to value the non-controlling interest at full (or fair) value. **(20 marks)**

11 War   45 mins

(a) When an acquisition takes place, the purchase consideration may be in the form of share capital. Where no suitable market price exists (for example, shares in an unquoted company) how may the fair value of the purchase consideration be estimated? **(4 marks)**

(b) On 1 May 20X7, War Co acquired 70% of the ordinary share capital of Peace Co by issuing to Peace Co's shareholders 500,000 ordinary $1 shares at a market value of $1.60c per share. The costs associated with the share issue were $50,000.

As at 30 June 20X7, the following financial statements for War Co and Peace Co were available.

INCOME STATEMENTS
FOR THE YEAR ENDED 30 JUNE 20X7

	War Co	Peace Co
	$'000	$'000
Revenue	3,150	1,770
Cost of sales	(1,610)	(1,065)
Gross profit	1,540	705
Distribution costs	(620)	(105)
Administrative expenses	(325)*	(210)
Interest payable	(70)	(30)
Dividends from Peace Co	42	–
Profit before taxation	567	360
Income tax expense	(283)	(135)
Profit for the year	284	225

*Note. The issue costs of $50,000 on the issue of ordinary share capital are included in this figure.

Dividends paid during the year were: War Co: $38,000
                                        Peace Co: $60,000

STATEMENTS OF FINANCIAL POSITION AT 30 JUNE 20X7

	War Co $'000	Peace Co $'000
Assets		
Non-current assets		
Property, plant and equipment	1,750	350
Investment in Peace Co	800	–
	2,550	350
Current assets		
Inventory	150	450
Receivables	238	213
Cash	187	112
	575	775
Total assets	3,125	1,125
Equity and liabilities		
Shares of $1 each	750	100
Share premium	300	150
Retained earnings	625	450
	1,675	700
Non-current liabilities	1,050	175
Current liabilities	400	250
Total equity and liabilities	3,125	1,125

You have been asked to prepare the consolidated financial statements, taking account of the following further information.

(i)   There was no impairment in the value of goodwill.

(ii) War Co accounts for pre-acquisition dividends by treating them as a deduction from the cost of the investment. Peace Co paid an ordinary dividend of 60c per share on 1 June 20X7. No dividends were proposed as at 30 June 20X7.

(iii) The profit of Peace Co may be assumed to accrue evenly over the year.

(iv) The property, plant and equipment of Peace Co had a net realisable value of $400,000 at the date of acquisition. Their fair value was $500,000. It has been decided that, as Peace Co was acquired so close to the year end, no depreciation adjustment will be made in the group accounts; the year end value will be taken as the carrying value of the property, plant and equipment in the accounts of Peace Co. The remaining assets and liabilities of Peace Co were all stated at their fair value as at 1 May 20X7.

(v)   Peace Co did not issue any shares between the date of acquisition and the year end.

(vi) There were no intercompany transactions during the year.

Required

Prepare the consolidated statement of financial position and the consolidated income statement of the War Group Co for the year ended 30 June 20X7. If it is the group policy to value the non-controlling interest at its proportionate share of the fair value of the subsidiary's identifiable net assets.   **(21 marks)**

(Total = 25 marks)

12 Fallowfield and Rusholme

27 mins

Fallowfield acquired a 60% holding in Rusholme three years ago when Rusholme's retained earnings balance stood at $16,000. Both businesses have been very successful since the acquisition and their respective income statements for the year ended 30 June 20X8 are as follows:

	Fallowfield $	Rusholme $
Revenue	403,400	193,000
Cost of sales	(201,400)	(92,600)
Gross profit	202,000	100,400
Distribution costs	(16,000)	(14,600)
Administrative expenses	(24,250)	(17,800)
Dividends from Rusholme	15,000	
Profit before tax	176,750	68,000
Income tax expense	(61,750)	(22,000)
Profit for the year	115,000	46,000

STATEMENT OF CHANGES IN EQUITY (EXTRACT)

	Fallowfield Retained earnings $	Rusholme Retained earnings $
Balance at 1 July 20X7	163,000	61,000
Dividends	(40,000)	(25,000)
Profit for the year	115,000	46,000
Balance at 30 June 20X8	238,000	82,000

Additional information

During the year Rusholme sold some goods to Fallowfield for $40,000, including 25% mark up. Half of these items were still in inventories at the year-end.

Required

Produce the consolidated income statement of Fallowfield Co and its subsidiary for the year ended 30 June 20X8, and an extract from the statement of changes in equity, showing retained earnings. Goodwill is to be ignored. **(15 marks)**

13 Panther Group

Panther operated as a single company, but in 20X4 decided to expand its operations. Panther acquired a 60% interest in Sabre on 1 July 20X4 for $2,000,000. The statements of comprehensive income of Panther and Sabre for the year ended 31 December 20X4 are as follows:

	Panther $'000	Sabre $'000
Revenue	22,800	4,300
Cost of sales	(13,600)	(2,600)
Gross profit	9,200	1,700
Distribution costs	(2,900)	(500)
Administrative expenses	(1,800)	(300)
Finance costs	(200)	(70)
Finance income	50	–
Profit before tax	4,350	830
Income tax expense	(1,300)	(220)
PROFIT FOR THE YEAR	3,050	610
Other comprehensive income for the year, net of tax	1,600	180
TOTAL COMPREHENSIVE INCOME FOR THE YEAR	4,650	790

Since acquisition, Panther purchased $320,000 of goods from Sabre. Of these, $60,000 remained in inventories at the year end. Sabre makes a mark-up on cost of 20% under the transfer pricing agreement between the two companies. The fair value of the identifiable net assets of Sabre on purchase were $200,000 greater than their book value. The difference relates to properties with a remaining useful life of 20 years.

On the acquisition date Panther advanced a loan to Sabre amounting to $800,000 at a preferential interest rate of 5%. The loan is due for repayment in 20X9.

Statement of changes in equity (extracts) for the two companies:

	Panther Reserves $'000	Sabre Reserves $'000
Balance at 1 January 20X4	12,750	2,480
Dividend paid	(900)	–
Total comprehensive income for the year	4,650	790
Balance at 31 December 20X4	16,500	3,270

Panther and Sabre had $400,000 and $150,000 of share capital in issue throughout the period respectively.

Required

Prepare the consolidated statement of comprehensive income and statement of changes in equity (extract for reserves) for the Panther Group for the year ended 31 December 20X4.

No adjustments for impairment losses were necessary in the group financial statements.

Assume income and expenses (other than intragroup items) accrue evenly. **(15 marks)**

14 Hever 45 mins

Hever has held shares in two companies, Spiro and Aldridge, for a number of years. As at 31 December 20X4 they have the following statements of financial position:

	Hever $'000	Spiro $'000	Aldridge $'000
Non-current assets			
Property, plant & equipment	370	190	260
Investments	218	–	–
	588	190	260
Current assets:			
Inventories	160	100	180
Trade receivables	170	90	100
Cash	50	40	10
	380	230	290
	968	420	550
Equity			
Share capital ($1 ords)	200	80	50
Share premium	100	80	30
Retained earnings	568	200	400
	868	360	480
Current liabilities			
Trade payables	100	60	70
	968	420	550

You ascertain the following additional information:

(1)   The 'investments' in the statement of financial position comprise solely Hever's investment in Spiro ($128,000) and in Aldridge ($90,000).

(2)   The 48,000 shares in Spiro were acquired when Spiro's retained earnings balance stood at $20,000.

The 15,000 shares in Aldridge were acquired when that company had a retained earnings balance of $150,000.

(3)   When Hever acquired its shares in Spiro the fair value of Spiro's net assets equalled their book values with the following exceptions:

	$'000
Property, plant and equipment	50 higher
Inventories	20 lower (sold during 20X4)

Depreciation arising on the fair value adjustment to non-current assets since this date is $5,000.

(4)   During the year, Hever sold inventories to Spiro for $16,000, which originally cost Hever $10,000. Three-quarters of these inventories have subsequently been sold by Spiro.

(5)   No impairment losses on goodwill had been necessary by 31 December 20X4.

Required

Produce the consolidated statement of financial position for the Hever group (incorporating the associate). It is the group policy to value the non-controlling interest at its proportionate share of the fair value of the subsidiary's identifiable net assets.   **(25 marks)**

15 Trontacc   18 mins

Trontacc Co is a company whose activities are in the field of major construction projects. During the year ended 30 September 20X7, it enters into three separate construction contracts, each with a fixed contract price of $1,000,000. The following information relates to these contracts at 30 September 20X7:

	Contract		
	A	B	C
	$'000	$'000	$'000
Payments on account (including amounts receivable)	540	475	400
Costs incurred to date	500	550	320
Estimate costs to complete the contract	300	550	580
Estimate percentage of work completed	60%	50%	35%

Required

(a)   Show how each contract would be reflected in the statement of financial position of Trontacc Co at 30 September 20X7 under IAS 11.

(b)   Show how each contract would be reflected in the statement of comprehensive income of Trontacc Co for the year ended 30 September 20X7 under IAS 11.   **(10 marks)**

16 C Co   27 mins

C Co is a civil engineering company. It started work on two construction projects during the year ended 31 December 20X0. The following figures relate to those projects at the end of the reporting period.

	Maryhill bypass	Rottenrow Centre
	$'000	$'000
Contract price	9,000	8,000
Costs incurred to date	1,400	2,900
Estimated costs to completion	5,600	5,200
Value of work certified to date	2,800	3,000
Progress billings	2,600	3,400

An old mineshaft has been discovered under the site for the Rottenrow Centre and the costs of dealing with this have been taken into account in the calculation of estimated costs to completion. C Co's lawyers are reasonably confident that the customer will have to bear the additional costs which will be incurred in stabilising the land. If negotiations are successful then the contract price will increase to $10m.

C Co recognises revenues and profits on construction contracts on the basis of work certified to date.

Required

(a) Calculate the figures which would appear in C Co's financial statements in respect of these two projects.

(b) It has been suggested that profit on construction contracts should not be recognised until the contract is completed. Briefly explain whether you believe that this suggestion would improve the quality of financial reporting for long-term contracts.

(15 marks)

17 Provisions   45 mins

IAS 37 *Provisions, contingent liabilities and contingent assets* was issued in 1998. Prior to its publication, there was no International Accounting Standard that dealt with the general subject of accounting for provisions.

Extract prepares its financial statements to 31 December each year. During the years ended 31 December 20X0 and 31 December 20X1, the following event occurred.

Extract is involved in extracting minerals in a number of different countries. The process typically involves some contamination of the site from which the minerals are extracted. Extract makes good this contamination only where legally required to do so by legislation passed in the relevant country.

The company has been extracting minerals in Copperland since January 20W8 and expects its site to produce output until 31 December 20X5. On 23 December 20X0, it came to the attention of the directors of Extract that the government of Copperland was virtually certain to pass legislation requiring the making good of mineral extraction sites. The legislation was duly passed on 15 March 20X1. The directors of Extract estimate that the cost of making good the site in Copperland will be $2 million. This estimate is of the actual cash expenditure that will be incurred on 31 December 20X5.

Required

(a) Explain why there was a need for an accounting standard dealing with provisions, and summarise the criteria that need to be satisfied before a provision is recognised.   **(12 marks)**

(b) Compute the effect of the estimated cost of making good the site on the financial statements of Extract for BOTH of the years ended 31 December 20X0 and 20X1. Give full explanations of the figures you compute.

The annual discount rate to be used in any relevant calculations is 10%.

The relevant discount factors at 10% are:

Year 4 at 10%   0.683
Year 5 at 10%   0.621

(13 marks)

(Total = 25 marks)

18 Alpha   45 mins

In producing the Framework for the Preparation and Presentation of Financial Statements (Framework) and some of the current International Accounting Standards, the International Accounting Standards Board (IASB) has had to address the potential problem that the management of some companies may choose to adopt inappropriate accounting policies. These could have the effect of portraying an entity's financial position in a favourable manner. In some countries this is referred to as 'creative accounting'. Included in the Framework, and a common feature of many recent International Accounting Standards, is the application of the principle of 'substance over form'.

Required

(a)   Describe in broad terms common ways in which management can manipulate financial statements to indulge in 'creative accounting' and why they would wish to do so.   **(7 marks)**

(b)   Explain the principle of substance over form and how it limits the above practice; and for each of the following areas of accounting describe an example of the application of substance over form.

     (i)   Group accounting
     (ii)   Financing non-current assets
     (iii)   Measurement and disclosure of current assets   **(8 marks)**

(c)   Alpha, a public listed corporation, is considering how it should raise $10 million of finance which is required for a major and vital non-current asset renewal scheme that will be undertaken during the current year to 31 December 20X6. Alpha is particularly concerned about how analysts are likely to react to its financial statements for the year to 31 December 20X6. Present forecasts suggest that Alpha's earnings per share and its financial gearing ratios may be worse than market expectations. Mr Wong, Alpha's Finance Director, is in favour of raising the finance by issuing a convertible loan. He has suggested that the coupon (interest) rate on the loan should be 5%; this is below the current market rate of 9% for this type of loan. In order to make the stock attractive to investors the terms of conversion into equity would be very favourable to compensate for the low interest rate.

Required

     (i)   Explain why the Finance Director believes the above scheme may favourably improve Alpha's earnings per share and gearing.

     (ii)   Describe how the requirements of IAS 33 *Earnings per share* and IAS 32 *Financial instruments: presentation* are intended to prevent the above effects.   **(10 marks)**

                                                          (Total = 25 marks)

19 Jenson   45 mins

(Adapted from past ACCA exam paper 2.5 Pilot paper)

The timing of revenue (income) recognition has long been an area of debate and inconsistency in accounting. Industry practice in relation to revenue recognition varies widely, the following are examples of different points in the operating cycle of businesses that revenue and profit can be recognised.

(a)   On the acquisition of goods
(b)   During the manufacture or production of goods
(c)   On delivery/acceptance of goods
(d)   When certain conditions have been satisfied after the goods have been delivered
(e)   Receipt of payment for credit sales
(f)   On the expiry of a guarantee or warranty

In the past the 'critical event' approach has been used to determine the timing of revenue recognition. The International Accounting Standards Board (IASB) in its Framework for the Preparation and Presentation of Financial Statements (Framework) has defined the 'elements' of financial statements, and it uses these to determine when a gain or loss occurs.

Required

(a)   Explain what is meant by the critical event in relation to revenue recognition and discuss the criteria used in the Framework for determining when a gain or loss arises.   **(5 marks)**

(b)   For each of the stages of the operating cycle identified above, explain why it may be an appropriate point to recognise revenue and, where possible, give a practical example of an industry where it occurs.   **(12 marks)**

(c) Jenson has entered into the following transactions/agreements in the year to 31 March 20X5.

(i) Goods, which had a cost of $20,000, were sold to Wholesaler for $35,000 on 1 June 20X4. Jenson has an option to repurchase the goods from Wholesaler at any time within the next two years. The repurchase price will be $35,000 plus interest charged at 12% per annum from the date of sale to the date of repurchase. It is expected that Jenson will repurchase the goods.

(ii) Jenson owns the rights to a fast food franchise. On 1 April 20X4 it sold the right to open a new outlet to Mr Cody. The franchise is for five years. Jenson received an initial fee of $50,000 for the first year and will receive $5,000 per annum thereafter. Jenson has continuing service obligations on its franchise for advertising and product development that amount to approximately $8,000 per annum for each franchised outlet. A reasonable profit margin on the provision of the continuing services is deemed to be 20% of revenues received.

(iii) On 1 September 20X4 Jenson received subscriptions in advance of $240,000. The subscriptions are for 24 monthly publications of a magazine produced by Jenson. At the year end Jenson had produced and despatched six of the 24 publications. The total cost of producing the magazine is estimated at $192,000 with each publication costing a broadly similar amount.

Required

Describe how Jenson should treat each of the above examples in its financial statements in the year to 31 March 20X5. **(8 marks)**

(Total = 25 marks)

20 Bulwell   18 mins

Bulwell Aggregates Co wish to expand their transport fleet and purchased three heavy lorries with a list price of $18.000 each. Robert Bulwell has negotiated lease finance to fund this expansion, and the company has entered into a finance lease agreement with Granby Garages Co on 1 January 20X1. The agreement states that Bulwell Aggregates will pay a deposit of $9,000 on 1 January 20X1, and two annual instalments of $24,000 on 31 December 20X1, 20X2 and a final instalment of $20,391 on 31 December 20X3.

Interest is to be calculated at 25% on the balance outstanding on 1 January each year and paid on 31 December each year.

The depreciation policy of Bulwell Aggregates Co is to write off the vehicles over a four year period using the straight line method and assuming a scrap value of $1,333 for each vehicle at the end of its useful life.

Required

Show the entries in the income statement and statement of financial position for the years 20X1, 20X2, 20X3. This is the only lease transaction undertaken by this company.

Calculations to the nearest $. **(10 marks)**

21 Financial assets and liabilities   18 mins

(a) On 1 January 2005, an entity issued a debt instrument with a coupon rate of 3.5% at a par value of $6,000,000. The directly attributable costs of issue were $120,000. The debt instrument is repayable on 31 December 2011 at a premium of $1,100,000.

What is the total amount of the finance cost associated with the debt instrument? **(3 marks)**

(b) On 1 January 20X3 Deferred issued $600,000 loan notes. Issue costs were $200. The loan notes do not carry interest, but are redeemable at a premium of $152,389 on 31 December 20X4. The effective finance cost of the loan notes is 12%.

What is the finance cost in respect of the loan notes for the year ended 31 December 20X4? **(3 marks)**

(c)   On 1 January 20X1, EFG issued 10,000 5% convertible bonds at their par value of $50 each. The bonds will be redeemed on 1 January 20X6. Each bond is convertible to equity shares at the option of the holder at any time during the five year period. Interest on the bond will be paid annually in arrears.

The prevailing market interest rate for similar debt without conversion options at the date of issue was 6%.

The discount factors for 6% at year 5 is 0.747.

The cumulative discount factor for years 1-5 at 6% is 4.212.

At what value should the equity element of the hybrid financial instrument be recognised in the financial statements at EFG at the date of issue?   **(4 marks)**

(Total = 10 marks)

22 Lis   18 mins

On 1 January 20X3 Lis Co entered into a lease agreement to rent an asset for a 6 year period, at which point it will be returned to the lessor and scrapped, with annual payments of $18,420 made in advance. The market price of the asset on the same date was $86,000. The present value of minimum lease payments amounts to $84,000, discounted at the implicit interest rate shown in the lease agreement of 12.5%.

Lis Co expects to sell goods produced by the asset during the first 5 years of the lease term, but has leased the asset for 6 years as this is the requirement of the lessor, and in case this expectation changes.

Required

Explain how the above lease would be accounted for the year ending 31 December 20X3 including producing relevant extracts from the statement of comprehensive income and statement of financial position.

You are not required to prepare the notes to the financial statements.   **(10 marks)**

23 Carpati

The following information relates to Carpati Co:

(1)   The net book value of plant and equipment at 30 September 20X6 is $1,185,000.
(2)   The tax written down value of plant and equipment at 1 October 20X5 was $405,000.
(3)   During the year ended 30 September 20X6, the company bought plant and equipment of $290,000, which is eligible for tax depreciation.
(4)   Carpati Co bought its freehold property in 20W5 for $600,000. It was revalued in the 20X6 accounts to $1,500,000. Ignore depreciation on buildings. No tax allowances were available to Carpati Co on the buildings.

Required

Draft the note for the statement of financial position at 30 September 20X6 omitting comparatives, in respect of deferred tax.

Work to the nearest $'000. Assume a current income tax rate of 30%. Tax depreciation is at 25% on a reducing balance basis. The income tax rate enacted for 20X7 is 28%.

24 Pilum

18 mins

A statement showing the retained profit of Pilum Co for the year ended 31 December 20X4 is set out below:

	$	$
Profit before tax		2,530,000
Less: income tax expense		(1,127,000)
		1,403,000
Transfer to reserves		(230,000)
Dividends:		
Paid preference interim dividend	138,000	
Paid ordinary interim divided	184,000	
Declared preference final dividend	138,000	
Declared ordinary final dividend	230,000	
		(690,000)
Retained		483,000

On 1 January 20X4 the issued share capital of Pilum Co was 4,600,000 6% preference shares of $1 each and 4,120,000 ordinary shares of $1 each.

Required

Calculate the earnings per share (on basic and diluted basis) in respect of the year ended 31 December 20X4 for each of the following circumstances. (Each of the three circumstances (a) to (c) is to be dealt with separately):

(a) On the basis that there was no change in the issued share capital of the company during the year ended 31 December 20X4.

(b) On the basis that the company made a rights issue of $1 ordinary shares on 1 October 20X4 in the proportion of 1 for every 5 shares held, at a price of $1.20. The market price for the shares at close of trade on the last day of quotation cum rights was $1.78 per share.

(c) On the basis that the company made no new issue of shares during the year ended 31 December 20X4 but on that date it had in issue $1,500,000 10% convertible loan stock 20X8 – 20Y1. This loan stock will be convertible into ordinary $1 shares as follows:

20X8 90 $1 shares for $100 nominal value loan stock
20X9 85 $1 shares for $100 nominal value loan stock
20Y0 80 $1 shares for $100 nominal value loan stock
20Y1 75 $1 shares for $100 nominal value loan stock

Assume where appropriate that the income tax rate is 30%.   **(10 marks)**

25 Biggerbuys

45 mins

Biggerbuys has carried on business for a number of years as a retailer of a wide variety of consumer products. The entity operates from a number of stores around the country. In recent years the entity has found it necessary to provide credit facilities to its customers in order to maintain growth in revenue. As a result of this decision the liability to its bankers has increased substantially. The statutory financial statements for the year ended 30 June 20X9 have recently been published and extracts are provided below, together with comparative figures for the previous two years.

INCOME STATEMENTS FOR THE YEARS ENDED 30 JUNE

	20X7	20X8	20X9
	$m	$m	$m
Revenue	1,850	2,200	2,500
Cost of sales	(1,250)	(1,500)	(1,750)
Gross profit	600	700	750
Other operating costs	(550)	(640)	(700)
Operating profit	50	60	50
Interest from credit sales	45	60	90
Interest payable	(25)	(60)	(110)
Profit before taxation	70	60	30
Tax payable	(23)	(20)	(10)
Profit for the year	47	40	20

STATEMENTS OF FINANCIAL POSITION AT 30 JUNE

	20X7	20X8	20X9
	$m	$m	$m
Property, plant and equipment	278	290	322
Inventories	400	540	620
Trade receivables	492	550	633
Cash	12	12	15
	1,182	1,392	1,590
Share capital	90	90	90
Reserves	282	292	282
	372	382	372
Bank loans	320	520	610
Other interest bearing borrowings	200	200	320
Trade payables	270	270	280
Tax payable	20	20	8
	1,182	1,392	1,590

Other information

(1) Depreciation charged for the three years in question was as follows.

Year ended 30 June	20X7	20X8	20X9
	$m	$m	$m
	55	60	70

(2) The other interest bearing borrowings are secured by a floating charge over the assets of Biggerbuys. Their repayment is due on 30 June 20Y9.

(3) Dividends of $30m were paid in 20X7 and 20X8. A dividend of $20m has been proposed.

(4) The bank loans are unsecured. The maximum lending facility the bank will provide is $630m.

(5) Over the past three years the level of credit sales has been:

Year ended 30 June	20X7	20X8	20X9
	$m	$m	$m
	300	400	600

The entity offers extended credit terms for certain products to maintain market share in a highly competitive environment.

Given the steady increase in the level of bank loans which has taken place in recent years, the entity has recently written to its bankers to request an increase in the lending facility. The request was received by the bank on 15 October 20X9, two weeks after the financial statements were published. The bank is concerned at the steep escalation in the level of the loans and has asked for a report on the financial performance of Biggerbuys for the last three years.

Required

As a consultant management accountant employed by the bankers of Biggerbuys, prepare a report to the bank which analyses the financial performance of the company for the period covered by the financial statements. Your report may take any form you wish, but you are aware of the particular concern of the bank regarding the rapidly increasing level of lending. Therefore it may be appropriate to include aspects of prior performance that could have contributed to the increase in the level of bank lending. (25 marks)

26 Webster
45 mins

(Adapted from past ACCA exam paper 2.5 Pilot paper)

Webster is a publicly listed diversified holding company that is looking to acquire a suitable engineering company. Two private limited engineering companies, Cole and Darwin, are available for sale. The summarised financial statements for the year to 31 March 20X9 of both companies are as follows.

INCOME STATEMENT

	Cole $'000	Cole $'000	Darwin $'000	Darwin $'000
Sales revenue (note (a))		3,000		4,400
Opening inventory	450		720	
Purchases (note (b))	2,030		3,080	
	2,480		3,800	
Closing inventory	(540)		(850)	
		(1,940)		(2,950)
Gross profit		1,060		1,450
Operating expenses		(480)		(964)
Profit from operations		580		486
Loan note interest		(80)		–
Overdraft interest		–		(10)
Net profit for year		500		476

STATEMENT OF FINANCIAL POSITION

	Cole $'000	Cole $'000	Darwin $'000	Darwin $'000
Non-current assets				
Property, plant and equipment (note (c) and (d))		2,340		3,100
Current assets				
Inventory	540		850	
Accounts receivable	522		750	
Bank	20		–	
		1,082		1,600
Total assets		3,422		4,700
Equity and liabilities				
Equity				
Equity shares of $1 each		1,000		500
Reserves				
Revaluation reserve		–		700
Retained earnings – 1 April 20X8		684		1,912
Profit – year to 31 March 20X9		500		476
		2,184		3,588
Non-current liabilities				
10% Loan note		800		–
Current liabilities				
Accounts payable	438		562	
Overdraft	–		550	
		438		1,112
Total equity and liabilities		3,422		4,700

Webster bases its preliminary assessment of target companies on certain key ratios. These are listed below together with the relevant figures for Cole and Darwin calculated from the above financial statements:

	Cole		Darwin	
Return on capital employed	(500+80)/(2,184+800)		(476/3,588)	
	×100	19·4 %	× 100	13·3 %
Asset turnover	(3,000/2,984)	1·01 times	(4,400/3,588)	1·23 times
Gross profit margin		35·3 %		33·0 %
Net profit margin		16·7 %		10·8 %
Accounts receivable collection period		64 days		62 days
Accounts payable payment period		79 days		67 days

Note. Capital employed is defined as shareholders' funds plus non-current debt at the year end; asset turnover is sales revenues divided by gross assets less current liabilities.

The following additional information has been obtained.

(a)   Cole is part of the Velox Group. On 1 March 20X9 it was permitted by its holding company to sell goods at a price of $500,000 to Brander, a fellow subsidiary. The sale gave Cole a gross profit margin of 40% instead of its normal gross margin of only 20% on these types of goods. In addition Brander was instructed to pay for the goods immediately. Cole normally allows three months credit.

(b)   On 1 January 20X9 Cole purchased $275,000 (cost price to Cole) of its materials from Advent, another member of the Velox Group. Advent was also instructed by Velox to depart from its normal trading terms, which would have resulted in a charge of $300,000 to Cole for these goods. The Group's finance director also authorised a four-month credit period on this sale. Cole normally receives two months credit from its suppliers. Cole had sold all of these goods at the year-end.

(c)   Non-current assets:

Details relating to the two companies' non-current assets are:

	Cost/revaluation	Depreciation	Book value
	$'000	$'000	$'000
Cole: property	3,000	1,860	1,140
plant	6,000	4,800	1,200
			2,340
Darwin: property	2,000	100	1,900
plant	3,000	1,800	1,200
			3,100

The two companies own very similar properties. Darwin's property was revalued to $2,000,000 at the beginning of the current year (ie 1 April 20X8). On this date Cole's property, which is carried at cost less depreciation, had a book value of $1,200,000. Its current value (on the same basis as Darwin's property) was also $2,000,000. On this date (1 April 20X8) both properties had the same remaining life of 20 years.

(d)   Darwin purchased new plant costing $600,000 in February 20X9. In line with company policy a full year's depreciation at 20% per annum has been charged on all plant owned at year-end. The equipment is still being tested and will not come on-stream until next year. The purchase of the plant was largely financed by an overdraft facility, which resulted in the interest cost shown in the income statement. Both companies depreciate plant over a five-year life and treat all depreciation as an operating expense.

(e)   The bank overdraft that would have been required but for the favourable treatment towards Cole in respect of items in (a) and (b) above, would have attracted interest of $15,000 in the year to 31 March 20X9.

Required

(a) Restate the financial statements of Cole and Darwin in order that they may be considered comparable for decision making purposes. State any assumptions you make. **(10 marks)**

(b) Recalculate the key ratios used by Webster and, referring to any other relevant points, comment on how the revised ratios may affect the assessment of the two companies. **(10 marks)**

(c) Discuss whether the information in notes (a) to (d) above would be publicly available, and if so, describe its source(s). **(5 marks)**

(Total = 25 marks)

27 Dundee

25 mins

The summarised accounts of Dundee Co for the year ended 31 March 20X7 are as follows:

Statements of financial position at 31 March

	20X7 $m	20X6 $m
Non-current assets		
Property, plant and equipment	4,200	3,700
Current assets		
Inventories	1,500	1,600
Trade receivables	2,200	1,800
	3,700	3,400
	7,900	7,100
Equity		
Share capital	1,200	1,200
Retained earnings	2,200	1,900
	3,400	3,100
Non-current liabilities		
Deferred tax	1,070	850
Finance lease liabilities	1,300	1,200
	2,370	2,050
Current liabilities		
Trade payables	1,250	1,090
Current tax	225	205
Finance lease liabilities	500	450
Bank overdraft	155	205
	2,130	1,950
	7,900	7,100

Statement of comprehensive income for the year ended 31 March 20X7

	$m
Revenue	4,300
Cost of sales	(2,000)
Gross profit	2,300
Operating expenses	(1,000)
Finance costs	(250)
Profit before tax	1,050
Income tax expense	(450)
PROFIT/TOTAL COMPREHENSIVE INCOME FOR THE YEAR	600
Dividends paid in the period	300

Notes

(1) Depreciation charged for the year totalled $970 million. There were no disposals of property, plant and equipment in the period.

(2) There was no accrual of interest at the beginning or at the end of the year.

(3) Dundee Co finances a number (but not all) of its property, plant and equipment purchases using finance leases. In the period, property, plant and equipment which would have cost $600 million to purchase outright was acquired under finance leases.

Required

Prepare the statement of cash flows for Dundee Co for the year ended 31 March 20X7 as per IAS 7 using the indirect method. **(14 marks)**

28 Elmgrove   45 mins

As financial accountant for Elmgrove, you are responsible for the preparation of a statement of cash flows for the year ended 31 March 20X9.

The following information is available.

ELMGROVE
STATEMENT OF FINANCIAL POSITION AS AT 31 MARCH 20X9

	20X9 $m	20X8 $m
Non-current assets		
Property, plant and equipment	327	264
Current assets		
Inventories	123	176
Trade receivables	95	87
Short term investments	65	30
Cash at bank and in hand	29	–
	312	293
	639	557
Equity		
Share capital – $1 shares	200	120
Share premium	30	–
Revaluation surplus	66	97
Retained earnings	71	41
	367	258
Non-current liabilities		
10% Debentures	100	150
Current liabilities	172	149
	639	557

ELMGROVE
INCOME STATEMENT FOR THE YEAR ENDED 31 MARCH 20X9

	$m
Revenue	473
Cost of sales	(229)
Gross profit	244
Distribution costs	(76)
Administrative expenses	(48)
Finance income	6
Finance costs	(17)
Profit before tax	109
Income tax expense	(47)
Profit for the year	62
Dividends paid in the period	32

The following notes are also relevant.

1   *Property, plant and equipment*

Property, plant and equipment held by Elmgrove are items of plant and equipment and freehold premises. During 20X9 items of plant and equipment which originally cost $40m were disposed of, resulting in a loss of $6m. These items have a net book value of $28m at the date of disposal.

2   *Short term investments*

The short-term investments meet the definition of cash equivalents per IAS 7 *Statement of cash flows.*

3   *Current liabilities*

Current liabilities consist of the following.

	20X9	20X8
	$m	$m
Bank overdraft	–	22
Trade payables	126	70
Interest payable	7	3
Income tax payable	39	54
	172	149

4   *10% debentures*

On 1 August 20X8 $50m of 10% debentures was converted into $50m of $1 ordinary shares.

5   *Depreciation*

The depreciation charge for the year, included in the income statement, was $43m.

Required

(a)   Using the information provided, prepare a statement of cash flows for Elmgrove for the year ended 31 March 20X9 using the indirect method.   **(20 marks)**

(b)   Write a memorandum to a director of Elmgrove summarising the major benefits a user receives from a published statement of cash flows.   **(5 marks)**

(Total = 25 marks)

29 CPP and CCA

27 mins

(a) 'It is important that management and other users of financial accounts should be in a position to appreciate the effects of inflation on the business with which they are concerned.'

Required

Consider the above statement and explain how inflation obscures the meaning of accounts prepared by the traditional historical cost convention, and discuss the contribution which CPP accounting could make to providing a more satisfactory system of accounting for inflation.

(b) Compare the general principles underlying CPP and CCA accounting.

(c) Define the term 'realised holding gain'.

(15 marks)

1 Conceptual framework

(a) The **going concern assumption** is that an entity will continue in operational existence for the foreseeable future. This means that the financial statements of an entity are prepared on the assumption that the entity will **continue** trading. If this were not the case, various adjustments would have to be made to the accounts: provisions for losses; revaluation of assets to their possible market value; all non-current assets and liabilities would be reclassified as current; and so forth.

Unless it can be assumed that the business is a going concern, other accounting assumptions cannot apply.

For example, it is meaningless to speak of consistency from one accounting period to the next when this is the final accounting period.

The **accruals basis** of accounting states that items are recognised as assets, liabilities, equity, income and expenses when they satisfy the definitions and recognition criteria in the *Framework*. The effect of this is that revenue and expenses which are related to each other are matched, so as to be dealt with in the same accounting period, without regard to when the cash is actually paid or received. This is particularly relevant to the purchase of non-current assets. The cost of a non-current asset is spread over the accounting periods expected to benefit from it, thus matching costs and revenues. In the absence of the going concern convention, this cannot happen, as an example will illustrate.

Suppose a company has a machine which cost $10,000 two years ago and now has a net book value of $6,000. The machine can be used for another three years, but as it is highly specialised, there is no possibility of selling it, and so it has no market value.

If the going concern assumption applies, the machine will be shown at **cost less depreciation** in the accounts (ie $6,000), as it still has a part to play in the continued life of the entity. However, if the assumption cannot be applied, the machine will be given a nil value and other assets and liabilities will be similarly revalued on the basis of winding down the company's operations.

(b) One of the ideas behind the *Framework* is to **avoid the fire-fighting approach**, which has characterised the development of accounting standards in the past, and instead develop an underlying philosophy as a basis for consistent accounting principles so that each standard fits into the whole framework. Research began from an analysis of the fundamental objectives of accounting and their relationship to the information needs of accounts users. The *Framework* has gone behind the requirements of existing accounting standards, which define accounting treatments for particular assets, liabilities, income and expenditure, to define the nature of assets, liabilities, income and expenditure.

2 Regulators

Tutorial note. It is best to use headings to divide up your answer, as we do here.

Stock Exchange

A quoted company is a company whose shares are bought and sold on a stock exchange. This involves the signing of an agreement which requires compliance with the rules of that stock exchange. This would normally contain amongst other things the stock exchange's detailed rules on the information to be disclosed in quoted companies' accounts. This, then, is one regulatory influence on a quoted company's accounts. The stock exchange may enforce compliance by monitoring accounts and reserving the right to withdraw a company's shares from the stock exchange: ie the company's shares would no longer be traded through the stock exchange. In many countries there is, however, no statutory requirement to obey these rules.

Local legislation

In most countries, companies have to comply with the local companies legislation, which lays down detailed requirements on the preparation of accounts. Company law is often quite detailed, partly because of external influences such as EU Directives. Another reason to increase statutory regulation is that quoted companies are under great pressure to show profit growth and an obvious way to achieve this is to manipulate accounting policies. If this involves breaking the law, as opposed to ignoring professional guidance, company directors may think twice before bending the rules – or, at least, this is often a government's hope.

Standard-setters

Professional guidance is given by the national and international standard-setters. Prescriptive guidance is given in accounting standards which must be applied in all accounts intended to show a 'true and fair view' or 'present fairly in all material respects'. International Financial Reporting Standards and national standards are issued after extensive consultation and are revised as required to reflect economic or legal changes. In some countries, legislation requires details of non-compliance to be disclosed in the accounts. 'Defective' accounts can be revised under court order if necessary and directors signing such accounts can be prosecuted and fined (or even imprisoned).

The potential for the IASB's influence in this area is substantial. It must pursue excellence in standards with absolute rigour to fulfil that potential.

3 Standard setters

(a)   The users of financial information – creditors, management, employees, business contacts, financial specialists, government and the general public – are entitled to information about a business entity to a greater or lesser degree. However, the needs and expectations of these groups will vary.

The preparers of the financial information often find themselves in the position of having to reconcile the interests of different groups in the best way for the business entity. For example whilst shareholders are looking for increased profits to support higher dividends, employees will expect higher wage increases; and yet higher profits without corresponding higher tax allowances (increased capital allowances for example) will result in a larger tax bill.

Without accounting standards to prescribe how certain transactions should be treated, preparers would be tempted to produce financial information which meets the expectations of the favoured user group. For example creative accounting methods, such as off balance sheet finance could be used to enhance a company's statement of financial position to make it more attractive to investors/lenders.

The aim of accounting standards is that they should regulate financial information in order that it shows the following characteristics.

(i)   Relevance
(ii)   Reliability
(iii)   Understandability
(iv)   Comparability

(b)   A number of reasons could be advanced why the financial statements of not-for-profit entities should not be subject to regulation.

- They do not have shares that are being traded, so their financial statements are not produced with a share price in mind.
- They do not have chief executives with share options seeking to present favourable figures to the market.
- They are not seeking to make a profit, so whether they have or not is perhaps irrelevant.
- They are perceived to be on slightly higher moral ground than profit-making entities, so are less in need of regulation.

However a closer look at this brings up the following points.

- Charities may not be invested in by the general public, but they are funded by the public, often through direct debits.

- Charities are big business. In addition to regular public donations they receive large donations from high-profile backers.

- They employ staff and executives at market rates and have heavy administrative costs. Supporters are entitled to know how much of their donation has gone on administration.

- Any misappropriation of funds is serious in two ways. It is taking money from the donating public, who thought they were donating to a good cause, and it is diverting resources from the people who should have been helped.

- Not all charities are *bona fide*. For instance, some are thought to be connected to terrorism.

For these reasons, it is important that the financial statements of not-for-profit entities are subject to regulation.

4 Polymer

POLYMER CO: INCOME STATEMENT FOR THE YEAR ENDED 31 MAY 20X8

	$
Revenue	1,526,750
Cost of sales (W3)	(1,048,000)
Gross profit	478,750
Distribution costs (W4)	(124,300)
Administrative expenses (W5)	(216,200)
Finance costs (W6)	(18,400)
Profit before tax	119,850
Income tax expense	(40,000)
PROFIT FOR THE YEAR	79,850

POLYMER CO: STATEMENT OF FINANCIAL POSITION AS AT 31 MAY 20X8

	$
ASSETS	
Non-current assets	
Property, plant and equipment (W7)	452,250
Intangible assets	215,500
	667,750
Current assets	
Inventories (W8)	425,750
Receivables (W9)	171,880
Cash and cash equivalents	5,120
	602,750
Total assets	1,270,500
EQUITY AND LIABILITIES	
Equity	
Share capital	300,000
Share premium reserve	100,000
Retained earnings (283,500 + 79,850)	363,350
General reserve	50,000
Revaluation surplus	50,000
	863,350
Non-current liabilities	
10% debentures	100,000
8.4% cumulative preference shares	100,000
	200,000

		$
Current liabilities		
Trade and other payables (W10)		115,900
Short-term borrowings		51,250
Current tax payable		40,000
		207,150
Total equity and liabilities		1,270,500

Workings

1 Depreciation

Cost of sales:	8% × 150,000	12,000
Administration	10% × 50,000	5,000
:	1/4 × 20% × 50,000	2,500
		7,500
Distribution:	3/4 × 20% × 50,000	7,500

2 *Depreciation (amortisation) of lease*
$75,000 × 1/50   1,500

3 *Cost of sales*

	$
Opening inventories (108,400 + 32,750 + 184,500)	325,650
Purchases	750,600
Carriage inwards	10,500
Manufacturing wages	250,000
Manufacturing overheads	125,000
Depreciation of plant (W1)	12,000
Closing inventories (W9)	(425,750)
	1,048,000

4 *Distribution costs*

	$
Per question	116,800
Depreciation (W1)	7,500
	124,300

5 *Administrative expenses*

		$
Per question		158,100
Legal expenses	54,100	
less: solicitors' fees capitalised	(5,000)	
		49,100
Depreciation (W1)		7,500
Amortisation of lease (W2)		1,500
		216,200

6 *Finance costs*

	$
Interest expense on loan notes ($100,000 × 10%)	10,000
Preference dividend	8,400
	18,400

7 Property, plant and equipment

	Freehold land	Leasehold property	Plant & equipment	Furniture & fixtures	Motor vehicles	Total
	$	$	$	$	$	$
NBV per TB						
Cost or valuation	250,000	75,000	150,000	50,000	75,000	
Accumulated dep'n	–	(15,000)	(68,500)	(15,750)	(25,000)	
Net book value	250,000	60,000	81,500	34,250	50,000	
Solicitor's fees	5,000					
Depreciation charge	–	(1,500)	(12,000)	(5,000)	(10,000)	
NBV 31 May 20X8	255,000	58,500	69,500	29,250	40,000	452,250

8 Inventories

	$
Raw materials	112,600
Work in progress	37,800
Finished goods	275,350
	425,750

9 Receivables

	$
Trade receivables (177,630 – 5,750 allowance for receivables)	171,880

10 Trade and other payables

	$
Trade payables	97,500
Loan interest payable	10,000
Preference dividend payable	8,400
	115,900

5 Winger

Tutorial note. As with consolidated accounts questions, a question on the preparation of a single company's accounts needs a methodical approach. Lay out proformas and fill the numbers in gradually by systematically working through the question. Points are as follows

(a) Exclude 'sale or return' goods from both sales and cost of sales.

(b) The profit on sale of property needs to be correctly accounted for.

(c) Exclude from the finance lease interest charge the $20m down payment – interest does not accrue on this.

(d) When calculating the lease payable, you need to accrue one year's interest but no more. You know that $20m is due within one year, so the non-current liability is the balance of the total amount due.

(a) WINGER
INCOME STATEMENT FOR THE
YEAR ENDED 31 MARCH 20X1

	$'000
Sales revenues (358,450 – 27,000)	331,450
Cost of sales (W1)	(208,550)
Gross profit	122,900
Distribution expenses	(28,700)
Administration expenses	(15,000)
Profit on disposal of land and buildings (95,000 – 80,000)	15,000
Loss on abandonment of research project	(30,000)
Finance cost (W3)	(11,200)
Profit before tax	53,000
Income tax (15,000 – 2,200)	(12,800)
Profit for the year	40,200

(b) STATEMENT OF FINANCIAL POSITION
AS AT 31 MARCH 20X1

	$'000	$'000
Assets		
Tangible non current assets		
Property (200,000 – 6,000 (W2))		194,000
Plant and equipment (W4)		160,000
		354,000
Current assets		
Inventories (28,240 + 22,500 (W1))	50,740	
Accounts receivable (55,000 – 27,000 (W1))	28,000	
Cash	10,660	
		89,400
Total assets		443,400
Equity and liabilities		
Equity		
Equity shares 25c each		150,000
Retained earnings (W5)		129,800
		279,800
Non-current liabilities		
Leasing obligations (W6)	47,200	
8% loan notes	50,000	
		97,200
Current liabilities		
Trade and other accounts payable (W7)	51,400	
Income tax payable	15,000	
		66,400
Total equity and liabilities		443,400

Workings

1	*Cost of sales*	$'000
	Per question	185,050
	Less sale/return goods (27,000 × 100/120)	(22,500)
	Add depreciation (W2)	46,000
		208,550

2	Depreciation	$'000
	Building (100,000 ÷ 50)	2,000
	Heating system (20,000 ÷ 10)	2,000
	Lifts (30,000 ÷ 15)	2,000
		6,000
	Leased plant (80,000 × 20%)	16,000
	Owned plant (154,800 − 34,800) × 20%	24,000
		46,000

3	Finance cost	$'000
	Loan note interest (50,000 × 8%)	4,000
	Finance lease (80,000 − 20,000) × 12%	7,200
		11,200

4	Plant and equipment	$'000
	Cost: owned plant	154,800
	leased plant	80,000
		234,800
	Depreciation: owned plant (34,800 + 24,000 (W2))	(58,800)
	Leased plant (80,000 × 20%)	(16,000)
		160,000

5	Retained earnings	$'000
	Balance b/f	71,600
	Profit for the year	40,200
	Profit on disposal of property (45,000 − 15,000)	30,000
	Dividend paid	(12,000)
		129,800

6	Leasing obligations	$'000
	Total payments due	80,000
	Less amount paid	(20,000)
		60,000
	Add accrued interest (60,000 × 12%)	7,200
	Total creditor	67,200
	Due within one year	20,000
	Due after one year	47,200

7	Trade and other payables	$'000
	Trial balance	29,400
	Lease creditor (W6)	20,000
	Accrued loan note interest	2,000
		51,400

(c) Companies often used to justify the non-depreciation of buildings on several grounds, including:

(i)   That the current value of the buildings was **higher than cost**.

(ii)   That the level of **maintenance** meant that no deterioration or consumption had taken place.

(iii) That the depreciation charge would **not be material.**

However, IAS 16 requires the **depreciable amount** of an asset to be charged against profit over its useful life. That depreciable amount is obtained by comparing the cost of the asset with its **estimated residual value** at the end of its useful economic life. By requiring the residual value to be estimated at **current prices**, the standard removes any **potential inflationary effects** which would otherwise increase the residual value and hence reduce, even to zero, the depreciable amount. This overcomes the argument that high residual values remove the need for depreciation, unless the value of a second-hand asset has greater value than the same asset new – an unlikely proposition.

The argument regarding **immateriality** of the depreciation charge because of a long economic life may have some validity. Although it is not addressed directly by IAS 16, accounting standards generally only apply to **material items,** according to the *Framework*. However, under this principle, it will be necessary to consider not only each year's potential depreciation charge, but also the **accumulated depreciation** that would need to be provided against the asset. Over time, this latter amount would inevitably become material and the 'long life' argument would cease to hold.

Thus, Winger's **previous policy** was not appropriate and the change to depreciate assets was necessary to comply with IAS 16.

The directors' proposed treatment of the deferred development expenditure is also incorrect. It needs to be written off because its **value** has become **impaired due to adverse legislation, not a change of accounting policy**. It now has no effective value. There has therefore not been a change of accounting policy, so it cannot be treated as a prior period adjustment. It must be written off to the income statement.

6 Hewlett (Study text Question 6)

HEWLETT CO
STATEMENT OF COMPREHENSIVE INCOME FOR THE YEAR ENDED 31 DECEMBER 20X2

	$'m
Revenue	2,648
Cost of sales (W1)	(1,765)
Gross profit	883
Distribution costs (W1)	(514)
Administrative expenses (W1)	(363)
Finance costs (4% × 150)	(6)
Fair value gain on investment properties (586 – 548)	38
Rental income	48
Profit before tax	86
Income tax expense (note iv)	(27)
PROFIT FOR THE YEAR	59
Other comprehensive income:	
Gain on property revaluation	484
TOTAL COMPREHENSIVE INCOME FOR THE YEAR	543

STATEMENT OF FINANCIAL POSITION AS AT 31 DECEMBER 20X2

	$'m
ASSETS	
Non-current assets	
Property, plant and equipment (W2)	874
Investment properties (note x)	586
	1,460
Current assets	
Inventories (388 – (15 – 8))	381
Trade receivables	545
Cash and cash equivalents	28
	954
	2,414
EQUITY AND LIABILITIES	
Equity	
Share capital	125
Share premium	244
Retained earnings	413
General reserve	545
Revaluation surplus	473
	1,800

Non-current liabilities

4% loan notes 20X8	150

Current liabilities

Trade payables	434
Income tax payable (note v)	27
Interest payable ((4% × 150) – 3)	3
	464
	2,414

STATEMENT OF CHANGES IN EQUITY FOR THE YEAR ENDED 31 DECEMBER 20X2

	Share capital	Share premium	Retained earnings	General reserve	Revaluation surplus	Total
	$'m	$'m	$'m	$'m	$'m	$'m
Balance at 1 January 20X2	100	244	349	570	–	1,263
Changes in equity for 20X2						
Issue of share capital (W4)	25			(25)		–
Dividends (W5)			(6)			(6)
Total comprehensive income for the year			59		484	543
Transfer to retained earnings (W2)			11		(11)	–
Balance at 31 December 20X2	125	244	413	545	473	1,800

*   The initial application of a policy to revalue assets under IAS 16 is a change in accounting policy dealt with as a revaluation in accordance with IAS 16, rather than IAS 8 (which would require restatement of the opening figures).

Workings

1   *Expenses*

	Cost of sales	Distribution	Admin
	$'m	$'m	$'m
Per TB	1,669	514	345
Opening inventories	444		
Depreciation of buildings (W2)			18
Depreciation of plant and equipment (W2)	24		
Impairment loss on plant (W3)	4		
Loss on sale of equipment (12 – 7)	5		
Closing inventories (388 – (15 – 8))	(381)		
	1,765	514	363

2   *Property, plant and equipment*

	Land	Buildings	Plant & equipment	Total
	$'m	$'m	$'m	$'m
Cost	60	320	258	
Accumulated depreciation	–	(64)	(126)	
NBV b/d at 1 January 20X2	60	256	132	
Change in accounting policy (bal)	40	444		484
	100	700	132	
Disposal of equipment (15 – 3)			(12)	
	100	700	120	
Depreciation during year				
Buildings ($700m/(50 – 10))	–	(18)		
Plant & equipment ($120m × 20%)			(24)	
Impairment loss on plant (W3)			(4)	
NBV c/d at 31 December 20X2	100	682	92	874

		$'m
Realisation of revaluation surplus on buildings:		
Surplus		444
Realised over remaining 40 years (444/40):		11

3 *Impairment loss on plant*

	$'m
Carrying value	22
Recoverable amount (Value in use: (3.8m × 3.993) + (4.2m × 0.677))	(18)
	(4)

Recoverable amount is the higher of value in use ($18m) and fair value less costs to sell ($16m).

4 *Bonus issue*

DR General reserve ($100m /$0.50 × 1/4 = 50m shares × $0.50)	$25m
CR Share capital	$25m

5 *Dividends (proof)*

	$'m
Interim ($100m /$0.50 = 200m shares × $0.03)	6 per trial balance

The final dividend has not been paid and is not a liability of the company at the year end.

7 Gains

Gains Co – Statement of changes in equity for the year ended 31 December 20X9

	Share capital $'000	Share premium $'000	Retained earnings $'000	Revaluation surplus $'000	Total $'000
Balance at 1 January 20X9	2,800	1,150	2,120	750	6,820
Change in accounting policy			40	(40)	–
Restated balance	2,800	1,150	2,160	710	6,820
Changes in equity for 20X9					
Issue of share capital	600	(40)	–	–	560
Dividends			(200)		(200)
Total comprehensive income for the year (686 – (W1) 50)	–	–	636	–	636
Transfer to retained earnings (W2)			35	(35)	–
Balance at 31 December 20X9	3,400	1,110	2,631	675	7,816

Workings

1 Loss on investment property (160 – 110)   (50)

2 *Calculation of profit realised on sale of revalued asset*

	$
Revaluation recognised in past	50,000
Less: amounts transferred to retained earnings:	
(80,000/10 – 30,000/10) × 3	(15,000)
	35,000

8 Multiplex

> **Tutorial note**. Impairment is a difficult subject, so make sure you understand where you went wrong – if at all!

The impairment losses are allocated as required by IAS 36 *Impairment of assets*.

	Asset @ 1.1.20X0 $'000	1st loss (W1) $'000	Assets @ 1.2.20X0 $'000	2nd loss (W2) $'000	Revised asset $'000
Goodwill	200	(200)	–	–	–
Operating licence	1,200	(200)	1,000	(100)	900
Property: stations/land	300	(50)	250	(50)	200
Rail track/coaches	300	(50)	250	(50)	200
Steam engines	1,000	(500)	500	–	500
	3,000	(1,000)	2,000	(200)	1,800

Workings

1   *First impairment loss*

$500,000 relates directly to an engine and its recoverable amount can be assessed directly (ie zero) and it is no longer part of the cash generating unit.

IAS 36 then requires goodwill to be written off. Any further impairment must be written off the remaining assets pro rata, except the engine which must not be reduced below its net selling price of $500,000.

2   *Second impairment loss*

The first $100,000 of the impairment loss is applied to the operating licence to write it down to net selling price.

The remainder is applied pro rata to assets carried at other than their net selling prices, ie $50,000 to both the property and the rail track and coaches.

9 Barcelona and Madrid

CONSOLIDATED STATEMENT OF FINANCIAL POSITION AS AT 30 SEPTEMBER 20X6

	$m
Non-current assets	
Property, plant & equipment (2,848 + 354)	3,202
Patents	45
Goodwill (W2)	43
	3,290
Current assets	
Inventories (895 + 225)	1,120
Trade and other receivables (1,348 + 251)	1,599
Cash and cash equivalents (212 + 34)	246
	2,965
	6,255
Equity attributable to owners of the parent	
Share capital	920
General reserve (W4)	796
Retained earnings (W3)	2,243
	3,959
Non-controlling interest (490 × 40%)	196
	4,155

Non-current liabilities	
Long-term borrowings (558 + 168)	726
Current liabilities	
Trade and other payables (1,168 + 183)	1,351
Current portion of long-term borrowings	23
	1,374
	6,255

Workings

1　*Group structure*

　　　　Barcelona
　　　　　|　　　　60% (30.6.X2)
　　　　Madrid

2　*Goodwill*

	$m	$m
Consideration transferred (250m × 50% × $1.06)		159
Non-controlling interest at acquisition (165 × 40%)		66
Net assets at acquisition:		
Share capital	50	
General reserve	11	
Retained earnings	104	
		(165)
Goodwill at acquisition		60
Impairment losses to date		(17)
Goodwill at end of reporting period		43

Goodwill – alternative working

	$m	$m
Consideration transferred		159
Net assets at acquisition (as above)	165	
Group share 60%		(99)
Goodwill at acquisition		60
Impairment		17
Goodwill at end of reporting period		43

3　*Retained earnings*

	Barcelona $m	Madrid $m
Per question	2,086	394
Pre-acquisition	–	(104)
	2,086	290
Madrid – share of post acquisition earnings (290 × 60%)	174	
Less: goodwill impairment losses to date	(17)	
	2,243	

4　*General reserve*

	Barcelona $m	Madrid $m
Per question	775	46
Pre-acquisition	–	(11)
	775	35
Madrid – share of post acquisition general reserve (35 × 60%)	21	
	796	

10 Reprise

REPRISE GROUP CONSOLIDATED STATEMENT OF FINANCIAL POSITION AS AT 31 MARCH 20X4

	$'000
Non-current assets	
Land and buildings	3,350
Plant and equipment (1,010 + 2,210)	3,220
Motor vehicles (510 + 345)	855
Goodwill (W4)	826
	8,251
Current assets	
Inventories (890 + 352 – (W2) 7.2)	1,234.8
Trade receivables (1,372 + 514 – 39 – (W3) 36)	1,811
Cash and cash equivalents (89 + 39 + 51)	179
	3,224.8
	11,475.8
Equity attributable to owners of the parent	
Share capital	1,000
Revaluation surplus	2,500
Retained earnings (W7)	5,257.3
	8,757.3
Non-controlling interest (W6)	896.5
	9,653.8
Non-current liabilities	
10% debentures	500
Current liabilities	
Trade payables (996 + 362 – (W3) 36)	1,322
	11,475.8

Workings

1   *Group structure*

R
|
| 75%   ∴ non-controlling interest = 25%
|
E

2   *Unrealised profit on inventories*

Unrealised profit included in inventories is:

$$\$31,200 \times \frac{30}{130} = \$7,200$$

3   *Trade receivables/trade payables*

Intragroup balance of $75,000 is reduced to $36,000 once cash-in-transit of $39,000 is followed through to its ultimate destination.

4   *Goodwill*

	$'000	$'000
Consideration transferred		2,000
Non-controlling interest (125,000 × $4.40)		550
		2,550
Net assets acquired as represented by:		
Share capital	500	
Retained earnings	1,044	
		(1,544)
Goodwill at acquisition		1,006
Impairment losses to date		(180)
Goodwill at end of reporting period		826

Goodwill – alternative working

	$'000	$'000
Consideration transferred		2,000
Net assets acquired	1,544	
Group share 75%		(1,158)
Goodwill attributable to parent		842
Impairment (180 × 75%)		(135)
		707
Goodwill attributable to NCI (W5)		164
Impairment (180 × 25%)		(45)
		119
Total goodwill (707 + 119)		826

5   *Goodwill attributable to non-controlling interest*

	$'000
Non-controlling interest at fair value (W4)	550
Share of net assets at acquisition (1,544 × 25%)	(386)
	164

6   *Non-controlling interest at year end*

	$'000
Share of Encore's net assets at 31 March 20X4	
(3,110 × 25%)	777.5
Goodwill (W5)	164
	941.5
Goodwill impairment (180 × 25%)	(45)
	896.5

Note: Goodwill impairment charged to the NCI is in proportion to the NCI shareholding.

7   *Consolidated retained earnings*

	Reprise	*Encore*
	$'000	$'000
Per question	4,225	2,610
PUP (W2)	(7.2)	
Pre-acquisition retained earnings		(1,044)
	4,217.8	1,566
Encore – share of post acquisition retained earnings		
(1,566 × 75%)	1,174.5	
Less goodwill impairment losses to date (180 × 75%)	(135)	
	5,257.3	

11 War

> **Tutorial note.** This question may look intimidating because it involves an acquisition part of the way through the year, some fair value issues and both the consolidated income statement and statement of financial position. It is, however, fairly straightforward.

(a)   IFRS 3 *Business combinations* states that shares offered as consideration should be valued at fair value, which for listed shares will be market price on the date of acquisition. However, the standard acknowledges that the market price may be difficult to determine if it is unreliable because of an inactive market. In particular, where the shares are not listed, there may be no suitable market. In such cases the value must be estimated using the best methods available. This may involve the use of:

(i)   The value of similar listed securities

(ii)   The present value of the cash flows of the shares

(iii)   Any cash alternative which was offered

(iv)   The value of any underlying security into which there is an option to convert

It may be necessary to undertake a valuation of the company in question should none of the above methods prove feasible.

Direct expenses incurred such as professional fees of lawyers and accountants also form part of the cost of the combination. However, issue costs of equity are treated as a deduction from the proceeds of the equity issue, rather than part of the cost of the combination.

(b)   WAR GROUP
CONSOLIDATED STATEMENT OF FINANCIAL POSITION AS AT 30 JUNE 20X7

	$'000
Assets	
Non-current assets	
Property, plant and equipment (1,750 + 350 + 150)	2,250
Goodwill (W3)	189
	2,439
Current assets	
Inventories	600
Receivables	451
Cash at bank and in hand	299
	1,350
Total assets	3,789
Equity and liabilities	
Ordinary shares of $1 each	750
Share premium (W6)	250
Retained earnings (W5)	659
Non-controlling interest (W4)	255
	1,914
Non-current liabilities	1,225
Current liabilities	650
Total equity and liabilities	3,789

WAR GROUP
CONSOLIDATED INCOME STATEMENT FOR THE YEAR ENDED 30 JUNE 20X7

	$'000
Revenue	3,445
Cost of sales	(1,788)
Gross profit	1,657
Distribution costs	(638)
Administrative expenses (W7)	(310)
Operating profit	709
Interest payable	(75)
Profit before tax	634

Income tax		(306)
Profit for the year		328

Attributable to:

Owners of the parent		317
Non-controlling interest		11
		328

Workings

1   *Fair value adjustment*

	$'000
Peace Co: property, plant and equipment at fair value	500
Carrying value	350
Fair value adjustment	150

> **Top tip.** Before you can work out the goodwill, you need to work out the pre-acquisition element of the dividend, as this will give you the cost of the investment.

2   *Pre-acquisition dividend*

Dividend paid by Peace to War: $42,000

Pre-acquisition element $^{10}/_{12} \times \$42,000 = \$35,000$

3   *Goodwill*

	$'000	$'000
Consideration transferred		800
Less pre-acquisition dividend (W2)		(35)
		765
Non-controlling interest (823 × 30%)		247
Share capital	100	
Share premium	150	
Fair value adjustment (W1)	150	
Retained earnings		
Prior year: 450 – 165 (225 – 60)	285	
Current year: $^{10}/_{12} \times 165$	138	
Total net assets		(823)
Goodwill		189

Goodwill – alternative working

	$'000	$'000
Consideration transferred		765
Total net assets	823	
Group share 70%		(576)
Goodwill		189

4   *Non-controlling interest at year end (statement of financial position)*

	$'000
Peace Co net assets (1,125 – 175 – 250)	700
Fair value adjustment (W1)	150
	850
× 30%	255

5   *Retained earnings*

	War Co	Peace Co
	$'000	$'000
Per statement of financial position	625	450
Pre-acquisition dividend	(35)	
Issue costs	50	
Pre-acquisition profits:		

Prior year (450 – 165 (W3))		(285)
10 months to 1 May 20X7 ((450 – 285)× 10/12)		(138)
		27
Group share of Peace (70% × 27)	19	
Group retained earnings	659	

6   *Share premium account*

	$'000
War Co	300
Less issue costs	(50)
	250

7   *Administrative expenses*

	$'000
War Co	325
Peace Co ($^2/_{12}$ × 210)	35
	360
Less issue costs	(50)
	310

8   *Non-controlling interest (income statement)*

$225,000 × $^2/_{12}$ × 30% = $11,250

12 Fallowfield and Rusholme

CONSOLIDATED INCOME STATEMENT FOR THE YEAR ENDED 30 JUNE 20X8

	$
Revenue (403,400 + 193,000 – 40,000)	556,400
Cost of sales (201,400 + 92,600 – 40,000 + 4,000)	(258,000)
Gross profit	298,400
Distribution costs (16,000 + 14,600)	(30,600)
Administrative expenses (24,250 + 17,800)	(42,050)
Profit before tax	225,750
Income tax expense (61,750 + 22,000)	(83,750)
Profit for the year	142,000
Profit attributable to:	
Owners of the parent	125,200
Non-controlling interest (W2)	16,800
	142,000

STATEMENT OF CHANGES IN EQUITY (EXTRACT)

	Retained earnings
	$
Balance at 1 July 20X7 (W3)	190,000
Dividends	(40,000)
Profit for the year	125,200
Balance at 30 June 20X8 (W4)	275,200

Workings

1   *Group structure*

Fallowfield

60%   3 years ago
Pre-acquisition ret'd earnings: $16,000

Rusholme

2	*Non-controlling interest*	$
	Rusholme – profit for the period	46,000
	Less: PUP (40,000 × ½ × 25/125)	4,000
		42,000
	Non-controlling share 40%	16,800

3   *Retained earnings brought forward*

		Fallowfield $	Rusholme $
	Per question	163,000	61,000
	Pre-acquisition retained earnings	–	(16,000)
		163,000	45,000
	Rusholme – share of post acquisition retained earnings (45,000 × 60%)	27,000	
		190,000	

4   *Retained earnings carried forward*

		Fallowfield $	Rusholme $
	Per question	238,000	82,000
	PUP	–	(4,000)
	Pre-acquisition retained earnings		(16,000)
		238,000	62,000
	Rusholme – share of post acquisition retained earnings (62,000 × 60%)	37,200	
		275,200	

13 Panther Group

PANTHER GROUP

CONSOLIDATED STATEMENT OF COMPREHENSIVE INCOME FOR THE YEAR ENDED 31 DECEMBER 20X4

	$'000
Revenue [22,800 + (4,300 × 6/12) – 320]	24,630
Cost of sales [13,600 + (2,600 × 6/12) – 320 + (W2) 10 + (W4) 5]	(14,595)
Gross profit	10,035
Distribution costs (2,900 + (500 × 6/12))	(3,150)
Administrative expenses (1,800 + (300 × 6/12))	(1,950)
Finance costs [200 + ((70 – (W3) 20) × 6/12)]	(225)
Finance income (50 – (W3) 20)	30
Profit before tax	4,740
Income tax expense [1,300 + (220 × 6/12)]	(1,410)
PROFIT FOR THE YEAR	3,330
Other comprehensive income for the year, net of tax [1,600 + (180 × 6/12)]	1,690
TOTAL COMPREHENSIVE INCOME FOR THE YEAR	5,020

Profit attributable to:	
Owners of the parent (3,330 – 112)	3,218
Non-controlling interest (W5)	112
	3,330

Total comprehensive income attributable to:	
Owners of the parent (5,020 – 148)	4,872
Non-controlling interest (W5)	148
	5,020

CONSOLIDATED STATEMENT OF CHANGES IN EQUITY FOR THE YEAR ENDED 31 DECEMBER 20X4 (EXTRACT)

	$'000 Reserves
Balance at 1 January 20X4 (Panther only)	12,750
Dividend paid	(900)
Total comprehensive income for the year	4,872
Balance at 31 December 20X4 (W6)	16,722

Workings

1 *Timeline*

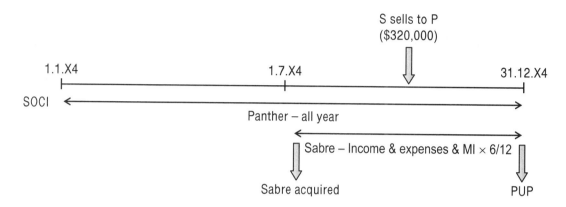

2 *Unrealised profit on intragroup trading*

$$\text{Sabre to Panther} = \$60,000 \times \frac{20\%}{120\%} = \$10,000$$

Adjust cost of sales and non-controlling interest in books of seller (Sabre).

3 *Interest on intragroup loan*

$\$800,000 \times 5\% \times 6/12 = \$20,000$

Cancel in books of Panther and Sabre.

4 *Fair value adjustments*

	At acq'n 1.7.X4 $'000	Movement	$'000	At year end 31.12.X4 $'000
Property	200	(200/20 × 6/12)	(5)	195

5 *Non-controlling interest*

	$'000		$'000
Profit for the year ((610 + (W3) 20*) × 6/12)]	315		
Less: Post acquisition interest* (W3)	(20)		
Less: PUP (W2)	(10)		
Additional depreciation on fair value adjustment (W4)	(5)		
	280	× 40%	112
Other comprehensive income (180 × 6/12)	90	× 40%	36
Total comprehensive income			148

* The interest on the loan is specific to the post-acquisition period. Therefore, it is added back before time apportioning the remainder of the profits, and then deducted in full as it is a post-acquisition expense.

6   Group reserves carried forward (proof)

	Panther $'000	Sabre $'000
Reserves per question	16,500	3,270
PUP (W2)		(10)
Fair value change (W3)		(5)
Pre acquisition reserves		
[2,480 + ((610 + (W3) 20 + 180) × 6/12)]		(2,885)
		370
Sabre – share of post acquisition reserves (370 × 60%)	222	
	16,722	

14 Hever

CONSOLIDATED STATEMENT OF FINANCIAL POSITION AS AT 31 DECEMBER 20X4

	$'000
Non-current assets	
Property, plant & equipment (370 + 190 + (W3) 45)	605
Goodwill (W4)	2
Investment in associate (W5)	165
	772
Current assets	
Inventories (160 + 100 – (W2) 1.5)	258.5
Trade receivables (170 + 90)	260
Cash (50 + 40)	90
	608.5
	1,380.5
Equity attributable to owners of the parent	
Share capital	200
Share premium reserve	100
Retained earnings (W7)	758.5
	1,058.5
Non-controlling interest (W6)	162
	1,220.5
Current liabilities	
Trade payables (100 + 60)	160
	1,380.5

Workings

1   Group structure

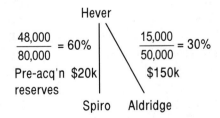

∴ In the absence of information to the contrary, Spiro is a subsidiary, and Aldridge an associate of Hever.

2   *Unrealised profit on inventories*

Mark-up = 6,000 ∴ ¼ × 6,000 = $1,500

3 *Fair values – adjustment to net assets*

	At Acquisition	Movement	At balance sheet date
Property, plant and equipment	50	(5)	45
Inventories	(20)	20	0
	30	15	45

4 *Goodwill on consolidation – Spiro*

	$'000	$'000
Consideration transferred		128
Non-controlling interest (210 × 40%)		84
Net assets at acquisition		
Share capital	80	
Retained earnings	20	
Share premium	80	
Fair value adjustments (W3)	30	
		(210)
Goodwill arising on consolidation		2

Goodwill – alternative working

	$'000	$'000
Consideration transferred		128
Net assets	210	
Group share 60%		(126)
Goodwill arising on consolidation		2

5 *Investment in associate*

	$'000
Cost of associate	90
Share of post-acquisition retained reserves ((400 – 150) × 30%)	75
	165

Note: it is not necessary to calculate the goodwill arising on the investment in Aldridge as there are no impairment losses.

6 *Non-controlling interest*

	$'000	$'000
Net assets	360	
Fair value adjustment (W3)	45	
	405	
Non-controlling share (40%)		162

7 *Retained earnings*

	Hever $'000	Spiro $'000	Aldridge $'000
Per question	568	200	400
PUP (W2)	(1.5)	–	–
Fair value adjustment (W3)		15	
Pre-acquisition retained earnings		(20)	(150)
		195	250
Spiro – share of post acquisition earnings (195 × 60%)	117		
Aldridge – share of post acquisition earnings (250 × 30%)	75		
Less: goodwill impairment losses to date	(0)		
Less: impairment losses on associate to date	(0)		
	758.5		

15 Trontacc

(a)   Treatment of construction contracts in the statement of financial position of Trontacc Co at 30 September 20X7

	A	B	C	Total
	$'000	$'000	$'000	$'000
Gross amounts due from customers (Note 1)	80	–	–	80
Trade receivables (Note 2)	–	–	–	–
Gross amounts due to customers (Note 1)	–	(25)	(45)	(70)

Note 1

	A	B	C
	$'000	$'000	$'000
Gross amounts due from/to customers			
Contract costs incurred	500	550	320
Recognised profits less losses	120	(100)	35
	620	450	355
Less: progress billings to date	(540)	(475)	(400)
	80	(25)	(45)

Note 2

	A	B	C
	$'000	$'000	$'000
Trade receivables			
Progress billings to date	540	475	400
Less: cash received	(540)	(475)	(400)
	–	–	–

(b)   Treatment of construction contracts in the statement of comprehensive income of Trontacc for the year ended 30 September 20X7

	Contract			
	A	B	C	Total
	$'000	$'000	$'000	$'000
	(W1)	(W2)	(W3)	
Revenue	600	500	350	1,450
Expenses	(480)	(550)	(315)	(1,345)
Expected loss	–	(50)	–	(50)
Gross profit/(loss)	120	(100)	35	55

Workings

1   *Contract A*

	$'000
Statement of comprehensive income	
Revenue (60% × 1,000)	600
Expenses (60% of 800	(480)
Gross profit	120

2   *Contract B*

	$'000
Statement of comprehensive income	
Revenue (50% × 1,000)	500
Expenses (all costs to date)	(550)
Expected losses	(50)
Gross profit	(100)

3   *Contract C*

	$'000
Statement of comprehensive income	
Revenue (35% × 1,000)	350
Expenses (35% × 900)	(315)
Gross profit	35

16 C Co

(a)

	Maryhill bypass $'000	Rottenrow centre $'000
Revenue	2,800	3,000
Profit/(loss) (W1)	622	(100)
Cost of sales	2,178	3,100
Current liabilities		
Gross amounts due to customers (W2)	578	600

Workings

1   Maryhill: $(9,000 - (1,400 + 5,600)) \times \dfrac{2,800}{9,000} = 622$

Rottenrow: $8,000 - (2,900 + 5,200) = (100)$

2

	Maryhill $'000	Rottenrow $'000
Costs incurred to date	1,400	2,900
Recognised profits/(losses)	622	(100)
Progress billings	(2,600)	(3,400)
	(578)	(600)

(b)   Construction contracts are recognised as such when they cover at **least two accounting periods**. If they were not to be treated as they are under IAS 11, then the costs incurred during the early years of the contract would be recognised but with no corresponding revenue. This would lead to several years of losses then one year of high profits regardless of how profitable the contract really was. The advantage of this approach however would be that there would be no need to use estimates and forecasts.

The current treatment **matches an element of the revenue to the costs incurred**. There is an attempt to maintain **prudence** by ensuring that any **foreseeable** losses are **accounted for immediately**. This gives a fairer representation of the underlying financial substance of the transaction and makes it easier for the user of the accounts to assess the financial position of the company.

17 Provisions

(a)   **Why there was a need for an accounting standard dealing with provisions**

IAS 37 *Provisions, contingent liabilities and contingent assets* was issued to prevent entities from using provisions for creative accounting. It was common for entities to recognise material provisions for items such as future losses, restructuring costs or even expected future expenditure on repairs and maintenance of assets. These could be combined in one large provision (sometimes known as the 'big bath'). Although these provisions reduced profits in the period in which they were recognised (and were often separately disclosed on grounds of materiality), they were then released to enhance profits in subsequent periods. To make matters worse, provisions were often recognised where there was no firm commitment to incur expenditure. For example, an entity might set up a provision for restructuring costs and then withdraw from the plan, leaving the provision available for profit smoothing.

The criteria that need to be satisfied before a provision is recognised

IAS 37 states that a provision should not be recognised unless:

(i) An entity has a present obligation (legal or constructive) as a result of a past event, and

(ii) It is probable that an outflow of resources embodying economic benefits will be required to settle the obligation, and

(iii) A reliable estimate can be made of the amount of the obligation.

An obligation can be legal or constructive. An entity has a constructive obligation if:

(i) It has indicated to other parties that it will accept certain responsibilities (by an established pattern of past practice or published policies), and

(ii) As a result, it has created a valid expectation on the part of those other parties that it will discharge those responsibilities.

(b) Extract should recognise a provision for the estimated costs of making good the site because:

(i) It has a present obligation to incur the expenditure as a result of a past event. In this case the obligating event occurred when it became virtually certain that the legislation would be passed. Therefore the obligation existed at 31 December 20X0, and

(ii) An outflow of resources embodying economic benefits is probable, and

(iii) It is possible to make a reliable estimate of the amount.

Effect on the financial statements

For the year ended 31 December 20X0:

- A provision of $1,242,000 (2,000,000 × 0.621) is reported as a liability.

- A non-current asset of $1,242,000 is also recognised. The provision results in a corresponding asset because the expenditure gives the company access to an inflow of resources embodying future economic benefits; there is no effect on the income statement for the year.

For the year ended 31 December 20X1:

- Depreciation of $248,400 (1,242,000 × 20%) is charged to the income statement. The non-current asset is depreciated over its remaining useful economic life of 5 years from 31 December 20X0 (the site will cease to produce output on 31 December 20X5).

- Therefore at 31 December 20X1 the net book value of the non-current asset will be $993,600 (1,242,000 − 248,400).

- At 31 December 20X1 the provision will be $1,366,000 (2,000,000 × 0.683).

- The increase in the provision of $124,000 (1,366,000 − 1,242,000) is recognised in the income statement as a finance cost. This arises due to the unwinding of the discount.

18 Alpha

> **Tutorial note.** Creative accounting and substance over form are important concepts. You must relate your answer to the situation given in part (c) of the question and not just write a general essay. One or two examples would be enough in (a).

(a) **Creative accounting**, the manipulation of figures for a desired result, takes many forms. Off-balance sheet finance is a major type of creative accounting and it probably has the most serious implications.

It is very rare for a company, its directors or employees to manipulate results for the purpose of fraud. The major consideration is usually the effect the results will have on the share price of the company. If the share price falls, the company becomes vulnerable to takeover. Analysts, brokers and economists, whose opinions affect the stock markets, are often perceived as having an outlook which is both short-term and superficial. Consequently, companies will attempt to produce the results the market expects or wants. The companies will aim for steady progress in a few key numbers and ratios and they will aim to meet the market's stated expectation.

The number of methods available for creative accounting and the determination and imagination of those who wish to perpetrate such acts are endless. It has been seen in the past that, wherever an accounting standard or law closes a loophole, another one is found. This has produced a change of approach in regulators and standard setters, towards general principles rather than detailed rules.

Here are a few examples of creative accounting.

(i) **Income recognition and cut-off**
Manipulation of cut-off is relatively straightforward. For instance a company may delay invoicing in order to move revenue into the following year.

(ii) **Revaluations**
The optional nature of the revaluation of non-current assets leaves such practices open to manipulation. The choice of whether to revalue can have a significant impact on a company's statement of financial position.

(iii) **Window dressing**
This is where transactions are passed through the books at the year end to make figures look better, but in fact they have not taken place and are often reversed after the year end. An example is where cheques are written to creditors, entered in the cash book, but not sent out until well after the year end.

(iv) **Change of accounting policies**
This tends to be a last resort because companies which change accounting policies know they will not be able to do so again for some time. The effect in the year of change can be substantial and prime candidates for such treatment are depreciation, inventory valuation, changes from current cost to historical cost (practised frequently by privatised public utilities) and foreign currency losses.

(v) **Manipulation of accruals, prepayments and contingencies**
These figures can often be very subjective, particularly contingencies. In the case of impending legal action, for example, a contingent liability is difficult to estimate, the case may be far off and the lawyers cannot give any indication of likely success, or failure. In such cases companies will often only disclose the possibility of such a liability, even though the eventual costs may be substantial.

(b) The phrase 'substance over form' has been described as follows.

'Transactions and other events should be accounted for and presented in accordance with their substance and financial reality and not merely with their legal form.'

This is a very important concept and it has been used to determine accounting treatment in financial statements through accounting standards and so prevent off balance sheet transactions.

(i) **Group accounting** is perhaps the most important area of off balance sheet finance which has been prevented by the application of the substance over form concept. A number of IASs have tackled abuses by enforcing the substance over form concept.

The most important point is that the definition of a subsidiary (under IAS 27) is based upon the **principle of control rather than purely ownership.** Where an entity is controlled by another, the controlling entity can ensure that the benefits accrue to itself and not to other parties. Similarly, one of the circumstances where a subsidiary may be excluded from consolidation is where there are severe long-term restrictions that prevent effective control.

(ii) Finance leases and their accounting treatment under IAS 17 *Leases* are an example of the application of substance over form.

Operating leases do not really pose an accounting problem. The lessee pays amounts periodically to the lessor and these are charged to the income statement. The lessor treats the leased asset as a non-current asset and depreciates it in the normal way. Rentals received from the lessee are credited to the income statement in the lessor's books.

For assets held under **finance leases** this accounting treatment would not disclose the reality of the situation. If a lessor leases out an asset on a finance lease, the asset will probably never be seen on his premises or used in his business again. It would be inappropriate for a lessor to record such an asset as a non-current asset. In reality, what he owns is a stream of cash flows receivable from the lessee. The asset is a receivable rather than a non-current asset.

Similarly, a lessee may use a finance lease to fund the 'acquisition' of a major asset which he will then use in his business perhaps for many years. The substance of the transaction is that he has acquired a non-current asset, and this is reflected in the accounting treatment prescribed by IAS 17, even though in law the lessee may never become the owner of the asset.

(iii) With regard to **measurement or disclosure of current assets**, a common example where substance over form is relevant are sale and repurchase agreements. There are arrangements under which the company sells an asset to another person on terms that allow the company to repurchase the asset in certain circumstances. A common example of such a transaction is the sale and repurchase of maturing whisky inventories. The key question is whether the transaction is a straightforward sale, or whether it is, in effect, a secured loan. It is necessary to look at the arrangement to determine who has the rights to the economic benefits that the asset generates, and the terms on which the asset is to be repurchased.

If the seller has the right to the benefits of the use of the asset, and the repurchase terms are such that the repurchase is likely to take place, the transaction should be accounted for as a loan.

Another example is the factoring of **trade receivables**. Where debts are factored, the original creditor sells the receivables to the factor. The sales price may be fixed at the outset or may be adjusted later. It is also common for the factor to offer a credit facility that allows the seller to draw upon a proportion of the amounts owed.

In order to determine the correct accounting treatment it is necessary to consider whether the benefit of the receivables has been passed on to the factor, or whether the factor is, in effect, providing a loan on the security of the receivables. If the seller has to pay interest on the difference between the amounts advanced to him and the amounts that the factor has received, and if the seller bears the risks of non-payment by the debtor, then the indications would be that the transaction is, in effect, a loan.

(c) (i) The Finance Director may be right in believing that renewing the non-current assets of the company will contribute to generating higher earnings and hence improved earnings per share. However, this will not happen immediately as the assets will need to have been in operation for at least a year for results to be apparent. Earnings will be higher because of the loan being at a commercially unrealistic rate, namely 5% instead of 9%.

As regards gearing, the Finance Director may well wish to classify the convertible loan stock as equity rather than debt; thus gearing will be lower. He may argue that because the loan is very likely to be converted into shares, the finance should be treated as equity rather than as debt.

(ii) IAS 33 *Earnings per share* requires the calculation of **basic earnings per share**. The Finance Director believes that the convertible loan he is proposing will not affect EPS and that an interest cost of 5% will not impact heavily on gearing.

However, IAS 32 will require the interest cost to be based on 9% and IAS 33 also requires the calculation and disclosure of **diluted EPS**.

The need to disclose diluted earnings per share arose because of the limited value of a basic EPS figure when a company is financed partly by convertible debt. Because the right to convert carries benefits, it is usual that the interest rate on the debt is lower than on straight debt. Calculation of EPS on the assumption that the debt is non-convertible can, therefore, be misleading since:

(1)   Current EPS is higher than it would be under straight debt

(2)   On conversion, EPS will fall – diluted EPS provides some information about the extent of this future reduction, and warning shareholders of the reduction which will happen in the future

IAS 32 *Financial instruments: presentation* affects the proposed scheme in that IAS 32 requires that convertible loans such as this should be split in the statement of financial position and presented partly as equity and partly as debt. Thus the company's gearing will probably increase as the convertible loan cannot be 'hidden' in equity.

19 Jenson

> **Tutorial note.** This is an important conceptual subject and it is closely linked with the IASB's *Framework*, which you should have discussed, rather than IAS 18, the accounting standard on revenue recognition. You need to use your imagination to come up with examples in (b).

(a)   In revenue recognition, the 'critical event' is the point in the earnings process or operating cycle at which the transaction is deemed to have been **sufficiently completed** to allow the **profit** arising from the transaction, or a distinct component part of it, to be **recognised** in income in a particular period. This has to be addressed in order to allocate transactions and their effects to different accounting periods and is a direct result of the episodic nature of financial reporting. For most companies the **normal earnings cycle** is the purchase of raw materials which are transformed through a manufacturing process into saleable goods, for which orders are subsequently received, delivery is made and then payment received.

In the past the approach has been to **match costs with revenues** and record both once the critical event has passed; in most systems this critical event has been full or **near full performance of the transaction**, so that no material uncertainties surround either the transaction being completed or the amounts arising from the transaction. This is encompassed in the notion of prudence, so that revenue is recognised only in cash or near cash form. However, any point in the cycle could be deemed to be the critical event. This approach leaves the statement of financial position as a statement of uncompleted transaction balances, comprising unexpired costs and undischarged liabilities.

In contrast, the IASB's **Framework** defines income and expenses in terms of increases in economic benefits (income) and outflow or depletion of assets (expenses), not in terms of an earnings or matching process. The statement of financial position thus assumes primary importance in the recognition of earnings and profits. Income **can only be recognised** if there is an **increase** in the equity (ie net assets) of an entity not resulting from contributions from owners. Similarly, an expense is recognised if there is a **decrease** in the ownership interest of an entity not resulting from distributions to owners. Thus income arises from recognition of assets and derecognition of liabilities, and expenses arise from derecognition of assets and recognition of liabilities. The IASB explains that it is not possible to reverse this definitional process, ie by defining assets and liabilities in terms of income and expenses, because it has not been possible to formulate robust enough base definitions of income and expenses (partly because the choice of critical event can be subjective). Nevertheless commentators often attempt to link the two approaches by asserting that **sufficient evidence** for recognition or derecognition will be met at the critical event in the operating cycle.

(b)   *On the acquisition of goods*

This would be **unlikely** to be a critical event for most businesses. However, for some the acquisition of the raw materials is the most important part of the process, eg extraction of gold from a mine, or the harvesting of coffee beans. Only where the goods in question could **be sold**

immediately in a liquid market would it be appropriate to recognise revenue, ie they would have to have a **commodity value.**

During the manufacture or production of goods

This is also **unlikely** to be the critical event for most businesses because **too many uncertainties** remain, eg of damaged goods or overproduction leading to obsolete inventory. An **exception** would **be long-term contracts** for the construction of specific assets, which tend to earn the constructing company revenues over the length of the contract, usually in stages, ie there is a **series of critical events** in the operating cycle (according to the Framework). It would **not** be appropriate to recognise all the revenue at the end of the contract, because this would reflect profit earned in past periods as well as the present period. Profit is therefore recognised during manufacture or production, usually through certification by a qualified valuer. Some would argue that this is not really a critical event approach, but rather an 'accretion approach'.

On delivery/acceptance of goods

Goods are frequently sold on **credit**, whereby the vendor hands over the inventory asset and receives in its place **a financial asset of a debt** due for the price of the goods. At that point legal title passes and **full performance** has taken place. In general, the bulk of the risks of the transaction have gone and the only ones remaining relate to the creditworthiness of the purchaser and any outstanding warranty over the goods. Many trade sales take place in this way, with periods of credit allowed for goods delivered, eg 30 days. This therefore tends to be the critical event for many types of business operating cycles.

Where certain conditions have been satisfied after the goods have been delivered

In these situations the customer has a right of return of the goods without reason or penalty, but usually within a time and non-use condition. A good example is clothes retailers who **allow non-faulty goods to be returned.** Another example is where the goods need only be paid for once they are sold on to a third party. Traditionally, recognition of revenue is delayed until, eg **the deadline to allowed return passes.** However, in circumstances where goods are never returned, it might be argued that the substance of the transaction is a sale on delivery.

Receipt of payment for credit sales

Once payment is received, only warranty risk remains. A company may wait until this point to recognise income if receipt is considered uncertain, eg when goods have been sold to a company resident in a country that has exchange controls. It would otherwise be **rare** to delay recognition until payment.

On the expiry of a guarantee or warranty

Many businesses may feel unable to recognise revenue in full because of **outstanding warranties,** eg a construction company which is subject to fee retention until some time after completion of the contract. Other businesses, such as car manufacturers, may make a **general provision** for goods returned under warranty as it will not be possible to judge likely warranty costs under individual contracts.

(c)   (i)   This agreement is worded as a **sale**, but it is fairly obvious from the terms and assessed substance that it is in fact a **secured loan.** Jenson should therefore continue to recognise the inventory in the statement of financial position and should treat the receipt from Wholesaler as a loan, not revenue. Finance costs will be charged to the income statement, of $35,000 × 12% × 9/12 = $3,150.

(ii)   Years 2 to 5 of the franchise contract would be **loss making** for Jenson and hence, under IAS 18, part of the initial fee of $50,000 should be **deferred over the life of the contract.** Since Jenson should be making a profit margin of 20% on this type of arrangement, revenues of $10,000 will be required to match against the costs of $8,000. The company will receive $5,000 pa and so a further $5,000 × 4 = $20,000 of the initial fee should be deferred, leaving $50,000 − $20,000 = $30,000 to be recognised in the first year. However, this may not represent a liability under IAS 37 *Provisions, Contingent Liabilities and*

Contingent Assets, where a liability is defined as an obligation to transfer economic benefits as a result of past transactions or events. It will be necessary to consider the terms of the initial fee and whether it is returnable.

(iii)   The cost of the first 6 months' publications is $192,000 ÷ 24 × 6 = $48,000. On an accruals basis, income of $240,000 ÷ 24 × 6 = $60,000 should be recognised. This would leave deferred income of $240,000 − $60,000 = $180,000 in Jenson's statement of financial position (ie as a liability). As in (ii), however, this may not represent a liability. In fact, the liability of the company may only extend to the cost of the future publications, ie $192,000 − $48,000 = $144,000. This would allow Jenson to **recognise all the profit** on the publications **immediately**. In want of an updated accounting standard on revenue recognition, it will be necessary to consider the extent of Jenson's commitments under this arrangement.

20 Bulwell

INCOME STATEMENTS (EXTRACTS)

	20X1	20X2	20X3	20X4
	$	$	$	$
Finance cost	11,250	8,063	4,078	
Depreciation on lorries	12,500	12,500	12,500	12,500

STATEMENTS OF FINANCIAL POSITION AT 31 DECEMBER (EXTRACTS)

	20X1	20X2	20X3	20X4
	$	$	$	$
Non-current assets				
Lorries: at cost	54,000	54,000	54,000	54,000
Depreciation	12,500	25,000	37,500	50,000
	41,500	29,000	16,500	4,000
Current liabilities				
Finance lease obligations	15,937*	16,313	–	–
Non-current liabilities				
Finance lease obligations	16,313	–	–	–

* (24,000 − 8,063)

Working

	$
Finance lease	
Original cost ($18,000 × 3)	54,000
Deposit	(9,000)
Balance 1.1.20X1	45,000
Interest 25%	11,250
Payment 31.12.20X1	(24,000)
Balance 31.12.20X1	32,250
Interest 25%	8,063
Payment 31.12.20X2	(24,000)
Balance 31.12.20X2	16,313
Interest 25%	4,078
Payment 31.12.20X3	(20,391)
	–

21 Financial assets and liabilities

(a)

	$
Issue costs	120,000
Interest $6,000,000 \times 3.5\% \times 7$	1,470,000
Premium on redemption	1,100,000
Total finance cost	2,690,000

(b)   The premium on redemption of the loan notes represents a finance cost. The effective rate of interest must be applied so that the debt is measured at amortised cost (IAS 39).

At the time of issue, the loan notes are recognised at their net proceeds of $599,800 (600,000 – 200).

The finance cost for the year ended 31 December 20X4 is calculated as follows:

	$
1.1.20X3 Proceeds of issue (600,000 – 200)	599,800
Interest at 12%	71,976
Balance 31.12.20X3	671,776
Interest at 12%	80,613
Balance at 31.12.210X4	752,389

The finance cost for the year ended 31.12.20X4 is $80,613.

(c)

> **Top tip.** The method to use here is to find the present value of the principal value of the bond, $500,000 (10,000 × $50) and the interest payments of $25,000 annually (5% × $500,000) at the market rate for non-convertible bonds of 6%, using the discount factors. The difference between this total and the principal amount of $500,000 is the equity element.

	$
Present value of principal $500,000 × 0.747	373,500
Present value of interest $25,000 × 4.212	105,300
Liability value	478,800
Principal amount	500,000
Equity element	21,200

22 Lis

The lease appears to be a finance lease for the following reasons:

- the present value of minimum lease payments amounts to 98% ($84,000/$86,000) of the fair value of the asset at inception of the lease, which can be regarded as 'substantially all'
- the asset will be used by Lis Co for the whole of its *economic* life, as it will be scrapped by the lessor at the end of the lease.

Consequently the asset should be capitalised in the statement of financial position. The asset should be depreciated over the shorter of its useful life (5 years) and the lease term (6 years).

A lease liability will be shown in the statement of financial position reduced by lease payments made in advance and increased by interest calculated using the interest rate implicit in the lease, 12.5%.

Both the asset and lease liability will initially be recognised at $84,000, the present value of minimum lease payments, as this is lower than the fair value of the asset. In present value terms the lessor is making a $2,000 loss by not selling the asset at its market value of $86,000, but may have reasons for doing so or the market may be illiquid.

FINANCIAL STATEMENT EXTRACTS

	$
Statement of comprehensive income (extract)	
Depreciation (W1)	16,800
Finance costs (W2)	8,198

Statement of financial position (extract)

	$
Non-current assets	
Leasehold assets (W1)	67,200
Non-current liabilities	
Finance lease liability (W2)	55,358
Current liabilities	
Finance lease liability (W2) (73,778 – 55,358)	18,420

Workings

1   *Net book value of leased asset*

	$
Depreciation of asset: $84,000/5 years useful life	16,800
Net book value at year end ($84,000 – $16,800)	67,200

The asset is depreciated over the shorter of its useful life (5 years) and lease term (6 years).

2   Finance lease

		$
1.1.X3	Present value of minimum lease payments	84,000
1.1.X3	Payment in advance	(18,420)
		65,580
1.1.X3 – 31.12.X3	Interest at 12.5% ($65,580 × 12.5%)	8,198
31.12.X3	**Finance lease liability c/d**	**73,778**
1.1.X4	Payment in advance	(18,420)
1.1.X4	**Finance lease liability c/d after next instalment**	**55,358**

The interest element ($8,198) of the current liability can also be shown separately as interest payable.

23 Carpati

Deferred tax liability

	20X6
	$'000
Accelerated tax depreciation (W1)	186
Revaluation (W2) *	252
	438

* The deferred tax on the revaluation gain will be charged to the revaluation surplus as IAS 12 requires deferred tax on gains recognised in other comprehensive income to be charged or credited to other comprehensive income.

Workings

1   *Tax depreciation*

	$'000	$'000
At 30 September 20X6:		
Carrying value		1,185
Tax base:		
At 1 October 20X5	405	
Expenditure in year	290	
	695	
Less: tax depreciation (25%)	(174)	
		(521)
Cumulative temporary difference		664
@ 28%=		186

2   *Revaluation surplus*

Temporary difference ($1,500,000 – $600,000) @ 28%. = $252,000

> **Tutorial note**. IAS 12 requires the deferred tax liability on revaluations to be recognised *even if* the entity does not intend to dispose of the asset since the value of the asset is recovered through use which generates taxable income in excess of tax depreciation allowable.

24 Pilum

(a)   Earnings per share

	$
Profit before tax	2,530,000
Less: income tax expense	(1,127,000)
Profit for the year	1,403,000
Less: preference dividends	(276,000)
Earnings	1,127,000
Earnings per share =	1,127,000
	4,120,000
	27.4c

(b)   The first step is to calculate the theoretical ex-rights price. Consider the holder of 5 shares.

	No	$
Before rights issue	5	8.90
Rights issue	1	1.20
After rights issue	6	10.10

The theoretical ex-rights price is therefore $10.10/6 = $1.68.

The number of shares in issue before the rights issue must be multiplied by the fraction:

$$\frac{\text{Fair value immediately before exercise of rights}}{\text{theoretical ex - rights price}} = \frac{\$1.78}{\$1.68}$$

Weighted average number of shares in issue during the year:

Date	Narrative	Shares	Time period	Bonus fraction	Total
1.1.X4	b/d	4,120,000	× 9/12	1.78/1.68	3,273,929
1.10.X4	Rights issue	824,000			
		4,944,000	× 3/12		1,236,000
					4,509,929

$$\text{EPS} = \frac{\$1,127,000}{4,509,929}$$

$$= 25.0\text{c}$$

(c) The maximum number of shares into which the loan stock could be converted is 90% × 1,500,000 = 1,350,000. The calculation of diluted EPS should be based on the assumption that such a conversion actually took place on 1 January 20X4. Shares in issue during the year would then have numbered (4,120,000 + 1,350,000) = 5,470,000 and revised earnings would be as follows:

	$	$
Earnings from (a) above		1,127,000
Interest saved by conversion (1,500,000 × 10%)	150,000	
Less: attributable tax (150,000 × 30%)	(45,000)	
		105,000
		1,232,000

$$\therefore \text{ Diluted EPS} = \frac{1,232,000}{5,470,000}$$

$$= 22.5\text{c}$$

24 Biggerbuys

REPORT

To: The bankers of Biggerbuys
From: Consultant management accountant
Subject: Financial performance 20X7 – 20X9
Date: 30 October 20X9

1   Introduction

1.1   In accordance with your instructions, I set out below a review of the entity's financial performance over the last three years.

1.2   The main focus of this report is on the reasons for the increase in the level of bank loans.

1.3   Appropriate accounting ratios are included in the attached appendix.

2   Bank lending

2.1   The main reason for the steep increase in bank lending is due to the entity not generating sufficient cash from its operating activities over the past three years.

2.2   For the year ended 30 June 20X8, the entity had a **net cash deficiency on operating activities** of $18m.

2.3   In addition, for at least the past two years, the cash generated from operating activities has not been sufficient to cover interest payable. Therefore those payments, together with tax and dividends, have had to be covered by borrowings.

2.4   As at 30 June 20X9, bank borrowings were $610m out of a total facility of $630m. Payment of the proposed dividends alone would increase the borrowings to the limit.

3   Operating review

3.1   Although revenue has been rising steadily over the period, operating profit has remained almost static.

3.2   Over this period the profit margin has risen, but not as much as would be expected. The cost of sales have risen in almost the same proportion as sales. This may be due to increased costs of raw materials, as inventories have risen steeply; but the turnover of inventory has been falling or static over the same period.

3.3 There has also been a large increase in trade receivables. Both the increase in inventories and trade receivables have had to be financed out of operating activities leading to the present pressure on borrowings.

3.4 Although the number of days sales in trade receivables has fallen steadily over the period, the trade receivables at the end of June 20X9 still represent nearly a year's credit sales. This is excessive and seems to imply a poor credit control policy, even taking into account the extended credit terms being granted by the company.

4 Recommendations

4.1 The entity needs to undertake an urgent review of its credit terms in order to reduce the levels of trade receivables.

4.2 Inventory levels are also extremely high (representing over four months' sales) and should be reviewed.

4.3 Operating costs also need to be kept under control in order to generate more cash from sales.

Please contact me if you need any further information.

Signed: An Accountant

Appendix: Accounting ratios

		20X7	20X8	20X9
1	Profit margin			
	$\dfrac{\text{Profit before interest}}{\text{Revenue}} \times 100$	$\dfrac{(50+45)}{1,850}\times100\%$	$\dfrac{(60+60)}{2,200}\times100\%$	$\dfrac{(50+90)}{2,500}\times100\%$
		= 5.1%	= 5.5%	= 5.6%
2	Operating costs			
	$\dfrac{\text{Other operating costs}}{\text{Revenue}} \times 100$	$\dfrac{550}{1,850}\times100\%$	$\dfrac{640}{2,200}\times100\%$	$\dfrac{700}{2,500}\times100\%$
		= 29.7%	= 29.1%	= 28.0%
3	Inventory turnover			
	$\dfrac{\text{Cost of sales}}{\text{Inventory}}$	$\dfrac{1,250}{400}$	$\dfrac{1,500}{540}$	$\dfrac{1,750}{620}$
		= 3.1 times	= 2.8 times	= 2.8 times
4	Trade receivables turnover			
	$\dfrac{\text{Trade receivables}}{\text{Credit sales}} \times 365$	$\dfrac{492}{(300+45)}\times365$	$\dfrac{550}{(400+60)}\times365$	$\dfrac{633}{(600+90)}\times365$
		= 523 days	= 436 days	= 334 days

5	Cash generated from operations	20X8 $m	20X9 $m
	Profit before interest	120	140
	Depreciation	60	70
	Increase in inventory	(140)	(80)
	Increase in trade receivables	(58)	(83)
	Increase in trade payables	–	10
		(18)	57

		20X7	20X8	20X9
6	ROCE			
	$\dfrac{\text{Profit before interest}}{\text{Net assets} + \text{borrowings}}\times100\%$	$\dfrac{95}{(372+520)}\times100\%$	$\dfrac{120}{(382+720)}\times100\%$	$\dfrac{140}{(372+930)}\times100\%$
		= 10.6%	= 10.9%	= 10.7%
7	Interest cover			
	$\dfrac{\text{Profit before interest}}{\text{Interest payable}}$	$\dfrac{95}{25}$	$\dfrac{120}{60}$	$\dfrac{140}{110}$
		= 3.8	= 2.0	= 1.3

	20X7	20X8	20X9
8 Gearing			
$\dfrac{\text{Borrowings}}{\text{Net assets}+\text{borrowings}}$	$\dfrac{520}{892}$	$\dfrac{720}{1,102}$	$\dfrac{930}{1,302}$
	= 58.3%	= 65.3%	= 71.4%
9 Asset turnover			
$\dfrac{\text{Revenue}}{\text{Net assets}+\text{borrowings}}$	$\dfrac{1,850}{892}$	$\dfrac{2,200}{1,102}$	$\dfrac{2,500}{1,302}$
	= 2.1 times	= 2.0 times	= 1.9 times

26 Webster

Top tip. This question is at the upper end of the scale of difficulty which you are likely to encounter, particularly part (a). Study the answer carefully.

(a)   INCOME STATEMENTS (RESTATED)

	Cole		Darwin	
	$'000	$'000	$'000	$'000
Revenue (3,000 – 125) (Note 1)		2,875		4,400
Opening inventory	450		720	
Purchases (Note 2)	2,055		3,080	
Closing inventory	(540)		(850)	
		1,965		2,950
Gross profit		910		1,450
Operating expenses	480		964	
Depreciation (Note 3)	40		(120)	
Loan interest	80		–	
Overdraft interest (W3)	15		–	
		(615)		(844)
Net profit		295		606

STATEMENT OF FINANCIAL POSITION (RESTATED)

	Cole		Darwin	
	$'000	$'000	$'000	$'000
Assets				
Non current assets				
Property, plant, equipment (W1)		3,100		2,620
Current assets				
Inventory	540		850	
Receivables (W2)	897		750	
Bank (W3)	–		60	
		1,437		1,660
		4,537		4,280
Equity and liabilities				
Equity shares ($1)		1,000		500
Revaluation surplus (800 – 40)		760		700
Retained earnings to 31 March 20X9				
(684 + 295 + 40)/(1,912 + 606)		1,019		2,518
		2,779		3,718
Non current liabilities				
10% loan note		800		–
Current liabilities				
Trade payables (W4)		163		562
Overdraft (W3)		795		–
		4,537		4,280

Workings

1   *Non-current assets*

		Cost/valuation	Depreciation	NBV
		$'000	$'000	$'000
Cole:	property	2,000	100	1,900
	plant	6,000	4,800	1,200
				3,100
Darwin:	property	2,000	100	1,900
	plant (3,000 – 600)	2,400	1,680	720
				2,620

2   *Receivables*
Cole: 522 + 375 (Note 1) = 897

3   *Bank*

	Cole	Darwin
	$'000	$'000
As stated	20	(550)
Reversal of sale (Note 1)	(500)	
Payment for purchases (Note 2)	(300)	
Payment for plant (Note 3)		600
Payment/saving of interest to statement of financial position	15	10
	(795)	60

4   *Payables*
Cole 438 –275 (Note 2) = 163

Tutorial notes

1   Sale to Brander is at gross margin 40%, therefore the cost of sale is $500 × 60% = $300.

Had a normal margin of 20% applied, the cost of this sale would represent 80% of the selling price. The normal selling price would be $\dfrac{300}{0.8}$ = $375.

Sales and receivables would reduce by $125 and the proceeds of $500 would not have been received.

2   Purchase of goods from Advent on normal terms would have increased purchases by $25. Using the normal credit period would mean these goods would have been paid for by the year end, increasing the overdraft and reducing trade payables.

3   The plant bought in February 20X9 has not yet generated income for Darwin, so it is sensible to ignore it in the acquisition comparison.

The effects are:

- Cost of plant – $600, overdraft affected
- Depreciation reduced $600 × 20% = $120

The depreciation charged changes:

	Cole	Darwin
	$'000	$'000
As stated for property	(60)	
Depreciation on revaluation	100	
Reduction (above)		(120)
	40 increase	(120) (decrease)

(b)

Ratios	Cole		Darwin	
Return on capital employed:	(295+80)/(2,779+800)	= 10.5%	606/3,718	= 16.3%
Asset turnover	2,875/(4,537 − 958)	= 0.8 times	4,400/(4,280 − 562)	=1.2 times
Gross profit %	910/2,875	= 31.7%	(unchanged)	= 33%
Net profit %	295/2,875	= 10.3%	606/4,400	= 13.8%
Receivables collection (days)	897/2,875 ×365	= 114	(unchanged)	= 62
Payables period (days)	163/2,055 ×365	= 29	(unchanged)	= 67

Using the unadjusted figures, Cole would be preferred, as its key ratios given are better than those of Darwin. Cole achieves better profitability due to greater unit margins. Both companies have poor asset turnover implying under-utilisation or inefficient methods.

Both companies manage working capital in a similar fashion. Webster should examine liquidity ratios:

Cole: 1,082/438 = 2.5
Darwin: 1,600/1,112 = 1.4

The acid test ratio of Cole is 1.23 whereas Darwin's is 0.67.

Using the adjusted accounts, the above position is reversed showing Darwin to be more profitable and to manage its assets more efficiently. Cole's true liquidity position is not so healthy – Cole controls receivables poorly and appears to pay suppliers earlier.

Darwin's poor liquidity position is probably due to financing non-current assets from its overdraft. Alternative refinancing would be beneficial.

Cole's parent company has produced an initially favourable set of ratios by creating favourable payment terms and trading conditions, and Darwin's original ratios were distorted by revaluations and the timing of new plant purchases.

Other factors to consider include:

(i)   The asking price
(ii)   The future prospects, profits and cash flow forecasts
(iii)   The state of forward order books
(iv)   The quality of the management and labour force
(v)   Other possible acquisitions

(c)   This answer assumes the accounts would be prepared in compliance with extant IASs and that they would be publicly available.

Notes (a) and (b). This data would need to be disclosed under IAS 24 *Related party disclosures*. Specifically disclosure would be required of:

(i)   The relationship
(ii)   The nature of the transaction
(iii)   The volume of transactions
(iv)   Outstanding items
(v)   Pricing policy
(vi)   Other data to enable users of accounts to understand the transactions such as margins/terms

Note (c). Under IAS 16 *Property, plant and equipment* where assets are revalued, these values would be included in the statement of financial position together with supporting information. IAS 16 also encourages disclosure of fair values if materially different from carrying values.

Note (d). Movements on non current assets would disclose acquisitions, but dates of purchase and financing would not normally be disclosed.

Note (e). This information would not be given and could not be calculated from published accounts.

27 Dundee

Dundee Co
Statement of cash flows for the year ended 31 March 20X7

	$m	$m
Cash flows from operating activities		
Profit before taxation	1,050	
Adjustments for:		
Depreciation	970	
Interest expense	250	
	2,270	
Decrease in inventories (1,500 – 1,600)	100	
Increase in trade receivables (2,200 – 1,800)	(400)	
Increase in trade payables (1,250 – 1,090)	160	
Cash generated from operations	2,130	
Interest paid	(250)	
Income taxes paid (W2)	(210)	
Net cash from operating activities		1,670
Cash flow from investing activities		
Purchase of property, plant and equipment (W1)	(870)	
Net cash used in investing activities		(870)
Cash flows from financing activities		
Payment of finance lease liabilities (W3)	(450)	
Dividends paid	(300)	
Net cash used in financing activities		(750)
Net increase in cash and cash equivalents		50
Cash and cash equivalents at beginning of year		(205)
Cash and cash equivalents at end of year		(155)

Workings

1   Purchase of property, plant and equipment

PROPERTY, PLANT AND EQUIPMENT

	$		$
b/d	3,700	Depreciation	970
Addition – finance leases	600		
∴ Additions – cash	870	c/d	4,200
	5,170		5,170

2   Income taxes paid

INCOME TAX PAYABLE

		$			$
∴ paid		210	b/d	DT	850
c/d	DT	1,070		CT	205
	CT	225	P/L		450
		1,505			1,505

3 *Payments under finance leases*

FINANCE LEASE LIABILITIES

	$			$
∴ paid	450	b/d	> 1 yr	1,200
c/d > 1 yr	1,300		< 1 yr	450
< 1 yr	400	Property, plant & equipment		600
	2,250			2,250

28 Elmgrove

Marking scheme

Marks

(a)

Format/presentation	2	
Cash generated from operations (½ per item)	4	
Interest paid	2	
Income taxes paid	1½	
Purchase of property, plant and equipment	2	
Sale of property, plant and equipment	1	
Interest received	1	
Issue of share capital	2½	
Dividend paid	1	
	17	
Property, plant and equipment note	1	
Cash and cash equivalents note	2	
Available/Maximum		20

(b)

Memo format	1	
Identify users	1	
Ability to generate cash	1	
Ability to repay debts	1	
Helps decision making	1	
Easier to understand		
than the income statement	1	
Aids comparison	1	
Available	7	
Maximum		5
		25

Suggested solution

(a)   ELMGROVE – STATEMENT OF CASH FLOWS FOR THE YEAR ENDED 31 MARCH 20X9

	$m	$m
Cash flows from operating activities		
Profit before taxation	109	
Adjustments for		
Loss on disposal	6	
Depreciation	43	
Interest income	(6)	
Interest expense	17	
	169	
Decrease in inventories (123 – 176)	53	
Increase in trade receivables (95 – 87)	(8)	
Increase in trade payables (126 – 70)	56	
Cash generated from operations	270	
Interest paid (W2)	(13)	
Income taxes paid (W3)	(62)	
Net cash from operating activities		195
Cash flows from investing activities		
Purchase of property, plant and equipment (W1)	(165)	
Proceeds from sale of property, plant and equipment (28 – 6)	22	
Interest received	6	
		(137)
Net cash used in investing activities		
Cash flows from financing activities		
Proceeds from issuance of share capital (W4)	60	
Dividend paid	(32)	
Net cash from financing activities		28
Net increase in cash and cash equivalents		86
Cash and cash equivalents at beginning of the period		8
Cash and cash equivalents at end of the period		94

Workings

1   *Property, plant and equipment additions*

PROPERTY, PLANT AND EQUIPMENT

	$m		$m
Balance b/d (NBV)	264	Revaluation surplus	31
		Depreciation	43
		Disposal	28
∴ Additions	165	Balance c/d (NBV)	327
	429		429

2   *Interest paid*

INTEREST PAYABLE

	$m		$m
		Balance b/d	3
∴ Paid	13	Income statement	17
Balance c/d	7		
	20		20

3   *Income taxes paid*

INCOME TAXES PAYABLE

	$m		$m
		Balance b/d	54
∴ Paid	62	Income statement	47
Balance c/d	39		
	101		101

4   *Issue of shares*

	$m
Issue of shares	
Share capital (plus premium) 31/3/X9	230
Share capital 31/3/X8	120
Increase	110
Debentures converted into shares	(50)
Shares issued for cash	60

IAS 7 requires that investing and financing activities that do not require the use of cash, such as converting debt to equity, should be excluded from the statement of cash flows.

(b)   MEMO

To: Memorandum to the directors of Elmgrove
From: AN Accountant
Date: 1.4.20X9

Subject: Major benefits to the users of financial statements from the publication of statements of cash flows.

The users of financial statements can basically be divided into the following groups.

(i)   Shareholders
(ii)   Management
(iii)   Creditors and lenders
(iv)   Employers

The needs of these groups are not identical and hence not all benefits listed below will be applicable to all users.

Benefits

(i)   Statements of cash flows direct attention to the survival of the entity which depends on its ability to generate cash.
(ii)   Statements of cash flows indicate the ability of an entity to repay its debts.
(iii)   They give information which can be used in the decision making and stewardship process.
(iv)   They are more easily understood than income statements that depend on accounting conventions and concepts.
(v)   Statements of cash flows give a better means of comparison between different companies.

29 CPP and CCA

> **Tutorial note.** It is unlikely that a detailed computation will be asked for, but you must have an understanding of the principles of CPP and CCA, the differences between them and the ways in which they try to improve on HCA.

(a) In accounting, the value of income and capital is measured in terms of money. In simple terms, profit is the difference between the closing and opening statement of financial position values (after adjustment for new sources of funds and applications such as dividend distribution). If, because of inflation, the value of assets in the closing statement of financial position is shown at a higher monetary amount than assets in the opening statement of financial position, a profit has been made. In traditional accounting, it is assumed that a monetary unit of $1 is a stable measurement; inflation removes this stability.

CPP accounting attempts to provide a more satisfactory method of valuing profit and capital by establishing a stable unit of monetary measurement, $1 of current purchasing power, as at the end of the accounting period under review.

A distinction is made between monetary items, and non-monetary items. In a period of inflation, keeping a monetary asset (eg trade receivables) results in a loss of purchasing power as the value of money erodes over time. Non-monetary assets, however, are assumed to maintain 'real' value over time, and these are converted into monetary units of current purchasing power as at the year end, by means of a suitable price index. The equity interest in the statement of financial position can be determined as a balancing item.

The profit or deficit for the year in CPP terms is found by converting sales, opening and closing inventory, purchases and other expenses into year-end units of $CPP. In addition, a profit on holding net monetary liabilities (or a loss on holding net monetary assets) is computed in arriving at the profit or deficit figure.

CPP arguably provides a more satisfactory system of accounting since transactions are expressed in terms of 'today's money' and similarly, the statement of financial position values are adjusted for inflation, so as to give users of financial information a set of figures with which they can:

(i) Decide whether operating profits are satisfactory (profits due to inflation are eliminated)
(ii) Obtain a better appreciation of the size and 'value' of the entity's assets

(b) CPP and CCA accounting are different concepts, in that CPP accounting makes adjustments for general inflationary price changes, whereas CCA makes adjustments to allow for specific price movements (changes in the deprival value of assets). Specific price changes (in CCA) enable a company to determine whether the operating capability of a company has been maintained; it is not a restatement of price levels in terms of a common unit of money measurement. The two conventions use different concepts of capital maintenance (namely operating capability with CCA, and general purchasing power with CPP).

In addition CPP is based on the use of a general price index. In contrast, CCA only makes use of a specific price index where it is not possible to obtain the current value of an asset by other means (eg direct valuation).

(c) In CCA, holding gains represent the difference between the historical cost of an asset and its current cost. If the asset is unsold, and appears in the statement of financial position of a company at current cost, there will be an 'unrealised' holding gain, which must be included in a current cost reserve. When the asset is eventually sold, the profit (equal to the sale price minus the historical cost) may be divided into:

(i) An operating profit which would have been made if the cost of the asset were its current value
(ii) A *realised* holding gain which has arisen because of the appreciation in value of the asset between the date of its acquisition and the date of its sale

Index

Note. **Key Terms** and their page references are given in **bold**.

Review Form & Free Prize Draw – Paper F7 Financial Reporting (International) (6/08)

All original review forms from the entire BPP range, completed with genuine comments, will be entered into one of two draws on 31 January 2009 and 31 July 2009. The names on the first four forms picked out on each occasion will be sent a cheque for £50.

Name: _____   Address: _____

_____

_____

How have you used this Text?
(Tick one box only)

☐ Home study (book only)

☐ On a course: college _____

☐ With 'correspondence' package

☐ Other _____

Why did you decide to purchase this Text? *(Tick one box only)*

☐ Have used BPP Texts in the past

☐ Recommendation by friend/colleague

☐ Recommendation by a lecturer at college

☐ Saw advertising

☐ Saw information on BPP website

☐ Other _____

During the past six months do you recall seeing/receiving any of the following?
(Tick as many boxes as are relevant)

☐ Our advertisement in *ACCA Student Accountant*

☐ Our advertisement in *Pass*

☐ Our advertisement in *PQ*

☐ Our brochure with a letter through the post

☐ Our website www.bpp.com

Which (if any) aspects of our advertising do you find useful?
(Tick as many boxes as are relevant)

☐ Prices and publication dates of new editions

☐ Information on Text content

☐ Facility to order books off-the-page

☐ None of the above

Which BPP products have you used?

Text	☑	Success CD	☐	Learn Online	☐
Kit	☐	i-Learn	☐	Home Study Package	☐
Passcard	☐	i-Pass	☐	Home Study PLUS	☐

Your ratings, comments and suggestions would be appreciated on the following areas.

	Very useful	Useful	Not useful
Introductory section (Key study steps, personal study)	☐	☐	☐
Chapter introductions	☐	☐	☐
Key terms	☐	☐	☐
Quality of explanations	☐	☐	☐
Case studies and other examples	☐	☐	☐
Exam focus points	☐	☐	☐
Questions and answers in each chapter	☐	☐	☐
Fast forwards and chapter roundups	☐	☐	☐
Quick quizzes	☐	☐	☐
Question Bank	☐	☐	☐
Answer Bank	☐	☐	☐
Index	☐	☐	☐

Overall opinion of this Study Text	Excellent ☐	Good ☐	Adequate ☐	Poor ☐

Do you intend to continue using BPP products?   Yes ☐   No ☐

On the reverse of this page are noted particular areas of the text about which we would welcome your feedback.
The BPP author of this edition can be e-mailed at: marymaclean@bpp.com

Please return this form to: Lesley Buick, ACCA Publishing Manager, BPP Learning Media, FREEPOST, London, W12 8BR

Review Form & Free Prize Draw (continued)

TELL US WHAT YOU THINK

Free Prize Draw Rules

1 Closing date for 31 January 2009 draw is 31 December 2008. Closing date for 31 July 2009 draw is 30 June 2009.

2 Restricted to entries with UK and Eire addresses only. BPP employees, their families and business associates are excluded.

3 No purchase necessary. Entry forms are available upon request from BPP Learning Media. No more than one entry per title, per person. Draw restricted to persons aged 16 and over.

4 Winners will be notified by post and receive their cheques not later than 6 weeks after the relevant draw date.

5 The decision of the promoter in all matters is final and binding. No correspondence will be entered into.